TRANSACTIONAL SKILLS

HOW TO STRUCTURE AND DOCUMENT A DEAL

Second Edition

■ ■ ■

Stephen L. Sepinuck

Frederick N. & Barbara T. Curley Professor
Director, Commercial Law Center
Gonzaga University School of Law

John Francis Hilson

Former Professor
UCLA School of Law

WEST
ACADEMIC
PUBLISHING

© 2019 LEG, Inc. d/b/a West Academic
    444 Cedar Street, Suite 700
    St. Paul, MN 55101
    1-877-888-1330

West, West Academic Publishing, and West Academic are trademarks of West Publishing Corporation, used under license.

Printed in the United States of America

ISBN: 978-1-64242-608-3

To Sandra, who has taught me what companionship truly is.

    SLS

To Sean and Patrick, you inspire me and make me proud.

    JFH

PREFACE

This book is designed for use both in law schools and in large law firms with associate training programs. In creating it, we have drawn on our many decades of collective experience in teaching courses on the transactional practice of law and in training junior associates. Although the book contains explanatory text, it is designed primarily as a problem-based approach to the acquisition of transactional lawyering skills. We believe that learning in general, and skills acquisition in particular, requires active engagement, repetition, and frequent feedback. This book is designed to facilitate that approach.

We invite all who use this book to send us their comments about it. Only with those can we possibly improve the next edition. We also invite users to visit the web page for the book – www.transactionalskills.com – for updates and for links to useful resources.

Finally, we welcome you to transactional lawyering. We love this type of law practice, we hope that affection is evident in at least some of the pages that follow, and we further hope that this book will help prepare you for whatever transactional work comes your way.

Disclaimer: This book is intended to provide accurate information on the subjects covered. However, the book is provided for informational purposes only; its publication and distribution do not constitute the provision of legal or professional advice or services by either the authors or the publisher. If legal or professional services are required, the services of a competent professional should be sought.

TABLE OF CONTENTS

PART TWO – SIMULATIONS

TABLE OF CASES

TABLE OF STATUTES

TRANSACTIONAL SKILLS
HOW TO STRUCTURE AND DOCUMENT A DEAL

Second Edition

Part One – The Basics of Contract Drafting

CHAPTER ONE
INTRODUCTION

———————

Many people simplistically bifurcate the work of lawyers into two categories: (i) dispute resolution, which includes mediation, arbitration, litigation, appellate work, and regulatory hearings; and (ii) transactional practice, which involves negotiating, structuring, and documenting deals and agreements (whether involving real estate, mergers and acquisitions, finance, or securities). Movies and television have popularized the work of lawyers who handle controversies and have all but ignored transactional aspect of lawyering. Yet, while accurate statistics are hard to come by, some estimate that half of the work of lawyers in the United States is transactional in nature. Moreover, all lawyers engage in some transactional practice. The lawyers who specialize in tort or divorce need to be able to draft and review settlement agreements. Prosecutors and defenders need to be able to draft plea agreements. All attorneys in private practice need to be able to draft fee agreements between themselves and their clients.

Unfortunately, traditional legal education focuses on litigation.[1] Most doctrinal courses, such as Contracts and Property, are taught using the case method, which examines the subject by looking at disputes that resulted in litigation. Even the courses that provide training in lawyering skills, such as Legal Research and Writing, Trial Advocacy, and Moot Court, typically explore the practice of law through of the lens of litigation.

This book and its focus are different. They are designed to provide training and experience in the transactional practice of law. While much of the material in this book begins with and builds on contract law and contract principles, this book is more than an advanced text on contracts. Instead, this book will help you develop the skills needed to successfully engage in the transactional practice of law. Although the book contains numerous references and citations to cases, these references are merely to illustrate or support a point made in the text. The bulk of the book consists of background material leading up to exercises involving numerous types of transaction documents: leases, promissory notes, guarantees, and agreements of many kinds.

———————

[1] While many law schools now offer one or more courses on transactional practice, either as a required or elective part of the curriculum, even at those law schools the number of such courses is still small when contrasted with the litigation offerings.

There are some topics that are important to a transactional lawyer but which are not covered in this book. For example, there is little discussion of the tax ramifications of the various ways in which transactions are structured or of how bankruptcy may upset the expectations of one of the parties to a transaction. Even though these topics have not been included, it is important to understand that each of these areas is very important when working on a transaction. Consider, for example:

- Once a lawyer and client have determined that the client will proceed with a proposed acquisition, the lawyer should consider whether there are other, tax-advantaged ways in which to structure the transaction.

- Once a client decides to engage in a particular transaction, the client's lawyer should consider what might happen to the client or the transaction if the counterparty were to become a debtor in a bankruptcy case.

In each instance, these and other legal issues might be critical to how the transaction documents are drafted and even to whether the parties successfully consummate the transaction. Thus, a transactional lawyer who lacks the relevant expertise needs to confer with a tax lawyer or a bankruptcy lawyer early on in order to make sure that the client's expectations will be met and the client's interests properly protected.

The practice of transactional law is similar to dispute resolution in many ways. In both settings, lawyers must have a thorough understanding of the applicable legal rules and the policies underlying them. They must be honest, fulfill promises, listen well, communicate clearly, maintain confidences, admit error, and accept criticism and correction with grace and an open mind. It also helps to be courteous and punctual. This book might help you develop these skills, but it will focus on the other skills and abilities needed by lawyers involved in transactional practice. These other skills include:

- The ability to imagine all of the events that might later interfere with the transaction or the parties' relationship, including,

  - the ability to perform risk analysis, and

  - the judgment needed to determine which issues to provide for in the transaction documents and which to ignore;

- The ability to produce appropriate documentation for a transaction, including,

- knowing the distinctions among, and the appropriate use of, the different types of contract terms (*e.g.*, covenants, conditions, representations, warranties, discretionary authority, declarations), and

- the ability to properly draft each type of term;

- The ability to identify and eliminate ambiguity in the language of written agreements, including,

  - the ability to spot and resolve ambiguity, inconsistency, and other drafting problems in your drafting, and

  - the ability to spot the same issues in the work of others;

- Understanding the rules of contract interpretation, including,

  - how the rules might work against your client, and

  - how to turn the rules into an advantage rather than a disadvantage; and

- Understanding so-called "boilerplate" provisions, including,

  - knowing what each such provision actually means and does, and

  - appreciating how these often overlooked provisions can be vital to ensuring that an agreement meets your client's goals.

Underscoring all of these skills is an attitudinal difference between dispute resolution and transaction practice. Most disputes involve an unwilling participant (typically, the defendant if the dispute has progressed to litigation). They also often involve what is – or at least, what appears to be – a "zero-sum scenario." That is, one party's gain is offset by the other party's loss. Even this does not account for the fact that one or both of the parties will be responsible for attorney's fees, so that resolution of the dispute might leave the parties, collectively, in a worse position than before the dispute began. Transactional practice is frequently different because the parties share a common objective and each party expects to benefit from the transaction. For example:

- A technology firm wants to use its technology to generate revenue, while still retaining ownership of the technology, and a prospective customer wants access to the technology, so they enter into a license agreement;

- A landlord wants to lease its building in return for the payment of rent and a prospective tenant wants to secure space, so they enter into a lease;

- A bank wants to lend money so as to earn interest and a prospective borrower wants to obtain a loan, so they enter into a loan agreement; and

- A seller wants to sell a business and a prospective buyer wants to buy the business, so they enter into a purchase and sale agreement.

This does not mean that there will be no controversies about how to consummate the transaction; it means merely that most of the controversies will be about the deal terms, not about whether the parties will or should do a deal with each other.

In short, the goal of a litigator is to help the client win (and the other side to lose) in the resolution of a controversy, whereas the goal of a transactional lawyer is to facilitate the transaction while protecting the client's interests. In some instances, the transactional lawyer's best advice will be for the client to walk away from the transaction. But clients rarely appreciate that advice, even when it is in their best interests.[2]

A second principal difference between dispute resolution and transactional practice is that the facts concerning a dispute most often occurred in the past[3] while in a transaction the facts have not yet occurred. Thus, lawyers handling a controversy often must comb through the available evidence to identify the facts that support their client's position.[4] They investigate. Transactional lawyers, on the other hand, focus upon the object of the deal, especially from the client's perspective, and consider what might go wrong. They imagine. Consider the following Exercise, the first of many you will be asked to tackle in this book.

---

[2] It is therefore a major reputational problem for a transactional lawyer to be known as "a deal killer."

[3] Occasionally, a party might seek prospective relief for a wrong that has not yet occurred. For example, a wife might seek a temporary restraining order against further contact from a violent husband or the owner of a trademark might seek an injunction against future infringement. Even in those cases, however, granting the requested relief will typically depend on whether predicate facts justify it.

[4] Recall the old saw:
    If the law is not on your side, argue the facts,
    If the facts are not on your side, argue the law, and
    If the facts and law are not on your side, pound the table.
The import of that quip is that a lawyer handling a controversy often tries to fit the existing facts or the law into a narrative that suits the client's interests.

Exercise 1-1[5]

Four law school classmates have decided that they would like to rent a house together as way of reducing their living expenses. The class will be split into four groups, each representing one of four proposed roommates. The proposed roommates are all third-year law students who attend the same school. Here are their names and some minor biographical information:

Andrea – Her home is in New Jersey; her family is very well off; she is an only child; she is quiet and is the smartest of the group; she is the one who needs to study the least but does study the most; she is near the top of the class; she drives a late-model American car.

Jim – His home is in Wisconsin; his family is working class; he receives a small scholarship; he is one of three siblings; he is gregarious and well-liked by most people; he is very athletic, having played varsity baseball in college; he drives a 17-year-old Toyota; he is ranked in the middle of his class.

Paul – His home is in New Hampshire; his family is working class; he is one of four siblings; he studies all the time; he is on law review; he drives an old Chevrolet; he is highly ambitious.

Stacy – Her home is in California; her family is well off; she is an only child; she is an extrovert; she drives a late-model Porsche; she is a chain smoker; she has not been a serious student.

The house that the classmates plan to rent has the following characteristics:
- It is furnished;
- It has a kitchen with a breakfast area and a living room with a fireplace, sofa, two arm chairs, and one television;
- It has one master bedroom with an attached bathroom, two standard bedrooms with a communal bathroom; and a makeshift bedroom in the basement;
- It needs to be heated in the winter and air conditioned in the warm weather months;
- It has a two car garage;
- Free parking is available on the street, but it is restricted on specified days to facilitate street cleaning and trash collection;

---

[5]   Inspired by William E. Foster and Emily Grant, *Memorializing the Meal: An Analogical Exercise for Transactional Drafting*, 36 U. HAW. L. REV. 403 (2014).

- It is approximately 1.5 miles from the law school; public transportation is available, but it is not particularly practical given the route to the law school;
- The lease will have a one-year term, from August 1 until July 31, and rent will be $4,000 per month; and
- A security deposit equal to one month's rent is required at the time the parties execute the lease.

Identify the issues and contingencies that the proposed roommates should discuss and which of these an agreement among them should address. Do not attempt to resolve the issues or contingencies; merely identify them.

Lastly, after a transactional lawyer has identified the risks inherent in a transaction – that is, both the legal issues and the potential future problems that might arise – the lawyer must assess each of them. Not all risks are equal, so this assessment requires judgment and an ability to separate the "wheat from the chaff."[6] More specifically, a transactional lawyer needs to be able to weigh each risk against the objective of the client – whether essential, important, or desirable -- that the risk jeopardizes.[7]

The lawyer must then consider whether there are ways – or devise new strategies – to eliminate or minimize the risks. Sometimes, this implicates ethical issues (*i.e.*, a lawyer should never advise a client to commit a criminal or fraudulent act to address a risk). More commonly, it might mean adding or altering a term to the transaction agreement or even changing the structure of the transaction. However, the lawyer is unlikely to be able to eliminate all risk. Accordingly, the lawyer should confer with the client to identify and manage the most salient risks. In doing this, it is not that the lawyer needs to stop thinking like a lawyer, but that the lawyer must also think like a client.

If no amount of creativity can satisfactorily mitigate the risks, then the lawyer needs to provide advice and judgment to the client as to whether the identified legal

---

[6]   *See* Tina L. Stark, *Thinking Like a Deal Lawyer*, 54 J. LEGAL EDUC. 223, 229 (2004) ("most lawyers . . . have been taught issue spotting. But if that is all that a lawyer does, she will justly earn a reputation as a deal killer. To be effective, she must assess the probability that a risk will occur and, if it is significant, find a way to limit it.").

[7]   *See* ROGER FISHER AND WILLIAM URY, GETTING TO YES: NEGOTIATING AGREEMENT WITHOUT GIVING IN (2011).

issues significantly jeopardize one or more of the client's essential objectives.[8] To be clear, assessing and weighing risks is not the same as making the decision. The client will expect the lawyer to identify and explain the risks – especially the legal risks – associated with a transaction. The decision whether to accept a risk is the client's.

If the discussion so far has not whetted your appetite for transactional practice, and you are intent instead on being a litigator, it is worth remembering two things: (i) most litigation is resolved through a settlement; and (ii) as noted on page 5, litigators who prepare settlement agreements are engaged in transactional practice. For an example of what this might mean, consider the following:

> A patent holder ("PH") brought suit against a competitor's subsidiaries ("D1" and "D2"), claiming that they infringed a valuable patent owned by PH. After discovery concluded and motions were heard and ruled upon, the parties informally agreed to settle the matter rather than to proceed to trial.
>
> The terms of the settlement call for:
>
> (1) D1 and D2 to pay PH $50,000 at the time that the settlement agreement is signed and $250,000 in specified installments over a period of years;
>
> (2) PH to grant D1 and D2 a license of the patent for a period of years, with D1 and D2 to pay specified license fees during that period; and
>
> (3) each party to provide the other with a general release.
>
> These terms arguably constitute a fairly straightforward business arrangement. Even so, before memorializing them in writing, the litigator – now turned transactional lawyer – needs to consider a number of issues, including each of the following:
>
> (a) Are the license agreement and the deferred settlement payments cross-defaulted? Thus, if the Ds fail to make a payment under the license agreement, does that allow PH to both terminate the license agreement and accelerate the unpaid balance of the deferred settlement payments? Similarly, if the Ds fail to make a deferred

---

[8] Remember, however, that a risk with a 0.01% probability of creating a $5 billion problem is not a $500,000 issue. It is still a $5 billion issue. Think of the Exxon Valdez, the BP oil spill, *etc. See* Philip E. Tetlock and Dan Gardner, SUPERFORECASTING: THE ART AND SCIENCE OF PREDICTION 145 (2015) ("whether the correct probability is 5% or 1% . . . matters if the consequences of the improbable are great enough. Imagine an Ebola outbreak. Or funding the next Google.").

settlement payment, does that allow PH to both accelerate the unpaid balance of those payments and terminate the license agreement?

(b) Is the license exclusive or non-exclusive and is it worldwide or is it limited to a specified geographical area?

(c) With respect to the deferred settlement payments and the license fees, are D1 and D2 to be jointly and severally liable, jointly liable, or is one primarily liable and the other is secondarily liable?[9]

(d) Are the payment obligations of D1 and D2 to be guaranteed by their parent company?

(e) Is PH to release its claims against D1 and D2 on the date that the settlement agreement is executed and the $50,000 is paid or only if and when the deferred installments are paid in full? That is to say, is there a novation or should the release be conditioned upon receipt of all of the payments? If the latter is the case, query whether the release is also to be conditioned upon receipt of the license fees or whether the payment of the license fees is in the nature of an independent obligation.[10]

As this example illustrates, the settlement terms that the parties agreed upon are akin to a term sheet that business people work out in connection with a proposed transaction. In both cases, the key business terms have been outlined, but the details about how those terms are to be implemented need to be explored and determined in large part by the lawyer, regardless of whether that lawyer is primarily a litigator.

---

[9]   For more information regarding the distinctions between these different types of liability, see the discussion beginning on page 42.

Note, if one of the subsidiaries will be primarily liable and the other secondarily liable – either due to the express terms of the settlement agreement or because this is how the law will interpret the nature of their obligations – the agreement should include suretyship waivers by the entity that is secondarily liable.

[10]   Irrespective of how those issues are resolved, as a drafting matter, the settlement agreement should avoid phrasing the release so that it covers PH's claims for the deferred settlement payments or the license fees.

CHAPTER TWO
THE COMPONENTS OF AN AGREEMENT

A. THE STRUCTURE OF WRITTEN AGREEMENTS

Most written agreements have the same basic structure:
1. Title
2. Preamble
3. Recitals
4. Definitions
5. Contract Body
   A. Deal-Specific Terms
   B. General Terms
6. Signature Blocks

1. Title

The title usually identifies the type of agreement, such as "Sales Agreement" or "Lease." It is useful for locating the document in a file folder or drawer filled with other documents, but usually lacks any independent significance. In those few circumstances where the nature of the parties' arrangement is unclear from the language used in the body of the document and yet important to determining their rights, the label the parties attach to their relationship might signify their intent but is unlikely to be determinative. Instead, the economic reality of their transaction often governs what type of agreement the parties have formed.[1]

Notice that the discussion above refers to the written document as an "agreement," not as a "contract." While you might encounter documents labeled as a "contract" of one type or another (*e.g.*, a "Sales Contract"), such a label is potentially misleading. Under the Uniform Commercial Code, which governs many commercial transactions, an "agreement" is the bargain of the parties in fact, whereas a "contract" is the legal obligation that arises from an agreement.[2] The

---

[1] *See, e.g.*, U.C.C. §§ 1-203, 9-109(a)(1).

[2] *See* U.C.C. § 1-201(b)(3), (12).

Restatement (Second) of Contracts defines the two terms similarly.[3] Thus, whether an agreement exists is a factual issue; whether an agreement creates a contract is a legal issue. Put another way, parties sign agreements; they do not sign contracts.[4]

2. Preamble

The preamble identifies the parties and the date (although the date is often placed instead on the signature page, particularly if the parties will sign separately, at different times).

> This Agreement ("Agreement") is made this fifth day of April, 2015, by and between Franklin Properties, LLC, a Washington limited liability company ("Landlord") and Office Supply Store, Inc., a California corporation ("Tenant").

Notice the three parenthetical phrases, each in quotes. This is a manner of creating a defined term. Thus, in the example above, all further references in the written document to "Landlord" (with a capital "L") will mean Franklin Properties, LLC. Similarly, all further references to "Tenant" will mean Office Supply Store, Inc. It is, of course, not necessary to define the parties in such a manner. The agreement could use the parties' full names throughout the document. Alternatively, it could define them using an abbreviated name for each party (*e.g.*, "Franklin," and "OSS"). However, it is customary to use terms that correspond to the parties' relationship to each other, such as landlord and tenant, buyer and seller, or lender and borrower. This practice makes the document easier to understand and helps third parties not get confused about the role each party plays in the transaction.

---

[3] *See* RESTATEMENT (SECOND) OF CONTRACTS §§ 1 (defining a contract as "a promise or a set of promises for the breach of which the law gives a remedy or the performance of which the law in some way recognizes as a duty."), 3.

[4] *But cf.* Preston M. Torbert, *A Study of the Risks of Contract Ambiguity*, 2 PEKING UNIV. TRANSNATIONAL L. REV. 1, 40 (2014) (implying that because the word "agreement" in the title of a document might refer to a binding or nonbinding document, the parties should use the word "contract" when they intend to be bound).

3. Recitals

Recitals are often used to explain the background to the agreement: why the parties are entering into the agreement and what they hope to achieve. For example, a guaranty agreement might contain recitals such as:

> Whereas, Child wants a loan from Bank to start a new business,
>
> Whereas, Bank is willing to lend funds to Child to start the new business only if Parent guarantees the debt, and
>
> Whereas Parent is willing to guaranty Bank's loan to Child.

Recitals might also be used to identify the consideration for the agreement. For example, the recitals in that same guaranty agreement might continue in either of the following ways:

> In consideration of the foregoing, **Parent and Bank agree as follows**:

> In consideration of $10.00, receipt of which is hereby acknowledged, and other good and valuable consideration, **the parties hereby agree as follows**:

In most, but not all, states, these recitals (all the text in black in the three blocks above; not the text in blue) have no legal significance. They are not enforceable provisions.[5] They do not provide rights or detail remedies. This is particularly true

---

[5]   *See, e.g.*, Abraham Zion Corp. v. Lebow, 761 F.2d 93, 103 (2d Cir. 1985) (quoting Genovese Drug Stores v. Connecticut Packing Co., 732 F.2d 286, 291 (2d Cir. 1984)) ("Although a statement in a 'whereas' clause may be useful in interpreting an ambiguous operative clause in a contract, it cannot 'create any right beyond those arising from the operative terms of the document' "); Skaff v. Progress Int'l, LLC, 2014 WL 5454825 (S.D.N.Y. 2014) (recital clause in security agreement indicating that the collateral was limited to deposit accounts did not affect broader security interest granted in merger agreement); Paloian v. Grupo Serla S.A. de C.V., 433 B.R. 19, 32 (N.D. Ill. 2010) (recitals are not binding unless referred to the operative portions of the agreement); Trafton v. Rocketplane Kistler, Inc., 2010 WL 771511, *4 (E.D. Wis. 2010) ("The fact that one of the 'whereas' recitals sets forth both sides' expectations does not create some kind of condition precedent. It is well-established, moreover, that 'whereas' clauses exist merely to provide context and are not themselves part of the agreement"); Irwin v. West Gate Bank, 848

with respect to a recital of consideration; a mere recital that consideration exists or has been provided will not prevent either party from proving that consideration is in fact lacking.[6]

Given this, you might be wondering why contracting parties – and their lawyers – use recitals. The most common answer is tradition, which is really not an answer at all. Another reason is that, particularly in complex transactions, they provide context to help a later reader (possibly a judge) understand the terms that follow or the reason that the parties have entered into the agreement (*e.g.*, to settle a dispute). That context can occasionally be useful in construing terms that are unclear or ambiguous. A third reason for using a recital – perhaps the most important – is that it can occasionally help stave off a claim of misrepresentation, such as by indicating that each party was represented by counsel, had ample opportunity to review the agreement, and was not relying on any representation made by the other party.[7] The fact remains, however, that recitals are generally unnecessary. In some cases they are even worse than that. Sometimes an agreement contains a recital that should be a representation, a warranty, or both. We discuss representations and warranties below. For now, just remember that such terms should be clearly identified for what they are, not buried in a recital and thereby perhaps stripped of their meaning.

The text in blue in the blocks above are words of agreement. They are not recitals; they are, instead, the foundation of the document. Such words, or others to the same effect, are essential and should appear once in every written agreement.

N.W.2d 605 (Neb. 2014) (a recital of consideration, "[a]s a statement of fact, it may be explained or contradicted by extrinsic evidence").

Some jurisdictions, however, give legal effect to recitals. *See* Cal. Evid. Code § 622 ("[t]he facts recited in a written instrument are conclusively presumed to be true as between the parties thereto, or their successors in interest"); Or. Rev. Stat. § 42.300 ("Except for the recital of a consideration, the truth of the facts recited from the recital in a written instrument shall not be denied by the parties thereto").

[6] *See* RESTATEMENT (SECOND) OF CONTRACTS § 218 & cmt. e. *See also* Cal. Evid. Code § 622 (while most recitals conclusively bind the parties, a recital of consideration does not).

[7] Although recitals are not themselves representations, and therefore do not help establish the underlying facts necessary to support a claim for misrepresentation, they can be useful as an acknowledgment that undermines one or more of the elements of a claim of misrepresentation. *See* FSL Acquisition Corp. v. Freeland Systems, LLC, 686 F. Supp. 2d 921(D. Minn. 2010) (dealing with a disclaimer of reliance in an asset-purchase agreement).

4. Definitions

Brief written agreements might not need definitions. However, if a written agreement refers to the same concept many times, it is often useful to create a short term as a substitute for the concept, particularly if the concept itself takes many words to express. For example, if the owner of a business is agreeing to sell all the equipment and inventory of the business to a buyer, it would be very cumbersome to identify all the property to be sold in every place that the agreement refers to that property. Instead, the parties could simply define a single term to mean all the property that will be sold. For example:

> "Property" means all equipment, inventory, and other goods of the Seller located at 123 Main Street on December 1, 2015.

This technique is particularly useful when describing real property because legal descriptions of realty are notoriously long and complex. Instead of repeating the entire description in every place the agreement refers to the property, it is far simpler to state the legal description just once and use it to create a defined term that the written agreement will then use throughout.

Using defined terms does more than save space and make written agreements more readable. It also helps prevent error, such as might occur if the written agreement used slightly different words in different places to refer to the same concept. Lawyers and judges typically assume that different words mean different things, and they often struggle to force a different meaning into terms with only a slight variation in language. Therefore, wherever you mean the same thing, use the same words. Defined terms and their definitions help you do that. We will return to the art and skill involved in drafting definitions in Chapter Five.

5. The Body of the Written Agreement

The body of the agreement contains the operative portions of the agreement. This includes the deal-specific terms, such as the quantity of goods to be sold, the price to be paid for real estate, and the duration of a lease or employment agreement. It also includes everything else that either party promises to do or to refrain from doing, every right either party expressly grants to the other, and every representation or warranty that either party makes. The body of the agreement will usually also include other, more general provisions. These might include a choice of governing law, a choice of forum, information on where or how notifications are to be sent, rules on assignment and delegation, or a statement about whether headings in the written agreement are relevant to its interpretation.

Although not required, it is usually a good idea to present the terms in the body of the document in some logical sequence. For example, you could list all of the duties of one party followed by all of the duties of the other party. Alternatively, you could list their rights and responsibilities in roughly the chronological order that you expect them to arise.[8] Another common approach is to list the deal-specific terms before the more general terms that are likely to appear in many agreements of the type involved. A logical structure helps the drafter keep track of everything, and thus not omit something important. It also helps make sure there are no duplications or internal conflicts.

6. Signature Blocks

The last portion of a written agreement will be a place for all parties to affix their signatures. If an agreement is being signed by an individual, no identifying information is required, although it is both customary and beneficial to indicate the name of the individual where he or she is to sign the document. In contrast, when a document is being executed on behalf of an entity (*e.g.*, a corporation or a limited liability company), it is important that the signer's representative capacity is properly reflected.[9] Thus, if a party to an agreement is a corporation or limited liability company, then the signature block should clearly indicate that the individual signing is in fact doing so on behalf of the entity. For example:

Office Supply Store, Inc.,

by: _____
     Pat Smith, President

---

[8] *See* Estate of Fisher v. PNC Bank, 769 F. Supp. 2d 853 (D. Md. 2011) (interpreting provisions of a will to apply in chronological order).

[9] *See, e.g.,* Credit Suisse Securities (USA) LLC v. West Coast Opportunity Fund, LLC, 2009 WL 2356881 (Del. Ch. Ct. 2009) (individual who signed in his individual capacity an agreement promising not to pledge "directly or indirectly" certain corporate stock for one year did not thereby prevent a limited liability company which he owned and controlled from pledging its own stock to its broker).

For the same reasons, if an individual is entering into an agreement both in an individual capacity and in a representative capacity, the individual should sign multiple times, once in each capacity, and that capacity should be properly identified.[10] For example:

Pat Smith	Office Supply Store, Inc.
_____	by: _____
	Pat Smith, President

B. THE TYPES OF CONTRACT TERMS

The body of a written agreement usually contains several different types of terms. Some terms impose duties (creating a correlative right in the other party), some grant authority or discretion (a different type of right), some create a condition, and some do other things. To fully understand the parties' rights and responsibilities under a written agreement, it is essential to appreciate the different types of terms, how each type is used, and what its consequences are. The reader must also be able to identify what type of term each written provision is.

The following chart provides a brief description of the different types of terms. Although not all lawyers and courts use this terminology, the classification below is used throughout the remainder of this book.

---

[10]   *See* Troubled Asset Solutions, LLC v. Wilcher, 2018 WL 2045251 (Or. Ct. App. 2018) (an individual who, to secure a $5 million note, signed a deed of trust only in his capacity as the sole member of an LLC and not also in his individual capacity encumbered the LLC's real property but not his own, even though the document expressly identified three parcels owned by him as additional collateral; the lender was not entitled to have the deed of trust reformed because it was grossly negligent). *But cf.* Western Surety Co. v. La Cumbre Office Partners, LLC, 213 Cal. Rptr. 3d 460 (Cal. Ct. App. 2017) (because the official capacity of a person signing an agreement on behalf of a limited liability company does not need to be indicated, an LLC was bound an indemnity agreement signed by the managing member of its manager, even though the agreement mistakenly identified him as the LLC's managing member).

Despite the risk, it is not uncommon when numerous affiliated entities are entering into an agreement and an individual holds the same office with respect to each entity, for the signature block to list all of the entities and for the individual to sign once on behalf of all the entities. Of course, before constructing a signature block in this manner, it is essential to confirm that the individual holds precisely the same office as to each of the relevant entities.

Type of Term	Definition	Effect/Purpose
Covenant	A promise to do or refrain from doing something; a duty.	Creates contract liability if breached (*i.e.*, if not fulfilled).
Discretionary Authority	A right to choose whether to take an action or what action to take.	Creates permission for one party to choose between stated actions or to act pursuant to a specified standard.
Condition to the Agreement	A predicate to the existence of the agreement.	Unless and until the condition is satisfied, there is no deal.
Condition to an Obligation	A predicate to a duty.	Establishes the circumstance that must exist (or not exist) before a party must perform a specific duty. A condition might be outside the control of the parties or within the control of one of them. Failure of a condition is not a breach, unless it is also made a duty (*i.e.*, a covenant).
Condition to Discretionary Authority	A predicate to a right.	Establishes the circumstance that must exist (or not exist) before a party may exercise discretionary authority.
Present Transfer of Rights	A transfer of rights to property.	Constitutes all or part of one party's performance.
Waiver of Rights or Release of Claim	A surrender of rights provided for by law or contract, or the relinquishment of an existing claim.	Prevents a party from asserting a right or claim.

Type of Term	Definition	Effect/Purpose
Representation	A statement of a past or present (but not future) fact made by one party to the other.	Creates potential tort liability if untrue and might be grounds for rescission.
Warranty	A promise that a past, present, or future fact is true.	Creates contract liability if not true.
Declaration	A statement as to which the parties agree.	Defines terms or establishes rules applicable to the transaction or to the parties' relationship.

These different types of contract terms are the building blocks of agreements, each with different shape:

In general, the proper type of term must be used or the structure can become unstable and collapse. That said, it is sometimes possible to substitute one type of contract term for another, without a significant problem, just as one might use two square blocks in a place where a single rectangle is needed.[11] Before exploring the distinctions among the different types of contract terms, and the circumstances when one type of term can safely substitute for another, however, it is useful to discuss the language used to create each type of term.

---

[11] On the other hand, sometimes a single deal point should be drafted as two or more different types of contract terms in order to fully satisfy the client's objectives.

1. The Language Appropriate for Each Type of Term

Because contract terms are created with words, not wood, they are a bit like a wizard's spells: if the proper words are not invoked, the effort might lead to some very nasty and unintended results. This is not to say that rigid formalism is required. It means merely that, after determining what type of term each clause of an agreement should be, the drafter must be careful to use the word or words necessary in each case to create the type of term intended.

This might sound fairly simple and, indeed, it is. Nevertheless, errors abound.[12] In particular, you are likely to see errant uses of the word "will." Drafters frequently says things such as "the seller will deliver the goods," or "the buyer will pay each installment on the first business day of each month." Presumably, the drafter intended each of these sentences to impose a duty. That is, each was to be a covenant, a promise to perform. However, "will" is merely a prediction of future events; it does not evidence a promise or create a duty. To do that, the drafter of these sentences should have used "shall."[13]

On the other hand, you are more likely to see excessive and improper use of the word "shall." The word "shall" should be used only to create a covenant (*i.e.,* to impose a duty). Some drafters, however, reflexively use "shall" when they intend to create other types of contract terms, particularly declarations, perhaps under the erroneous belief that the word is necessary to indicate the binding nature of the term or the importance that the parties attached to it. This is known as a false imperative. Consider the following examples:

> This agreement **shall** be binding upon the parties' successors and assigns.

---

[12]   Drafters are not the only ones who make these errors; courts often make these errors as well. *See* Quality Wash Group V, Ltd., v. Hallak, 58 Cal. Rptr. 2d 592 (1996) (conflating representations and warranties).

[13]   *See, e.g.,* Brandt v. Lee, 2015 WL 506443 (Minn. Ct. App. 2015) (a letter, sent by the holder of a purchase option, stating "please take this as formal notification of my intent to exercise the option" was unclear as to whether it actually exercised the option or merely provided notification of the intent to do so). *Cf.* Ferry v. Black Diamond Video, Inc., 2016 WL 3381237 (D.N.J. 2016) (an email message indicating that the plaintiff "intended" to exercise his stock purchase rights might have been effective and thus motion to dismiss complaint for breach of contract was denied).

> If any provision of this agreement shall be deemed unenforceable, and
> if limiting the provision would make the provision valid, then the
> provision shall be deemed so limited.

The first example purports to put an obligation not on one of the parties, but on an inanimate object: the agreement itself. That is common but improper. The second example contains two misuses of the word "shall." The first use of the word is in a condition (if a provision is unenforceable), and thus does not involve a duty at all. The second use is in connection with an attempt to create an interpretive rule, which should be a declaration. However, the term is phrased as a covenant with the duty implicitly falling on the entity interpreting and enforcing the agreement: a court. This is improper because private parties cannot in their agreements issue binding commands to or impose duties on any third party, let alone a court or judge.

Although the improper use of "shall" is quite common, it can lead to significant problems. Consider the following three attempts to create a security interest (a type of consensual lien):

> Borrower hereby grants Lender a security interest in [specified
> property] to secure the loan.

> The loan is secured by [specified property].

> Borrower shall grant Lender a security interest in [specified property]
> to secure the loan.

The first, phrased as a present transfer of rights, is effective to create a security interest in the specified property.[14] The second, phrased as a declaration, is probably also sufficient.[15] The third, phrased as a covenant through the use of the word "shall," might not be adequate because, instead of indicating a present transfer

---

[14]   That is, the language will achieve the desired result provided there is no other impediment to the creation of the security interest in the specified property. *See* U.C.C. §§ 9-102(a)(74), 9-203(b) (respectively, defining "security agreement" and detailing the requirements for attachment of a security interest).

[15]   *See* In re Amex-Protein Dev. Corp., 504 F.2d 1056 (9th Cir. 1974).

of rights, it seems to require the Borrower to transfer a security interest in the future, a duty that the Borrower might or might not perform.[16]

Another example of a false imperative is the following choice-of-forum clause:

> Jurisdiction and venue for any action brought to enforce this Agreement shall lie in the Circuit Court for the Thirteenth Judicial Circuit of the State of Florida.

Use of the word "shall" suggests that the clause is a mandatory choice-of-forum clause, one that limits litigation to the stated forum. However, neither party is the subject of the sentence; instead the subjects are two inanimate things: jurisdiction and venue. As a result, the clause might simply be declaring that jurisdiction and venue in that court is proper, while not excluding the possibility that jurisdiction

---

[16] *See* National Oilwell Varco, L.P. v. Omron Oilfield & Marine, Inc., 676 F. App'x 967 (Fed. Cir. 2017) (affirming on other grounds the trial court's conclusion that the phrase "Contributor shall convey, assign, and transfer the Property to Partnership" was merely a promise to transfer in the future, not a present transfer); LHPT Columbus, LLC v. Capitol City Cardiology, Inc., 2014 WL 6657164 (Ohio Ct. App. 2014) (clause in wind-up agreement providing that "[t]he real estate leases . . . shall be assigned . . . by an Assignment of Lease . . . substantially in the form attached hereto" did not in fact assign the leases).

The same issue can arise with the use of "shall" in a statute. Consider a statute that provides as follows:

> All deeds conveying any lands situate in this State shall be recorded in the office for the recording of deeds in the county where such lands are situate.

Does "shall" create a duty to record every deed or is it merely intended to limit the place in which parties are to record a deed, if they choose to do so? This issue has been the subject of some very substantial litigation. *See* Montgomery Cty., Pa. v. MERSCORP, Inc., 904 F. Supp. 2d 436 (E.D. Pa. 2012). It is interesting to note that the actual statute at issue contained another "shall" that clearly did not create a duty – it meant simply "is" – but the court nevertheless concluded that the statute imposed a duty to record deeds. *Cf.* Harris Cty. v. MERSCORP, Inc., 791 F.3d 545 (5th Cir. 2015) (ruling that a Texas recording statute that uses the word "must" does not impose an affirmative duty to record, it merely dictates the manner in which documents are to be recorded). Without a duty to record, there is no cause of action. *See, e.g., id.;* Union Cty., Ill. v. MERSCORP, Inc., 920 F. Supp. 2d 923 (S.D. Ill. 2013); Jackson Cty., Mo. *ex rel.* Nixon v. MERSCORP, Inc., 915 F. Supp. 2d 1064 (W.D. Mo. 2013); Plymouth Cty. Iowa *ex rel.* Raymond v. MERSCORP, Inc., 886 F. Supp. 2d 1114 (N.D. Iowa 2012); Christian Cty. Clerk *ex rel.* Kem v. Mortgage Elec. Registration Sys. Inc., 2012 WL 566807 (W.D. Ky. 2012).

and venue might also be proper elsewhere. That is what a court interpreting this language ruled.[17]

To avoid confusion, drafters need to be careful and consistent when selecting the verb for the type of contract term desired. Specifically, unless you have some very good reason for doing otherwise, choose a verb according to the following chart.

Type of Term	Proper Word(s)
Covenant	"shall" or "promises to" (or "shall not" or "promises not to")
Discretionary Authority	"may" (or "need not")
Condition	"if" (or "must")
Present Transfer of Rights	"grants," "transfers," "assigns," or, if appropriate to the transaction, "sells," "leases," "licenses," "consigns," "pledges," or a similar, active verb.
Waiver or Release	"waives" or "releases"
Representation	"represents"
Warranty	"warrants"
Declaration	"is" or some other verb in the present tense (*e.g.,* "means" for a definition; "governs" for a choice-of-law clause).

A corollary to this admonition is to refrain from using each of the verbs referenced above in any other manner or in any other type of term.[18]

---

[17] *See* Thompson v. Founders Group Int'l, Inc., 886 P.2d 904 (Kan. Ct. App. 1994).

[18] *See* Mitteldorf v. B&W Appraisal Servs., Inc., 2017 WL 120905 (Cal. Ct. App. 2017) (refusing the regard the word "may" in an appraisal letter as a grant of discretion even though it is sometimes used in the conditional sense – that is, to mean "might").

2. Examples of Types of Terms

To illustrate the different types of contract terms, consider the following excerpt from an agreement for the purchase and sale of real property. Each term in the body of the agreement is labeled, in blue, with its type.

Purchase and Sale Agreement

This agreement ("Agreement") is made on January 6, 2015, by and between Jean R. Yawkey ("Seller") and John W. Henry ("Buyer").

1. *Property.* On or before March 1, 2015 (the "Closing Date") **[the creation of a defined term is a Declaration]**, Seller agrees to sell to Buyer and Buyer agrees to purchase from Seller the following described property **[mutual Covenants; that is each party is promising to do something]** (the "Property") **[Declaration]**:

[Description of Property]

2. *Purchase Price.* The purchase price is $600,000, payable as follows:

    (a) a deposit in the amount of $10,000 upon signing of this Agreement; and

    (b) $590,000 (the "Balance of the Purchase Price") on the Closing Date. **[Declaration]**

3. *Financing.* Buyer's duty to purchase is contingent on the Buyer obtaining mortgage financing, satisfactory to Buyer, in the amount of $590,000. **[Condition to an Obligation]** Buyer shall, within five days of the date hereof, apply for and diligently pursue a mortgage loan for such amount. **[Covenant]** If Buyer does not obtain a commitment for such a mortgage loan within 30 days of the date hereof **[Condition]**, Buyer shall so inform Seller **Covenant]** and, in such case, Seller will then have the option to provide the mortgage financing. **[Discretionary Authority]** If Seller elects not to provide the mortgage financing **[Condition]**, Buyer may cancel this Agreement **[Discretionary Authority]**. If Buyer cancels this Agreement under this paragraph **[Condition]**, Seller shall refund Buyer's deposit **[Covenant]**.

4. *Inspection.* Before the Closing Date, and after reasonable advance notification to Seller, Buyer and Buyer's representatives may inspect the Property. **[Discretionary Authority]** Buyer bears the cost of any such inspection. **[Covenant]**

5. *Condition of Property.* If for any reason Buyer is not satisfied with the results of any inspection [Condition], Buyer shall deliver to Seller [Covenant] a statement detailing the problems and either (i) a written notice of cancellation, canceling this Agreement; or (ii) a written proposal detailing what Seller must do to satisfy Buyer about the condition of the Property [Discretionary Authority]. If Buyer cancels this Agreement under this paragraph or Seller rejects Buyer's written proposal [Condition], Seller shall refund Buyer's deposit [Covenant]. If Seller accepts Buyer's written proposal [Condition], Seller shall comply with all terms in such proposal [Covenant].

6. *Closing.*

(a) On the Closing Date, Seller shall transfer to Buyer, by general warranty deed, good and marketable title to the Property, free and clear of all liens, encumbrances, easements, and restrictions, except as otherwise provided herein. [Covenant] If Seller is unable to deliver such title to Buyer on the Closing Date [Condition], Buyer may terminate this Agreement [Discretionary Authority].

(b) On the Closing Date, Buyer shall transfer to Seller, in immediately available funds, the Balance of the Purchase Price. [Covenant] If Buyer is unable to deliver such Balance of the Purchase Price to Seller in immediately available funds on the Closing Date [Condition], Seller may terminate this Agreement [Discretionary Authority].

7. *Default by Buyer.* If Buyer fails to perform Buyer's obligations under this Agreement [Condition], Seller may retain any deposits made by Buyer as agreed liquidated damages in full settlement of any claim for damages [Discretionary Authority].

8. *Broker's Commission.* This Agreement was brought about by George Sorkin ("Broker"). [Declaration] Seller is responsible for paying any commission or other fee due to Broker. [Declaration]

Exercise 2-1

One of the terms in the excerpt above is mislabeled. Identify which term is labeled incorrectly and what type of contract term it really is.

3. The Significance of the Distinctions: Choosing the Appropriate Term

Returning to the metaphor of contract terms as building blocks , in many cases, it is possible to draft a particular component of the parties' deal in any one of several different ways, each using a different type of contract term. For example, the last sentence of the Purchase and Sale Agreement preceding Exercise 2-1 is phrased as a declaration but it could just as easily have been drafted as a covenant: "Seller shall pay all commissions and other fees due to Broker arising out of this Agreement." Similarly, suppose, Buyer agreed to pay Seller $20,000 for a car, to be paid in two, equal installments. That payment obligation could be expressed as a covenant:

> Buyer shall pay Seller $10,000 on June 1 and another $10,000 on July 1.

Alternatively, it could be phrased as a covenant (the first sentence in the example below) and a declaration (the second sentence in the example below):

> Buyer shall pay Seller $20,000. $10,000 is due on June 1 and the remaining $10,000 is due on July 1.

On the whole, it might not matter which of these variations the parties use. For another example, assume that Dealer leased a car to Consumer for three years. In connection with that transaction, Consumer is to have the option to buy the car at the end of the lease term for $18,000. That option could be expressed as discretionary authority:

> At the end of the lease term, Consumer may purchase the car by paying Dealer $18,000.

Alternatively, it could be phrased as a covenant (the language in blue in the example below) subject to a condition (the language beginning with "if" in the example below):

> Dealer shall sell the car to Consumer at the end of the lease term if Consumer tenders $18,000 to Dealer.

Again, it might not matter which of these alternatives the parties use.

In many cases, however, the type of term used can make a huge difference. The distinction between a covenant and a condition, for example, is often very important. Consider a contract in which you hire a gardener to mow your lawn every week for twelve weeks. The gardener gets sick and fails to mow the lawn during the third week of the contract term. If the gardener merely promised to mow the lawn (a covenant), the failure to do so in week three would be a breach which would give rise to a claim for damages, perhaps measured by the cost of hiring someone else to mow the lawn that week. If, however, the agreement expressly made mowing the lawn each week a promise by the gardener and made the gardener's failure to mow the lawn a condition to your right to terminate the agreement, you could not only claim damages for breach, you could also terminate the agreement and find someone else to mow the lawn for the remaining nine weeks of the original contract term.[19]

Similarly, if a purchase and sale agreement required the seller to deliver good title to the property to be sold, the buyer would have a claim for damages if the seller beached because the property sold was encumbered by a lien. If, however, delivery of good title were a condition to the buyer's duty to go through with the transaction, the buyer could refuse to pay and cancel the deal. Notice that, from the buyer's perspective, neither of these two types of terms – covenant or condition – can by itself fully protect the buyer. If delivery of good title were merely a covenant, the buyer might remain obligated to purchase the property even though it was encumbered and even though a claim against the seller for damages might never be paid or might otherwise fail to fully compensate the buyer for the lost expectancy. On the other hand, if the requirement of good title were only a condition to the buyer's duty, and the buyer discovered the problem after paying for and receiving the property, the condition would no longer be operative. Hence, at least from the buyer's perspective, the requirement of good title should be both a covenant and a condition.[20]

---

[19] Even if the agreement did not *expressly* make mowing each week a condition to continuation of the arrangement, it might have done so *implicitly* through the legal doctrine known as material breach.

[20] The distinction between a covenant and a condition arose in a very interesting way in MDY Indus., LLC v. Blizzard Entm't, Inc, 629 F.3d 928 (9th Cir. 2010). The dispute involved alleged copyright infringement of the software that runs the World of Warcraft game. The plaintiff had created a program to allow users to automate play during the early levels of the game, thereby enabling their avatars to accumulate experience and assets within the game. This software violated the terms of use for the game. Because each game user's computer copies the game software into RAM every time it activates the game, and making

For one more example, consider a contract that imposes a duty on one party to notify the other. A failure to provide the requisite notification would be a breach. In many cases, the damages available for such a breach would be little or nothing. If, however, notification is a condition to the other party's obligation to perform, a failure to notify might have significant consequences.[21]

Sometimes, the type of clause used for a particular term can affect a party's rights in surprising ways. For example, in one case arising out of the 2008 financial crisis, one party to a credit-default swap claimed it had a duty to find a new surety when the credit rating of the initial surety fell – a duty from which it claimed it was excused by the doctrine of impossibility – while the counterparty argued that the agreement merely gave the first party the option (discretionary authority) of finding a replacement, a right to which the doctrine of impossibility was not relevant. Thus, the parties were left in the ironic position of one party arguing that it was obligated and the other party arguing that the first party was not obligated.[22]

---

that copy would be an infringement of copyright if not authorized, the game developer claimed that the plaintiff had facilitated copyright infringement. The issue then revolved around whether: (i) users covenanted to comply with the terms of use, for which damages would be the appropriate remedy for breach; or (ii) compliance was a condition to the user's software license, which would negate the license giving rise to injunctive relief for violation of copyright. The court concluded that the terms of use made compliance a covenant, not a condition, and thus there was no violation of copyright.

[21] *See* Cajun Constructors, Inc. v. Velasco Drainage Dist., 380 S.W.3d 819, 825-26 (Tex. Ct. App. 2012):

> Although the term "condition precedent" is not used in [the agreement], subsection 10.05D states: " No claim for an adjustment in Contract Price . . . will be valid *if not submitted* in accordance with this paragraph 10.05." (emphasis added). Despite the fact that conditions precedent are disfavored such that courts will not construe a contract provision as a condition precedent unless compelled to do so by language that may be construed no other way, we conclude that this language constitutes a condition precedent. To construe this clause as anything other than a condition precedent would be to ignore its plain language. * * * Because Cajun did not comply with section 10.05's notice requirements, * * * it failed to satisfy the conditions precedent to suing Velasco for breach of contract. * * * Accordingly, Velasco established it was entitled to summary judgment.

[22] *See* Hoosier Energy Rural Elec. Coop. v. John Hancock Life Ins. Co., 582 F.3d 721 (7th Cir. 2009). Because of the posture of the case – a request for a preliminary injunction – the court declined to decide the matter.

4.   Representations & Warranties

The discussion so far has not covered representations and warranties but these are often critical components of an agreement. To understand what they are and what they do, it is first necessary to distinguish a representation from a declaration. Each is a kind of statement, rather than a promise or condition. The main distinction is that a declaration is a statement agreed to by both parties whereas a representation is a statement made by one party to the other. This distinction can be very important. Some declarations, such as definitions and rules of construction,[23] are useful when interpreting the written agreement of which they are a part. Such declarations can provide necessary meaning to the obligations of one or both parties.[24] Others – such as "this agreement is governed by New York law" or "all disputes are subject to binding arbitration" – can be enforced in court. However, declarations themselves do not give rise to an action for breach of contract or establish a basis for any other cause of action.

In contrast, a misrepresentation – that is, a false representation – can be actionable. So, for example, if you hired Plumber to tend to the water system in an apartment complex after Plumber falsely represented to be both experienced and licensed, you would likely have a basis for rescinding the agreement.

In most cases, the substance of a written statement makes it fairly obvious whether the statement is a declaration (agreed to by both parties) or representation (made by one party to the other). In rare cases it might be difficult to know what was intended, but good drafting can always avoid this problem.

A warranty can look a lot like a representation. For example, a statement in an apartment lease that "the appliances are in good working condition" could be a representation (a statement of fact) or a warranty (a promise of fact).[25] Yet the distinction between a representation and a warranty can be very important; in fact, it is the difference between tort and contract.[26]

---

[23]   One common rule of construction deals with section headings and provides: "Section headings are provided for convenience only and are not relevant to the meaning of this Agreement."

[24]   For example, a declaration of the price in a sales agreement or the interest rate in a loan agreement provides necessary meaning to the buyer's or borrower's covenant to pay.

[25]   It could also be a declaration. For example, the prospective tenant might, in the company of the landlord, have examined the appliances before executing the lease and the two parties might have agreed together that the appliances were all working properly.

[26]   In contrast, a promise by the landlord to maintain the appliances during the term of the

An action for damages based on a misrepresentation is a tort claim.[27] In contrast, while breach of warranty had its origin in tort, it is now generally viewed as a contract action.[28] As a result, imposing liability for a misrepresentation (an untrue statement of fact) is more difficult than imposing liability for a breached warranty. Both typically require proof that the statement was untrue and caused damages. However, an action for misrepresentation often also requires proof that the misrepresentation was material,[29] sometimes requires proof that the person making the misrepresentation knew or should have known that the statement was false, and usually requires proof that the other party reasonably or justifiably relied on the statement.[30] Liability for breach of warranty, in contrast, is a form of strict liability and does not require that the warrantor knew or had reason to know that the

---

lease and to promptly fix any appliance that malfunctions would be a covenant. While the distinction between a representation and a warranty can be very important, the distinction between a warranty (a promise of fact) and a covenant (a promise to do or not do) is often immaterial because both give rise to contract liability. *See infra* section B.5.

[27] *See, e.g.,* Ranes & Shine, LLC v. MacDonald Miller Alaska, Inc., 355 P.3d 503 (Alaska 2015) (treating misrepresentation as a tort subject to a different statute of limitations than a claim for breach or warranty).

A misrepresentation might also, under contract law, prevent a contract from being formed, make the contract voidable, or provide grounds for reformation. *See* RESTATEMENT (SECOND) OF CONTRACTS ch. 7, topic 1, Introductory Note. Indeed, a misrepresentation can make a contract voidable if it is material and the recipient justifiably relied on it, regardless of whether the maker knew or had reason to know of the representation's falsity. *Id*. § 164.

[28] *See* Lyon Fin. Servs., Inc. v. Ill. Paper and Copier Co., 732 F.3d 755 (7th Cir. 2013). *But cf.* Norcia v. Samsung Telecommunications Am., LLC, 845 F.3d 1279 (9th Cir. 2017) (purporting to distinguish contract law from warranty law).

[29] For a misrepresentation to be material does not mean that the representation must be materially incorrect, it means that the misrepresentation must relate to a fact material to the transaction or agreement. *See* RESTATEMENT (SECOND) OF TORTS § 522C(1).

[30] *See, e.g.,* DDJ Mgmt., LLC v. Rhone Group LLC, 931 N.E.2d 87 (N.Y. 2010) (reasonable reliance required for misrepresentation claim). *See also* Quality Wash Group V, Ltd. v. Hallak, 58 Cal. Rptr. 2d 592 (Cal. Ct. App. 1996) (ruling that a seller of a business was liable for breach of a warranty but not for misrepresentation).

Section 2-313 of the Uniform Commercial Code treats as a warranty any "affirmation of fact" that is made by a seller of goods, relates to the goods, and becomes part of the basis of the bargain. This arguably converts all or almost all representations about the goods into warranties. *See* CB Aviation, LLC v. Hawker Beechcraft Corp., 2011 WL 5386365 (E.D. Pa. 2011) (treating as a warranty a clause about an airplane which was phrased as a representation). Whether such statements also remain representations is unclear.

promised statement was untrue. It also does not require proof of reliance, reasonable or otherwise.[31]

On the other hand, the remedies available for an actionable misrepresentation are different, and sometimes greater, than those for breach of warranty. Specifically, the remedy for breach of warranty is typically some measure of expectancy damages, whereas the remedies for the tort of misrepresentation are typically some measure of reliance or restitution damages,[32] along with punitive damages if the misrepresentation was intentional.[33] Because of these differences, transactional lawyers frequently phrase factual statements as both representations and warranties to maximize the likelihood and extent of recovery should the fact prove to be inaccurate.

Finally, the scope of statements that a representation and a warranty can cover is different. A representation must be a statement of past or present fact; it cannot be about a future fact.[34] A warranty can be a promise about the past, present, or future. In addition, a representation generally cannot be about the law.[35] That is

---

[31] *See, e.g.,* Lyon Fin. Servs., Inc. v. Ill. Paper and Copier Co., 848 N.W.2d 539 (Minn. 2014).

[32] Expectancy damages are designed to give the aggrieved party the benefit of the bargain by putting that party in the position it would have been had the warranted statement been true. *See* RESTATEMENT (SECOND) OF CONTRACTS § 347. Reliance damages compensate the aggrieved party for the loss it suffered by restoring it to the position it was before the agreement was formed. *See id.* at § 349. Restitution damages, like reliance damages, also seek to restore the aggrieved party to its pre-contract position but the amount is determined by what the defendant received rather than what the plaintiff lost. *See id.* at §§ 370–373.

[33] Note, however, that in some cases tort remedies might be foreclosed by the economic loss doctrine. That doctrine, which is widely accepted but which varies significantly in scope, generally prohibits recovery in tort when a product defect or failure causes damage to itself but does not cause personal injury or damage to other property. The doctrine might also prohibit recovery in tort whenever the loss is compensable through a breach of contract claim. *But cf.* Cornelia Fifth Avenue, LLC v. Canizales, 2017 WL 1034644 (S.D.N.Y. 2017) (ruling that the economic loss doctrine did not apply to a misrepresentation claim).

[34] *See* RESTATEMENT (SECOND) OF CONTRACTS § 159 cmt. c. *See also* West Pac. Elec. Co. v. Dragados/Flatiron, 2018 WL 2088276 at *13 (E.D. Cal. 2018) (*citing Borba v. Thomas*, 138 Cal. Rptr. 565, 570 (Ct. App. 1977)).

[35] *See* Lyon Fin. Servs., Inc. v. Ill. Paper and Copier Co., 732 F.3d 755 (7th Cir. 2013); Barnes v. Reserve Energy Exploration, 68 N.E.3d 133, 141 (Ohio Ct. App. 2016) (under Ohio law, a representation of law cannot form the basis of an action for fraud in the absence of a fiduciary relationship). *Contra* RESTATEMENT (SECOND) OF CONTRACTS § 170 (relevant

because each party is presumed to know the law and thus cannot reasonably rely on a statement about the law by the other party. In contrast, a party might be able to warrant statements about the law.[36]

5. Warranties vs. Covenants

A note about the distinction between warranties and covenants is in order. Both are contractual promises – the former a promise of fact; the latter a promise to do or to refrain from doing something – and both create contract liability if breached. Nevertheless, there can be important differences between them. For example, a warranty of merchantability in a sale of goods deals with the quality of the goods at the time the seller tenders delivery. It is therefore breached, if at all, at that time. In contrast, a promise to fix or replace defective goods – a type of covenant – is breached only if and when the seller fails or refuses to fix or replace the goods. Consequently, the statute of limitations on a claim for breach of such a covenant would start to run later than would the limitations period on a claim for breach of the warranty of merchantability.[37]

6. Conditions

Conditions are ubiquitous. Almost every contract has one or more conditions, but it is vital to understand that conditions vary in at least three ways.

First, conditions vary in importance. Some conditions go to the very heart of the deal. In a bet on a sporting event, for example, each party's only duty is conditioned the outcome of the event. Similarly, the obligation of a lottery to pay a ticket holder is conditioned on the ticket having the winning numbers. Insurance contracts are another example in which one party's principal duty is subject to a condition. Although the policy holder's duty to pay is not conditioned, the insurer's duty to pay depends on whether and if the insured contingency occurs – the insured person dies; the insured vehicle is in an accident; the insured property is damaged by fire or vandals.

---

to contract-based remedies for misrepresentation, not damages).

[36] *See* Lyon Fin. Servs., Inc. v. Ill. Paper and Copier Co., 848 N.W.2d 539 (Minn. 2014).

[37] *See, e.g.,* Grosse Pointe Law Firm, PC v. Jaguar Land Rover North Am., LLC, 894 N.W.2d 700 (Mich. Ct. App. 2016).

In contrast, other conditions affect a minor aspect of the deal. The principal duty of an adjunct faculty member hired by a law school to coach a moot court team might be to provide guidance on written and oral advocacy before the regional competition. It the team wins the regional competition – a condition – the faculty member might have a further obligation to prepare the students for the national competition. The principal duty of a landlord is to provide the leased premised. The landlord might also have a duty to repair the plumbing but that duty is subject to the condition that a problem with the plumbing arises during the lease term.

Of course, the importance of a condition – or of the term to which a condition applies – is not a legal matter. It is instead a value judgment. The point of this discussion is merely that conditions, like other aspects of an agreement, can be very important, rather unimportant, or anywhere in between.

Second, conditions vary with respect to the type of term to which they apply. Many conditions, perhaps most, are a predicate to a covenant (*i.e.*, to a duty) owed by one of the parties. Each of the examples mentioned above is a condition to a covenant. However, a condition can be a predicate to several other types of contract terms. For example, a purchase and sale agreement for a business might make give the buyer the option to cancel the deal if a material adverse change occurs between the time the parties enter into the agreement and the time the transaction is to close. In such a case, the condition (a material adverse change) is a condition to discretionary authority (the buyer's option to cancel).[38] Alternatively, a lease might provide that if the landlord is, for a reason beyond the landlord's control, unable to provide the leased premises at the start of the lease term, rent will abate for the period of delay. That would be a condition (the landlord's inability to provide the premises) to a declaration (rent will abate).

On rare occasions, the very existence of an agreement can be subject to a condition. For example, an individual might agree to buy an item at a garage sale only if the individual's spouse, who is not present, consents.

Finally, a single deal point can be drafted as both a condition and a covenant. Drafting a term solely as a condition usually makes sense for a matter that is outside the control of either party. However, for a matter within one party's control, it might make sense to draft the term as both a covenant and a condition (often referred to as a "promissory condition"). A condition to what? – to one or more of the other party's duties.

---

[38] Alternatively, the agreement could be drafted so that the absence of a material adverse change was a condition to the buyer's duty (covenant) to consummate the purchase.

Consider an agreement between a homeowner and a plowing company to keep the homeowner's driveway clear of snow from December 1 through March 30. Under the agreement, if three or more inches of snow accumulate, the plowing company is to plow the driveway. On April 1, the homeowner is to pay $50 for each time the plowing company plowed. The terms can be classified as follows:

Accumulation of snow:	Condition only
Plowing:	Covenant & Condition[39]
Paying	Covenant only[40]

What if instead, the agreement called for the homeowner to pay within ten days after each time the plowing company plowed? Then perhaps the classification of the paying would change:

Accumulation of snow:	Condition only
Plowing:	Covenant & Condition
Paying	Covenant & Condition

That is, a court might now infer that timely payment by the homeowner after the plowing company clears the homeowner's driveway of snow (*i.e.*, the absence of a material breach) is a condition to the plowing company's duty to plow on future occasions.[41] Of course, if the parties intend a term to be both a covenant and a condition, they are well advised to expressly state that in their agreement, rather than to rely on the malleable concept of material breach to achieve the same result.

This is not to say that every event within a party's control should be both a covenant and a condition. But it is important to recognize making a term only a covenant or only a condition might not fully protect the other party. Not every covenant is performed. And while a failure to perform a covenant gives rise to a claim for breach, often the non-breaching party might want a right or remedy other than a claim. After all, litigation can be expensive, time consuming, and always carries the risk of failure. Similarly, the failure of condition can be an easy way to

---

[39] The covenant to plow is *conditioned on* the accumulation of snow, but that fact does not make the covenant a *condition to* something else. Nevertheless, plowing is a condition to the homeowner's duty to pay; that is why it is listed here as a condition.

[40] The homeowner's duty to pay is *conditioned on* plowing, but it is not a *condition to* anything else, and is therefore not a promissory condition. In other words, a promissory condition is a promise and a condition; that is different from a conditioned promise.

[41] *See* RESTATEMENT (SECOND) OF CONTRACTS §§ 224–229, 237.

discharge a duty, but is unlikely to be effective if failure will not occur or is unlikely to be discovered until after the duty is performed.

7. Waivers vs. Releases

Waiver is traditionally defined as either the voluntary or intentional relinquishment of a known right.[42] One example of a right that a transactional document might purport to waive is the right to a jury trial (a right typically provided for in a declaration). Another right that might be waived is the right of one party to require the other party to perform its obligations under the contract (a right created by a covenant). Perhaps more commonly, a party waives a condition to a duty or discretion under the contract. For example, a buyer of real property might waive a condition to the buyer's duty to buy that the buyer obtain mortgage financing (perhaps because the buyer is able to purchase without that financing).[43]

A person who issues a waiver need not understand the consequence of doing so; it is enough that the person is aware of the essential facts (*i.e.*, that the right exists or that the condition has not been satisfied). A waiver need not be supported by consideration, but a party may retract a waiver not supported by consideration with respect to any unperformed portion of the contract, provided the party retracting the waiver notifies to the other party before other party has materially changed its position.[44]

A release is the relinquishment of a claim by the person who holds the claim and the effect of the release is to extinguish any cause of action on account of such claim.[45] Releases are most frequently used in connection with the settlement of a

---

[42] RESTATEMENT (SECOND) OF CONTRACTS § 84 cmt. b.

[43] Note, the waiver of a right to a jury trial might be in the parties' initial transaction documents or in a later one (or, potentially, through conduct or oral communication). In contrast, a waiver of a contractual duty or a condition presupposes that the duty or condition already exists, and thus will normally be in a later document (or though conduct or oral communication).

[44] *See, e.g.*, U.C.C. §§ 2-209(5), 2A-208(4). *See also* RESTATEMENT (SECOND) OF CONTRACTS § 84 cmt. f.

[45] Pellett v. Sonotone Corp., 160 P.2d 783, 787 (Cal. 1945), *overruled on other grounds,* Aidan Ming-Ho Leung v. Verdugo Hills Hosp., 282 P.3d 1250 (Cal. 2012). In contrast, a covenant not to sue does not extinguish the claim and would permit the beneficiary to sue for breach of contract if the covenant were not performed. *Id.*

dispute where the parties want their dispute to be fully and finally resolved and the related causes of action eliminated.[46] Generally, a release does not require consideration if it is in writing.[47]

Waivers and releases differ from present transfers of rights in at least two important respects. First, the law often requires specific language to effect a transfer of property while rarely doing so to effect a waiver or release. For example, to transfer real property or to record a transfer of real property, the instrument of conveyance might have to describe the real property with some specificity. Similarly, while a security agreement can normally describe personal property collateral in general terms,[48] in a consumer transaction or when the collateral consists of a commercial tort claim, more specificity is required.[49] In contrast, waivers and releases typically require no special language.[50]

Second, while the law does occasionally restrict or prohibit the transfer of property, it is more common for the law to invalidate restrictions on transfer, so as to make property readily transferrable.[51] In contrast, the law frequently prohibits or restricts the waiver of legal rights.[52]

---

[46] A release is different than, and should be distinguished from, an assumption of risk. A release is retrospective in its application and an assumption of risk is prospective in its application. Even though provisions for assumption of risk are often phrased using language of release (*e.g.*, the ticket holder releases the parking lot operator), this is incorrect and some courts have recognized that the terms are often inappropriately viewed as "interchangeable." Leon v. Family Fitness Center, Inc., 71 Cal. Rptr. 2d 923, 926-27 (Cal. Ct. App. 1998).

[47] *See* Cal. Civ. Code § 1541 ("An obligation is extinguished by a release therefrom given to the debtor by the creditor, upon a new consideration, or in writing, with or without new consideration.").

[48] *See* U.C.C. § 9-108(a), (b).

[49] *See* U.C.C. § 9-108(e).

[50] *See, e.g.*, Restatement (Third) of Suretyship and Guaranty § 48 cmt. b. (no particular language or form is required to waive suretyship defenses).

[51] *See infra* Chapter Four, note 80 and accompanying text.

[52] *See, e.g.*, U.C.C. §§ 9-602, 9-624.

8. Declarations

Although declarations do not create contractual duties – and, therefore, cannot be breached – they can nevertheless be very important in defining or determining the parties' rights. For example, an agreement for the purchase and sale of goods might include a statement about when the risk of loss passes from the seller to the buyer. If the goods suffer a casualty, that statement will dictate who must bear the loss.[53]

Similarly, a clause declaring that a buyer of real property "has examined the property and accepts it in its present condition" probably puts on the buyer the risk that the property complies with applicable regulations, even if both parties were mistaken about that fact.[54] In short, such a clause negates the buyer's right to avoid the contract due to mistake.

Chapter Four of this book, which deals with boilerplate terms, explores several other common types of contractual declarations – *e.g.*, merger clauses, severability clauses, and *force majeure* clauses – that can significantly affect the parties' rights. Thus, the fact that a clause is drafted as a declaration is not an invitation to disregard it.

It is now time to apply this discussion about the various types of contract terms by completing the following exercises.

Exercise 2-2

Your client, Lonborg, a landscaper, has reached a preliminary oral agreement with Tiant to provide landscaping for Tiant's new apartment complex, pursuant to plans prepared by Tiant's architect. Review the deal points identified below and determine for each how it should be translated into contract language. Specifically, for each term, determine which type

---

[53] Although such a declaration does not directly impose a duty on either party, it can indirectly affect the parties' duties. For example, if the goods are destroyed while the seller still had the risk of loss, the seller might be excused from performing. *See* U.C.C. § 2-613. If so, the seller would have no duty to tender the goods and the buyer would have no duty to pay the price. In contrast, if the goods are destroyed after the risk of loss passed to the buyer, the buyer would generally be obligated to pay the price. *See* U.C.C. § 2-709(1)(a).

[54] *See* Lenawee Cty. Bd. of Health v. Messerly, 311 N.W.2d 203 (Mich. 1982); RESTATEMENT (SECOND) OF CONTRACTS § 154(a).

of term (from the list below) it should be. Note, it might be appropriate and desirable for any individual deal point to be expressed as more than one type of term.

- Representation
- Covenant
- Condition to an obligation
- Condition to discretion

- Warranty
- Discretionary authority
- Declaration
- Present transfer of rights

A. Tiant will pay Landscaper a total of $35,000: $10,000 upon signing the agreement and $25,000 upon completion of the work.

B. Work will commence on or before April 1.

C. Lonborg will complete work by June 15 unless weather conditions make that impossible.

D. All of the plants that Lonborg installs will be free from disease and will survive the first winter after installation.

E. Lonborg is a licensed contractor.

F. If Lonborg fails to timely pay any of Lonborg's subcontractors working on this project, Tiant may terminate the agreement.

G. Massachusetts law governs the parties' rights and duties under the agreement.

H. Prior to installation of any plant called for under the plans, Tiant may substitute another plant of the same or lower cost.

Exercise 2-3

Caterer operates a large, commercial catering business. Last week, Caterer reached a preliminary oral agreement to sell the entire business to Buyer. You will be preparing the written agreement for the parties to sign. In preparation for that, review the deal points identified below and for each prepare a written explanation of why it should or should not be each of the following:

- Representation
- Covenant

- Warranty
- Condition to an obligation

Do not draft the agreement or the deal points; simply determine which type of contract term each deal point should be and why. Note, it might be appropriate and desirable for any individual deal point to be expressed as more than one type of contract term.

A. The financial statements about the business previously provided by Caterer to Buyer are correct.

B. The business will suffer no material adverse change between the time the parties sign the written agreement and the time they close the transaction (*i.e.*, when the seller transfers the business assets and the buyer pays the purchase price). Assume that "material adverse change," while vague, is a term commonly used in agreements of this type and needs no definition.

C. No key personnel will leave the business prior to the closing. Assume that "key personnel" is a term that will be defined elsewhere in the agreement.

Exercise 2-4

Your client plans to acquire an exclusive license to some encryption technology, while also providing funds to the licensor to improve the technology. In drafting the license agreement, which one of the following alternative terms dealing with updates to the technology would be preferable, and why?

> Every update, modification, or improvement to the Licensed Technology will, upon creation, be the property of Licensee.

> Licensor shall, immediately after creating any update, modification, or improvement to the Licensed Technology, assign such update, modification, or improvement to the Licensee.

C. A NOTE ON CONTRACTING WITH MULTIPLE PARTIES

When a transaction involves multiple parties on one side – that is, when one party wishes to contract simultaneously with multiple individuals or entities – a question necessarily arises about the nature of the liability of the multiple parties. Is each of them responsible for every promise they collectively make? Should they be?

Transactional lawyers sometimes ignore these questions by simply creating, usually in the preamble, a defined term for all of the parties on one side of the transaction. For example, if a married couple were selling their jointly owned home, the agreement might define the two of them as the "Sellers," (or worse, as the "Seller"). This implicitly makes each spouse a promisor of all of their collective promises, and thus apparently creates joint and several liability. Other times, transactional lawyers purport to address these questions expressly by including in the agreement a simple statement that the multiple parties are entering into the transaction "jointly and severally." Unfortunately, this simple statement might resolve the first question (by indicating what the parties' liability is) but possibly without giving due consideration to the second question (whether that is appropriate). Not every promise should be treated the same way.

Before going any further, it is necessary to understand the relevant terminology. In traditional parlance, there were two main types of contract liability: (i) several; and (ii) joint and several.[55] The differences can be explained as follows:

Several – There are multiple promises, with each promisor making a separate promise. Example: X loans A and B $100 and the agreement among them provides that "A and B each severally promises to pay X $50." There are two separate promises, one by A and the other by B, each for $50. The problems with this type of liability are that (i) a breach by one of them does not constitute a breach by the other; and (ii) the promisee is not entitled to full recourse against either of them.

Joint and Several -- There is a single promise and each promisor is separately liable for the whole promise. Example: "A and B jointly and severally promise to pay X $100." This is the type of liability most beneficial to the promisee because it permits the promisee to recover the whole promise from any single promisor and does not make any promisor an indispensable party to an action against any of the others.

In loan agreements, it is extremely common for all the obligors to be jointly and severally liable for the total debt, unless there is some tax or other reason for structuring the transaction differently. Moreover, the warranties and covenants are

---

[55] *See* RESTATEMENT (FIRST) OF CONTRACTS § 111(1) (1932) (expressing the distinctions more clearly than does the Restatement (Second)).

Traditionally, there was a third alternative: joint (but not several) liability. It involves a single promise with each of the joint promisors obligated for all of it, but it made each promisor an indispensable party to any action on the promise, which could be a problematic requirement for the promisee. By statute and judicial decision in most jurisdictions, the distinction between "joint" and "joint and several" has largely been abolished. *See* RESTATEMENT (SECOND) OF CONTRACTS §§ 289(3), 290. *But see* Cal. Civ. Code § 1430.

also usually drafted as joint and several obligations of all the obligors. This helps ensure that the creditor can pursue any of them when any warranty or covenant is breached.

In other types of deals, transactional attorneys should carefully consider which obligations should be joint and several and which should be merely several. In other words, they should consider which warranties and covenants should be made by all the promisors – so that each promisor is fully responsible regardless of who among them caused the breach – and which should be made by only one or some of the promisors.

For example, consider a situation in which the two owners of a corporation or limited liability company that operates a small business contract to sell their shares or membership rights. In the purchase and sale agreement, which both owners and the buyer sign, it would be entirely appropriate for both of the owners to make – jointly and severally – the representations and warranties relating to the financial condition of the business. On the other hand, if both owners will, as part of the transaction, covenant not to compete with the buyer, it would probably not be appropriate for that covenant to be made jointly and severally. It is not clear why one co-seller should be liable for the breach of that covenant – perhaps several months or years later – by the other co-seller.[56]

Exercise 2-5

Evans owns 50% of the common stock in Bosox Bar & Grille, Inc. Pedroia owns the other 50%. They have tentatively agreed to sell their shares to Betts. In the purchase and sale agreement, should they make a single, joint and several covenant to sell or should each seller make a separate (*i.e.*, several) covenant to sell the shares that seller owns, and why?

---

[56] In contrast, because representations are limited to past and present facts, it is likely to be less of a problem if all of the parties making the same representation do so jointly and severally. Moreover, because the most common remedy for a misrepresentation is rescission, not monetary damages, it is appropriate for representations to made jointly and severally. Doing so helps to ensure that rescission is available against all the parties on one side of a transaction.

CHAPTER THREE
THE PROPER USE OF FORMS

Both lawyers and non-lawyers frequently use forms in preparing written agreements. Forms for this purpose are available from many different sources. Some fairly simple forms are available for free online or for sale at office supply stores. More complex forms are included in form books available in most law libraries. Some forms are created by industry trade groups or by bar association committees and task forces. Many law firms have numerous forms, especially for those types of transactions that the firm regularly negotiates and documents for the same client or different clients engaged in similar deals. Law firms also often use an agreement from a prior deal as a model for a new transaction, thereby converting an earlier agreement into something akin to a form (*i.e.*, a precedent-based form). *Reasons to be careful w/ forms*

Regardless of the type or source of a form, competent attorneys must be very careful in how they use a form. This is true for several reasons. First, unless you are using a form that you or your law firm created – and perhaps even then – you cannot be certain that the form is well drafted. Is the language clear? Are there ① latent ambiguities? Is it premised on a correct understanding of applicable law? Has the law changed since the form was created? The mere fact that the form exists does not absolve the lawyer from thinking carefully about these questions.

Second, a form might have been written to favor a particular party or side to a ② transaction: for example, the buyer, the landlord, or the lender. Using such a form when you represent the other side can be quite problematic. Third, rarely are all the ③ clauses in a form relevant to or appropriate for a particular transaction. In other words, forms are usually over-inclusive. Similarly, forms rarely contain all the terms that should be included in the written agreement for a particular transaction. Thus, they are also usually under-inclusive. This is especially true when the "form" is a precedent-based document.

Despite these potential problems, attorneys can save a lot of time by using a form. The trick in using forms is not to treat them as templates with blanks to be blindly filled in. Using a form in such a manner is an invitation to error. Instead, a form should be a model that serves as a guideline on structure and format, a source of issues that the attorney should consider, and, only after the exercise of independent judgment, a possible source of contract language. Above all, never include in an agreement a term that you do not understand. If you do not know why a particular term is included in a form you are using, find out.

Exercise 3-1

A. Below are selected portions of a form commercial lease. Review it closely. Begin by identifying the typical transaction for which the document might be used and the purpose for the document in the transaction. Then, for each paragraph of the introduction and for each numbered section, determine what type or types of contract term it contains, what it means, and why it is included. Consult whatever sources or resources you need to thoroughly understand each provision. Note, this is not a well-drafted form. In future exercises you will be asked to improve and redraft portions of this form.

B. As you complete Part A, consider how reading a written agreement is different from reading a judicial opinion or a statute. What should a person do when reading a written agreement that need not be done when reading other legal sources?

Commercial Lease Agreement

This Commercial Lease Agreement ("Lease") is made by and between _____ ("Landlord") and _____ ("Tenant").

Landlord is the owner of land and improvements commonly known and numbered as _____ and legally described as follows (the "Building"):

[Legal Description of Building]

Landlord makes available for lease a portion of the Building designated as __ _____ (the "Leased Premises").

Landlord desires to lease the Leased Premises to Tenant, and Tenant desires to lease the Leased Premises from Landlord for the term, at the rental and upon the covenants, conditions, and provisions herein set forth.

THEREFORE, in consideration of the mutual promises herein contained and other good and valuable consideration, it is agreed:

1. **Term.** Landlord hereby leases the Leased Premises to Tenant, and Tenant hereby leases the same from Landlord, for a term beginning _____ and ending _____ (the "Lease Term"). Landlord shall use its best efforts

to give Tenant possession as nearly as possible at the beginning of the Lease Term. If Landlord is unable to timely provide the Leased Premises, rent shall abate for the period of delay. Tenant shall make no other claim against Landlord for any such delay.

2. **Rental.** Tenant shall pay to Landlord during the Lease Term rent of _____ per year, payable in installments of _____ per month. Each installment payment shall be due in advance on the first day of each calendar month during the Lease Term to Landlord at _____ or at such other place designated by written notice from Landlord to Tenant. The rental payment amount for any partial calendar month included in the Lease Term shall be prorated on a daily basis. On the date of the execution of this Lease, Tenant shall also pay to Landlord a security deposit (the "Security Deposit") in the amount of _____ .

3. **Sublease and Assignment.** Tenant shall have the right, without Landlord's consent, to assign this Lease to a corporation into which Tenant may merge or consolidate, to any subsidiary of Tenant, to any corporation under common control with Tenant, or to a purchaser of substantially all of Tenant's assets. Except as set forth above, Tenant shall not sublease all or any part of the Leased Premises, or assign this Lease in whole or in part without Landlord's consent, such consent not to be unreasonably withheld or delayed.

4. **Repairs.** During the Lease Term, Tenant shall make, at Tenant's expense, all necessary repairs to the Leased Premises. Repairs shall include such items as routine repairs of floors, walls, ceilings, and other parts of the Leased Premises damaged or worn through normal occupancy, except for major mechanical systems or the roof, subject to the obligations of the parties otherwise set forth in this Lease.

5. **Alterations and Improvements.** Tenant, at Tenant's expense, shall have the right following Landlord's consent to remodel, redecorate, and make additions, improvements, and replacements of and to all or any part of the Leased Premises from time to time as Tenant may deem desirable, provided the same are made in a workmanlike manner and utilizing good quality materials. Tenant shall have the right to place and install personal property, trade fixtures, equipment, and other temporary installations in and upon the Leased Premises, and to fasten the same to the premises. All personal property, equipment, machinery, trade fixtures, and temporary installations, whether acquired by Tenant at the commencement of the Lease Term or placed or installed on the Leased Premises by Tenant thereafter,

shall remain Tenant's property free and clear of any claim by Landlord. Tenant shall have the right to remove the same at any time during the Lease Term provided that all damage to the Leased Premises caused by such removal shall be repaired by Tenant at Tenant's expense.

6. *Property Taxes.* Landlord shall pay, prior to delinquency, all general real estate taxes and installments of special assessments coming due during the Lease Term on the Leased Premises, and all personal property taxes with respect to Landlord's personal property, if any, on the Leased Premises. Tenant shall be responsible for paying all personal property taxes with respect to Tenant's personal property at the Leased Premises.

7. *Insurance.* Landlord shall maintain fire and extended coverage insurance on the Building and the Leased Premises in such amounts as Landlord shall deem appropriate. Tenant shall be responsible, at its expense, for fire and extended coverage insurance on all of its personal property, including removable trade fixtures, located in the Leased Premises.

8. *Utilities.* Tenant shall pay all charges for water, sewer, gas, electricity, telephone, and other services and utilities used by Tenant on the Leased Premises during the Lease Term unless otherwise expressly agreed in writing by Landlord. In the event that any utility or service provided to the Leased Premises is not separately metered, Landlord shall pay the amount due and separately invoice Tenant for Tenant's pro rata share of the charges. Tenant shall pay such amounts within fifteen (15) days of invoice. Tenant acknowledges that the Leased Premises are designed to provide standard office use electrical facilities and standard office lighting. Tenant shall not use any equipment or devices that utilize excessive electrical energy or which may, in Landlord's reasonable opinion, overload the wiring or interfere with electrical services to other tenants.

9. *Signs.* Following Landlord's consent, Tenant shall have the right to place on the Leased Premises, at locations selected by Tenant, any signs which are permitted by applicable zoning ordinances and private restrictions. Landlord may refuse consent to any proposed signage that is in Landlord's opinion too large, deceptive, unattractive, or otherwise inconsistent with or inappropriate to the Leased Premises or use of any other tenant. Landlord shall assist and cooperate with Tenant in obtaining any necessary permission from governmental authorities or adjoining owners and occupants for Tenant to place or construct the foregoing signs. Tenant

shall repair all damage to the Leased Premises resulting from the removal of signs installed by Tenant.

10. ***Entry.*** Landlord shall have the right to enter upon the Leased Premises at reasonable hours to inspect the same, provided Landlord shall not thereby unreasonably interfere with Tenant's business on the Leased Premises.

11. ***Building Rules.*** Tenant will comply with the rules of the Building adopted and altered by Landlord from time to time and will cause all of its agents, employees, invitees, and visitors to do so; all changes to such rules will be sent by Landlord to Tenant in writing. The initial rules for the Building are attached hereto as Exhibit "A" and incorporated herein for all purposes.

12. ***Damage and Destruction.***

A. If the Leased Premises or any other part of the Building is damaged by fire or other casualty resulting from any act or negligence of Tenant or any of Tenant's agents, employees, or invitees, rent shall not be diminished or abated while such damages are under repair, and Tenant shall be responsible for the costs of repair not covered by insurance.

B. Except as provided in subsection A above, if the Leased Premises or any part thereof or any appurtenance thereto is so damaged by fire, casualty, or structural defects that the same cannot be used for Tenant's purposes, then Tenant shall have the right within ninety (90) days following damage to elect by notice to Landlord to terminate this Lease as of the date of such damage. In the event of minor damage to any part of the Leased Premises, and if such damage does not render the Leased Premises unusable for Tenant's purposes, Landlord shall promptly repair such damage at the cost of Landlord. In making the repairs called for in this paragraph, Landlord shall not be liable for any delays resulting from strikes, governmental restrictions, inability to obtain necessary materials or labor, or other matters which are beyond the reasonable control of Landlord. Tenant shall be relieved from paying rent and other charges during any portion of the Lease Term that the Leased Premises are inoperable or unfit for occupancy, or use, in whole or in part, for Tenant's purposes. Rentals and other charges paid in advance for any such periods shall be credited on the next ensuing payments, if any, but if no further payments are to be made, any such advance payments shall be refunded to Tenant.

13. ***Default.*** If at any time Tenant defaults in the payment of rent when due to Landlord as herein provided, and if said default continues for fifteen (15) days after written notice thereof shall have been given to Tenant by Landlord, or if default shall be made in any of the other covenants or conditions to be kept, observed, and performed by Tenant, and such default shall continue for thirty (30) days after notice thereof in writing to Tenant by Landlord without correction thereof then having been commenced and thereafter diligently prosecuted, Landlord may declare the Lease Term ended and terminated by giving Tenant written notice of such intention, and if possession of the Leased Premises is not surrendered, Landlord may re-enter said premises. Landlord shall have, in addition to the remedy above provided, any other right or remedy available to Landlord on account of any Tenant default, either in law or equity. Landlord shall use reasonable efforts to mitigate its damages.

14. ***Quiet Possession.*** Landlord covenants and warrants that, upon performance by Tenant of its obligations hereunder, Landlord will keep and maintain Tenant in exclusive, quiet, peaceable, undisturbed, and uninterrupted possession of the Leased Premises during the Lease Term.

Question

The two sentences in § 6 are phrased very differently. The same is true of the two sentences in § 7. Is this appropriate or is it poor drafting, and why?

A. ACQUIRING THE NECESSARY LEGAL KNOWLEDGE – ANNOTATING THE FORM

Drafting a written agreement or other legal document – even if starting with a form provided by a reputable source – requires more than an understanding of what each term in the document does. It requires knowledge of the law that applies to the transaction or document. For example, a lawyer needs to know what rights the law would impliedly grant in connection with the planned transaction and what duties it would impose in order to determine whether a waiver of any rights or duties is necessary. The lawyer will also need to know what language is needed and what other rules must be complied with to effectively waive those rights or duties.

Returning to the distinction between "agreement" and "contract" discussed in Chapter Two, it might be useful to think of it visually. In general, a diagram of the scope of an agreement and the scope of the resulting contract looks as follows:[1]

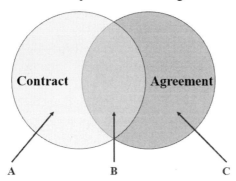

The two scopes overlap significantly (the diagram is not drawn to scale): every term to which the parties have agreed and that is enforceable is within the scope of both circles, and thus falls in the Area B of the diagram, where the two circles overlap. The terms to which the parties have agreed but which are not enforceable are in Area C. Most important for our discussion, the terms that the law implies, but to which the parties have not expressly or implicitly agreed,[2] are in Area A. In short, the law might, depending on the nature of the transaction and the breadth of the parties' agreement, imply terms into the contract.

For example, consider a simple transaction for the sale of goods governed by Article 2 of the Uniform Commercial Code (as enacted by the state whose law governs). The terms in Area A might include (among other things):

- a warranty of title, § 2-312
- a warranty of merchantability, § 2-314
- conditions to each party's duty, §§ 2-507(1), 2-511(1)
- rules on how the seller is to tender the goods, §§ 2-503, 2-504
- a time and place for shipment or delivery, §§ 2-308, 2-309(1)
- a requirement of delivery in one lot, § 2-307
- rules allocating the risk of loss, §§ 2-509, 2-510

---

[1]   In the unlikely event that the entire agreement is unenforceable – for example, an agreement to buy and sell contraband – then there would be no overlap between the two circles. Alternatively, the agreement might be a subset of the contract if every agreed-to term is enforceable and additional terms are implied by law.

[2]   The parties' agreement might include terms inferred from usage of trade, course of dealing, or course of performance. *See* U.C.C. § 1-201(b)(3).

Each of these rules can be changed by agreement. While a simple sale of goods might be conducted without the assistance of a lawyer, a transactional attorney would need to be familiar with these rules when drafting a form for either party to use in its business or when drafting an agreement – whether from scratch or by modifying a form – for a specific transaction.

Indeed, if a lawyer lacks the requisite knowledge, the lawyer has a professional and ethical duty to acquire that knowledge before completing the task. The ABA Model Rules of Professional Conduct, upon which many state rules of professional conduct are based, require that lawyers provide competent representation and then expressly state that competency "requires the legal knowledge . . . reasonably necessary for the representation."[3] The official comment adds that a lawyer may handle legal problems of a type with which the lawyer is unfamiliar but qualifies that permission by noting that the lawyer must acquire the requisite legal knowledge "through necessary study."[4]

For many deals, the transaction or document will be governed by a statute, and thus the place to start when seeking the requisite knowledge is the statute itself. A second useful thing to do, after becoming familiar with the statute, is to annotate the form you are considering using. To annotate a form, you identify each critical provision, those that you do not understand, and those that have no obvious purpose or whose language seems archaic or awkward. You then consult the statute and other relevant legal authorities to determine why the clause is there and whether it achieves its desired purpose. In practice, there might not be sufficient time or the client might not wish to pay for such an exercise. Even in such a circumstance, however, the lawyer using a form needs to read every provision in the document and understand the purpose and meaning of each provision. To the extent that the meaning or purpose of a provision is not evident, the lawyer needs to ask someone who knows or perform the necessary research.

This can be a daunting task. Sometimes even extensive investigation will produce no clear reason for a particular provision. If the form is old, or is a recent modification of an old document, it might have terms that predate current law and are no longer needed or are now invalid. Nevertheless, the act of annotating the form might help you determine which terms should be removed, what language should be updated, and which provisions must remain unchanged.

---

[3]   ABA Model Rule of Professional Conduct 1.1

[4]   *Id.* cmt. 2.

Exercise 3-2

You represent Art Dealer, who sells fine art (paintings and sculptures) at a retail establishment in Spokane, Washington and at art shows held at convention centers around the country. Art Dealer uses the form credit sales agreement set forth below. Begin by identifying the typical transaction for which the document might be used and the purpose for the document in the transaction. Then, annotate each of the three terms in blue. In other words, for each sentence or phrase in blue, identify its purpose, explain why it is or is not necessary given the applicable law, and explain how, if at all, it should be revised. Before doing this: (i) review the annotation below of the sentence in § 5, as an example of how to annotate a provision; and (ii) consult whatever legal authorities you deem relevant. Do not merely intuit the answer; you will need to research the law to complete this exercise.

CREDIT SALES AGREEMENT

[Identification of parties, recitals, definitions]

* * *

1.   ***Goods Purchased & Sold.*** Seller hereby sells to Buyer and Buyer hereby purchases from Seller the following: _____

_____
(the "Artwork") for a price of $_____ (the "Price"), subject to the terms and conditions below.

2.   ***Payment.*** Buyer shall pay the Price to Seller within 60 days of the date of the delivery of the Artwork by Seller to Buyer (the "Payment Date"). Interest accrues on any amount remaining unpaid after the Payment Date, until paid, at the lesser of 12 percent per annum or the maximum legal rate.

3.   ***When Title Passes.*** Title to the Artwork passes at the time, but not before, Buyer pays the Price in full. Prior to the payment of the Price in full, Seller remains the owner of the goods.

4.   ***No Warranties.*** Seller makes no warranty in connection with this transaction and expressly disclaims the warranties of title and merchantability.

---

5. ***Preservation of Defenses.*** Any holder of this contract is subject to all claims and defenses which Buyer could assert against Seller. Recovery hereunder by Buyer shall not exceed amounts paid by Buyer hereunder.

6. ***Choice of Law.*** This Agreement is governed by and is to be interpreted under the law of the State of Washington.

7. ***Right to Cancel.*** Buyer may cancel this transaction at any time prior to midnight of the second business day after the date hereof.

8. ***Entire Agreement.*** This Agreement constitutes the entire agreement between Buyer and Seller pertaining to the subject matter contained herein.

Annotation of § 5

"Any holder of this contract is subject to all claims and defenses which the buyer could assert against the seller. Recovery hereunder by the buyer shall not exceed amounts paid by the buyer hereunder."

This clause is about preserving the buyer's defenses against an assignee of the right to payment. In other words, if the seller assigns to a third party (an assignee) the right to receive payment from the buyer, any defense the buyer might have – such as if the goods are defective or otherwise than as promised – to the buyer's duty to pay the seller will be a defense to the duty to pay the assignee. This clause is required under the Federal Trade Commission's Holder-In-Due-Course regulations, 16 C.F.R. § 433.2, in any consumer credit contract. However, the clause is supposed to be printed in bold and, apparently, in all capital letters. Moreover, the language of this clause is not quite what is required. As a result, use of a form with this language in a consumer credit contract would probably be an unfair and deceptive act or practice that could subject the seller to sanctions by the FTC.

Note also that the seller would not want to use this clause, or a revised version of it, unless it was necessary to do so. Thus, if the seller were selling artwork to a business entity or selling to an individual who planned to use the artwork for business purposes, in which case the transaction would not be governed by the FTC rules, *see* 16 C.F.R. §§ 433.1(b), 433.2, there would be no need for the clause and the seller would prefer to be able to assign the contract to a third party free of claims and defenses.

Exercise 3-3

You represent Internet Retailer, which is based in Michigan and which sells goods to consumers over the internet. Internet Retailer uses the form sales agreement set forth below. Annotate each of the four terms in blue. In other words, for each sentence or phrase in blue, identify its purpose, explain why it is or is not necessary given the applicable law, and explain how, if at all, it should be revised. Before doing this, consult whatever legal authorities you deem relevant. Do not merely intuit the answer; you will need to research the law to complete this exercise.

SALES AGREEMENT

[Identification of parties, recitals, definitions]

* * *

3.   *Delivery.* **All goods are sold FOB the Seller's place of business at Ann Arbor, Michigan.**

5.   *Limitation of Liability.* **The Seller will not be liable for any indirect, special, consequential, or punitive damages (including lost profits) arising out of or relating to this agreement or the transactions it contemplates (whether for breach of contract, tort, negligence, or other form of action).**

16. *Electronic Signatures.* **Either or both parties may sign this agreement electronically.**

18. *Time.* **Time is of the essence.**

Exercise 3-4

You represent the bank that uses the form promissory note set forth below. Begin by identifying the typical transaction for which the document might be used and the purpose for the document in the transaction. Then, annotate each of the six terms in blue. In other words, for each sentence or phrase in blue, identify its purpose, explain why it is or is not necessary given the applicable law, and explain how, if at all, it should be revised. Before doing this, consult whatever legal authorities you deem relevant. Do not merely intuit the answer; you will need to research the law to complete this exercise.

PROMISSORY NOTE

For value received the undersigned (hereinafter "Maker") promises to pay to the order of First National Bank of Anchorage (hereinafter "Lender"), the principal sum of _____ Dollars, together with interest from the date hereof until paid on all sums which are and which may become owing hereon from time to time, upon the following terms and conditions:

1. *Interest.* Unless there shall be a default, interest shall accrue from the date hereof and be paid at the rate of ___ percent per annum, computed on a 365/360 day basis; provided, however, that in the event of any default, as hereinafter defined, all sums then and thereafter owing hereon, at the option of the Lender, shall bear interest at the rate of _____ percent per annum, computed on a 365/360 day basis (the "Default Rate").

2. *Payments.* Maker shall pay the principal amount of this promissory note (the "Note") in _____ equal installments on or before the _____ day of each month until it has been paid in full. On each date on which a payment of principal is due, Maker shall also pay all interest that has accrued as of that date. Each payment made on this Note shall be applied first to interest accrued to the date of payment and then to principal.

3. *Late Payment Charge.* If any installment is not paid within _____ days after it becomes due, then Maker agrees to pay a late charge equal to _____ percent per annum of the delinquent installment to cover the extra expense involved in handling delinquent payments. This is in addition to and not in lieu of any other rights or remedies Lender may have by virtue of any breach or default.

4. ***Default; Attorney's Fees and Other Costs and Expenses.*** In the event of any default, all sums owing and to become owing hereon, at the option of the Lender, shall become immediately due and payable and shall bear interest thereafter at the Default Rate per annum. Maker agrees to pay all costs and expenses which Lender may incur by reason of any default, including without limitation reasonable attorney's fees with respect to legal services relating to any default or to a determination of any rights or remedies of Lender under this Note and reasonable attorney's fees relating to any actions or proceedings which Lender may institute or in which Lender may appear or participate and in any appeals therefrom.

5. ***Liability.*** Maker hereby waives demand, presentment for payment, protest, and notice of protest and of nonpayment.

6. ***Maximum Interest.*** Notwithstanding any other provision of this Note, interest, fees, and charges payable by reason of the indebtedness evidenced hereby shall not exceed the maximum, if any, permitted by any governing law.

7. ***Applicable Law.*** This Note shall be construed according to the laws of the State of Alaska.

Exercise 3-5

You represent the bank that uses the form guaranty below. Begin by identifying the typical transaction for which the document might be used and the purpose for the document in the transaction. Then, annotate each of the four terms in blue. In other words, for each sentence or phrase in blue, identify its purpose, explain why it is or is not necessary given the applicable law, and explain how, if at all, it should be revised. Before doing this, consult whatever legal authorities you deem relevant. Do not merely intuit the answer; you will need to research the law to complete this exercise.

GUARANTY AGREEMENT

[Identification of parties, recitals, definitions]

* * *

1. ***Obligations Guarantied.*** Guarantor hereby guarantees to Creditor the final and full payment in cash of the Guarantied Obligations. **This is a guaranty of payment and not merely of collection.** In addition, Guarantor will be liable to Creditor for and shall pay Creditor all costs and expenses, including reasonable attorney's fees, incurred by Creditor in enforcing the obligations of Guarantor under this Agreement.

2. ***Nature of Guaranty.*** The obligations of the Guarantor under this Agreement are **continuing, absolute, unconditional, and irrevocable.**

3. ***Waivers.*** To the fullest extent permitted by law, Guarantor waives: * * *

4. ***Revival and Reinstatement.*** **If the payment of the Guarantied Obligations or a transfer by Borrower or Guarantor to Creditor of any property should for any reason subsequently be declared to be void or voidable under any state or federal law relating to creditors' rights (collectively, a "Voidable Transfer"), and if Creditor is required to repay or restore, in whole or in part, any such Voidable Transfer, then, as to any such Voidable Transfer, or the amount thereof that Creditor is required to repay or restore, and as to all reasonable costs, expenses, and attorney's fees of Creditor related thereto, the liability of the Guarantors will automatically be revived, reinstated, and restored and will exist as though such Voidable Transfer had never been made.**

5. ***Successors and Assigns.*** This Agreement will be binding on the heirs, administrators, and representatives of Guarantor and will inure to the benefit of the successors and assigns of Creditor.

6. ***Choice of Law.*** This Agreement is governed by and is to be interpreted under the law of the State of California

7. ***Waiver of Right to Jury.*** **Guarantor hereby waives Guarantor's**

> rights to a jury trial of any claim or cause of action based on,
> arising out of, or relating to this Agreement, the Guarantied
> Obligations, or any of the transactions contemplated herein,
> including contract claims, tort claims, breach of duty claims, and
> all other common law or statutory claims.
>
> 8. ***Entire Agreement.*** This Agreement constitutes the entire
> agreement between the Guarantor and Creditor pertaining to the
> subject matter contained herein.

While it is vital for a transactional attorney to annotate any form the attorney plans to use, it is also important to remember one major limitation associated with this endeavor. The annotations will explain only what is included in the form; they fail to deal with essential terms that the form might lack.

Consider a form guaranty agreement governed by California law that contains the following clause:

> Guarantor assumes all responsibility for being and keeping itself informed of Borrower's financial condition and other circumstances bearing upon the risk of nonpayment and Guarantor agrees that Creditor has no duty to advise Guarantor of any information known to Creditor now or in the future regarding such condition or risks.

In the process of annotating that form, a lawyer might learn that the clause is prompted by the decision in *Sumitomo Bank of California v. Iwasaki*,[5] in which the California Supreme Court ruled that a creditor which received a continuing guaranty owes a duty during the course of the suretyship to disclose facts known by the creditor if: (i) the creditor has reason to believe that those facts materially increase the risk beyond that which the surety intended to assume; and (ii) if there is a reasonable opportunity to communicate them. Like most suretyship defenses, though, this one can be waived by agreement. The clause above is an example of such a waiver.

So, a lawyer who needs a guaranty agreement that will be governed by New York law and who starts with a form that contains the clause above might reasonably conclude that the clause is unnecessary and delete it. On the other hand,

---

[5]   447 P.2d 956 (Cal. 1968).

consider a lawyer who needs a guaranty agreement to be governed by California law and starts with a form designed for use in New York and which omits this clause. How is the lawyer to know to add it? Annotating the form is not likely to provide that knowledge.

B. ACQUIRING THE NECESSARY LEGAL KNOWLEDGE – UPDATING THE FORM

Changes in the law – whether through legislation or judicial decision – often necessitate changes to forms. For this reason, transactional attorneys need to be constantly vigilant and diligent in their review of legal developments. The California Supreme Court decision in *Sumitomo Bank,* discussed above, provides a somewhat dated example of this. Another more recent illustration arises out of the bankruptcy court decision in *In re Adelphia Communications Corp.*[6] In that case, the debtor had entered into loan agreements that provided for what is colloquially known as "grid interest." The interest rates on loans varied periodically based on two factors: prevailing market rates and the debtor's financial condition and performance as indicated in the debtor's financial statements. In essence, a grid or table with these two factors was used to adjust periodically the interest rates. Unfortunately for the lenders, the debtor submitted fraudulent financial statements. As a result, the debtor paid the lenders less interest than it should have: a lot less, somewhere between $187 million and $300 million.

When the debtor went into bankruptcy, the lenders filed a claim for the lost interest. The bankruptcy court looked at the loan agreements and concluded that interest was to be based on what the debtor's financial condition "is reported to be" in its financial statements, not on what the debtor's true financial condition was, and that nothing in the agreements provided for the interest rate to be recalculated if the reported information was inaccurate. Thus, the court denied the lenders' claim.

The case made headlines in the legal community and no doubt within days – if not hours – transactional attorneys representing banks changed their form loan agreements to make it clear that the lenders were entitled to a retroactive interest rate adjustment if the debtor submitted fraudulent or incorrect financial statements. As it turned out, the court's decision was reversed on appeal.[7] Nevertheless, it would not be surprising to find that many forms still contain whatever language was

---

[6]   342 B.R. 142 (Bankr. S.D.N.Y. 2006).

[7]   In re Adelphia Communications Corp., 2008 WL 3919198 (S.D.N.Y. 2008).

inserted into loan agreements in reaction to the bankruptcy court decision.[8] After all, while the inserted language may be unnecessary, it is likely harmless. The larger point here is that legal changes (whether statutory or through case law) occur and they might render language in a form obsolete or ineffective or might require the inclusion of additional language that was not previously part of the form.

Exercise 3-6

Read *Redco Construction v. Profile Properties, LLC*, 271 P.3d 408 (Wyo. 2012). You are an attorney in Wyoming who represents several construction companies. The form agreement you use when a client contracts with a tenant to repair or improve real property includes a representation and warranty by the tenant that the landlord has authorized the tenant to enter into the agreement with the construction company. How, if at all, would you revise the form as result of the *Redco* decision?

Exercise 3-7

Read *Biotronik A.G. v. Conor Medsystems Ireland, Ltd*, 11 N.E.3d 676 (N.Y. 2014). You are a lawyer that represents a business that enters into agreements that grant exclusive distributorships. The agreements you draft typically disclaim your clients' liability for all "indirect, special, and consequential damages." How, if at all, would you revise this language?

Problem 3-8

Read *Morello v. AR Resources, Inc.*, 2018 WL 3928806 (D.N.J. 2018). You are in house counsel for AR Resources. Revise the portion of the company's collection letter quoted in the case so that it will not violate the Fair Debt Collection Practices Act.

---

[8]   After one court ruled that a fraudulent transfer savings clause was ineffective, *see* In re TOUSA, Inc., 422 B.R. 783, 863-65 (Bankr. S.D. Fla. 2009), commentators predicted that "lenders will likely keep [such] savings clauses in their documents, in the hope that . . . they will be upheld despite what the court said in TOUSA." John C. Weitnauer, *TOUSA and its Consequences*, SR048 ALI-ABA 1507 (2010).

CHAPTER FOUR
BOILERPLATE

The term "boilerplate" refers to standard terms or clauses that are frequently included in most written agreements, typically near the end. They usually deal with the allocation of costs, interpretation or modification of the agreement, the agreement's effect on third parties, or dispute resolution. Classic examples include a merger clause, which helps to invoke the full force of the parol evidence rule, as well as terms dealing with severability, amendment, waiver, assignment and delegation, excuse, attorney's fees, choice of law, and choice of forum. Often, transactional attorneys and their clients pay little attention to these clauses. That is a mistake. Many of the provisions commonly referred to as boilerplate can significantly impact a client's rights.

> [Plaintiff] calls the . . . clauses "boilerplate," and they were; transactions lawyers have language of this sort stored up for reuse. But the fact that language has been used before does not make it less binding when used again. Phrases become boilerplate when many parties find that the language serves their ends. That's a reason to enforce the promises, not to disregard them.[1]

A complete study of every boilerplate term and the law that governs it is beyond the scope of this book. Instead, what follows is a brief exploration of several subjects commonly addressed with boilerplate clauses. The goal of this material is modest: to show through these examples the attention that a transactional attorney should give to boilerplate terms. That attention requires knowledge of the applicable law, consideration about the appropriateness of the term to a specific transaction, and careful review of the language used.

----

[1]   Rissman v. Rissman, 213 F.3d 381, 385 (7th Cir. 2000).

A. INTERPRETATION AND MODIFICATION

1. Parol Evidence & Merger Clauses

When all the parties to a transaction have adopted the same written expression of the agreement, the parol evidence rule protects the integrity of that writing by restricting each party's ability to contradict or supplement the terms expressed in that writing. In other words, the parol evidence rule operates as a gatekeeper that determines what evidence a fact finder may consider in determining to what terms the parties have agreed. If the parol evidence rule bars a party from attempting to prove that the agreement includes a particular term outside of the writing, the agreement will be enforced as written, without regard to the parol term to which the parties have allegedly agreed.

The parol evidence rule is based on the assumption that when parties record their agreement in writing, they usually intend the writing to supersede the terms that they discussed or even agreed to in prior communications or negotiations. Therefore, unless the writing is obviously preliminary in nature or has a clear omission, the parol evidence rule considers evidence of any term alleged by one of the parties to have been agreed to, but not reflected in the writing, to be questionable. The rule treats evidence that directly contradicts the writing as particularly suspect.

The parol evidence rule is also premised, at least in part, on the fact that testimony about oral terms is inherently unreliable. People rarely remember the exact words that were spoken. They might remember what they *meant* and might remember what they *understood* the other party to have said, but those things might differ in important ways from the precise words used. In short, memories about oral terms are likely to be faulty and imperfect. What is more, it is usually the parties themselves who provide oral testimony about negotiations, but the parties have an interest in the outcome of their dispute. Thus, they might have an incentive to craft their testimony is ways that achieve a desired result. Moreover, because oral testimony must be evaluated by the fact finder – either the judge or a jury – it will invariably be filtered through whatever conscious and subconscious biases the fact finder has. Perhaps jurors will credit more strongly the testimony of people like themselves (whether measured by gender, race, ethnicity, or affluence). Perhaps a judge will draw similar inferences about credibility based on experience gained on the bench.

When the only evidence of the agreement is oral,[2] courts accept all the offered testimony and do the best they can to sort through it. But when the parties have a written memorial of their agreement, the parol evidence rule mandates that courts prefer the written record over the parties' recollections. As one court put it, "[t]he parol evidence rule is founded on experience and public policy and created by necessity, and it is designed to give certainty to a transaction which had been reduced to writing by protecting the parties against the doubtful veracity and the uncertain memory of interested witnesses."[3]

Note that while the word "parol" literally means "oral," for this purpose its meaning is much broader. The parol evidence rule covers not only terms allegedly agreed to orally, but also evidence of written terms that are extrinsic to the written memorial of agreement. In other words, when a written memorial of an agreement exists, the parol evidence rule limits a party's ability to offer extrinsic evidence of prior or contemporaneous terms to supplement or contradict the written memorial, whether the evidence be written or oral.[4]

One note of caution is in order. When a proffered term gets past the parol evidence rule, that does not mean it will necessarily be treated as part of the parties' agreement. It means merely that the fact finder will be permitted to receive and evaluate evidence of the term. Just as satisfaction of the statute of frauds does not prove the existence of an agreement – it merely allows a party the chance to prove the existence of an agreement – satisfaction of the parol evidence rule does not prove the existence of a term. Instead it merely allows evidence of a term to be admitted.

---

[2]   This assumes no problem with the statute of frauds.

[3]   Citizens State Bank-Midwest v. Symington, 780 N.W.2d 676 (N.D. 2010) (quoting Gajewski v. Bratcher, 221 N.W.2d 614, 626 (N.D. 1974)).

[4]   While the Restatement makes no distinction between written and oral parol evidence, the two types of parol evidence are not always treated equally. For example, Articles 2 and 2A of the Uniform Commercial Code, which codify the parol evidence rule with respect to contracts for the sale or lease of goods, exclude evidence of prior and contemporaneous oral agreements and of prior written agreements, but they do not exclude evidence of contemporaneous written agreements. *See* U.C.C. §§ 2-202, 2A-202. Indeed, in some states, courts are compelled to read together writings relating to the same matters, between the same parties, and made as parts of substantially one transaction. *See, e.g.*, Cal. Civ. Code § 1642. Thus, writings executed or adopted contemporaneously with the written memorial of the parties' agreement might be beyond the reach of, and unaffected by, the parol evidence rule. Moreover, all courts will probably consider a written document expressly referenced in the written memorial of the parties' agreement.

(a) The Operation of the Parol Evidence Rule

The parol evidence rule is occasionally codified in a statute, but more commonly is part of the common law of contracts. Although the exact contours and nuances of the common-law rule vary from jurisdiction to jurisdiction, for the most part the rule requires courts to do two things: (i) classify the writing which memorializes the agreement; and (ii) classify the type of evidence that one party seeks to admit.

(b) Classifying the Writing

The parol evidence rule has three different classifications for a writing that memorializes the agreement of the parties: (i) fully integrated; (ii) partially integrated; and (iii) non-integrated.[5] Fully integrated agreements get the most protection under the parol evidence rule, partially integrated agreements get some, and non-integrated agreements fall outside the parol evidence rule entirely.

A written agreement is integrated – either partially or fully – if it constitutes "a final expression of one or more terms of the agreement."[6] In other words, an agreement is integrated if one or more of the agreed terms is recorded in (*i.e.,* integrated into) a writing. No particular form need be used for a writing to be an integrated one. Moreover, the writing need not contain all of the terms. The key elements are that it be final – that is, that it not be created during negotiations with the expectation that the terms reflected in it might change – and that it be adopted in some way by both parties.[7] Such adoption could be in the form of a signature but need not be. It could also be through a failure to object.[8]

A fully integrated agreement is one adopted by the parties as "a complete and exclusive statement of the terms of their agreement."[9] Any integrated agreement

---

[5]   *See* RESTATEMENT (SECOND) OF CONTRACTS §§ 209, 210.

[6]   RESTATEMENT (SECOND) OF CONTRACTS § 209(1).

[7]   *See* U.C.C. § 2-202 (referring to a writing "intended by the *parties* as a final expression of their agreement") (emphasis added).

[8]   *See* RESTATEMENT (SECOND) OF CONTRACTS § 209, ill. 2.

[9]   RESTATEMENT (SECOND) OF CONTRACTS § 210(1).

that is not fully integrated is classified as partially integrated.[10] Thus, a partially integrated agreement is a final expression of some, but not all, of the terms to which the parties have agreed; a fully integrated agreement is a final expression of all of the terms of the agreement.

As might already be apparent, there is a sort of chicken and egg problem here. If the proffered parol evidence is true, then the integrated writing cannot really be a complete and exclusive statement of the terms agreed upon. Thus we get to one of the principal problems in dealing with the parol evidence rule. How is a court to determine whether an integrated agreement is fully or partially integrated?

Many older cases used – and some courts continue to use – the "four corners" approach. Under this approach, reflected in the First Restatement of Contracts, the judge determines the nature of the writing by looking only at the "four corners" of the writing itself, paying no attention to the specific circumstances of the parties or the credibility of the proffered parol evidence. If the writing appears to be complete on its face, it is treated as fully integrated. This "four corners" approach to integration emphasizes the logical and objective resolution of disputes in accordance with formal rules. It also is faithful to the underlying purpose of the parol evidence rule: to treat the written record as more reliable and more authoritative of the parties' agreement. If judges were to look at the proffered parol evidence in determining whether a writing was fully integrated, they would necessarily have to evaluate the reliability of the parol evidence, which is precisely what the rule is designed to avoid.

Nevertheless, there are problems with the four corners approach. After all, how is a court to determine if a written agreement is complete on its face? Frequently, the judge will try to determine if the writing lacks any critical terms. However, that is not the correct question. The issue is not whether the writing contains everything that the parties *should have* agreed to – which is what that inquiry addresses – but whether it covers everything they *did* agree to. The parties' actual agreement might cover more or less than what parties entering into a similar transaction would normally agree upon. A writing that omits some critical terms might nevertheless represent the parties' entire agreement. Similarly, a writing that seems complete might in fact omit some terms, particularly if the omitted terms deal with a separate transaction or are otherwise only marginally related to the recorded terms.

Over time, the "four corners" test has yielded to a more contextual approach. Under this approach, adopted by the Second Restatement, courts may consider parol evidence when determining whether a writing is fully integrated, partially

---

[10]   RESTATEMENT (SECOND) OF CONTRACTS § 210(2).

integrated, or not integrated at all.[11] Nevertheless, remnants of the "four corners" approach are still alive in some jurisdictions.

(c) The Relevance of a Merger Clause

Sometimes, one or both parties want to ensure that a written memorialization of their agreement will be treated as a fully integrated agreement, so as to invoke the greatest amount of protection under the parol evidence rule. To do this, they add language to the writing that states, in one form or another, that the writing contains the entire agreement of the parties. These clauses are frequently referred to as "merger" or "integration" clauses because they often state that all prior agreements are "merged" or "integrated" into the writing.

Courts typically regard a merger clause as highly probative[12] – but not conclusive[13] – of whether a writing is fully or partially integrated. At least one jurisdiction also requires a merger clause to be conspicuous, at least if it will be used to exclude evidence of an express warranty.[14] Conversely, the absence of a

---

[11] RESTATEMENT (SECOND) OF CONTRACTS § 214(a), (b). Indeed, the comments expressly state that this "may be proved by any relevant evidence." *Id.* at § 210, cmt. b.

[12] *See, e.g.*, Amicas, Inc. v. GMG Health Sys., Ltd., 676 F.3d 227 (1st Cir. 2012) (summarily treating a set of writings that contained an integration clause as fully integrated, and thus precluding evidence of agreements reached during negotiations, even though the clause was on a pre-printed form and the party seeking to admit the evidence was not represented by counsel).

[13] *See, e.g.,* Bena v. Schleicher, 2017 WL 1907741 (Wash. Ct. App. 2017) (using parol evidence to conclude that a writing with a merger clause was not fully integrated); Kanno v. Marwit Capital Partners II, L.P., 227 Cal. Rptr. 3d 334 (Cal. Ct. App. 2017) (a merger clause is merely rebuttable evidence that the agreement containing it is fully integrated; although each of the three agreements executed in connection with the purchase of a business contained a merger clause, none was fully integrated; the fact there were three agreements for the same transaction demonstrated that the parties did not intend for any one agreement to be a complete integration). Rota-McLarty v. Santander Consumer USA, Inc., 2011 WL 2133698 (D. Md. 2011) (despite the presence of a merger clause, a retail installment sales contract was not fully integrated and was to be read with the seller's standard order form that the buyer signed at the same time).

[14] *E.g.*, Seibel v. Layne & Bowler, Inc., 641 P.2d 668, 671 (Or. Ct. App. 1982). *See also* George Packing Co. v. FMC Techs., Inc., 2011 WL 7082545 (D. Or. 2011) (following *Seibel* by concluding that a lease with an inconspicuous merger clause was not intended by the parties to be the complete and exclusive statement of their agreement).

merger clause does not necessarily mean that the parties did not intend the writing to fully integrate their agreement, but its absence is a factor that a court may consider.[15]

In the power of merger clauses also lies their danger. A sophisticated and powerful party in charge of drafting an agreement might, in addition to including a merger clause, include language that strongly favors its interests, omit terms previously agreed to that favor the other party, or even add a term that contradicts the explicit understanding of the parties. These provisions might go unnoticed or, if noticed, unchallenged by the less sophisticated or less powerful contracting party. The hazard is not limited to the unsophisticated, however. A complex commercial agreement might take weeks or even months to draft, negotiate, and revise. Often, the lawyers work late into the night leading up to the closing in an effort to finalize the contractual language. Occasionally, surprises come up at the closing table, and the parties scurry to find a last-minute accommodation to prevent the transaction from collapsing. Woe to the lawyer, not to mention the client, who in the rush to completion fails to make sure that everything agreed to is properly recorded into a written agreement that contains a merger clause.

Exercise 4-1

You are drafting a written agreement for a client and wish to include a merger clause. Which of the following clauses would suffice and which would not? Which clause would you be most likely to use? What problems might the other clauses cause? How would you draft the clause?

1. This Agreement represents the final agreement of the parties.
2. This Agreement is the complete and exclusive statement of the terms of the parties' agreement; there are no other agreements not reflected herein.
3. All of the parties' negotiations are merged into this Agreement.
4. This Agreement supersedes all prior agreements, whether written or oral, relating to the subject matter hereof.
5. This Agreement may not be modified except by a writing signed by both parties.

---

[15]   *Cf.* Bresler v. Wilmington Trust Co., 2015 WL 1402377 (D. Md. 2015) (" In the absence of an integration clause, parol evidence was clearly admissible").

(d) Classifying the Evidence

In general, parol evidence may not be admitted to: (i) contradict a fully or partially integrated written agreement; or (ii) supplement a fully integrated written agreement.[16] By negative implication, and pursuant to the general principle that all relevant evidence is admissible, parties are free to submit parol evidence to supplement a partially integrated written agreement or to either supplement or contradict a writing that does not qualify as an integrated agreement.

Thus, we start with two classes of parol evidence: (i) evidence that contradicts the written agreement; and (ii) evidence that supplements the written agreement. To these we need to add a third category: (iii) evidence proffered to explain the terms in the writing. Although the Restatement treats such evidence as admissible, regardless of the nature of the writing,[17] not all courts agree. Some refuse to admit evidence to explain a term in a fully or partially integrated agreement unless the term is ambiguous or unclear on its face. Moreover, courts that normally admit parol evidence to explain an integrated written agreement might not do so if the agreement contains a merger clause expressly forbidding the use of extrinsic explanatory evidence.[18]

Unfortunately, we are not yet done classifying the potential types of parol evidence. The parol evidence rule rests on the assumption that the writing reflects a valid contract. Suppose two friends at a bar, both slightly inebriated, begin a friendly argument about who owns the nicer car, each preferring the one owned by the other. As a dare, one of them offers to sell his car to the other for $1,000, a price well below its true value. The other friend agrees and they sign a writing to that effect on one of the napkins available at the bar. Should evidence be admissible to show that the whole thing was a joke and therefore should not be

---

[16] *See* RESTATEMENT (SECOND) OF CONTRACTS §§ 215, 216.

[17] *See* RESTATEMENT (SECOND) OF CONTRACTS § 214(c). *See also* Pacific Gas & Elec. Co. v. G.W. Thomas Drayage & Rigging Co., 442 P.2d 641, 644 (Cal. 1968) ("The test of admissibility of extrinsic evidence to explain the meaning of a written instrument is not whether it appears to the court to be plain and unambiguous on its face, but whether the offered evidence is relevant to prove a meaning to which the language of the instrument is reasonably susceptible."). *Cf.* Trident Center v. Connecticut Gen. Life Ins. Co., 847 F.2d 564 (9th Cir. 1988) (criticizing but nevertheless applying this rule).

[18] *See, e.g.*, Hot Rods, LLC v. Northrop Grumman Sys. Corp., 196 Cal. Rptr. 3d 53 (Cal Ct. App. 2015) (enforcing a clause providing that the parties "intend that this Agreement constitutes the complete and exclusive statement of its terms and that no extrinsic evidence whatsoever may be introduced in any judicial proceedings involving this Agreement.").

enforceable?[19] Similarly, if you were forced to sign a written agreement because someone was holding a gun to your head, should you not be allowed to admit evidence of that coercion to avoid contract liability? Generally speaking, parol evidence is admissible to demonstrate that an alleged contract is either void or voidable.[20]

Application of this exception is, however, sometimes problematic, particularly when the evidence is offered to show that the agreement was induced through fraud or misrepresentation. Suppose for example, that Armas has brought suit against Burrelson to enforce a written agreement. Burrelson wants to introduce evidence of prior negotiations. Perhaps that evidence will show that Armas made a material and false representation of fact during negotiations that induced Burrelson to enter into the agreement.[21] If courts admit evidence of alleged misrepresentations, and allow juries to consider that evidence, the exception for misrepresentation has the potential to swallow the parol evidence rule. Yet courts are understandably reluctant to enforce the parol evidence rule to exclude evidence of misrepresentation, and thereby let a party profit from such behavior.

---

[19] *See* Lucy v. Zehmer, 84 S.E.2d 516 (Va. 1954). *Compare* Leonard v. Pepsico, Inc., 88 F. Supp. 2d 116 (S.D.N.Y. 1999), *aff'd,* 210 F.3d 88 (2d Cir. 2000).

[20] *See* RESTATEMENT (SECOND) OF CONTRACTS § 214(d). *See also* Riverisland Cold Storage, Inc. v. Fresno-Madera Production Credit Ass'n, 291 P.3d 316 (Cal. 2013) (fraud exception to the parol evidence rule is not limited to matters as to which the writing is silent and can include fraud directly at variance with a promise in the writing); Italian Cowboy Partners, Ltd. v. Prudential Ins. Co. of Am., 341 S.W.3d 323 (Tex. 2011) (merger clause in commercial lease was not a disclaimer of tenant's reliance on property manager's oral assurances that there had been no problems with building and did not bar fraud claim); Citizens State Bank-Midwest v. Symington, 780 N.W.2d 676 (N.D. 2010) (parol evidence rule does not bar evidence of fraud, mistake, or accident); Adelaar v. Sprout Foods, Inc., 2013 WL 3168663 (S.D.N.Y. 2013) (the parol evidence rule does not bar evidence of mistake, even when the doctrine of mistake is invoked to reform – rather than to avoid – the written agreement).

Of course, as is true with respect to almost every general legal principle, states have enacted various narrow exceptions to this rule. For example, Missouri's Credit Agreement Statute of Frauds, Mo. Rev. Stat. § 432.047, prevents borrowers using parol evidence of fraudulent misrepresentations as a defense to liability on a written credit agreement. *See* Smithville 169 v. Citizens Bank & Trust Co., 2013 WL 434028 (W.D. Mo. 2013). Lawyers must be on a constant lookout for such statutes.

[21] *See, e.g.,* Mid-Wisconsin Bank v. Koskey, 819 N.W.2d 563 (Wis. Ct. App. 2012) (bank's statement to guarantor that it would pay off the existing lender and obtain a first lien on the collateral was not an actionable promise because of the guaranty's integration clause but was a misrepresentation entitling the guarantor to rescind the guaranty).

One way contracting parties might be able to effectively extend the parol evidence rule to cover evidence of misrepresentation is if the writing includes a merger clause that states not merely that the writing incorporates the entire agreement – *i.e.*, that all *promises* are contained in the writing – but also that there were no material *representations* beyond those included in the writing and that neither party relied on any oral statements by the other.[22] A typical example of such an expanded merger clause reads as follows:

> This Agreement contains the complete and exclusive understanding of the parties with respect to the subject matter hereof. There are no promises, understandings, or representations of the parties not included herein.

A clause such as this is often referred to as a *general* merger clause. It *might be* effective in some jurisdictions to expand the scope of the parol evidence to cover evidence of fraud or misrepresentation. However, in other jurisdictions, to achieve this result courts require that the merger clause be phrased from the perspective of the listener or reader, not from the perspective of the speaker or writer. In other words, instead of purporting to disclaim the existence of representations or warranties outside the written agreement, the clause must disclaim reliance on any statements outside the agreement.[23]

---

[22]   *See* Novare Group, Inc. v. Sarif, 718 S.E.2d 304 (Ga. 2011) (buyers of real property with spectacular views that seller was planning to obstruct with development across the street had no claim for misrepresentation or rescission because the written agreements expressly stated that: (i) the views might change over time; (ii) oral representations of the sellers could not be relied upon; (iii) the buyers did not in fact rely upon any oral representations; and (iv) the entire agreement between the parties was set forth in the terms of the written contract). *See also* Sequel Capital, LLC v. Pearson, 2012 WL 2597759 (N.D. Ill. 2012) (lender could not avoid settlement agreement for fraud based on written misrepresentation because the agreement contained a clause stating that the parties were "solely relying upon their own judgment . . . and not as a result of any fraud, duress or coercion" and that all prior agreements and understandings between the parties, whether written or oral, were void). *But cf.* Italian Cowboy Partners, Ltd. v. Prudential Ins. Co. of Am., 341 S.W.3d 323 (Tex. 2011) (clause in commercial lease stating that neither the landlord nor its agents have made any representations or promises with respect to the premises, along with merger clause, was insufficient to prevent claim based on fraud because the clause did not disclaim *reliance* on the landlord's statements).

[23]   *See, e.g.*, FdG Logistics LLC v. A & R Logistics Holdings, Inc., 131 A.3d 842 (Del. Ch. Ct. 2016); Prairie Capital III, L.P. v. Double E Holding Corp., 132 A.3d 35 (Del Ch. Ct. 2015). *See also* JM Vidal, Inc. v. Texdis USA, Inc., 764 F. Supp. 2d 599 (S.D.N.Y. 2011);

Other jurisdictions will refuse to exclude evidence of misrepresentation despite the presence of a *general* merger clause but will bar such evidence if the writing contains a *specific* merger clause: that is, a clause that expressly disclaims any representations as to the specific subject matter to which the parol evidence relates.[24] An example of such a clause in a commercial lease might be phrased as follows:

> This Agreement contains the complete and exclusive understanding of the parties with respect to the subject matter hereof. There are no promises, understandings, or representations not included herein relating to the identity, business, or intentions of any other tenants or prospective tenants.

Drafting a specific merger clause is a challenge because there might be no easy way to know or determine in advance the subject matter of the alleged misrepresentation.

In the absence of an effective merger clause, we have a fourth category of admissible parol evidence: (iv) evidence relevant to whether the agreement is avoidable for fraud or misrepresentation. Moreover, even if the writing contains a well-drafted merger clause, the parol evidence rule will not keep out evidence of other invalidating causes, such as illegality, duress, or mistake.

To this we add one final category: (v) evidence of a condition precedent. Most courts admit evidence that both parties intended that the written agreement be subject to a condition.[25] For example, suppose Schilling and Clemens sign an

---

Harbinger Capital Partners Master Fund I, Ltd. v. Wachovia Capital Markets, LLC, 2010 WL 2431613 (N.Y. Sup. Ct. 2010).

[24] *See, e.g.*, Korff v. Hilton Resorts Corp., 506 F. App'x 473 (6th Cir. 2013) (based on NY law); Novare Group, Inc. v. Sarif, 718 S.E.2d 304 (Ga. 2011). *See also* Jennifer Niesen, *Drafting a Bullet-Proof Merger Clause*, 2 THE TRANSACTIONAL LAWYER 1 (Apr. 2012).

Somewhat similarly, if the alleged misrepresentation is directly contradicted by the written agreement, courts will usually conclude that reliance is unreasonable as a matter of law. Group One Dev., Inc v. Bank of Lake Mills, 2017 WL 2937709 (S.D. Tex. 2017) (although the borrowers claimed to have been fraudulently induced to enter into a loan agreement by oral representations that the loan was "unsecured," the borrowers could not, as a matter of law, have reasonably relied on those representations because they were directly contradicted by the terms of the agreement).

[25] *See* RESTATEMENT (SECOND) OF CONTRACTS § 217; Valentine v. Wells Fargo Bank, 2011 WL 13134193 (N.D. W. Va. 2011) (under New York law, the parol evidence rule did not bar evidence of an alleged condition precedent to an interest rate swap agreement even though the signed, written agreement contained a merger clause and identified conditions precedent

agreement for Schilling to employ Clemens for one year at a specified salary. At the same time, they orally agree that the agreement will be effective only if a background check reveals that Clemens has never been convicted of a crime. Evidence of the oral condition is generally admissible.[26]

(e) Summary

The following chart summarizes what is to happen under the common-law parol evidence rule, once the judge classifies the writing and classifies the proffered parol evidence.

integration (court)

Determined by:

		Nature of the Writing		
		Fully Integrated	**Partially Integrated**	**Not Integrated**
Nature of the Proffered Evidence	**Contradictory**	Not Admissible	Not Admissible	Admissible
	Supplemental	Not Admissible	Admissible	Admissible
	Explanatory *214 C*	Admissible*	Admissible*	Admissible
	Basis for *214 D* **Avoidance**	Admissible**	Admissible**	Admissible
	Condition Precedent *217*	Generally Admissible†	Admissible†	Admissible

collateral agreement | Not integrated

*   Some courts require that the writing be ambiguous or unclear before they admit evidence to explain a fully (or partially) integrated writing.[27]

---

to the parties' payment obligations).

[26] *See* RESTATEMENT (SECOND) OF CONTRACTS § 217, ills. 1, 2. It is unclear whether this rule applies to contracts for the sale or lease of goods. For such contracts, the parol evidence rule has been codified by statutes that make no mention of an exception for a condition precedent. *See* U.C.C. §§ 2-202, 2A-202.

[27] Article 2 of the U.C.C. has no such requirement, at least if the explanatory evidence

** A clause disclaiming both the existence of and reliance on any representation not included in the writing might preclude evidence of a representation offered as part of an effort to show that the agreement is avoidable due to misrepresentation.[28]   Alternatively, a specific merger clause disclaiming representations relating to a specific subject might bar evidence of a statement relating to that subject.

† A clause indicating that the writing is unconditional might lead to the exclusion of evidence of a condition precedent.[29]

Exercise 4-2

You represent a used car dealership. Because the bulk of the compensation that dealership pays to its sales staff is based on commission, the sales staff have an incentive to make statements and promises, purportedly on behalf of the dealership, to entice customers to buy. Draft a merger clause for inclusion in the dealership's form sales agreement that will, to the greatest extent possible, insulate the dealership from liability or responsibility for any such statements or promises.

Exercise 4-3

Company is in need of a large infusion of working capital. Company's president and Lender have reached tentative agreement for: (i) Lender to make a $100 million loan to Company; and (ii) the president to provide Lender with an option to purchase the president's stock in Company. You represent Company and Company's president. Lender's counsel has sent you a draft of the Loan Agreement and a draft of the Stock Purchase Option Agreement. Each draft contains a merger clause. Is there any reason that should concern you? *See Schron v. Grunstein*, 917 N.Y.S.2d 820 (N.Y.

---

consists of course of performance, course of dealing, or usage of trade. *See* U.C.C. § 2-202 cmt. 1.

[28]   Such a clause would not bar evidence offered to show duress or illegality and might not prevent admission of evidence of mistake or, possibly, fraud.

[29]   *See, e.g.,* Bloor v. Shapiro, 32 B.R. 993 (S.D.N.Y. 1983).

Sup. Ct. 2011). If so, how should the merger clauses be drafted to eliminate or reduce that concern?

2. Severability & Savings Clauses

(a) The Common Law Approach to Severance

Courts have long severed an unenforceable provision from the remainder of an otherwise valid agreement, leaving the remainder in effect, provided the unenforceable provision is not an "essential part of the agreed exchange."[30] To determine whether a provision is essential, courts attempt to give effect to the intention of the parties, inquiring as to whether the "parties would not have entered into the agreement absent that provision."[31]

(b) The Effect of a Severability Clause

A severability clause functions against this common-law backdrop. A typical severability clause reads as follows:

> If any provision of this Agreement is held invalid, illegal or unenforceable, the remaining provisions of this Agreement will remain effective.

The frequency with which such a clause can be found in form agreements suggests that drafters put them in almost reflexively, without any significant thought. That is unfortunate because such a clause does not address the crucial issue underlying severability – essentiality – and consequently leaves courts with two options, both of which should be potentially troublesome for the transactional attorney.

The first option is to give the severability clause its most natural reading, which is to sever *any* unenforceable provision. In other words, this option treats the clause

---

[30] RESTATEMENT (SECOND) OF CONTRACTS § 184(1).

[31] Panasonic Co. v. Zinn, 903 F.2d 1039, 1041 (5th Cir. 1990); *see also* Hughes v. Schaefer, 452 A.2d 428 (Md. 1982) (clauses in municipal loan agreements requiring the trustees' approval for future loans were an invalid restriction on the city's powers but were not essential to the overall transaction and were therefore severable).

as a declaration that no provision of the agreement is truly essential. Obviously, that is unlikely to be consistent with the parties' intent. Not all invalid provisions should be severed. Consider, for example, an agreement for the purchase and sale of a small business in which the seller promises not to compete with the buyer for a specified time in a specified proximity to the business sold. In all likelihood, the non-compete clause is essential to the deal. That is, much of the purchase price might be attributable to the promise not to compete. If the non-compete clause is unenforceable, the buyer might not wish to be bound by the remainder of the agreement. That is, the buyer might not want to be obligated to pay the full price.

The second option for courts is to disregard the severability clause and evaluate the essentiality of the unenforceable provision.[32] This approach is problematic because it renders the severability clause a nullity.

Thus, a traditional severability clause is either too broad or irrelevant. It can also lead a court to treat multiple agreements executed at the same time and as part of the same overall transaction as independent, which might not be consistent with the parties' intent.[33] For these reasons, several authorities recommend that a severability clause identify the essential terms and make them exceptions to severance.[34] Courts have shown themselves to be responsive to such drafting.[35]

---

[32] *See* Small v. Parker Healthcare Mgmt. Org., 2013 WL 5827822 (Tex. Ct. App. 2013).

[33] *See* In re Kline, 2013 WL 587339 (Bankr. D. Or. 2013). In that case, parties to an asset purchase agreement contemporaneously executed two commercial leases. The APA, promissory note, and the leases contained cross-default clauses. After the buyers filed for bankruptcy protection, they proposed to assume one of the leases. The seller objected, claiming that the debtors had to cure the default under the note and APA to assume the lease. Relying in part on the severability clause, the court ruled that the debtors' obligations under the different agreements were severable and thus they did not have to cure the default under the APA to assume the lease. The court might have reached the same result even if there had been no severability clause, *see* In re Plitt Amusement Co., 233 B.R. 837 (Bankr. C.D. Cal. 1999) (reaching a similar result for much the same reason but also concluding that the obligations were severable as a matter of federal bankruptcy law and that "artful drafting" would not change that result); *but cf.* In re Buffets Holdings, Inc., 387 B.R. 115 (Bankr. D. Del. 2008) (individual leases governed by a master lease were not severable and had to be assumed or rejected together). Nevertheless, the fact remains that the severability clause in *Kline* did not help the seller, who in all likelihood drafted it.

[34] *E.g.*, NEGOTIATING AND DRAFTING CONTRACT BOILERPLATE §§ 17.05–17.06 (Tina L. Stark, ed., 2003).

[35] *See, e.g.*, Hill v. Names & Addresses, Inc., 571 N.E.2d 1085 (Ill. Ct. App. 1991). *See also* Schuiling v. Harris, 747 S.E.2d 833 (Va. 2013) (noting the absence of any terms

Exercise 4-4

In each of the transactions described below, the clause mentioned is or might be unenforceable. If you were drafting the agreement for the transaction, should the clause be severable? Why or why not? If you need additional information to make this determination, what information do you need?

A. A divorce settlement agreement that provides for a division of marital property. The agreement contains a term whereby each spouse waives the right to alimony.

B. An agreement for the purchase and sale of a restaurant. The agreement includes a liquor license among the items to be purchased and sold.

C. An employment agreement for a geneticist assigned to the research and development department of a major manufacturer of pharmaceuticals. The agreement contains a covenant not to compete for three years following termination of employment.

D. An agreement for a bank to serve as the collateral agent for a group of lenders financing a movie studio. The agreement contains a covenant for the lenders to indemnify the bank for all liabilities arising out of or relating to the bank's role as collateral agent except those attributable to the bank's illegal conduct.

E. A loan commitment between a commercial bank and a large corporation seeking funding for a major acquisition. The agreement contains a clause obligating the corporation to pay the bank a $10 million breakup fee if the corporation goes through with the acquisition using an alternative source of funding.

(c) Savings Clauses

Some transactional attorneys take a different approach to potentially unenforceable clauses. Instead of indicating that an unenforceable clause is to be severed, they invite courts to rewrite the clause so that it becomes enforceable. This is probably most common with respect to a covenant not to compete, which will typically be unenforceable if unreasonably broad in duration or geographic scope. For example, the agreement might contain a clause such as one of the following:

---

specified as essential in its ruling to sever an unenforceable provision and enforce the remainder of the agreement).

> ***Non-competition Savings Clause.*** If a court determines that [the clause restricting competition] is unenforceable because of its duration or geographic scope, the parties shall modify the duration or area of [the restriction], or allow a court of competent jurisdiction to so modify [the restriction], in the least amount necessary to render [the restriction] enforceable.

> ***Non-competition Savings Clause.*** The parties intend that [the clause restricting competition] to be as expansive in duration and geographic scope as the law permits. If a court determines that [the restriction] is unenforceable because its duration is too long or its geographic scope is too great, then the [restriction] will remain valid and fully enforceable to the extent that the law permits.

It is important to understand, however, what while some courts are willing to rewrite the restriction,[36] others will refuse the parties' invitation to rewrite the agreement.[37] Thus, depending on the jurisdiction, such a savings clause might not be helpful, although it is unlikely to be harmful.

Even if the courts in the applicable jurisdiction will rewrite an unenforceable restriction, transactional attorneys must be aware of the approach that the courts will follow when performing that task. While some will edit the clause in any manner to achieve the parties' stated desire, others follow what is known as the "blue pencil" rule. Under this approach, a court will not rephrase an overly broad restrictive covenant, but will instead strike out grammatically severable words and phrases.[38] Thus, the clause will be saved only if the reason for its infirmity can be removed by excising words.

---

[36] *See, e.g.*, PharMethod, Inc. v. Caserta, 382 F. App'x 214 (3d Cir. 2010) (applying Pa. law); Franklin v. Forever Venture, Inc., 696 N.W.2d 545 (S.D. 2005).

[37] *See, e.g.*, Kolani v. Gluska, 75 Cal. Rept. 2d 257 (Cal. Ct. App. 1998).

[38] *See, e.g.*, Valley Med. Specialists v. Farber, 982 P.2d 1277, 1286 (Ariz. 1999). *See also* Kimball v. Anesthesia Specialists of Baton Rouge, Inc., 809 So. 2d 405 (La. Ct. App. 2001) (if a non-compete clause contains both a description of a localized area that complies with statutory law and an overly broad and invalid geographic limitation, the latter could be severed, but if the agreement lacks the former, a court cannot rewrite the clause so as to make it comply with the statute); ML Manager, LLC v. Pinsonneault, 2014 WL 222833 (Ariz. App. Ct. 2014) (because a promissory note had a severability clause, and its provision for unreasonable late charges was grammatically severable from the remainder of the note, the late charges could be severed under the "blue pencil" rule).

Exercise 4-5

Dentist has been practicing dentistry in Tuscon, Arizona for 37 years. Five years ago, Dentist hired Apprentice, a recent dentistry school graduate, to work with Dentist. Dentist has now decided to retire and to sell the dentistry practice to Apprentice for $750,000. The sale price will include all the dentistry equipment and the leasehold on the offices where they work. You represent Apprentice and are preparing the purchase and sale agreement. The current draft of the agreement includes a covenant by Dentist not to solicit any patients or employees of the practice for a period of five years. It also includes the following covenant not to compete:

> Dentist shall not, for a period of five years from the Closing Date, engage in the practice of dentistry or otherwise provide dentistry services, other than on a pro bono basis or in connection with teaching dentistry at an accredited school of dentistry, anywhere within 50 miles of [location of the dentistry office sold to Apprentice].

You have researched Arizona law on the enforceability of non-compete clauses and know that they must be reasonable in duration, geographic reach, and scope of activities covered.[39] You are confident that the draft is reasonable with respect to the scope of activities covered. You further know that duration and broad geographic scope are less likely to be an issue with respect to a covenant made in connection with the sale of a business than with respect to a covenant made in connection with an employment agreement. Nevertheless, the lack of clear guidance about what is a reasonable duration and a reasonable geographic scope is a cause of concern.

Given that Arizona follows the "blue-pencil" approach,[40] revise the clause to ensure that it will be enforceable to the maximum extent possible. What other changes could you make to the agreement to protect Apprentice in the event that a court rules that the non-compete clause is too broad? Draft those changes.

---

[39]　*See, e.g.*, Unisource Worldwide, Inc. v. Swope, 964 F. Supp. 2d 1050 (D. Ariz. 2013).

[40]　*See supra* n.36.

Another common savings clause deals with the possibility that the interest rate charged on an indebtedness might be usurious. Instead of inviting a court to substitute a different and permissible interest rate, this type of clause typically calls for the rate and fees to be reduced or refunded to the extent necessary to avoid usury.

> ***Usury Savings Clause.*** Notwithstanding any provisions in this Note to the contrary, no interest, charges, or other payments in excess of those permitted by law shall accrue or become payable hereunder and any excessive payments which may be made shall be applied to principal in reduction of the balance of this Note.

However, caution is in order before relying on such a usury savings clause. Several states treat a usury savings clause as ineffective to prevent the loan from being usurious.[41] Other states give effect to a usury savings clause.[42] Of course, if the only potential problem with a usury savings clause were that it might be ineffective, there would be no reason – other than perhaps professional ethics – not to include such a clause in a loan agreement. However, there is at least one significant potential downside to placing a usury savings clause in a loan agreement. While some courts have stated that a usury savings clause evidences the lender's intent not to charge usurious interest,[43] others have suggested that a usury savings clause actually manifests the lender's intent to charge usurious interest, a fact that might lead to more severe consequences.[44] Moreover, in states that follow the blue-

---

[41] *See, e.g.,* NV One, LLC v. Potomac Realty Capital, LLC, 84 A.3d 800 (R.I. 2014); Simsbury Fund, Inc. v. New St. Louis Assocs., 611 N.Y.S.2d 557 (N.Y. App. Div. 1994); Swindell v. FNMA, 409 S.E.2d 892 (N.C. 1991); Dupree v. Virgil R. Coss Mortgage Co., 267 S.W. 586 (Ark. 1925). *Cf.* Herkimer Inv., LLC v. Goldstein, 2012 WL 2923342 at *7 (N.J. Super. Ct. App. Div. 2012) (suggesting that the nature of the transaction and the sophistication of the parties is relevant to whether a usury savings clause is effective).

[42] In Texas, for example, courts have allowed such a clause to avoid a usury violation, at least in some cases. For a comprehensive list of such cases, see Woodcrest Assocs., Ltd. v. Commonwealth Mortgage Corp., 775 S.W.2d 434, 437-38 (Tex. Ct. App. 1989); In re Perry, 425 B.R. 323 (Bankr. S.D. Tex. 2010). However, if the loan agreement or promissory note is usurious on its face, or the lender does not invoke the clause when needed, the clause will not rescue the lender from the consequences of usury. *See, e.g.,* Armstrong v. Steppes Apartments, Ltd., 57 S.W.3d 37, 47 (Tex. Ct. App. 2001).

[43] *See, e.g.,* Kennon v. McGraw, 281 S.W.3d 648, 652 (Tex. Ct. App. 2009).

[44] *See, e.g.,* 514 Broadway Inv. Trust, *ex rel.* Blechman v. Rapoza, 816 F. Supp. 2d 128

pencil rule, a typical usury savings clause might not be adequate and instead drafters would need to find other ways to deal with the potential problem.[45]

Other types of savings clauses are similarly of questionably efficacy, even though they remain common.[46] Thus, transactional attorneys should not rely on a savings clause to ensure that the transaction is legal and that the parties' obligations are enforceable. Instead, those who draft an agreement should be cognizant of the applicable law and make sure that the agreement complies with it. Moreover, if a written agreement has both a severability clause and a savings clause, then the agreement should contain an ordering principle to guide the court as to which clause to apply first. Presumably, the savings clause is to control over the severability clause; an unenforceable clause should be severed only if it cannot first be saved.

(D.R.I. 2011). *See also* Jersey Palm-Gross, Inc. v. Paper, 639 So. 2d 664, 671 (Fla. Ct. App. 1994), *aff'd*, 658 So. 2d 531 (Fla. 1995), in which the appellate court indicated that a usury savings clause might be "determinative" on the issue of intent if the interest charged is close to the legal rate or the transaction is not clearly usurious at the outset but becomes usurious after the occurrence of a future contingency, but not stating whether the clause tends to prove or disprove intent. The clause would seem to disprove intent in the latter case but might tend to prove it in the former. On appeal, the Florida Supreme Court ruled that the existence of a usury savings was one factor to consider but the clause did not necessarily indicate that the lender lacked the intent to charge usurious interest.

[45] ML Manager, LLC v. Pinsonneault, 2014 WL 222833 (Ariz. App. Ct. 2014) (because the promissory note at issue had a severability clause and the clause providing for unreasonable late charges was grammatically severable from the remainder of the note, the trial court properly eliminated the late charges under the "blue pencil" rule).

[46] For example, upstream guaranties (that is, a subsidiary's guaranty of a parent company's indebtedness) and any security interest granted to support that an upstream obligation bear the risk of being avoided as a fraudulent transfer or fraudulent incurrence of debt if the subsidiary is insolvent or rendered insolvent thereby. To address this risk, the guaranty might contain a savings clause, such as the following:

> ***Savings Clause.*** Guarantor's liability hereunder is limited to the maximum amount that would render Guarantor's obligations not subject to avoidance as a fraudulent transfer or fraudulent incurrence of debt under applicable law or under United States Bankruptcy Code.

However, the only known court decision dealing with such a clause ruled that it was invalid for multiple reasons. *See* In re TOUSA, Inc., 422 B.R. 783, 863-65 (Bankr. S.D. Fla. 2009).

3. Amendment

Agreements to modify or amend an existing contract face three potential problems. First, the common law generally requires that an amendment be supported by consideration. This requirement is not always enforced with respect to executory contracts, for which material performance remains due by both parties. It has also been abrogated in contacts for the sale or lease of goods[47] and, in some jurisdictions, more generally.[48]

Second, the agreement, as modified, must satisfy the applicable statute of frauds.[49] Thus, for example, if parties to a written agreement for the purchase and sale of goods wish to change one or more terms on delivery, price, warranties, dispute resolution, or the like, they may do so by oral agreement. If, however, they wish to increase the quantity of goods to be sold, the amendment must be in writing and signed by the party against whom enforcement is sought.[50]

Third, the original agreement might purport to require that any future amendment be in writing and be signed. The following clause is typical.

> ***Amendment.*** No amendment of this Agreement will be binding
> unless it is in writing and signed by [both parties] [the party against
> whom enforcement is sought].

However, such a clause prohibiting oral modifications is generally unenforceable.[51]

---

[47] *See* U.C.C. §§ 2-209(1), 2A-208(1).

[48] *See, e.g.*, Mich. Comp. Laws § 566.1 (but requiring the amendment to be in writing); N.Y. Gen. Oblig. Law § 5-1103 (same); S.D. Codified Laws § 53-8-7 (same). *See also* RESTATEMENT (SECOND) OF CONTRACTS § 89 (permitting the amendment to be enforced if doing so would be fair and equitable in light of circumstances unanticipated when the parties entered into the original agreement).

[49] *See, e.g.*, U.C.C. § 2-209(3); Cal. Civ. Code § 1698(c).

[50] *See* U.C.C. § 2-201(1).

[51] *See, e.g.*, Autotrol Corp. v. Continental Water Sys. Corp., 918 F.2d 689, 692 (7th Cir. 1990) (indicating that such a clause is unenforceable in Texas and that the "Texas approach is by no means idiosyncratic"); Quality Products and Concepts Co. v. Nagel Precision, Inc., 666 N.W.2d 251, 257 (Mich. 2003) ("it is well established in our law that contracts with written modification or anti-waiver clauses can be modified or waived notwithstanding their restrictive amendment clauses. This is because the parties possess, and never cease to possess, the freedom to contract even after the original contract has been executed"); GE

The theory is that the parties can either by agreement change or by conduct waive this requirement. However, a no-oral modifications clause is enforceable in contracts for the sale or lease of goods (although in a merchant-non-merchant transaction, such a clause must be separately signed if it is in a form provided by the merchant)[52] and is often enforceable in government contracts.[53] Moreover, some states have abrogated this rule by statute,[54] thereby giving effect to the language of the clause, although even in such states, part performance, waiver, or estoppel might provide a basis for enforcing an oral modification.[55]

4. Waiver

Just as a written agreement might seek to prevent or invalidate future oral modifications, it might also seek to invalidate unwritten waivers. Waiver is traditionally defined as the intentional relinquishment of a known right. That definition is a bit misleading, however, for several reasons. First, intent might be

---

Props., LLC v. Draggoo, 881 N.W.2d 359 at *4 (Wis. Ct. App. 2016); Celtic Bank v. Executive Title, Inc., 2016 WL 3027893 at *6 (N.D. Ill. 2016); Reid v. Boyle, 527 S.E.2d 137 (Va. 2000); First Nat'l Bank of Pa. v. Lincoln Nat'l Life Ins. Co., 824 F.2d 277, 280 (3d Cir. 1987) (applying Pa. law); Pacific Northwest Group A v. Pizza Blends, Inc., 951 P.2d 826, 828-29 (Wash. Ct. App. 1998) (involving a lease) (cited approvingly in Wells Fargo Bank v. Main, 2011 WL 449562 at *3 (Wash. Ct. App. 2011)).

[52] *See* U.C.C. §§ 2-209(2), 2A-208(2).

[53] *See, e.g.*, P&D Consultants, Inc. v. City of Carlsbad, 2010 WL 4680800 (Cal. Ct. App. 2010).

[54] *See* Cal. Civ. Code § 1698(c); Bare v. JPMorgan Chase Bank, 2013 WL 6073335 (Cal. Ct. App. 2013); N.Y. Gen. Oblig. Law § 15-301(1); Nassau Beekman, LLC v. Ann/Nassau Realty, LLC, 960 N.Y.S.2d 70 (N.Y. App. Div. 2013).

[55] *See, e.g.*, Aircraft Servs. Resales LLC v. Oceanic Capital Co., Ltd., 586 F. App'x 761 (2d Cir. 2014). *See also* Wells Fargo Bank v. Smith, 2012 WL 1288494 (Ohio Ct. App. 2012) (discussing waiver of a no-oral-modifications clause); U.C.C. §§ 2-209(4), 2A-208(3) (both acknowledging that an ineffective modification might operate as waiver); Fanucchi & Limi Farms v. United Agri Products, 414 F.3d 1075 (9th Cir. 2005) (indicating that even though under California law an agreement with a no-oral-modifications clause could not be modified by a later oral agreement, it could be novated – that is, replaced – by a later oral agreement); Wind Dancer Prod. Group v. Walt Disney Pictures, 215 Cal. Rptr.3d 835 (Cal. Ct. App. 2017) (parties may, by their conduct, waive a clause prohibiting oral modification to their written agreement).

inferred from a volitional statement or act. Thus, there is no requirement that the person making the waiver specifically intends to do so. Second, the known "right" need not concern a covenant or performance. It might – and often does – relate to a condition. Third, the person making the waiver need not know of the legal effect of the waiver, merely of the underlying facts. For example, a person who performs despite the failure of a condition precedent need not understand the consequence of doing so, provided the person is or should be aware that the condition has not been satisfied.

A typical clause purporting to limit or restrict waivers is as follows:

> ***Waiver.*** No waiver of any provision of this Agreement will be effective unless it is in writing and signed by [both parties] [the party against whom the waiver is to be enforced]. A waiver is effective, if at all, only with respect to the specific instance involved and does not constitute a waiver of any provision, right, or condition on any future occasion.

Notice that the two sentences in this clause purport to do very different things. The first sentence purports to invalidate oral waivers and waivers by conduct or inaction. The second purports to limit the scope of an effective waiver. It does this by purporting to prevent the waiver from applying to future events.

However, the first sentence might have only limited effectiveness. Just as the law in many states treats a no-oral-modifications clause as ineffective, it will similarly treat a no-oral-waivers clause as ineffective.[56] The theory underlying this

---

[56] *See, e.g.*, Kamco Supply Corp. v. On the Right Track, LLC, 49 N.Y.S.3d 721, 725 (N.Y. App. Div. 2017); Penncro Assocs., Inc. v. Sprint Spectrum L.P., 2006 WL 1320252 (D. Kan. 2006) *Cf.* 1301 Properties v. Abelson, 2016 WL 1367908 (N.Y. Sup. Ct. 2016) (applying equitable estoppel). *But cf.* Shields Ltd. P'ship v. Bradberry, 526 S.W.3d 471 (Tex. 2017) (although a landlord's rights under a lease agreement would normally be waived despite a general clause in the agreement purporting to prohibit waiver except in a signed writing, the landlord did not, by accepting late payments, waive the condition in the renewal clause requiring the tenant not to have defaulted because the nonwaiver clause specifically stated that acceptance of late rental payments did not constitute a waiver); Melrose Credit Union v. Soyferman, 2018 WL 1004988 (N.Y. Sup. Ct. 2018) (a debtor's defense of waiver, based on the secured party's acceptance of partial payment after default, did not create a triable issue because the note expressly provided that, even if the holder did not require full payment upon default, the holder "will still have the right to do so if I am in default at a later time"); Stephen L. Sepinuck, The Limited Efficacy of No-Implied-Waiver Clauses, 7 THE TRANSACTIONAL LAWYER 1 (Dec. 2017)

rule is that the parties can waive or be estopped from enforcing the requirement of a writing. Thus, in many jurisdictions the first sentence is of dubious validity. Nevertheless, in other jurisdictions a clause prohibiting oral waivers is effective.[57] Moreover, even if the first sentence is not fully effective to prevent oral waivers or waivers arising from conduct, it might be helpful in other ways, such as undermining the evidence of intent to waive, preventing the creation of a course or performance, or negating the basis for estoppel.[58]

Once made, an effective waiver can be retracted with respect to the executory portion of a contract, provided the other party has not relied to its detriment on the waiver.[59] To do this, the party wishing to retract the waiver must communicate that fact to the other party. Thus, for example, if a borrower paid several installment payments late but the lender has waived that default either through an express communication or by its conduct in accepting the payments, the lender may nevertheless insist that the borrower make future payments on time. To do this, the lender must normally notify the borrower of this fact. While the second sentence of the clause above might suggest that such notification is not needed, without such notification the borrower might be able to make out a basis for estoppel.

In short, claims of modification and waiver often go hand-in-hand with each other as well as with claims based on estoppel and course of performance. Contractual boilerplate directed at any one of these doctrines might have little or no relevance to the other three.

Exercise 4-6

Greenspace LLC wishes to hire Verdant Construction Co. to build a high-rise office building on some real property Greenspace owns. Because the plans call for the use of some new construction techniques designed to minimize the environmental impact of the project, both parties anticipate that, during construction, problems will arise that require modification of the plans. Because any change easily could involve increased cost or expense in the six- or seven-figure range, both parties want to make sure that any change is properly vetted, approved, and documented. The current draft of the agreement provides as follows:

---

[57] *See, e.g.*, Tillquist v. Ford Motor Credit Co., 714 F. Supp. 607, 611-12 (D. Conn. 1989).

[58] *See, e.g.*, National R.R. Passenger Corp. v. Expresstrak, LLC, 61 U.C.C. Rep. Serv. 2d 39 (D.D.C. 2006).

[59] *See, e.g.*, U.C.C. §§ 2-209(5), 2A-208(4).

> ***Modification.*** No amendment of this Agreement will be binding unless it is in writing and signed by both parties. No waiver of any provision of or right under this Agreement will be effective unless it is in writing and signed by the party against whom the waiver is to be enforced.

After researching the law of the applicable jurisdiction, you remain concerned that this clause might not be enforceable. Is there any additional term or language that would protect the parties from modifications or waivers arising from oral communications or conduct? If so, what would that term or language be?

B. RISK ALLOCATION

1. Indemnification

Indemnification is the process of shifting the responsibility for a loss or expense from one party (the "indemnitee) to another (the "indemnitor"). It is accomplished by the contractual promise of the indemnitor to pay an obligation for which the indemnitee is liable or to recompense the indemnitee for an obligation it has paid.

An indemnification clause is common in the documentation for many types of transactions. For example, a trust agreement might obligate the trust to pay any liabilities the trustee incurs while acting for the trust. The parties to an escrow agreement might promise to indemnify the escrow agent with respect to any claims associated with the subject matter of the escrow. A consortium of lenders might promise to indemnify their agent or an indenture trustee for actions the agent or trustee takes on behalf of the lenders. Notice that all of these examples involve an indemnitee that probably has a fiduciary relationship to the indemnitor(s). However, indemnification is not so limited. The seller of a business might promise to indemnify the buyer for any warranty claims made by the customers of the business with respect to transactions that predate the sale. In the agreement with the publishers of this book, the authors promised to indemnify them for any loss arising from violation of copyright.

Indemnification clauses are useful because they augment the rights or remedies that the indemnitee would have under the common law. For example, if the seller of a business warranted to the buyer that the business had no *undisclosed* contingent liabilities, the buyer would have no cause of action or right of recovery if a contingent liability that was disclosed ripened. If the authors of this book represented to the publishers that the book does not infringe anyone's copyrights, the publishers would have a right to recover only if they could prove both that the book does infringe and that they reasonably relied on the authors' representation.

It is important to distinguish indemnification from warranty and guaranty. As the following diagram shows, warranties are two-party affairs under which the warrantor promises the obligee that a specified fact – *e.g.*, that goods sold conform to specifications; that leased premises are habitable; that good title is being conveyed; that contracts with third parties are genuine and enforceable – is true.

Warrantor $\xrightarrow{\textit{warranty}}$ **Obligee**
(*e.g.*, buyer, lessee, creditor)

If the statement later proves to be untrue, the warrantor will have contract liability to the obligee, which liability might include both direct economic loss as well as reasonably foreseeable and unavoidable consequential damages. Warranties can be used in almost any transaction but are particularly common in sales agreements, leases, and loan agreements.

Guaranties and indemnities are, in contrast, three-party arrangements. A guarantor promises to pay the debt of a third party to an obligee.

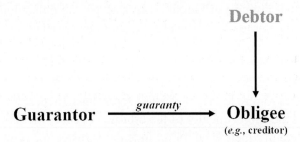

An indemnitor promises to reimburse the obligee for its payment or liability to a third party.

While warranties, guaranties, and indemnities are all, essentially, risk-allocation devices, the legal rules applicable to each are different. Guaranties – whether labeled as such or not – are subject to numerous suretyship defenses.[60] Indemnification agreements are not subject to suretyship defenses but many states have statutory and common-law limitations on indemnity agreements. These limitations invalidate many agreements to indemnify for liability resulting from the indemnitee's own reckless, intentional, or illegal conduct. Some prohibit indemnification based on the indemnitee's negligence.[61] A transactional lawyer who fails to recognize a promise as an indemnity might fail to appreciate that the promise is restricted or nullified by statute.

A typical indemnification clause might be phrased as follows:

> ***Indemnification.*** Indemnitor shall indemnify, defend, and hold harmless Indemnitee against all losses, liabilities, and claims arising out of or relating to [description of conduct, event, or transaction].

The scope of the clause will, of course, be affected substantially by the description of the conduct, event, or transaction inserted in place of the bracketed phrase. However, the two sets of words in blue are also important, and a transactional lawyer needs to understand and appreciate the differences among them.

A duty to "defend" is different from a duty to "indemnify." The latter covers actual liability of the indemnitee to a third party; the former covers the costs of defending a claim brought against the indemnitee, even if that claim is unsuccessful. As should be apparent, a duty to bear the expense of defending the indemnitee can be quite significant and might in some cases exceed the amount claimed. Moreover, a duty to defend typically requires the indemnitor to pay the defense costs as and when incurred, not after the matter is concluded.

While many authorities state that "indemnify" and "hold harmless" are synonymous,[62] some authorities regard the phrases as different. Specifically, the

---

[60] *See* RESTATEMENT (THIRD) OF SURETYSHIP AND GUARANTY § 1(3)(a), (b) (suretyship obligation can arise regardless of the form of the transaction or the terms used to describe the obligation), § 37 (delineating the various suretyship defenses).

[61] *See* Kamy Molavi, A Review and Update of Anti-Indemnity Statutes (Sept. 2012) (available at //www.dri.org/dri/course-materials/2012-construction/pdfs/11_Molavi.pdf.); NEGOTIATING AND DRAFTING CONTRACT BOILERPLATE § 10.04 (Tina L. Stark, ed., 2003).

[62] *See, e.g.*, Winchester Repeating Arms Co. v. United States, 51 Ct. Cl. 118 (Ct. Cl. 1916); BLACKS'S LAW DICTIONARY 286 (9th ed. 2009); KENNETH A. ADAMS, A MANUAL OF STYLE

duty to indemnify obligates the indemnitor to reimburse the indemnitee, while a duty to hold harmless limits the indemnitee's liability to the indemnitor, effectively barring the indemnitor from bringing suit against the indemnitee. Put another way, "indemnification" deals with *third-party claims* against the indemnitee:

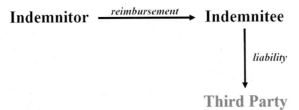

In contrast, "hold harmless" deals with the *indemnitor's claims* against the indemnitee:[63]

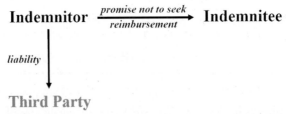

Of course, the fact that this distinction is not well understood suggests that a transactional attorney should not rely on it and should instead use other language to eliminate claims by the indemnitor against the indemnitee.

With respect to "losses, liabilities, and claims," case law suggests that "losses" refers to amounts actually paid. "Liabilities" is broader and covers amounts due as well as amounts paid. And "claims" is broader still and applies any time a third party has initiated a legal action. Moreover, although indemnification clauses

---

FOR CONTRACT DRAFTING §§ 13.323–13.334 (3d ed. 2013); NEGOTIATING AND DRAFTING CONTRACTUAL BOILERPLATE § 10.07[1] (Tina L. Stark, ed., 2003). *See also* In re Francis, 505 B.R. 914 (9th Cir. BAP 2014) (marital settlement agreement requiring the ex-husband to hold his ex-wife harmless on a credit card debt required him to indemnify her).

[63] *See, e.g.,* Queen Villas Homeowners Ass'n v. TCB Property Mgmt., 56 Cal. Rptr. 3d 528, 534 (Cal. Dist. Ct. App. 2007). *See also* Majkowski v. American Imaging Mgmt. Serv., LLC, 913 A.2d 572, 592 n.55 (Del. Ch. Ct. 2006); Hilary Bradbury, *Beyond Boilerplate: Drafting and Understanding Indemnification Clauses*, 51 Advocate (Idaho) 13 (January 2008); MELLINKOFF'S DICTIONARY OF AMERICAN LEGAL USAGE 286 (1992).

typically deal with the indemnitee's liability to a third party, if phrased broadly enough the clause can also cover the direct losses of the indemnitee.[64]

Exercise 4-7

A consortium of lenders has agreed to finance Megacorp's $1.5 billion acquisition of Gargantuan Industries. To secure the loan, Megacorp will provide the lenders with a lien on much of its personal and real property. The lenders have agreed among themselves that Central Bank, which will be making a substantial portion of the loan, will serve as agent for all the lenders. As agent, Central Bank will be responsible for receiving and distributing Megacorp's payments on the loan, preserving and protecting the lenders' interest in the collateral, and enforcing the loan if Megacorp defaults. The initial draft of the loan agreement – to which Megacorp, each of the Lenders, and Central Bank as agent will be a party – contains the following clause:

Indemnification. The Lenders hereby jointly and severally agree to pay, protect, reimburse, indemnify and hold harmless Agent from and against any and all claims, demands, liabilities, damages, losses, costs, charges and expenses (including reasonable fees, expenses, and disbursements of counsel and allocated costs of internal counsel) that Agent incurs or becomes subject to as a consequence, directly or indirectly, of its actions under this Agreement, other than as a result of the gross negligence or willful misconduct of Agent.

A. If your last name begins with a letter from A to J, you represent Central Bank. Identify the ways in which this clause might be too narrow or otherwise problematic. Redraft the clause to appropriately broaden the lenders' duty and remove any other identified problem.

---

[64] *See, e.g.*, Hot Rods, LLC v. Northrop Grumman Sys. Corp., 196 Cal. Rptr. 3d 53 (Cal Ct. App. 2015) (interpreting an indemnification clause to cover direct losses because the clause covered "any claims," which was defined to include a claim brought by any "person" and because the clause also covered "damages, costs, [and] losses"); Starbrands Capital LLC v. Original MW Inc., 2015 WL 5305215 (D. Mass. 2015) (indemnification clause was not limited to claims made by third parties against the indemnitee because the clause extended to "all losses, liabilities, damages and expenses" relating to the specified conduct).

B. If your last name begins with a letter from K to Z, you represent one of the other lenders. Identify the ways in which this clause might be too broad or otherwise problematic. Redraft the clause to appropriately narrow the lenders' duty and remove any other identified problem.

2. Excuse

Contract law is rife with doctrines that can be used to excuse one or both of the parties from some or all of the party's unperformed contractual duties. Most of these doctrines deal with circumstances in existence at the time the parties entered into their agreement. The following is a partial list:[65]

Excuses Based on Circumstances
Existing When the Agreement Was Formed

Duress
Fraud or Misrepresentation
Illegality or Public Policy
Incapacity
Mistake
Unconscionability

We have already seen that some boilerplate provisions attempt to limit these excuses. For example, a severability clause or savings clause might be used to minimize the chance that illegality or public policy will provide a basis for fully excusing one party. A well-drafted merger clause, along with the parol evidence rule, might reduce the likelihood of an excuse based on misrepresentation. For the most part, however, excuses based on these doctrines are immune to clever drafting techniques.

Contract law also has several excuse doctrines designed to deal with circumstances arising after a contract is formed. These include:[66]

---

[65] *See* RESTATEMENT (SECOND) OF CONTRACTS §§ 12–16 (incapacity), 151–158 (mistake) 169–173 (misrepresentation), 174–177 (duress and undue influence), 178–199 (public policy), 208 (unconscionability) (1981).

[66] *See* RESTATEMENT (SECOND) OF CONTRACTS §§ 261–271. Section 266 provides for excuses based on impracticability and frustration of purpose arising from events existing at the time of contracting but which the parties had no reason to know.

Excuses Based on Circumstances
Arising After the Agreement Was Formed

Death of a Party
Frustration of Purpose
Impracticability or Impossibility
Intervening Illegality

Each of these doctrines can be expanded or limited by agreement of the parties. If you think about it, that should not be surprising. Contracts are, at heart, risk allocation devices. Consider, for example, an agreement to buy and sell property or services. By entering into the agreement and making their reciprocal promises, the parties have necessarily accepted certain risks. The buyer has, to some extent, accepted the risk that the buyer might not need or want the property or services at the time the seller is to provide them or that their market value might decline in the interim. The seller, in turn, has accepted the risks that the seller might not be able to provide the property or services on time or at all, that the seller's cost of performing might exceed the contract price, or that the market value of the property or services might rise. The parties are free, however, to adjust or reallocate these risks in a variety of ways. For example, the agreement might give either or both parties a right to terminate the agreement if a specified event occurs.

In the absence of agreement, the doctrines listed above allocate the risk that some – typically unforeseen and unlikely event – will significantly impact a party's ability to perform or significantly undermine a party's intended purpose in entering into the agreement. They therefore provide a partial or complete excuse when certain post-contracting events occur.

For example, a party's contractual duties can be suspended or discharged if, through no fault of the party, performance is made impracticable by the occurrence of an event the non-occurrence of which was a basic assumption on which the contract was made.[67] Unfortunately, that rule is rather vague and very difficult to apply with any certainty. A severe shortage or raw materials due to war, embargo, local crop failure, or an unforeseen shutdown of the intended source of supply might qualify, but a mere increase in the difficulty or expense of performing does not.[68] Drawing the line between these things is extremely difficult.

---

[67] *See* RESTATEMENT (SECOND) OF CONTRACTS § 261. *See also* U.C.C. §§ 2-613 *through* 2-616.

[68] RESTATEMENT (SECOND) OF CONTRACTS § 261 cmt. d.

To provide greater clarity, or to alter the allocation of risk, the parties might wish to provide their own rules to deal with such events. One common way in which parties do so is through a term commonly referred to as a *"force majeure"* clause.[69] The following clause is a typical example.

Force Majeure.

(a) Neither party will be responsible for any failure to perform its obligations under this Agreement if the party's performance is prevented in whole or in part by a Force Majeure Event, whether foreseen or unforeseen.

(b) A party prevented from performing an obligation under this Agreement by a Force Majeure Event (the "Excused Party") must immediately notify the other party, giving full particulars of the Force Majeure Event and the reasons that the Force Majeure Event prevents the Excused Party from performing its obligation. The Excused Party must use reasonable efforts to mitigate the effect of the Force Majeure Event upon the performance of its obligations under this Agreement.

(c) A "Force Majeure Event" means: an act of God (including fire, flood, tsunami, earthquake, volcanism, landslide, tornado, hurricane or other natural disaster); war (whether declared or not); invasion; act of a foreign enemy; terrorist activity or threats; riot; rebellion; revolution; insurrection; requisition; confiscation; nationalization; blockage; embargo; biological hazard or contamination; radioactive contamination; labor dispute; or strike.

There are several things to note about this clause. First, by purporting to *define* the circumstances constituting a Force Majeure Event, rather than to *describe* such circumstances, the clause is inherently limited. Unlisted circumstances do not qualify.[70] Yet, as time passes and new calamities occur, risks might become apparent that no one previously thought to include in the clause. Who would have thought, prior to 2008, that the credit markets would collapse virtually overnight? Yet they did. Should that event excuse a party to a credit agreement from

---

[69] *See, e.g.,* Baroi v. Platinum Condo. Dev., LLC, 874 F. Supp. 2d 980 (D. Nev. 2012) (contractual *force majeure* clause can be broader than the common-law impossibility defense without rendering the contract or consideration illusory).

At least one state has a *force majeure* statute. *See* Miss. Code § 75-2-617.

[70] *See, e.g.,* Tug Blarney, LLC v. Ridge Contracting, Inc., 14 F. Supp. 3d 1255 (D. Alaska 2014); In re Cablevision Consumer Litig., 864 F. Supp. 2d 258 (E.D.N.Y. 2012).

complying with a contractual duty to provide a substitute surety?[71] Which of the events that are listed in the clause above might not have been listed in a similar clause two or three decades ago?[72] What events that are not listed should the clause contain? Should piracy be included if the contract involves the shipment of goods around Africa?

To avoid this problem, the *force majeure* clause could be drafted in a manner that is not limiting. This result could be achieved either by changing "means" to "includes" or by adding at the end a catchall phrase, such as "or similar cause." However, these approaches add uncertainty and can lead to litigation about what other events qualify.[73]

Second, through the phrase "whether foreseen or unforeseen," the clause above expressly negates any requirement that the event be unforseen or unforeseeable. Under the common law, foreseeablility is a major factor in an excuse based on impracticability. A *force majeure* clause that does not expressly negate that factor might be interpreted to provide an excuse only for unforeseeable events.[74]

Third, the clause above provides an excuse only if a Force Majeure Event "prevents" performance, in whole or in part. Parties might want to make relief more readily available. If so, they might substitute a phrase such as "materially and adversely affects a party's ability to perform" or "substantially hinders, obstructs, or impedes a party's ability to perform." Alternatively, they might wish to provide relief for an event that merely delays performance.

---

[71] *See* Hoosier Energy Rural Elec. Coop. v. John Hancock Life Ins. Co., 582 F.3d 721 (7th Cir. 2009) (declining to decide the matter). *See also* Great Lakes Gas Transmission L.P. v. Essar Steel Minnesota, LLC, 871 F. Supp. 2d 843 (D. Minn. 2012) (inability to obtain financing due to credit crisis was not a *force majeure* event within the meaning of the parties' agreement but discussing cases going both ways).

[72] We would be surprised if, prior to the Chernobyl disaster in 1986, many drafters included "radioactive contamination" in the litany of Force Majeure Events. We would be a bit less surprised, but not shocked, if prior to the terrorist attacks on September 11, 2001, drafters included "terrorist activity or threats" in the list.

[73] *See infra* page 145 (discussing the maxim of *ejusdem generis*). *See also* Ergon-West Virginia, Inc. v. Dynegy Marketing & Trade, 706 F.3d 419 (5th Cir. 2013); Beardslee v. Inflection Energy, LLC, 761 F.3d 221 (2d Cir. 2014); Kel Kim Corp. v. Central Markets, Inc., 519 N.E.2d 295 (N.Y. 1987).

[74] *See* VICI Racing, LLC v. T-Mobile USA, Inc., 763 F.3d 273 (3d Cir. 2014) (declining to decide what Delaware law is on this point). *Cf.* Starke v. United Parcel Serv., Inc., 513 F. App'x 87 (2d Cir. 2013) (suggesting that a *force majeure* clause that was not expressly limited to unforeseeable causes was not so limited).

Exercise 4-8

Montana Mining Company ("MMC") has known for several years that its property contains significant deposits of palladium. Only recently, however, have the technologies been developed to make it economical to extract that metal. To protect itself from fluctuations in the price of palladium, MMC wishes to enter into a long-term supply contract under which it will promise to sell and deliver specified amounts of palladium each month for the next six years to Bentley Manufacturing, Inc., a maker of catalytic converters based in Michigan. The first draft of the sales agreement contains a *force majeure* clause worded like the sample above.

A. If your last name begins with a letter from A to J, you represent MMC. Identify circumstances and events that might prevent or hinder MMC from performing under the contract, but which do not qualify as a Force Majeure Event. Redraft the clause to cover those circumstances and events.

B. If your last name begins with a letter from K to Z, you represent Bentley Manufacturing. Identify the circumstances and events that qualify as a Force Majeure Event, but which should not excuse MMC from performing under the contract. Redraft the clause to exclude those circumstances and events.

C. EFFECT ON OTHER PARTIES

1. Assignment & Delegation

Contracts by their very nature create rights and obligations. Each promise creates a duty of the promisor and a correlative right in the promisee. Contracts with mutual promises – which are the bulk of contracts – create rights and duties for both parties.

In the modern commercial world, contracting parties often want to transfer their contractual rights or duties to others. Sometimes, such transfers involve all of the rights and duties with respect to one or more contracts. When a business is to be sold, for example, the seller often transfers all of the outstanding contractual rights and duties of the business to the buyer. More commonly, only a portion of the rights or duties is transferred. Consider, for example, General Contractor, who enters into an agreement with Owner to construct a new office building on Owner's property. In the agreement, General Contractor promises to build the building pursuant to certain specifications and Owner promises to make a series of payments. In the normal course of affairs, General Contractor might want to transfer both some of its contractual rights and some of its contractual duties. Specifically, General Contractor might need to pay its employees before Owner is required to make payment under the construction contract. To get the funds to pay the employees, General Contractor might wish to transfer (*e.g.,* sell) the right to future payment from Owner to a bank or finance company (presumably at a discount). Similarly, General Contractor might not have the expertise needed to perform all of the construction work. It might therefore need to transfer the duty to perform the electrical or plumbing work to an electrician or plumber.

In short, contract rights are essentially a type of incorporeal property. They can be bought and sold just as other types of property – real estate or goods – can be bought and sold. The analogy is imperfect, though. If you sell a car or a house, the only two people affected by the transaction are you and the buyer. If you sell a right to receive performance under a contract, you not only alter the rights of yourself and the buyer, you are potentially also affecting the promisor under the contract. This is even more clearly the case when contractual duties are transferred. Imagine what would happen if the law school teacher who contracted with a school to teach a course on transactional skills were to transfer the obligation to teach to a recent college graduate who had never attended law school. No doubt, neither the school nor the students enrolled in the course would be happy.[75]

The law deals with the transfer of contractual rights and duties through a variety of rules. Before examining those rules, it is important to understand the applicable terminology. The transfer of a contractual *right* is called an "assignment"; the transfer of a contractual *duty* is referred to as a "delegation." The transferee of an assignment is an "assignee" and the transferee of a duty is a "delegate." The diagrams that follow might help.

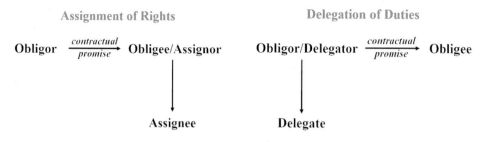

Assignment of Rights   Delegation of Duties

---

[75] *Cf.* RESTATEMENT (SECOND) OF CONTRACTS § 318, ill. 5.

(a) Assignment of Rights

If no statute controls, the common law generally permits a party to assign a contractual right, subject to three exceptions.[76] The first exception – that the substitution of the assignee for the assignor would materially change the duty of the obligor or materially increase the risk imposed on the obligor – rarely arises. The Restatement provides only one example:

> B contracts to support A for the remainder of A's life. A cannot by assignment confer on C a right to have B support C.[77]

A could, however, assign the right to receive payments from B for the remainder of *A's* life.[78] In other words, as long as the nature of the obligor's performance does not change, it generally matters little to whom that obligation is owed.

The second exception covers assignments prohibited by public policy. The classic example of a public policy limit on assignment is champerty: the trafficking in legal claims. The common law has a long-standing and strong dislike for anything that promotes litigation and has historically invalidated attempts to assign all or part of an interest in a lawsuit. This policy still applies with respect to tort claims, particularly those involving personal injury,[79] but has abated somewhat with respect to contract claims.

The final exception to the free assignability of contract rights is if the contract has a valid prohibition on assignment. In fact, many written agreements purport to prohibit assignment and many transactional attorneys almost reflexively incorporate in their drafts a clause purporting to restrict or prohibit assignment. However, many contractual restrictions on assignment are invalidated by statute.[80] Moreover, even

---

[76] RESTATEMENT (SECOND) OF CONTRACTS § 317(2). Of course, not all states follow all of the Restatement rules. *See, e.g.*, In re Mortgages Ltd., 427 B.R. 780 (D. Ariz. 2010) (Arizona does not follow § 328; an assignment of the contract does not delegate duties).

[77] RESTATEMENT (SECOND) OF CONTRACTS § 317, ill. 3.

[78] *See* RESTATEMENT (SECOND) OF CONTRACTS § 317, ill. 4.

[79] *See, e.g.*, Gurski v. Rosenblum and Filan, LLC, 885 A.2d 163 (Conn. 2005) (invalidating assignment of a legal malpractice claim to the person who had sued her podiatrist for negligent treatment and won a judgment due to the alleged malpractice of the podiatrist's lawyers).

[80] Article 9 of the Uniform Commercial Code governs the assignment of most contractual rights to payment and overrides most contractual restrictions and many legal restrictions on

in the absence of such a statute, most courts, when interpreting agreements, follow several principles that limit the scope or effectiveness of a clause purporting to restrict assignment.[81]

Exercise 4-9

Supplier contracts to sell Homeowner at a stated price all the heating oil Homeowner needs to heat Homeowner's house for the next four months.

A. The agreement between the parties has no restriction on assignment.
   1. May Supplier assign the right to payment from Homeowner? *See* U.C.C. § 2-210(2).
   2. Homeowner sells the home to Buyer. May Homeowner assign to Buyer the right to receive heating oil from Supplier?
   3. May Homeowner assign the right to receive heating oil to Neighbor? If so, is Neighbor entitled to receive the amount of heating oil needed to heat Homeowner's house or the amount needed to heat Neighbor's house? *See* Restatement (Second) of Contracts § 334, ill. 3.

B. How, if at all, does the answer to each question in Part A change if the agreement between Supplier and Homeowner contains a clause prohibiting each party from "assigning the contract"? *See* Restatement (Second) of Contracts § 322(1); U.C.C. § 2-210(4).

C. How, if at all, does the answer to each question in Part A change if the agreement between Supplier and Homeowner contains a clause prohibiting each party from "assigning its rights under the contract"? *See* Restatement (Second) of Contracts § 322(2); U.C.C. §§ 2-210(2), 9-406(d).

D. How, if at all, does the answer to each question in Part A change if the agreement between Supplier and Homeowner contains a clause prohibiting each party from "assigning its rights under the contract" and providing that any attempted assignment of such rights is "void"?

---

assignment. *See* U.C.C. §§ 9-406, 9-408. Article 2 generally permits both buyers and sellers of goods to assign their contract rights. *See* U.C.C. § 2-210(2).

[81] *See* RESTATEMENT (SECOND) OF CONTRACTS § 322.

Exercise 4-10

Auditor contracts to provide accounting services to Broker. The written agreement between them includes the following:

> Broker shall not, directly or indirectly, assign this Agreement or any rights or claims against Auditor arising under this Agreement to anyone. Any assignment or transfer by Broker in violation of this paragraph is void.

Broker's business collapses after major accounting irregularities are disclosed, with the result that Broker has a malpractice claim against Auditor. Does the contract between Auditor and Broker prohibit the assignment of that malpractice claim? Rewrite the clause to make it clearer that it does apply to the malpractice claim.

(b) Delegation of Duties

The rules on delegation – that is, the ability of the obligor to discharge its duty through performance by the delegate – are more restrictive than the rules on assignment. In addition to prohibiting a delegation that is contrary to public policy or to the terms of the contract, they also prohibit delegation whenever the obligee has a substantial interest in having the obligor personally perform. This last restriction covers most personal services contracts. As one court put it, had the Metropolitan Airports Commission "contracted with Luciano Pavarotti to sing in its passenger facilities in order to soothe the souls of weary travelers, it could not be compelled to accept performance from pop-star Michael Jackson."[82] Of course, it is not always easy to identify what is and what is not a contract for personal services. What is clear is that the payment of money is not normally a personal service. As the same court continued, "the payment of rent pursuant to a lease is hardly the type of performance that depends upon the identity of the party that is to perform, *i.e.*, the lessee."[83]

Of course, the agreement could modify this rule by permitting an obligor to delegate even though the obligee does have an interest in having the obligor

---

[82]   Matter of Midway Airlines, Inc., 6 F.3d 492, 495 (7th Cir. 1993).

[83]   *Id.*

perform. Consider the following exercise, based on a listserv posting by a teacher of contract law.

Exercise 4-11

Professor contracted with University Press to author a book on contract law. After Professor produced and submitted the manuscript, but before printing, University Press sold its law division to IT Company. Professor, who had publicized the book as forthcoming from University Press, believes that the change in publishers will make the book less prestigious and might reduce sales and royalties, hurt Professor's credibility, and reduce Professor's prospect for tenure.

The publication agreement provides that "University Press may assign this Agreement or any of its interests in it and may delegate its duties." What advice do you give to Professor?

Even when delegation is permissible, it does not absolve the obligor of its duty under the contract.[84] To obtain absolution, the assent of the obligee is needed. If that assent is given, the result is a "novation." A novation is, in essence a new agreement by which the obligee releases the obligor and agrees to accept the obligation of the delegate instead. A novation will not be inferred merely from the obligee's acceptance of the performance of the delegate; a more clear manifestation of assent is needed. As a result, in most instances in which a contractual duty is delegated, there is no novation. Thus, the original obligor remains obligated on the contract even after it has delegated its duty to perform. Whether the delegate is also obligated (in the absence of a novation) depends on a variety of factors that we will not explore.[85]

---

[84] RESTATEMENT (SECOND) OF CONTRACTS § 318(3). Indeed, what often results is a suretyship relationship under which the delegate becomes the primary obligor and the original obligor becomes a secondary obligor. *See* RESTATEMENT (THIRD) OF SURETYSHIP AND GUARANTY § 2(e).

[85] Typically, the delegate will become obligated only if the delegation was pursuant to a contract with the obligor (*i.e.*, the delegate is not agreeing to perform gratuitously) and the obligee qualifies as a third-party beneficiary of that contract. In a contract for the sale of goods, a person who accepts an assignment "of the contract" – and is therefore both an assignee and a delegate – becomes obligated to perform and can be sued for breach by either

2. Successors

A successor is an entity that succeeds by operation of law to all the rights and obligations of its predecessor. The classic example is the survivor in a corporate merger. A decedent's estate might also be a successor to the deceased. Unlike an assignee or delegate, which might acquire the assignor's rights or delegator's duties under only a single contract, a successor steps into the shoes of the predecessor with respect to all of the predecessor's contractual rights and obligations.

One boilerplate term commonly found in agreements of all types is a clause that purports to deal with both successors and assigns. A typical example is as follows:

> ***Successors and Assigns.*** This Agreement is binding on and inures to the benefit of the parties and their respective successors and assigns.

Unfortunately, when phrased in this manner, the clause probably serves no purpose. The principal treatise of contractual boilerplate identifies the following five potential purposes for such a clause:

1. To bind an assignee to perform
2. To require a non-assigning party to render performance to an assignee
3. To indicate that rights are assignable
4. To indicate that duties are delegable
5. To bind the parties to the contract

The treatise then explains why it is doubtful that the clause serves any of these purposes.[86] As a result, another notable contract drafting guru has concluded that the typical successors and assigns clause serves no useful purpose and should be scrapped. He then lamented that the clause's incoherence "helps ensure its survival – because drafters are unsure what function it serves, they're loath to delete it."[87]

---

of the original parties to the contract.

[86] NEGOTIATING AND DRAFTING CONTRACT BOILERPLATE § 4.03 (Tina L. Stark, ed., 2003). A traditionally worded successors clause apparently also does nothing to or for an entity that acquires one of the contracting parties in a manner that does not make the entity a successor. *See* Nature's Plus Nordic A/S v. Natural Organics, Inc., 980 F. Supp. 2d 400 (E.D.N.Y. 2013) (entity that purchased a party to a contract that included a clause purporting to bind successors and assigns did not have standing to bring a breach of contract claim in its own name).

[87] *Getting Rid of "Successors and Assigns" Provision*, Adams on Contract Drafting,

Before joining in this recommendation, it is worth noting that there might be a sixth purpose for a successors and assigns clause, a purpose closely related to the first two purposes identified above: to bind either the successor or the counterparty to an extension of the contractual relationship. For example, a security agreement might provide that the collateral secures future loans made by the secured party to the debtor and that the collateral includes after-acquired property of the debtor. A successors and assigns clause might be an attempt to ensure that a *successor to the debtor* is bound by those terms.

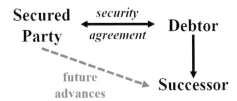

Alternatively, the clause might be an attempt to have the collateral secure future advances made by an assignee or *successor to the secured party*.

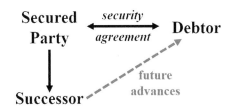

Similarly, a guaranty might promise repayment of future loans made by the creditor to the principal obligor. A successors and assigns clause might be an attempt to cover credit extended by an assignee of, or successor to, the creditor. However, it is far from clear that a typically worded successors and assigns clause would achieve either of these purposes.

With respect to the former, the clause is probably unnecessary. Article 9 of the Uniform Commercial Code expressly provides that a successor to the debtor – a "new debtor" in Article 9's parlance[88] – is bound by an after-acquired property clause.[89] While the Code and comments are conspicuously silent about whether future advances to the new debtor are secured by the collateral, that is probably

---

http://www.adamsdrafting.com/successors-and-assigns/ (Sept. 18, 2006).

[88] *See* U.C.C. §§ 9-102(a)(56), 9-203(d).

[89] *See* U.C.C. § 9-203(e).

because the liability of both the new debtor and the collateral for such advances goes without saying. After all, the new debtor is bound not merely by the security interest, but by the security agreement entered into by the original debtor.[90] Thus, if the security agreement with the original debtor purports to make the collateral secure future advances, that should be sufficient to cover advances the secured party makes to the new debtor.[91]

With respect to the second example, the typical clause is probably insufficient. While a successor steps into the shoes of the predecessor and an assignee acquires the rights of the assignor, encumbering the collateral with liability for future loans made by a successor or assignee could greatly prejudice a debtor who lacks notice of the succession or assignment. Consider a scenario in which Debtor grants a security interest to X to secure existing and future debts. Debtor then borrows from Y, not knowing that Y has become a successor or assignee of X. It would be rather inequitable for the collateral to secure that new indebtedness. While the parties no doubt can, by agreement, provide that it does, it is unlikely that a court would interpret a traditionally worded successors and assigns clause as having that effect.

Similarly, while a court might interpret a continuing guaranty as covering future loans made by a *successor* to the original creditor, it is unlikely that a court would interpret the guarantee – even one with a successors and assigns clause – as extending to an *assignee* of the original creditor because that could greatly expand the obligation of the guarantor in ways that were outside the reasonable contemplation of the parties.[92]

The lesson from this discussion is that if the parties intend to cover future advances made by or to a successor or assign, they should expressly so state in the

---

[90]   *See* U.C.C. § 9-203(d).

[91]   Moreover, this result is not unfair. A new debtor, as a successor that becomes liable as a matter of law for all the original debtor's contractual obligations, should be charged with notice of the security agreement. Accordingly, by accepting a future advance, a new debtor should expect that the advance is secured.

[92]   *See* McLane Foodservice, Inc. v. Table Rock Restaurants, LLC, 736 F.3d 375 (5th Cir. 2013). In general, guaranties are not assignable. However, this rule is not applied mechanically and an assignment of a guaranty will not release the guarantor unless "the essentials of the original contract have been changed and the performance required of the principal is materially different from that first contemplated." Southern Wine and Spirits of Illinois, Inc. v. Steiner, 8 N.E.3d 1065, 1069-70 (Ill. Ct. App. 2014). As so explained, the rule is not very different than the suretyship principle that provides that a surety is exonerated when the underlying obligation has been modified without the consent of the surety. *See* RESTATEMENT (THIRD) OF SURETYSHIP AND GUARANTY § 41(b)(i).

future advances clause, rather than relying on a traditionally worded successors and assigns clause. Such a clause serves no clear purpose and can be safely discarded.

Exercise 4-12

Corporation has a $10 million line of credit from State Bank. The debt is to be guaranteed by Owner. You are drafting the guaranty agreement and want to make sure that Owner will be obligated for all present and future obligations of Corporation to State Bank. You are aware that State Bank is in preliminary negotiations with National Bank about merging. You also know that State Bank might sell to another bank all or part of its loan to Corporation. Draft language to make it clear that the guaranty will cover not only any future amounts that State Bank lends to Corporation, but any amounts loaned by an entity that merges with State Bank or that acquires from State Bank an interest in its loan to Corporation.

D. DISPUTE RESOLUTION

1. Costs and Attorney's Fees

Throughout the United States, parties are normally expected to pay their own costs in negotiating, executing, performing, and enforcing their own contracts.[93] Pursuant to this general rule, parties must pay their own expenses in bringing or defending contract actions – even when successful – unless either a specific statute provides to the contrary or the contract both places and, under the law, is permitted to place, the burden on the other party.[94] Thus, parties wishing to reallocate these expenses must ensure that their contract contains a reallocation provision broad

---

[93] *See, e.g.,* TINA L. STARK, ED., NEGOTIATING AND DRAFTING CONTRACT BOILERPLATE § 12.05 (2003).

[94] There are some exceptions to this general rule. For example, some pre-contract costs might be recoverable in a successful claim for rescission of contract and reliance damages, because the goal of recovery in such a case is to place the aggrieved party in the position it would have occupied had the contract never been made. *See id.* at § 12.05[2]. Similarly, misconduct during litigation might result in sanctions, thereby shifting some costs to the misbehaving party.

enough to cover all the different types of expenses that the party to be recompensed might incur.

Exercise 4-13

Lender is providing working capital financing to Borrower, secured by a lien on virtually all of Borrower's assets. The Credit/Security Agreement includes the following provision intended to make the Borrower responsible for all of Lender's expenses and attorney's fees:

> Borrower shall indemnify, defend, and hold Lender harmless from any loss, cost, expense, or liability, including reasonable attorney's fees, incurred by Lender in performing or enforcing its rights under this Agreement.

What expenses, other than attorney's fees, might Lender incur? Does this clause cover them? What attorney services might Lender need in the course of the parties' relationship? Will the fees incurred for those services be covered by this clause?

(a) A Synopsis of the Law

Because attorney's fees clauses override a general policy of the law that each side bear its own costs, they are often construed rather strictly.[95] Consequently, a clause requiring reimbursement of "costs" or "expenses" will likely not be adequate to cover attorney's fees.[96]

More important, a contract clause expressly providing for reimbursement of attorney's fees might not, depending on how the clause is worded, cover all the

---

[95] *See, e.g.*, Gottlieb v. Such, 740 N.Y.S.2d 44, 44 (N.Y. App. Div. 2002).

[96] *See* Coastal Power Int'l Ltd. v. Transcontinental Capital Corp., 182 F.3d 163 (2d Cir. 1999); Allstate Ins. Co. v. Loo, 54 Cal. Rptr. 2d 541 (Cal. Ct. App. 1996); Jackson v. Hammer, 653 N.E.2d 809 (Ill. Ct. App. 1995). *But cf.* Boulevard Bank v. Philips Medical Systems Int'l B.V., 827 F. Supp. 510 (N.D. Ill. 1993) (clause in guaranty agreement allowing recovery of "collection costs" included attorney's fees).

attorney's fees incurred.[97] For example, a clause covering attorney's fees incurred "in connection with any action to enforce the agreement" might not reach a claim for rescission based on fraud or a related claim for damages in tort, such as for misrepresentation.[98] It might also not cover actions brought by or against others to establish priority to collateral,[99] or fees incurred prior to or in lieu of litigation. In some states such language would also not cover attorney's fees incurred on

---

[97] *See, e.g.*, SK Food Corp. v. Firstbank, 2017 WL 776116 (Tenn. Ct. App. 2017) (a prospective borrower's promise in a loan commitment letter to pay the bank's expenses, including reasonable attorney's fees, "incurred in the preparation and negotiation of documentation, did not cover the attorney's fees the bank incurred in successfully defending against the prospective borrower's claim for breach by refusing to lend); Magnusson v. Ocwen Loan Servicing, LLC, 2017 WL 6261482 (D. Utah 2017) (credit documents providing for the borrower to pay the lender's attorney's fees "in enforcing the note," in litigation that "that might significantly affect Lender's interest in the property," or incurred "for the purpose of protecting Lender's interest in the Property," did not cover attorney's fees incurred in successfully defending against the borrower's action for violation of the Home Affordable Modification Program because the litigation did not involve an effort to enforce the note and did not relate to the lender's lien on the collateral).

[98] *Compare* Bena v. Schleicher, 2017 WL 1907741 (Wash. Ct. App. 2017) (a suit to reinstate a promissory note was not an action "to collect" within the meaning of the contractual clause authorizing an award of attorney's fees); Marcus v. Fox, 723 P.2d 682 (Ariz. 1986) (rescission claim is not one "arising out of a contract"), *with* Diamond D Enters. USA, Inc. v. Steinsvaag, 979 F.2d 14 (2d Cir. 1992) (franchisor's contractual right to attorney's fees "incurred in enforcing" the agreement extended to those incurred in defending a fraud in inducement claim); Lerner v. Ward, 16 Cal. Rptr. 2d 486 (Cal. Ct. App. 1993) ("any action or proceeding arising out of this agreement" covered a fraud in inducement claim). *See also* Clark v. Missouri Lottery Comm'n, 463 S.W.3d 843 (Mo. Ct. App. 2015) (loan agreement that obligated the borrower to pay the fees of an attorney that the lender hired to collect did not cover attorney's fees that the lender incurred in successfully defending against the borrower's claim that the security agreement was ineffective); PC Crane Serv., LLC v. McQueen Masonry, Inc., 273 P.3d 396 (Utah Ct. App. 2012) (contract clause providing that lender was entitled to attorney's fees incurred in connection with legal action after default did not cover fees incurred in the borrower's action for recovery of amounts paid because the borrower had not defaulted).

[99] *See, e.g.*, Adkins v. Chrysler Fin. Corp., 344 F. App'x 144 (6th Cir. 2009) (security agreement providing for recovery of attorney's fees incurred "in connection with Secured Party's exercise of any of its rights and remedies under this Agreement" did not cover fees incurred in defending conversion action brought by another creditor).

appeal[100] or fees incurred in preparing a fee request or in litigating entitlement to fees, because recovery of those fees requires express reference to them.[101]

A similar problem can arise with respect to attorneys' fees incurred in connection with one party's bankruptcy proceeding. For example, a clause authorizing a lender to recover attorney's fees incurred "in connection with any action to enforce the agreement" might not be broad enough to reach fees incurred in reviewing or objecting to a plan of confirmation, defending a preference action, seeking relief from the automatic stay, challenging the debtor's discharge, or determining the dischargeability of the creditor's claim.[102]

(b) Prevailing Party

Some written agreements provide that, in the event of litigation, the "prevailing party" shall be entitled to reimbursement of attorney's fees. One problem with such clauses is that, even when there is only a single claim, it is often difficult to ascertain who is the prevailing party. For example, if the plaintiff obtains a judgment for only a small amount on a very large claim, is it fair to treat the plaintiff as prevailing?[103] Trial courts are supposed to determine which party

---

[100] *See* Synectic Ventures I, LLC v. EVI Corp., 261 P.3d 30 (Or. Ct. App. 2011) (creditor was not entitled to attorney's fees incurred in successful appeal because a contractual provision on attorney's fees must expressly reference appellate proceedings to cover fees incurred during an appeal).

[101] *See, e.g.,* IG Second Generation Partners, L.P. v. Kaygreen Realty Co., 980 N.Y.S.2d 479 (N.Y. App. Div. 2014); 214 Wall Street Assocs., LLC v. Medical Arts-Huntington Realty, 953 N.Y.S.2d 124 (N.Y. App. Div. 2012); 546–552 W. 146th St. LLC v. Arfa, 950 N.Y.S.2d 24, 26 (N.Y. App. Div. 2012). *See also* Allen Benson, *Fees on Fees – Drafting to Include Attorney's Fees Incurred in Seeking Fees*, 4 The Transactional Lawyer 1 (Aug. 2014).

[102] *See, e.g.,* In re England, 2018 WL 1614166 (Bankr. M.D. Ala. 2018). *But cf.* In re Sokolik, 635 F.3d 261 (7th Cir. 2011) (loan agreement in which debtor promised to pay "all reasonable collection costs, including attorney's fees and other charges, necessary for the collection of any amount not paid when due" covered attorney's fees incurred in successfully challenging the dischargeability of the debt).

Another issue that occasionally arises is whether the language of the attorney's fees clause encompasses fees incurred in preparing the fee request or litigating the entitlement to attorney's fees. *See* Thompson v. Pharmacy Corp. of Am., Inc., 334 F.3d 1242 (11th Cir. 2003).

[103] *See, e.g.,* Marine Enters., Inc. v. Security Pacific Trading Corp., 750 P.2d 1290 (Wash.

prevailed in reference to the extent each party realized its litigation objectives, whether through trial, settlement, or otherwise.[104] In so doing, courts are supposed to consider the parties' contentions in pleadings and in settlement discussions.[105] Because these are fact-intensive inquiries, a trial court's ruling on this point is often treated on review as a factual finding and, therefore, is rarely reversed. In some cases, neither party substantially prevails and thus neither gets its attorney's fees.[106]

Lenders often want their loan agreements to provide for reimbursement of their legal fees regardless of whether the lender is successful in bringing a claim against or defending a claim by the borrower. The enforceability of such clauses is questionable, however, if the lender is found to have materially breached the contract[107] or the state whose law governs has a statute providing for reciprocity with respect to attorney's fees.

Ct. App. 1988) (party who won a judgment for $5,701 in an action for $600,000 was not substantially prevailing party).

[104] *See, e.g.*, Santisas v. Goodin, 951 P.2d 399 (Cal. 1998).

[105] *See, e.g.*, Hsu v. Abbara, 891 P.2d 804 (Cal. 1995).

[106] *See, e.g.*, In re Mac-Go Corp., 541 B.R. 706 (Bankr. N.D. Cal. 2015) (although a creditor successfully defended against $900,000 in preference and fraudulent transfer claims – and was held liable for only $25,300 in avoidable post-petition transfers – there was no prevailing party within the meaning of Cal. Civ. Code § 1717, and thus the creditor had no right to attorney's fees); In re Brosio, 505 B.R. 903 (9th Cir. BAP 2014) (debtor who objected to the portion of a creditor's bankruptcy claim seeking $425 for attorney's fees was not a prevailing party under California Civil Code § 1717 after the creditor withdrew that portion of its request by filing an amended proof of claim because the court did not adjudicate anything and the amended claim was akin to a voluntary dismissal); Walton General Contractors, Inc. v. Chicago Forming Inc., 111 F.3d 1376 (8th Cir. 1997); Indoor Billboard Northwest Inc. v. M2 Sys. Corp., 2013 WL 3146850 (D. Or. 2013) (defendant that successfully argued that federal court had no subject matter jurisdiction and obtained dismissal of claim was not a prevailing party). *See also* Cal. Civ. Code § 1717(b)(1) (providing that a court may determine that there is no prevailing party). *Cf.* Wilkes v. Zurlinden, 984 P.2d 261 (Or. 1999) (each party prevailed in defending against the other's claim).

[107] *But see* In re Latshaw Drilling, LLC, 481 B.R. 765 (Bankr. N.D. Okla. 2012) (under New York law, lender was contractually entitled to attorney's fees incurred after it breached the loan agreement by failing to fund the loan).

(c) Reciprocity Statutes

At least six states have a statute that converts a unilateral attorney's fees provision into a bilateral one.[108] That is, by law, if one party to a contract is entitled to attorney's fees in successfully litigating an issue arising under the contract, then whichever party is successful will be entitled to attorney's fees from the other. Transactional attorneys need to be aware of these laws if there is any chance that one will apply.[109] An attorney's fees clause made reciprocal by law might interfere with a client's preferred dispute resolution strategy, particularly if the client is litigious and tends to take aggressive positions during litigation.[110] In short, attorneys need to be cognizant of the fact that the more broadly a contractual

---

[108] *See* Cal. Civ. Code § 1717; Fla. Stat. § 57.105(7); Mont. Code § 28-3-704; Or. Rev. Stat. § 20.096; Utah Code § 78B-5-826; Wash. Rev. Code § 4.84.330. *See also* Ct. Gen. Law § 42-150bb (making reciprocal a contractual clause making a consumer responsible for a commercial party's attorney's fees); Ariz Rev Stat. § 12-341.01 (authorizing the court to award attorney's fees to any successful party in a contract action); Tex. Civ. Prac. & Rem. Code § 38.001 (authorizing award of attorney's fees to successful party in a variety of contract actions).

Other states might invalidate a one-sided attorney's fees clause if the parties have unequal bargaining power and the clause might promote litigation or usury. *See, e.g.,* Moxley v. Pfundstein, 801 F. Supp. 2d 598 (N.D. Ohio 2011).

[109] *See* Capital One Bank v. Fort, 255 P.3d 508 (Or. Ct. App. 2011) (reciprocity statute was fundamental policy of the state and overrode choice-of-law clause in consumer's credit card contract). *Compare* First Intercontinental Bank v. Ahn, 798 F.3d 1149 (9th Cir. 2015) (because California Civil Code § 1717, which makes reciprocal a contractual clause awarding attorney's fees to only one of the contracting parties, is fundamental policy of the state, it applies to litigation in California even though the parties' promissory note had a valid clause choosing application of Georgia law); ABF Capital Corp. v. Grove Props. Co. 23 Cal. Rptr. 3d 803 (Cal. Ct. App. 2005) (similar, involving an agreement choosing application of New York law), *with* ABF Capital Corp. v. Berglass, 30 Cal. Rptr. 3d 588 (Cal. Ct. App. 2005) (because, under choice-of-law principles, New York law would be applicable to this litigation in California even if the parties had not contractually agreed to the application of New York law, the New York rule enforcing a unilateral attorney's fees provision governs and whether that rule violates California fundamental policy is irrelevant).

[110] It is worth noting that the reciprocity statute can operate to bind persons who were not parties to the contract. *See, e.g.,* Vineyard Bank v. DFI Funding, Inc., 2012 WL 1889266 (Cal. Ct. App. 2012) (mortgagee that foreclosed on and took title to the property could recover its attorney's fees from the other lender that claimed priority and initiated foreclosure proceedings because, had the other lender prevailed, its attorney's fees would have been secured by the property).

attorney's fees clause is drafted, the more broadly it might operate against the drafter. Note, however, that a reciprocity statute which applies to a particular contract might not be phrased broadly enough to cover tort claims, and thus a clause in the parties' agreement that is broad enough to cover attorney's fees incurred in connection with a tort claim might not, in fact, become reciprocal with respect to such a claim.[111]

Exercise 4-14

You are drafting a commercial real estate lease on behalf of the landlord and are working on a clause that makes the tenant responsible for the attorney's fees that the landlord incurs.

A. The applicable jurisdiction does not have a reciprocity statute that applies to commercial leases. You want the tenant to be responsible for any attorney's fees that the landlord might incur. Draft such a clause.

B. The applicable jurisdiction has a reciprocity statute applicable to commercial leases that provides as follows:

> Whenever the provisions of a contract give one party to the contract an express right to recover attorney's fees from another party to the contract, then in any action on the contract the prevailing party shall have the same right to recover attorney's fees from the losing party or parties.

What principle or principles should you follow in drafting the attorney's fees clause? Draft a clause that follows the principle or principles you identified.

---

[111] *See* Moallem v. Coldwell Banker Commercial Group, Inc., 31 Cal. Rptr. 2d 253 (Cal. Ct. App. 1994). *But cf.* Lane v. U.S. Bank, 2012 WL 3670467 (Cal. Ct. App. 2012) (clause entitling lender to attorney's fees "in connection with Borrower's default" and "for the purpose of protecting Lender's interest in the Property and rights under this Security Agreement" was broad enough to cover quasi-contract claims for unjust enrichment and imposition of a constructive trust, and such claims were "on the contract" within the meaning of the reciprocity statute).

(d) Prohibitions

As with just about anything related to contract law, lawyers must be on the lookout for statutes that restrict the parties' freedom to contract about attorney's fees. Reciprocity statutes do that in one way but other statutes might impose more significant restrictions, particularly with respect to consumer transactions. For example, Ohio law apparently renders unenforceable an attorney's fees clause in an agreement relating to a loan incurred primarily for personal, family, or household purposes.[112] In the Dakotas, an attorney's fees clause in a note, bond, mortgage, security agreement, guaranty, or other evidence of debt is void as against public policy.[113] The same is true in Nebraska even more generally: absent a statutory or judicial exception, a contractual clause making one party responsible for another's attorney's fees is void as against public policy.[114] An attorney's attempt to collect attorney's fees in such a transaction, even a seemingly innocuous request for them in a complaint, could violate the Fair Debt Collection Practices and subject the attorney to liability.[115]

---

[112] *See* Ohio Rev. Stat. § 1319.02; Foster v. D.B.S. Collection Agency, 463 F. Supp. 2d 783 (S.D. Ohio 2006) (citing predecessor to § 1319.02). What makes this somewhat troubling is that the statute does not expressly prohibit attorney's fees in consumer contracts, it merely authorizes them only in non-consumer contracts. Thus, the prohibition is really just a negative inference.

[113] *See* N.D. Cent. Code § 28-26-24; Farmers Union Oil Co. v. Maixner, 376 N.W.2d 43 (N.D. 1985) (statute applies to guarantees); S.D. Codified Laws § 15-17-39; International Multifoods Corp. v. Mardian, 379 N.W.2d 840, 845 (S.D. 1985) (statute applies to guarantees).

[114] *See, e.g.*, Stewart v. Bennett, 727 N.W.2d 424, 429 (Neb. 2007); Quinn v. Godfather's Invs., Inc., 348 N.W.2d 893 (Neb. 1984).
Courts in other jurisdictions disagree about whether to apply this rule if the parties have contractually chosen Nebraska law to apply to their relationship. Some treat the issue of attorney's fees as procedural, so that the law of the forum state applies, *e.g.*, Boswell v. RFD–TV the Theater, LLC, 498 S.W.3d 550 (Tenn. Ct. App. 2016), while others will apply Nebraska law to the issue and thereby deny a request for attorney's fees, *e.g.*, Amur Equip. Fin. Inc. v. CHD Transp. Inc., 2017 WL 5477379 (E.D. Cal. 2017).

[115] *See, e.g.*, Moxley v. Pfundstein, 2012 WL 4848973 (N.D. Ohio 2012).

2. Choice of Law

There are a variety of reasons parties might wish to choose which state's law governs their contractual relationship. Doing so might remove uncertainty and eliminate a subject on which briefing is necessary in the event of litigation. More significant, it allows parties, particularly those engaged in many multi-state or international transactions, to focus on compliance with one set of rules, rather than dozens. Most important, it can permit a party to seek refuge under the laws of the jurisdiction that are particularly favorable for its type of business. For example, a business with valuable trade secrets might want its agreements governed by the law of a jurisdiction which offers strong protection for them. A buyer of businesses might want its purchase agreements governed by the law of a jurisdiction that will enforce a broad covenant not to compete. A merchant that deals with consumers might want its contracts governed by a jurisdiction that interprets the obligation of good faith in a narrow and predictable manner and which does not permit punitive damages for most contract-related torts.

In general, contracting parties are free to select which jurisdiction's law will govern their relationship. The major limitation on this freedom, as expressed in the Restatement (Second) of Conflict of Laws, is that the jurisdiction selected must bear a "substantial relationship" to either the transaction or to the parties, or there must be some other reasonable basis for the parties' choice.[116] A second limitation arises whenever application of the chosen jurisdiction's law would violate a fundamental policy of the jurisdiction whose law would govern but for the parties' selection. In such cases the parties' selection will not be respected.[117] Courts are sometimes exceedingly willing to identify fundamental state policy, and thus invalidate a contractual choice of law.[118] A third limitation concerns contracts involving real

---

[116] *See* RESTATEMENT (SECOND) OF CONFLICT OF LAWS § 187(2)(a).

[117] *Id.* at § 187(2)(b). *See, e.g.*, Dahl v. Dahl, 345 P.3d 566 (Utah 2015) (application of the chosen Nevada law to determine whether a trust agreement created an irrevocable trust would violate fundamental policy of Utah – the form state for a divorce proceeding – in favor of an equitable distribution of marital assets).

A choice of law clause can be a double-edged sword. *See* 1-800-Got Junk? LLC v. Superior Court, 116 Cal. Rptr. 3d 923 (Cal. Ct. App. 2010) (franchisor that had drafted a franchise agreement choosing Washington law argued, unsuccessfully, for the agreement to be governed instead by the more favorable law of the forum state: California).

[118] *See, e.g.*, Rincon EV Realty LLC v. CP III Rincon Towers, Inc., 213 Cal. Rptr. 3d 410 (Cal. Ct. App. 2017) (although a loan agreement selected New York law as the governing law, and its waiver of the right to a jury is enforceable in New York, the agreement's jury

property. Not surprisingly, the law of the jurisdiction where the real property is located will govern the *effect* of the parties' agreement.[119] While parties are generally free to designate a jurisdiction whose law will govern the *interpretation* of their agreement involving real property,[120] prevailing practice is to let the law of the jurisdiction where the property is located govern this too.

State Statutory Variations on Choice of Law. At least five states – including California and New York – allow contracting parties to choose their respective bodies of law regardless of whether the state bears a substantial or reasonable relationship to the parties or the transaction, provided the contract involves a set minimum amount of money.[121] On the other hand, some have specific rules restricting contractual choice of law in certain types of contracts, such as franchise agreements or insurance policies.[122] Lawyers should check for such restrictions before drafting a choice-of-law provision.

---

waiver clause was unenforceable in California litigation because it violates a fundamental policy of the state and California has a materially greater interest in the matter than does New York); Nutracea v. Langley Park Invs. PLC, 2007 WL 135699 (E.D. Cal. 2007) (clauses in stock purchase agreement selecting New York law as the governing law and New York as the forum for all litigation between the parties were unenforceable because of California's strong policy in preventing fraud on California corporations and New York's minimal interest in the litigation); Madden v. Midland Funding, LLC, 237 F. Supp. 3d 130 (S.D.N.Y. 2017) (application of Delaware law pursuant to a choice-of-law clause in the parties' credit card agreement would violate a fundamental public policy of New York because Delaware does not cap the interest rate that parties may agree to whereas New York has a criminal usury statute); In re Miller, 341 B.R. 764 (Bankr. E.D. Mo. 2006) (default rate of interest on business loan, though valid under Iowa law that the parties had chosen in their agreement, violated Missouri law, was against fundamental policy of Missouri, and was therefore unenforceable).

[119] R**ESTATEMENT** (S**ECOND**) **OF** C**ONFLICT OF** L**AWS** §§ 223, 228.

[120] *Id.* at § 224(1).

[121] *See* Cal. Civ. Code § 1646.5 ($250,000); Del. Stat. tit. 6, § 2708 ($100,000); Fla. Stat. § 685.101 ($250,000);735 Ill. Comp. Stat. 105/5-5 ($250,000); N.Y. Gen. Oblig. Law § 5-1401(1) ($250,000).

The New York statute expressly overrides the choice-of-law rule in former Article 1 of the Uniform Commercial Code. Unfortunately, the legislature did not update the reference when it enacted revised Article 1 of the U.C.C. in 2014. *See* 2014 N.Y. Sess. Law ch. 505 (enacting, among other things, U.C.C. § 1-301). It remains unclear, therefore, whether the New York statute applies in a transaction governed by the U.C.C.

[122] *See* T**INA** L. S**TARK**, **ED.,** N**EGOTIATING AND** D**RAFTING** C**ONTRACT** B**OILERPLATE** § 6.02[c] (2003)

Caveats. First, reliance on an opt-in statute, such as that in New York, might be unfounded if the litigation occurs in another jurisdiction and the jurisdiction whose law is chosen (*e.g.*, New York) does not bear a substantial relationship to either the transaction or the parties. In other words, while New York courts can be expected to give effect to a contractual choice of New York law if the dollar threshold is satisfied, a court in another jurisdiction might not do so. Second, even when well drafted, a contractual choice-of-law clause will not govern contract formation questions.[123] After all, a court cannot logically give effect to the parties' contractual choice of law until it determines that the parties do in fact have a contract.[124] Similarly, questions about the scope of a choice-of-law provision are normally governed by the same law that governs the validity of the clause or contract.[125] Third, a contractual choice of law is unlikely to determine the law governing issues that arise more by operation of law than from the relationship of the parties.[126] Fourth, unless a contrary intent is manifest, some states interpret a choice-of-law clause as dealing only with substantive law, not procedural law. That distinction can be critical because statutes of limitations are regarded as procedural, and would therefore be taken from the law of the forum, rather than the chosen law.[127]

---

[123] *See, e.g.*, Life Plans, Inc. v. Security Life of Denver Ins. Co., 800 F.3d 343, 357 (7th Cir. 2015); B-S Steel of Kansas, Inc. v. Texas Industries, Inc., 439 F.3d 653, 661 n.9 (10th Cir. 2006).

[124] *See, e.g.,* Hanwha Corp. v. Cedar Petrochemicals, Inc., 760 F. Supp. 2d 426 (S.D.N.Y. 2011) (to determine if the parties formed a contract for the international sale of goods, the formation rules in the United Nations Convention on Contracts for the International Sale of Goods applied even though both parties had attempted to opt out of that treaty).

[125] *E.g.*, Finance One Public Co. Ltd. v. Lehman Bros. Special Fin., Inc., 414 F.3d 325 (2d Cir. 2006).

[126] *E.g.*, Berg Chilling Sys., Inc. v. Hull Corp., 435 F.3d 455 (3d Cir. 2006) (dealing with successor liability).

[127] *See, e.g.*, Pivotal Payments Direct Corp. v. Planet Payment, Inc., 2015 WL 9595285 (Del. Super. Ct. 2015) (because, under Delaware law, a choice-of-law provision in a contract does not apply to statutes of limitations unless the provision expressly says so, the parties' general selection of New York law did not make the N.Y. limitations period applicable, and thus the plaintiff's fraudulent inducement claim was time barred under Delaware law); Citizens Bank v. Merrill, Lynch, Pierce, Fenner and Smith, Inc., 2012 WL 5828623 (E.D. Mich. 2012) (applying Michigan procedural law, including its six-year statute of limitations, instead of the chosen law of New York, with its three-year limitations period, to tort and contract claims brought under New York law). *But cf.* RESTATEMENT (SECOND) OF CONFLICT OF LAW § 142

Finally, to opt out of a treaty or international convention, when that is permitted, the choice-of-law clause must do more than merely choose a particular state's law. That is because the treaty or convention is deemed to be part of that state's law.[128] The parties must expressly exclude application of the treaty or convention if they want it not to apply.

Drafting Considerations. As in all contract drafting, the wording of a clause can affect its scope. Wording is particularly important in choosing a governing law because some jurisdictions continue to interpret choice-of-law clauses narrowly.[129] Parties wishing to designate a governing law generally want that law to govern all aspects of their relationship. Consider, though, the following.

Exercise 4-15

Lender is providing working capital financing to Borrower. The Loan Agreement includes the following provision:

> This Agreement shall be governed by and construed in accordance with the laws of the State of New York.

What issues or claims might not be covered by this clause? How should the clause be drafted to make sure such issues and claims will be governed by New York law?[130]

(as amended in 1988) (indicating that any conflict with respect to the limitations period should be resolved in the same manner as other conflicts of law).

[128] BP Oil Int'l, Ltd. v. Empresa Estatal Petroleos, 332 F.3d 333 (5th Cir. 2003); Travelers Prop. Cas. Co. of Am. v. Saint-Gobain Technical Fabrics Canada Ltd., 474 F. Supp. 2d 1075 (D. Minn. 2007); American Mint LLC v. GOSoftware, Inc., 2006 WL 42090 (M.D. Pa. 2006); Ajax Tool Works, Inc. v. Can-Eng Mfg. Ltd., 2003 WL 223187 (N.D. Ill. 2003); Asante Techs., Inc. v. PMC-Sierra, Inc., 164 F. Supp. 2d 1142 (N.D. Cal. 2001). *But see* American Biophysics Corp. v. Dubois Marine Specialties, 411 F. Supp. 2d 61 (D.R.I. 2006).

[129] *E.g.*, Thompson and Wallace of Memphis, Inc. v. Falconwood Corp., 100 F.3d 429, 433 (5th Cir. 1996).

[130] *See, e.g. id.* (loan contract providing that the "agreement and its enforcement" were to be governed by New York law did not preclude application of Texas Deceptive Trade Practices Act and tort claims arising thereunder); Northeast Data Sys., Inc. v. McDonnell Douglas Computer Systems Co., 986 F.2d 607 (1st Cir. 1993) (contract clause providing that "[t]his Agreement and the rights and obligations of the parties hereto shall be governed by and

Another drafting issue is whether the choice-of-law clause must exclude the choice-of-law rules of the chosen jurisdiction.   Consider the following two alternatives:

> ". . . governed by the laws of the State of New York."

> ". . . governed by the laws of the State of New York (other than its choice-of-law rules)."

The latter formulation is thought to be safer because it avoids the argument and the possibility that a court would then look to New York choice-of-law principles and apply some other state's law. However, this "safer" phrasing is not necessary. The Restatement makes clear that when parties by contract select a governing law, absent some expression to the contrary, they are selecting its "local law," not its

---

construed in accordance with the laws of California" covered all contract claims, whether motivated by bad intent or not, but did not cover fraud in inducement claim because it "concerns the validity of the formation of the contract, it cannot be categorized as one involving the rights or obligations arising under the contract"); Valley Juice Ltd. v. Evian Waters of France, Inc., 87 F.3d 604 (2d Cir. 1996) (contract providing that "the Agreement is to be governed by the laws of the State of New York" did not apply to claim under Massachusetts Unfair Trade Practices Act); Maltz v. Union Carbide Chemicals & Plastics Co., 992 F. Supp. 286 (S.D.N.Y. 1998) (fact that agreement was "to be construed in accordance with the law of New York" did not apply to tort claims); Sunbelt Veterinary Supply, Inc. v. International Business Systems US, Inc., 985 F. Supp. 1352 (M.D. Ala. 1997) ("this agreement and the terms hereof shall be governed by and construed in accordance with the laws of the State of Florida" did not encompass tort claims); Shelley v. Trafalgar House Public Ltd., 918 F. Supp. 515 (D.P.R. 1997) ("this letter shall be subject to and construed in accordance with the laws of the State of New York" did not apply to tort claims). *But cf.* Masters Group Int'l, Inc. v. Comerica Bank, 352 P.3d 1101 (Mont. 2015) (forbearance Agreement stating that it "shall be governed and controlled in all respects by the laws of the State of Michigan" covered not only claims for breach of contract and breach of the covenant of good faith, but also tort claims for fraud arising out of a contract); Pyott-Boone Electronics Inc. v. IRR Trust for Donald L. Fetterolf, 918 F. Supp. 2d 532 (W. D. Va. 2013) (clause providing that "This Agreement shall be governed by the laws of the State of Delaware without regard to any jurisdiction's conflicts of laws provisions" encompasses all disputes that arise from or are related to the agreement); Nedlloyd Lines B.V. v. Superior Court, 11 Cal. Rptr. 2d 330 (Cal. 1992) (choice-of-law clause providing that the "agreement shall be governed by and construed in accordance with Hong Kong law" encompassed tortious breaches of fiduciary duties created by the agreement).

conflict-of-law rules.[131] Courts almost universally agree.[132]

More importantly, if New York law were selected not by virtue of its relationship to the parties or the transaction, but instead pursuant to the New York statute that permits contracting parties to opt into New York law,[133] the additional "safer" language might present a problem. Because that statute is itself a choice-of-law rule, excepting all choice of law rules might, some believe, remove the only basis for applying New York law.

3. Choice of Forum

A choice-of-forum clause indicates where the parties may or must litigate disputes that arise between them. Most such clauses make a binding or exclusive selection, thereby obligating the parties to litigate in the chosen forum. Occasionally, contracting parties wish merely to provide for the freedom to litigate in a particular forum, rather than to restrict all litigation to that forum. Because courts usually treat a clause as permissive unless the wording used clearly evidences that the selection is exclusive, attorneys should draft an exclusive forum-selection clause with care.[134]

As with clauses on attorney's fees or choice of law, the scope of a forum-selection clause will be affected by how it is worded. A clause covering "all disputes relating to this agreement or the relationship of the parties" will be much broader than one covering only "actions to enforce this agreement," because it will apply to related tort claims and claims for rescission.[135]

---

[131] *See* RESTATEMENT (SECOND) OF CONFLICT OF LAWS § 187(3) & cmt. h.

[132] *See, e.g.*, Chan v. Society Expeditions, Inc., 123 F.3d 1287 (9th Cir. 1997); Mastrobuono v. Shearson Lehman Hutton, Inc., 20 F.3d 713 (7th Cir. 1994), *rev'd on other grounds*, 514 U.S. 52 (1995); IRB-Brasil Resseguros, S.A. v. Inepar Invs., S.A., 982 N.E.2d 609 (N.Y. 2012).

[133] *See supra* note 121.

[134] *E.g.*, Triangle Cayman Asset Co. 2 v. Property Rental and Inv. Corp., 278 F. Supp. 3d 508 (D.P.R. 2017) (consent to jurisdiction in the General Court of Justice, in San Juan, Puerto Rico was not exclusive and did not prevent litigation in federal court in Puerto Rico). Ex parte Textron, Inc., 67 So. 3d 61 (Ala. 2011) (guarantors' consent to jurisdiction and venue in Rhode Island did not operate as an exclusive choice of forum); Excell, Inc. v. Sterling Boiler & Mech., Inc., 916 F. Supp. 1063 (D. Colo. 1996).

[135] *Cf.* In re Fisher, 433 S.W.3d 523 (Tex. 2014) (forum-selection clause in both a stock

One benefit of an exclusive choice-of-forum clause is that it reduces the expense of litigation. By ensuring that litigation will occur in the chosen place – presumably the home state of one or both of the parties – the clause minimizes travel costs relating to the litigation and avoids the problems and expense of finding or associating counsel admitted to practice in a distant location. A forum-selection clause can also reduce the prospect of litigation in multiple jurisdictions if there are numerous parties to the same contract.[136] There is, however, a much more important benefit to an exclusive choice-of-forum clause: it helps give efficacy to the parties' choice of law. Indeed, drafting an agreement with a choice-of-law provision unaccompanied by a choice-of-forum clause is like leaving home only partially dressed. It is a glaring omission that leaves the agreement ill-prepared for external conditions. Consider the following:

1.   Lender, a resident of State X, loans $100,000 to Borrower, a resident of State Y. The loan calls for interest at a rate that is permissible under the law of State X but which is usurious in State Y. The loan agreement specifies that the law of State X governs the parties' relationship. If litigation is commenced in State Y – a likely prospect no matter who brings the action – Lender bears the risk that a state or federal court in State Y will decide that State Y's usury laws represent a fundamental policy of the state and refuse to respect the choice-of-law clause.[137] If the court then rules that State Y's law governs, the court might invalidate the loan agreement or the interest rate. In contrast, if the agreement required all litigation to be conducted in State X, and parties litigated their dispute in State X, there would be little risk that the loan would be deemed usurious.

---

purchase agreement and the buyer's promissory note providing that the state and federal courts in Tarrant County, Texas were the exclusive forum for "any proceeding arising out of or relating to this Agreement" and covered the seller's action against the buyer's principals for breach of fiduciary duty and fraud because those actions were essentially efforts to collect on the promissory note and thus arose out of the contracts).

[136] *See* Boilermakers Local 154 Retirement Fund v. Chevron Corp., 73 A.3d 934 (Del. Ch. 2013) (upholding forum-selection clause in bylaws of a publicly traded corporation for (i) any derivative action or proceeding brought on behalf of the corporation or (ii) any action asserting a claim of breach of a fiduciary duty owed by any director, officer or other employee of the corporation to the corporation or the stockholders).

[137] *See, e.g.*, Madden v. Midland Funding, LLC, 237 F. Supp. 3d 130 (S.D.N.Y. 2017); Gregoria v. Total Asset Recovery, Inc., 2015 WL 115501 (E.D. Pa. 2015).

2. Investment Bank is a New Jersey corporation with its principal place of business in New York. It enters into a large interest rate swap with Importer, whose business is located primarily in Florida. All the negotiations took place in Florida and over the phone. Relying on the New York statute that allows parties to opt into New York law, the swap agreement provides that all matters arising under or relating to the swap are to be governed by the laws of the State of New York. A dispute arises and Importer brings an action against Investment Bank in Florida. A Florida court might refuse to enforce the contractual choice of law if it concludes that New York does not have a substantial relationship to either the parties or the transaction and that there is no other reasonable basis for applying New York Law.

Therefore, parties who select a governing law should always select the same jurisdiction as the *exclusive* forum for any litigation.[138]

Most states will enforce an exclusive choice-of-forum clause by dismissing an action brought in a forum other than the one selected.[139] In federal courts, the

---

[138] In addition to having a statute that allows parties to opt into New York law, the State of New York also has a statute that allows parties to agree to litigate in New York courts regardless of whether jurisdiction would otherwise be proper there if the parties have chosen New York law to govern. N.Y. Gen. Oblig. Law § 5-1402. Note, however, that this rule has a $1 million threshold, rather than the $250,000 threshold for selecting New York law to govern. *See also* Cal. Civ. Proc. Code § 410.40 (providing for litigation concerning a transaction of $1 million or more to occur in California if contract selects California law to govern).

[139] *See* RESTATEMENT (SECOND) OF CONFLICT OF LAWS § 80. *But see, e.g.,* Idaho Code § 29-110 (invalidating contractual terms that prohibit litigation in Idaho); IDACORP, Inc. v. American Fiber Sys., Inc., 2012 WL 4139925 (D. Id. 2012) (using Idaho's strong public policy against enforcement of forum selection clauses to deny motion to dismiss or to transfer action brought in federal court); Cerami-Kote, Inc. v. Energywave Corp., 773 P.2d 1143 (Id. 1989) (concluding that Idaho public policy required that a contractual choice of Florida as the sole forum for litigation of disputes not be enforced). *But see* Fisk v. Royal Caribbean Cruises, Inc., 108 P.3d 990 (Idaho 2005) (invalidating the Idaho statute with respect to certain maritime claims).

Courts disagree about whether attorney's fees are recoverable against a party that breaches an exclusive forum-selection clause if the agreement is silent on the issue. *Compare* Cornerstone Brands v. O'Steen, 2006 WL 2788414, at *4 (Del. Ch. Ct. 2006) (yes), *with* Brown Rudnick v. Surgical Orthomedics, 2014 WL 3439620 at *12-14 (S.D.N.Y. 2014); Versatile Housewares v. Thill Logistics, 819 F. Supp. 2d 230, 241-46 (S.D.N.Y. 2011); Westlake Vinyls v. Goodrich, 2014 WL 2816070, at *4-5 (W.D. Ky. 2014) (no).

matter can be dealt with through a motion to transfer to another federal forum or, if the clause selects a non-federal forum, through the doctrine of *forum non conveniens*.[140] At least at the federal level, a motion to transfer based on a choice-of-forum clause is to be granted in "all but the most exceptional cases."[141] However, forum-selection clauses are prohibited by statute in some types of contracts,[142] and a forum-selection clause might be invalidated if it results from fraud or overreaching, violates a strong public policy, or if enforcement of the clause would deprive a party of its day in court.[143] A clause can effectively deprive a party of its day in court, and be substantively unconscionable, if it makes a party – particularly one with few resources – litigate in a distant place.[144] It can also do so if, because of unforseen circumstances, the chosen forum is extremely inconvenient.[145]

---

[140] *See* Atlantic Marine Const. Co., Inc. v. U.S. Dist. Court for W. Dist. of Tex, 134 S. Ct. 568 (2013) (so ruling but also rejecting the argument that the clause may be enforced through a motion to dismiss).

[141] *Id.* at *9. Convenience to the parties is not a relevant consideration; "a district court may consider arguments about public-interest factors only." *Id.* at *12.

[142] *See, e.g.*, Cal. Bus. & Prof. Code § 20040.5; 815 Ill. Comp. Stat. 705/4 (both invalidating a provision in a franchise agreement that restricts venue to a forum outside the state).

[143] *E.g.*, Krenkel v. Kerzner Int'l Hotels Ltd., 579 F.3d 1279, 1281 (11th Cir. 2009); Afram Carriers, Inc. v. Moeykens, 145 F.3d 298, 301 (5th Cir. 1998) (*quoting* Mitsui & Co. (USA), Inc. v. Mira M/V, 111 F.3d 33, 35 (5th Cir. 1997)).

[144] This is especially true with respect to arbitration forums. *See* Nagrampa v. MailCoups, Inc., 469 F.3d 1257 (9th Cir. 2006) (arbitration provision was substantively unconscionable because it selected a forum at the franchisor's headquarters, 3,000 miles away from the franchisee's location and where the franchise agreement was to be performed); Brower v. Gateway 2000, Inc., 676 N.Y.S.2d 569 (N.Y. App. Div. 1998) (arbitration clause that required N.Y. consumer to arbitrate in Chicago was financially prohibitive and effectively barred consumer from enforcing his rights, and was therefore unconscionable).

[145] *See* TINA L. STARK, ED., NEGOTIATING AND DRAFTING CONTRACTUAL BOILERPLATE § 6.03[2] (2003). *See also* RESTATEMENT (SECOND) OF CONFLICTS OF LAWS § 80 cmt. c (indicating the selection might be unenforceable if: (1) it was "obtained by fraud, duress, the abuse of economic power or other unconscionable means," (2) the designated forum "would be closed to the suit or would not handle it effectively or fairly," or (3) the designated forum "would be so seriously an inconvenient forum that to require the plaintiff to bring suit there would be unjust"); Security Watch, Inc. v. Sentinel Sys., Inc., 176 F.3d 369 (6th Cir. 1999) (relying on the Restatement).

Even when a forum-selection clause is itself enforceable, other limits on its effectiveness might apply. For example, a forum-selection clause will not affect where venue lies for a bankruptcy proceeding.[146] In addition, a forum-selection clause will not prevent application of the doctrine of *forum non conveniens* to deny the parties their chosen forum; by agreeing to the forum-selection clause the parties have waived their right to assert their *own* inconvenience as a factor in support of dismissal or transfer, but inconvenience to non-parties, difficulty in accessing sources of proof, and judicial economy remain factors that might justify application of the doctrine.[147] While a forum-selection clause *might* be sufficient to create personal jurisdiction where there is none,[148] drafters of such clauses would be well advised to include an express consent to personal jurisdiction in the chosen forum and should be aware that a consent to personal jurisdiction might not be binding on an assignee or successor.

A choice-of-forum clause should specify whether actions may be brought in state courts, federal courts, or either. In choosing among these options, bear in mind that parties cannot in their contract create or expand upon the subject matter jurisdiction of federal courts. For this reason, providing for litigation exclusively in federal court is quite risky. If federal courts have no subject matter jurisdiction over the dispute, the contractual choice will likely be invalidated, perhaps leaving the parties free to litigate in any state court having personal jurisdiction over the parties. Similarly, if litigation in federal court is to be permitted or required, be careful not to specify a city or county in which no federal court sits. That might render the clause completely unenforceable or at least undermine the use of federal courts.[149]

---

[146] *See* 28 U.S.C. § 1408. Because bankruptcy courts apply the law of the jurisdiction in which they sit with respect to nonbankruptcy law issues, such venue can affect which state law governs. *See* In re Miller, 341 B.R. 764 (Bankr. E.D. Mo. 2006) (default rate of interest on business loan, though valid under Iowa law that the parties had chosen in their agreement, violated Missouri law, was against fundamental policy of Missouri, and was therefore unenforceable).

[147] *E.g.*, Trafalgar Capital Specialized Inv. Fund v. Hartman, 878 F. Supp. 2d 1274, 1286-87 (S.D. Fla. 2012) (applying 28 U.S.C. § 1404(a)).

[148] *See* Chan v. Society Expeditions, Inc., 39 F.3d 1398, 1406-07 (9th Cir. 1994); Heller Fin., Inc. v. Midwhey Powder Co., Inc., 883 F.2d 1286, 1292 (7th Cir. 1989) (both indicating that a forum-selection clause could operate as a consent to personal jurisdiction).

[149] *See* Phillips Elec. Co. of Durham, Inc. v. Hirani Eng'g and Land Surveying, P.C., 2009 WL 3787213 (M.D.N.C. 2009) (contractual designation of Durham County, NC as the venue

Transactional attorneys should also be careful when drafting an exclusive choice-of-forum clause not to inadvertently waive a party's right to remove an action to federal court. For example, in one case,[150] a patent license agreement included a clause providing that "[t]he Parties irrevocably consent to exclusive jurisdiction and venue of the state and federal courts in the State of Delaware." The court interpreted the clause as giving the plaintiff the unfettered choice to pick state or federal court in Delaware and remanded the case back to state court after the defendant had removed it to federal court in Delaware. The decision is questionable,[151] but nevertheless illustrates a potential trap for the transactional lawyer.

Some parties like to have what is occasionally referred to as a "floating forum clause." Such clauses provide for all suits to be brought in whatever jurisdiction one of the parties or its assigns resides. Thus, if that party assigns the contract, the choice of forum might switch to the residence of the assignee. There are at least three problems to such clauses, however. First, because such a clause will not always point to the same state, there is no way to ensure the applicability of the parties' choice of law.[152] Second, some courts require that a forum selection clause

---

for litigation prohibited action in federal court because there is no way to initiate an action in federal court in Durham); Bassett Seamless Guttering, Inc. v. GutterGuard, LLC, 2006 WL 156874 (M.D.N.C. 2006) (contract clause requiring litigation in Boulder, Colorado prohibited suit in federal court because Colorado has only one federal district court and even though a division of it sits in Boulder, all complaints must be filed in Denver).

[150] InterDigital, Inc. v. Wistron Corp., 2015 WL 4537133 (D. Del. 2015).

[151] The clause did not purport to waive the right to remove a Delaware state court action to a federal court in Delaware and even after removal, the action would still be within the exclusively selected fora. The court's interpretation was therefore unsupported by the words of the clause and likely to be inconsistent with the parties' intent.

[152] It is highly questionable whether parties could agree to a floating choice of law. *See* Sterling Nat'l Bank v. Kings Manor Estates, LLC, 2005 WL 2464167 (N.Y. City Civ. Ct. 2005) (invalidating such a clause). Contract rights are normally fixed at the time the agreement is reached, and to allow post-formation actions to alter the choice of law could greatly interfere with contract. *Cf.* Pharmacia & Upjohn Co. v. American Ins. Co., 719 A.2d 1265 (N.J. Super. Ct. App. Div. 1998).

Some transactional lawyers use a bifurcated choice-of-law clause. Such a clause chooses the law of the State X (typically, the law favored by the drafting party), but then provides for the law of the State Y to apply if the choice State X's law is not given effect. While there is no known decision dealing with such a clause, presumably each alternative would be analyzed separately under traditional choice-of-law principles.

expressly identify an ascertainable forum, and a floating forum-selection clause does not do that.[153] Third, some courts simply refuse to enforce such clauses.[154]

Finally, some thought should be given to the fact that a forum-selection clause, like most clauses in a written agreement, normally binds only the parties themselves, along with their successors and assigns.[155] Occasionally, however, it is desirable for a non-signatory – such as an affiliated entity, spouse, or guarantor – to be bound to litigate in the same forum. The best way to do that is, of course, by entering into a written agreement with that non-signatory, especially if the agreement containing the choice of forum disclaims the existence of a third-party beneficiary.[156]

---

[153] *See, e.g.*, Conopco, Inc. v. PARS Ice Cream Co., 2013 WL 5549614, at *5 (S.D.N.Y. 2013) (refusing to enforce a clause purporting to waive a lack of personal jurisdiction and improper venue regardless of where an action is brought); Gordian Group, LLC v. Syringa Exploration, Inc., 168 F. Supp. 3d 575 (S.D.N.Y. 2016) (refusing to enforce a clause in which one party "consents to venue and jurisdiction in any court in which [the counterparty] is sued or otherwise found or brought").

[154] *Compare* Preferred Capital, Inc. v. Power Eng'g Group, Inc., 860 N.E.2d 741 (Ohio 2007) (ruling such a clause unenforceable, at least if assignment was anticipated but not disclosed at the time the parties entered into the agreement); Preferred Capital, Inc. v. Sarasota Kennel Club, 489 F.3d 303 (6th Cir. 2007) (applying Ohio law to deny enforcement of floating forum selection clause), *with* IFC Credit Corp. v. Aliano, 437 F.3d 606 (7th Cir. 2006) (upholding such a clause); FTC v. IFC Credit, 543 F. Supp. 2d 925 (N.D. Ill. 2008) (same); Sterling Nat'l Bank v. Eastern Shipping Worldwide, Inc., 826 N.Y.S.2d 235 (N.Y. App. Div. 2006) (same). *See also* Polzin v. Appleway Equip. Leasing, Inc., 191 P.3d 476 (Mont. 2008) (upholding a lease clause providing for venue to be, at the option of the lessor, wherever the equipment is located or in Spokane, Washington); CMS Partners, Ltd. v. Plumrose USA, Inc., 101 S.W.3d 730 (Tex. Ct. App. 2003) (suggesting that it might matter whether the contract has been assigned).

[155] *See, e.g.*, Epitech, Inc. v. Kann, 139 Cal. Rptr. 3d 702 (Cal. Ct. App. 2012) (creditors were not third-party beneficiaries of agreement between the debtor and its financial advisor and thus their action against the advisor for misrepresentation was not subject to the arbitration clause in that agreement); Speedway Motorsports Int'l Ltd. v. Bronwen Energy Trading, Ltd., 706 S.E.2d 262 (N.C. Ct. App. 2011) (forum-selection clause in agreement between letter of credit applicant and the issuer was inapplicable to action between issuer and confirming bank). *But cf.* Amegy Bank v. Monarch Flight II, LLC, 870 F. Supp. 2d 441 (S.D. Tex. 2012) (secured party's claims for conspiracy and fraudulent transfer against debtor's wife and entities controlled by the debtor were subject to arbitration agreement between the secured party and the debtor).

[156] *See, e.g.*, Crastvell Trading Ltd. v. Marengere, 90 So. 3d 349 (Fla. Ct. App. 2012) (forum-selection clause in loan agreements was not binding on the debtors' affiliates or

Exercise 4-16

You are drafting a forum selection clause for a lease of commercial real estate. You are considering two alternatives:

> Any controversy between Owner and Tenant arising under this Lease must be determined in the state, county or city courts in which Owner's principal office is located.

> Any controversy between Owner and Tenant arising under this Lease must be determined in the courts in the state, county or city in which Owner's principal office is located.

How do these alternatives differ in meaning?

Exercise 4-17

You are re-drafting a form loan agreement for a large bank that does business throughout the country. The U.S. Court of Appeals for the Eighth Circuit has issued a decision about the Equal Credit Opportunity Act that is favorable to lenders, rejecting the analysis of a Sixth Circuit decision

---

controlling shareholder because the agreements expressly indicated that there were no third-party beneficiaries entitled to enforce the agreements).

Of course, merely entering into an agreement with the non-signatory is not always sufficient to bind that party to litigate in the chosen forum; it depends what that agreement says. *See* KFC Corp. v. Wagstaff, 502 B.R. 484 (W.D. Ky. 2013) (individuals who guaranteed the full and prompt payment of franchisees' debts to franchisor, but did not promise the full performance of all agreements, obligations, or covenants, were not bound by forum-selection clause in later-issued promissory notes that they did not sign); Jetstream of Houston, Inc. v. Aqua Pro Inc., 2010 WL 669458 (N.D. Ill. 2010) (guarantors were not bound by forum-selection clause in promissory notes in part because the guaranty agreement promised full and prompt payment of the debt, not performance of the debtor's contractual obligations). *But cf.* Frankford Crossing Shopping Ctr. Dallas, Tx. Ltd. P'ship v. Pho Partners, LLC, 942 F. Supp. 2d 366 (W.D.N.Y. 2013) (guarantor who, contemporaneously with the execution of a commercial lease, executed a broadly worded guaranty covering "the full and faithful performance and observance of all the covenants, terms, and conditions of the Lease" was bound by the forum-selection clause in the lease).

issued two months earlier.[157]   How, if at all, can you make sure that the bank's loan transactions will be governed by the Eighth Circuit precedent?

4. Arbitration

Parties are free to arbitrate almost any type of dispute pertaining to a contract. In addition, they may by agreement bind themselves to arbitrate disputes concerning private commercial rights created by many statutes, including those arising under the Securities Act of 1933, the Securities Exchange Act of 1934,[158] the Age Discrimination and Employment Act,[159] ERISA,[160] the Fair Labor Standards Act,[161] and the Magnuson-Moss Warranty Act.[162]   Indeed, arbitration agreements can be binding even in bankruptcy, where the strong federal policy in favor of arbitration can conflict with the goal of having a centralized and expeditious resolution of issues pertaining to the debtor's financial affairs.[163]   Although the Bureau of

---

[157]   *See* Hawkins v. Community Bank of Raymore, 761 F.3d 937 (8th Cir. 2014), *aff'd by an equally divided court*, 136 S. Ct. 1072 (2016); RL BB Acquisition, LLC v. Bridgemill Commons Dev. Group, LLC, 754 F.3d 380 (6th Cir. 2014).

[158]   *See* Rodriguez de Quijas v. Shearson/American Express, Inc., 490 U.S. 477 (1989) (concerning the 1933 Act); Shearson/American Express, Inc. v. McMahon, 482 U.S. 220 (1987) (concerning the 1934 Act).

[159]   *See* Gilmer v. Interstate/Johnson Lane Corp., 500 U.S. 20 (1991).

[160]   *See* Pritzker v. Merrill Lynch, Pierce, Fenner & Smith, Inc., 7 F.3d 1110 (3d Cir. 1993).

[161]   *See, e.g.*, Floss v. Ryan's Family Steak Houses, Inc., 211 F.3d 306, 313 (6th Cir. 2000), *cert. denied*, 531 U.S. 1072 (2001); Kuehner v. Dickinson & Co., 84 F.3d 316 (9th Cir. 1996). *Cf.* Albertson's Inc. v. United Food & Commercial Workers Union, 157 F.3d 758 (9th Cir. 1998) (individual employee's FLSA claim not required to be arbitrated merely because it falls under the arbitration clause of the employer's collective bargaining agreement with the union.).

[162]   *See* Davis v. Southern Energy Homes, Inc., 305 F3d 1268 (11th Cir. 2002), *cert. denied*, 538 U.S. 945 (2003); Walton v. Rose Mobile Homes LLC, 298 F.3d 470 (5th Cir. 2002).

[163]   *See* In re Electric Mach. Enter., Inc., 479 F.3d 791 (11th Cir. 2007) (non-core actions subject to an agreement to arbitrate must be arbitrated; core actions must be examined to determine whether "an inherent conflict exists between arbitration and the underlying purposes of the Bankruptcy Code"); MBNA America Bank v. Hill, 436 F.3d 104 (2d Cir. 2006) (debtor's core class actions against creditor for violations of the stay must be arbitrated); In re Mintze, 434 F.3d 222 (3d Cir. 2006) (debtor's action for rescission of home

Consumer Financial Protection, created in 2010 by the Dodd-Frank Wall Street Reform and Consumer Protection Act, is instructed to study the use of pre-dispute agreements to arbitrate in certain consumer contracts and authorized to promulgate regulations prohibiting, conditioning or limiting such agreements,[164] the Bureau has not yet conducted the study or proposed regulations on the matter.

Perhaps because so many different types of claims are now arbitrable, arbitration clauses have become a fixture of both commercial and consumer contracts. Today it is difficult – if not impossible – to open a deposit account with a bank or a securities account with a broker without agreeing to arbitrate any disputes that might arise. Nevertheless, before including an arbitration clause in a standardized form or a negotiated agreement, the parties and their counsel should consider the attributes of arbitration. Because most – and possibly all – of these attributes can be altered by agreement, any arbitration clause should be crafted to the particular contractual relationship and to the particular client's desires.

(a) The Principal Attributes of Arbitration

The process involved in any particular arbitration proceeding can and will vary depending on the nature of the dispute, the arbitrator or arbitration association selected, and, most importantly, the language of the parties' arbitration clause. Obviously, it is essential that any arbitration clause specify – either explicitly or through incorporation of the rules of some arbitration association – how the arbitrators will be selected,[165] who will bear the costs, and how the arbitration itself will be conducted. Two of the most common arbitration associations for domestic commercial disputes are the American Arbitration Association ("AAA") and the National Association of Securities Dealers ("NASD"). Each organization has fairly detailed rules and procedures governing the arbitrations they conduct.

---

equity loan must be arbitrated even though qualifying as a core proceeding). *Cf.* In re White Mountain Mining Co., 403 F.3d 164 (4th Cir. 2005) (bankruptcy court did not abuse its discretion by refusing to order – or permit – international arbitration of core proceeding by insider to determine that prepetition advances to debtor were debt, not equity).

[164] *See* 12 U.S.C. § 5518.

[165] For example, perhaps each party will select one and the two chosen will select a third. If the arbitration agreement does not specify how the arbitrator(s) will be selected and the parties do not otherwise agree, the applicable rules of an arbitration association will likely provide a mechanism. *See, e.g.*, AAA, Commercial Arbitration Rules and Mediation Procedures, Rules 1(a), 12 (2013).

In fact, the AAA has different rules and procedures for dealing with different types of disputes. Indeed, it has quite a large number of different sets of rules and procedures.[166] The most important is probably the Commercial Arbitration Rules and Mediation Procedures (Including Procedures for Large, Complex Commercial Disputes). These rules govern an AAA arbitration if either the parties' agreement specifies or if the dispute is a domestic commercial dispute and the parties have merely agreed to arbitrate pursuant to the rules of the AAA.[167] For that reason, much of the discussion below is based on these rules.

1. Discovery & Motion Practice. Arbitration is often expeditious compared to litigation. This is because much of the legal and political maneuvering commonplace in litigation is not available in arbitration. For example, there is little or no motion practice. A dispute might be resolved without a formal hearing, but there is usually no equivalent of a motion to dismiss or motion for summary judgment, actions that can delay a trial. Similarly, discovery in arbitration is fairly limited and thus fights about discovery are infrequent. The parties may file pleadings and exchange documents,[168] but interrogatories and depositions are rare and subject to the arbitrator's discretion.[169]

These attributes might be desirable for a particular client or transaction, or they might not. Some clients benefit from a speedy resolution of a dispute, but others might want to use the prospect of lengthy and expensive litigation as part of their negotiating strategy. Similarly, some clients might have secrets that they would not want to disclose – such as the internal e-mail message revealing a hidden and improper motive – while others might need access to the other party's internal records to successfully present a claim. A transactional attorney should consider what is most likely to be in the client's interests when deciding whether to include or agree to an arbitration clause and, if so, whether to expand the types of discovery that will be available.

2. No Juries, Rules of Evidence, or Class Actions. Arbitration is less formal than litigation. It is conducted without a jury. In part because of that, the parties need not comply with the rules of evidence. Instead, they may submit and the

---

[166] *See* www.adr.org.

[167] *See* AAA, Commercial Arbitration Rules and Mediation Procedures, Rule 1(a).

[168] *See* AAA, Commercial Arbitration Rules and Mediation Procedures, Rules 22(b), 33; NASD, Uniform Code of Arbitration, Rules 10314(a),(b), 10321(c).

[169] *See* AAA, Commercial Arbitration Rules and Mediation Procedures, Rule 22; NASD, Uniform Code of Arbitration, Rule 10321(a), (b). *See also* Philip D. O'Neill, *The Power of Arbitrators to Award Monetary Sanctions for Discovery Abuse*, 60 DISP. RES. J. 60 (2006).

arbitrator may consider any relevant and material evidence.[170] Contracting parties are no doubt free to require that arbitration proceedings be conducted in conformity with the rules of evidence, but that would be unusual.

A somewhat related point is that most arbitration associations do not have a procedure for class actions. This can be very significant. In consumer transactions, where the amount in controversy is often low, the typical consumer has insufficient economic incentive to bring an individual action. Class actions are often the only way consumers can effectively assert and enforce their contractual and statutory rights. If their contracts require the consumers to arbitrate, the consumers are essentially left without recourse. While this might render an arbitration clause unconscionable and unenforceable under state contract law, such arguments are notoriously difficult to win,[171] and the U.S. Supreme Court has ruled that the Federal Arbitration Act prevents states from treating an arbitration clause as unconscionable and unenforceable merely because the clause prohibits classwide proceedings.[172]

---

[170] *See* AAA, Commercial Arbitration Rules and Mediation Procedures, Rule 34; NASD, Uniform Code of Arbitration, Rule 10323.

[171] *See, e.g.,* Anders v. Hometown Mortgage Services, Inc., 346 F.3d 1024 (11th Cir. 2003) (limitations on remedies do not affect the enforceability of an arbitration agreement); Rosen v. SCIL, LLC, 799 N.E.2d 488 (Ill. Ct. App. 2003) (credit card arbitration agreement not unconscionable because it prohibited class actions). *But see* Fensterstock v. Education Fin. Partners, 611 F.3d 124 (2d Cir. 2010) (arbitration clause in student loan note that contained waiver of class action unconscionable under California law); In re Checking Account Overdraft Litigation., 718 F. Supp. 2d 1352 (S.D. Fla. 2010) (arbitration and class action waiver provisions of account holders' contract with bank unconscionable under Washington law); Ingle v. Circuit City Stores, Inc., 328 F.3d 1165 (9th Cir. 2003), *cert. denied*, 540 U.S. 1160 (2004) (arbitration clause in employment agreement unconscionable because of its one-way application, one-year limitations period, bar on class actions, and cost-splitting provisions); Ting v. AT&T, 319 F.3d 1126 (9th Cir.), *cert. denied*, 540 U.S. 811 (2003) (arbitration clause unconscionable because it barred class actions, split costs inappropriately, and mandated that results be kept confidential); Szetela v. Discover Bank, 118 Cal. Rptr. 2d 862 (Cal. Ct. App. 2002), *cert. denied*, 537 U.S. 1226 (2003) (striking a ban on class actions from arbitration clause).

[172] AT&T Mobility LLC v. Concepcion, 131 S. Ct. 1740 (2011) (the Federal Arbitration Act permits agreements to arbitrate to be invalidated by generally applicable contract defenses – such as fraud, duress, or unconscionability – but not by defenses that apply only to arbitration or that derive their meaning from the fact that an agreement to arbitrate is at issue). *But cf.* Brewer v. Missouri Title Loans, 364 S.W.3d 486 (Mo. 2012) (concluding, after *Concepcion*, that arbitration clause in consumer contract was unconscionable not because it prohibited class proceedings but because there was no opportunity to bargain

3. Privacy. Most arbitration proceedings are private. The proceedings themselves are not open to the public,[173] and the arbitrators are expected to maintain confidentiality.[174] If the contract so provides, the parties too will be required to keep confidential the results of and the information acquired during an arbitration proceeding. A corollary to this is that the decisions of arbitrators are generally not known, discoverable, or precedential. This can be a powerful incentive to include an arbitration clause in a written agreement. A party might not want the resolution of one dispute to become public, to have *stare decisis* effect, or to be persuasive authority for resolving similar disputes. Moreover, to the extent that an arbitrator might be persuaded by the decisions of prior arbitrators, the private nature of the proceedings might give one party a virtual monopoly on the relevant information. For example, a business that arbitrates disputes with its consumer customers will certainly have a record of all prior arbitrations, but individual consumers will not.

4. Basis of Decision. In general, an arbitrator's decision may be based on notions of justice and equity; it need not be consistent with the law.[175] Thus, for example, an action barred by the applicable statute of limitations might nevertheless lead to an arbitration award.[176] Accordingly, some arbitrations will result in decisions contrary to what the law requires. This is, of course, also true with respect to litigation, but appellate review of judicial decisions provides an opportunity to correct legal errors by the trial judge. Arbitration decisions are not generally reversible for legal error. Contracting parties that expect their counterparts to strictly comply with their contractual and legal duties might not want to grant such wide discretion to an arbitrator. They should, therefore, consider including in their arbitration clause a requirement that the arbitrator's decision be based upon and consistent with the parties' legal rights.[177] Alternatively, they could

---

about it, the consumer was required to bear his or her own costs, the company's most likely claims were excepted from the clause, and expert testimony indicated that attorneys would not represent consumers in such cases, a point borne out by the fact that no arbitration claims had been brought).

[173] *See* AAA, Commercial Arbitration Rules and Mediation Procedures, Rule 25.

[174] AAA, Code of Ethics for Commercial Arbitrators, Canon VI. In contrast, NASD Arbitration awards are made public. NASD, Uniform Code of Arbitration, Rule 10330(f).

[175] *See* AAA, Commercial Arbitration Rules and Mediation Procedures, Rule 47(a) ("The arbitrator may grant any remedy or relief that the arbitrator deems just and equitable and within the scope of the agreement of the parties").

[176] Broom v. Morgan Stanley DW Inc., 236 P.3d 182 (Wash. 2010).

[177] For additional strategies in dealing with the fact that the arbitrator is not required to apply

require that the arbitration process be like the process used to settle a salary dispute between a major league baseball player and a club: each side presents an offer and the arbitrators must select one of the offers, without alteration. This tends to make the parties' positions more reasonable.

5. Remedies Available. In general and unless agreed otherwise, an arbitrator may make any award the arbitrator deems just and equitable and which is within the scope of the agreement of the parties.[178] This includes specific performance (that is, an order compelling the breaching party to perform its contractual duties), interest starting at any date the arbitrator deems appropriate, assessment of costs and fees, and an award of attorney's fees if authorized by law or by the parties' agreement.[179]

Contrary to popular belief, arbitrators may award punitive damages. Even if the governing law selected by the parties would not allow for an award of punitive damages, as long as the arbitration procedures do not expressly prohibit them, punitive damages may be awarded.[180] Thus, parties wishing to foreclose the possibility of punitive damages should make that clear in their agreement.[181]

6. Appeal. By submitting a dispute to arbitration, the parties implicitly consent to entry of a judgment on that award by any court of competent jurisdiction.[182] They also implicitly agree that the award is not subject to judicial review for legal or factual error. Judicial review on appeal – at least in federal court – is typically restricted to instances where the award was procured by fraud or corruption, the arbitrator was patently partial to one side, the arbitrator's misconduct prejudiced

---

the law or the possibility that the arbitrator might misapply the law, see Stephen L. Sepinuck, *Managing the Risk of Legal Error in Arbitration*, 5 THE TRANSACTIONAL LAWYER 1 (June 2015).

[178] AAA, Commercial Arbitration Rules and Mediation Procedures, Rule 47(a).

[179] AAA, Commercial Arbitration Rules and Mediation Procedures, Rule 47(a), (c), (d).

[180] Mastrobuono v. Shearson Lehman Hutton, Inc., 514 U.S. 52 (1995); Stark v. Sandberg, Phoenix & Von Gontard, P.C., 381 F.3d 793, 803 (8th Cir. 2004), *cert. denied sub nom.* Stark v. EMC Mortgage Corp., 544 U.S. 1000 (2005).

[181] However, barring an arbitrator from awarding punitive damages in a consumer contract might be problematic. *See* York v. Dodgeland of Columbia, Inc., 749 S.E.2d 139 (S.C. Ct. App. 2013) (arbitration clause in consumer auto purchase agreement was unconscionable in part because it prohibited the arbitrator from awarding punitive or multiple damages, thereby causing the buyer to waive statutory remedies).

[182] *See* AAA, Commercial Arbitration Rules and Mediation Procedures, Rule 52(c).

one party's rights, or the arbitrator exceeded his or her authority.[183] Manifest disregard of the law *might* be an additional basis for a federal court to refuse to enforce an arbitration award, but that point remains in doubt.[184] What is clear is that parties cannot by agreement expand the bases for federal judicial review, such as

---

[183] *See* 9 U.S.C. § 10(a) (applicable only to federal courts). *See also* Cal. Civ. Proc. Code § 1286.2 (specifying the exclusive bases for a California court to vacate an arbitration award); General Mills, Inc. v. BCTGM Local 316G, 2014 WL 5100650 (N.D. Ill. 2014) (arbitrator exceeded her authority in case concerning employer's discharge of an employee by awarding damages to the union).

In some states, courts have greater authority when reviewing an arbitration *See, e.g.*, N.H. Rev. Stat. § 542:8 (permitting courts to correct or modify an award for "plain mistake"). *See also* Stephen K. Huber, *State Regulation of Arbitration Proceedings: Judicial Review of Arbitration Awards by State Courts*, 10 CARDOZO J. CONFLICT RESOL. 509 (2009); Hall St. Assocs. LLC v. Mattel, Inc., 552 U.S. 576, 590 (2008) (suggesting that the scope of judicial review might be different under state law); Schmidt v. UBS Fin. Servs., Inc., 10 N.E.3d 1145 (Mass. Ct. App. 2014) (§ 10 of the FAA does not apply in state court). *See also* Sargon Enters., Inc. v. Browne George Ross LLP, 223 Cal. Rptr. 3d 588 (Cal. Ct. App. 2017) (although a court may not normally review an arbitrator's ruling for legal error, it may review an award for exceeding that arbitrator's authority by violating one of the party's nonwaivable statutory rights; accordingly, the trial court should not have confirmed an arbitrator's award that held a party liable for breach of contract for filing a complaint despite having agreed to arbitrate because parties have a statutory right – even if they have entered into an arbitration agreement – to bring an action in court and let the court decide whether the dispute is arbitrable).

[184] *Compare* Stolt–Nielsen S.A. v. AnimalFeeds Int'l Corp., 559 U.S. 662, 672 n.3 (2010) (suggesting that an arbitration decision *may* be reversed for a manifest disregard of the law, which "requir[es] a showing that the arbitrators knew of the relevant [legal] principle, appreciated that this principle controlled the outcome of the disputed issue, and nonetheless willfully flouted the governing law by refusing to apply it"); LaTour v. Citigroup Global Markets, Inc., 544 F. App'x 748 (9th Cir. 2013) (upholding an arbitration award after reviewing it for manifest disregard of the law); Wachovia Sec. LLC v. Brand, 671 F.3d 472, 480-83 (4th Cir. 2012) (concluding after *Stolt-Nielsen* that manifest disregard of the law remains a basis for vacating an arbitration award); Schwartz v. Merrill Lynch & Co., Inc., 665 F.3d 444, 451-52 (2d Cir. 2011) (same); Broom v. Morgan Stanley DW Inc., 236 P.3d 182 (Wash. 2010) (a *facial* legal error is a basis for vacating an arbitral award because it indicates that the arbitrators exceeded their powers), *with* Medicine Shoppe Int'l, Inc. v. Turner Invs., Inc., 614 F.3d 485, 489 (8th Cir. 2010) (manifest disregard of the law is no longer a basis for vacating a arbitration award); Frazier v. CitiFinancial Corp., 604 F.3d 1313, 1324 (11th Cir. 2010) (same); Citigroup Global Mkts., Inc. v. Bacon, 562 F.3d 349, 355 (5th Cir. 2009) (same). *See also* Michael H. LeRoy, *Are Arbitrators Above the Law? The "Manifest Disregard of the Law" Standard*, 52 B.C. Law Rev. 137, 180-81 (2011).

by authorizing courts to review for any legal error[185] (nor, apparently, can they restrict the bases for judicial review).[186] This is one of the things that makes arbitration inherently risky.

The parties may, however, provide for *non-judicial* review of an arbitration decision. For example, they can permit an appeal of the arbitrator's findings of fact and conclusions of law to an appellate arbitrator or a panel of appellate arbitrators. Indeed, the rules of some arbitration organizations expressly envision an appeals process while those of others, such as the AAA, implicitly permit it.[187] If such review is desired, the arbitration clause should specify the grounds for reversal, the standard of review,[188] and the procedures to be followed.

(b) The Scope of an Arbitration Clause

Even if the parties want to arbitrate their disputes, arbitration might not be an appropriate or desirable procedure for dealing with all types of disputes or protecting all types of contractual rights. For example, a secured party might wish to preserve its ability to get a writ of replevin – something that in most jurisdictions

---

[185] *See* Hall St. Assocs. v. Mattel, Inc., 552 U.S. 576 (2008). Federal law apparently does not preempt state law on this point. Thus, states may authorize parties to provide, in their arbitration agreement, for judicial review of arbitration decisions for legal error. *See* Cable Connection, Inc. v. DIRECTV, Inc., 190 P.3d 586 (Cal. 2008). Nevertheless, most states, particularly those that have enacted the Uniform Arbitration Act, do not permit judicial review for legal error, even if the parties provide for it. *See, e.g.*, HL 1, LLC v. Riverwalk, LLC, 15 A.3d 725, 735 n.11 (Me. 2011).

[186] *See* Atlanta Flooring Design Ctrs., Inc. v. R.G. Williams Constr., Inc., 773 S.E.2d 868 (Ga. Ct. App. 2015) (because the statutory grounds vacating an arbitration award demonstrate Congressional intent to provide a minimum level of due process for parties to an arbitration, a contract provision stating that the parties expressly agreed not to challenge the validity of an arbitration award was contrary to public policy and thus unenforceable).

[187] *See* AAA, Optional Appellate Arbitration Rules, Rule A-1 (2013); Paul B. Marrow, *A Practical Approach to Affording Review of Commercial Arbitration Awards: Using an Appellate Arbitrator,* 60 DISP. RES. J. 10 (2005) (referring to rules of the International Institute for Conflict Prevention and Resolution, the Judicial Arbitration and Mediation Services, and the National Arbitration Forum).

[188] Such a review can be *de novo*, and thus more of a new arbitration rather than an appeal of the initial arbitration. *See* Condon v. Daland Nissan, Inc., 210 Cal. Rptr. 3d 655 (Cal. Ct. App. 2016).

can be accomplished quickly and on an *ex parte* basis even before a judgment is entered – without first seeking arbitration. Similarly, a licensor of intellectual property might wish to preserve its ability to seek and obtain a temporary restraining order and preliminary injunction.

Generally a contractual arbitration clause does not bar efforts to obtain a preliminary injunction; a court may grant preliminary injunctive relief pending arbitration, provided the requirements for such relief are met.[189] Indeed, the standard procedures of most arbitration organizations contemplate the availability of interim judicial relief.[190] One would think, therefore, that any effort to make this explicit in the arbitration clause would be proper, albeit perhaps unnecessary. Nevertheless, arbitration clauses that require one party to seek arbitration while permitting the other to seek recourse in the courts run the risk of being declared unconscionable.[191] This is true even if the clause is drafted so as to appear facially

---

[189] *See* Janvey v. Alguire, 647 F.3d 585 (5th Cir. 2011) (preliminary injunction is permissible before the court decides whether to order arbitration). *See also* Teradyne, Inc. v. Mostek Corp., 797 F.2d 43 (1st Cir. 1986); Roso-Lino Beverage Distribs., Inc. v. Coca-Cola Bottling Co. of New York, 749 F.2d 124 (2d Cir. 1984); Ortho Pharmaceutical Corp. v. Amgen, Inc., 882 F.2d 806 (3d Cir. 1989); Merrill Lynch, Pierce, Fenner & Smith, Inc. v. Bradley, 756 F.2d 1048 (4th Cir. 1985); Performance Unlimited, Inc. v. Questar Publishers, Inc., 52 F.3d 1373 (6th Cir. 1995); Merrill Lynch, Pierce, Fenner & Smith, Inc. v. Salvano, 999 F.2d 211, 213-14 (7th Cir. 1993); PMS Distrib. Co. v. Huber & Suhner, A.G., 863 F.2d 639 (9th Cir. 1988); Wine Not Int'l v. 2atec, LLC, 2006 WL 1766508 (M.D. Fla. 2006). *See also* Cal. Civ. Proc. Code § 1281.8(b). *Contra* Merrill Lynch, Pierce, Fenner & Smith, Inc. v. Hovey, 726 F.2d 1286 (8th Cir. 1984). *But see* Ferry-Morse Seed Co. v. Food Corn, Inc., 729 F.2d 589 (8th Cir. 1984) (affirming, subsequent to *Hovey*, the grant of a preliminary injunction in an arbitrable dispute).

[190] *See* AAA, Commercial Arbitration Rules and Mediation Procedures, Rules 37, 38; NASD, Uniform Code of Arbitration, Rule 10335.

[191] *See* Nagrampa v. MailCoups, Inc., 469 F.3d 1257 (9th Cir. 2006) (arbitration clause in franchise agreement was substantively unconscionable in part because it gave the franchisor access to a judicial forum to obtain provisional remedies to protect its intellectual property, while providing the franchisee with only the arbitral forum to resolve her claims); Royston, Rayzor, Vickery & Williams, L.L.P. v. Lopez, 443 S.W.3d 196 (Tex. Ct. App. 2013) (although one-sided arbitration clauses are generally enforceable, a clause in a law firm's agreement with its client requiring arbitration of all disputes except the firm's claims for unpaid fees was unconscionable); Rivera v. American Gen. Fin. Servs., Inc., 259 P.3d 803 (N.M. 2011) (arbitration clause in consumer loan contract that excepted foreclosure and repossession – the only remedies the creditor was likely to need – was unconscionably one-sided). *See also* Grosvenor v. Qwest Corp., 854 F. Supp. 2d 1021 (D. Colo. 2012) (arbitration clause in an internet subscriber agreement was illusory and not enforceable

neutral but its practical effect is to limit access to the courts for the types of claims that only one of the parties is likely to bring.[192]   Attorneys drafting arbitration clauses should therefore tread carefully in this area.

---

because the provider reserved the right to modify any of the agreement's provisions, including the arbitration clause, at its sole discretion); Batory v. Sears, Roebuck & Co., 456 F. Supp. 2d 1137 (D. Ariz. 2006); Caplin Enters., Inc. v. Arrington, 145 So. 3d 608 (Miss. 2014); Cordova v. World Fin. Corp. of New Mexico, 208 P.3d 901 (N.M. 2009); Horton v. California Credit Corp., 2009 WL 2488031 (S.D. Cal. 2009); Wisconsin Auto Title Loans, Inc. v. Jones, 714 N.W.2d 155 (Wis. 2006); Williams v. Aetna Fin. Co., 700 N.E.2d 859 (Ohio 1998); Taylor v. Butler, 142 S.W.3d 277 (Tenn. 2004); Iwen v. U.S. West Direct, 977 P.2d 989 (Mont. 1999); Arnold v. United Cos. Lending Corp., 511 S.E.2d 854 (W. Va. 1998). *But cf.* Family Sec. Credit Union v. Etheredge, 238 So. 3d 35 (Ala. 2017) (even if the trial court correctly concluded that the arbitration provision in vehicle financing contracts was substantively unconscionably because the financier reserved the right to avail itself of the courts while forcing the borrowers to arbitrate every conceivable claim, the provision was nevertheless enforceable because there was no evidence of procedural unconscionability); Berent v. CMH Homes, Inc., 466 S.W.3d 740 (Tenn. 2015) (while a one-side arbitration can be unconscionable, a clause that excepted from arbitration the seller's claims to enforce its security interest or to seek preliminary relief was not unconscionable because the seller provided a business justification for the exceptions); Dan Ryan Builders, Inc. v. Nelson, 737 S.E.2d 550 (W. Va. 2012) (contract law requires that a contract as a whole be supported by consideration and mutuality of obligation, not that a single arbitration clause within a multi-clause contract be; however, an arbitration clause might be unconscionable if the clause unfairly lacks mutuality); United States *ex rel.* Gillette Air Conditioning Co., Inc. v. Satterfield and Pontikes Constr. Inc., 2010 WL 5067683 (W.D. Tex. 2010) (arbitration clause that required subcontractor to arbitrate disputes, if contractor so elected, was enforceable because mutuality of obligation to arbitrate is not required and one-sided clause is not unconscionable); GE Commercial Distribution Fin. Corp. v. RER Performance, Inc., 476 F. Supp. 2d 116 (D. Conn. 2007) (exception in arbitration clause for replevin actions was enforceable, and thus lender could bring judicial action despite arbitration clause); Salley v. Option One Mortgage Corp., 925 A.2d 115 (Pa. 2007) (it is not presumptively unconscionable for arbitration clause in sub-prime home mortgage loan to have an exception for foreclosure by the lender); Delta Funding Corp. v. Harris, 912 A.2d 104 (N.J. 2006) (exclusion of foreclosure actions from arbitration clause did not render clause unconscionable, although cost-shift and attorney fee provisions might be unconscionable).

[192]   *See, e.g.*, Dalton v. Santander Consumer USA, Inc., 345 P.3d 1086 (N.M. Ct. App. 2014).

(c) Challenging an Arbitration Clause

When a party challenges the validity of an arbitration clause on a ground that would render the entire agreement invalid, the matter is to be decided by an arbitrator, not a court. In other words, a court must abstain from deciding the issue and enforce the arbitration clause. In contrast, when a party challenges the validity of an arbitration provision but does not challenge the validity of the broader agreement, the question is to be decided by the court, not an arbitrator.[193]

Because the Federal Arbitration Act codifies a strong national policy in favor of arbitrating private disputes, unconscionability claims focusing specifically on an arbitration clause face a very steep incline. Nevertheless, there is a growing body of law that recognizes that – at least in consumer transactions – arbitration clauses can be unconscionable, particularly if they require arbitration in a remote location or require payment of a fee in excess of the amount of the underlying transaction.[194]

---

[193] *See* Buckeye Check Cashing, Inc. v. Cardegna, 546 U.S. 440, 444-46 (2006). However, the parties may, in their agreement, also delegate this decision to an arbitrator. *See* Rent-A-Center, West, Inc. v. Jackson, 561 U.S. 63 (2010).

[194] *See, e.g.,* Ingle v. Circuit City Stores, Inc., 328 F.3d 1165 (9th Cir. 2003), *cert. denied,* 540 U.S. 1160 (2004) (arbitration clause in employment agreement unconscionable because of its one-way application, one-year limitations period, bar on class actions, and cost-splitting provisions); Ting v. AT&T, 319 F.3d 1126 (9th Cir.), *cert. denied,* 540 U.S. 811 (2003) (arbitration clause was unconscionable because it barred class actions, split costs inappropriately, and mandated that results be kept confidential); Newton v. American Debt Services, Inc., 854 F. Supp. 2d 712 (N.D. Cal. 2012) (arbitration clause in consumer's contract with debt settlement company was substantively unconscionable in part because it required arbitration in the debt settlement company's home city, thereby requiring the consumer to incur substantial expense, and gave the debt settlement company the unilateral right to choose the arbitrator); College Park Pentecostal Holiness Church v. General Steel Corp., 847 F. Supp. 2d 807 (D. Md. 2012) (arbitration clause was unconscionable to the extent it required the representatives of a financially modest church to travel 1,400 miles to arbitrate its claims, to pay the counterparty's attorney's fees and costs if it challenges arbitrability regardless of whether that challenge is successful, and to pay all the costs of arbitration regardless of success on the merits; clause was enforceable minus its unconscionable terms); Brinkley v. Monterey Fin. Servs., Inc., 196 Cal. Rptr. 3d 1 (Cal. Ct. App. 2015) (the portion of the arbitration clause in a consumer contract providing for the loser to pay all the fees and costs of the prevailing party was substantively unconscionable but could be severed from the remainder of the clause). Brower v. Gateway 2000, Inc., 676 N.Y.S.2d 569 (N.Y. App. Div. 1998) (arbitration clause was unconscionable because it made arbitration prohibitively expensive). *But cf.* Sanchez v. Valencia Holding Co., LLC, 353 P.3d 741 (Cal. 2015) (arbitration clause in consumer contract was not unconscionable even

Exercise 4-18

You are general counsel to a regional provider of internet services. You are considering adding a compulsory arbitration clause to each of the following form agreements that your company uses.

1. Agreements with suppliers who sell goods and services to the company on a recurring basis.
2. One-year and two-year agreements to provide internet service to consumers and small businesses.
3. Employment agreements with senior executives.

For each of these agreements, why should you include an arbitration clause? What reasons, if any, are there for not including an arbitration clause?

When drafting an arbitration clause – or a clause dealing with choice of law, choice of forum, or jury waiver – for an integrated transaction involving multiple agreements, it is important not to assume that a clause in one of the agreements will apply to a dispute involving one or more of the other agreements that lacks such a clause.[195] For example, the sale of a business might involve a purchase and sale agreement, a promissory note, a security agreement or mortgage, and one or more

---

though: (i) it prohibited class actions; (ii) it permitted self-help remedies, such as repossession; (iii) it permitted appeal to a three-arbitrator panel if the award is $0 or more than $100,000; and (iv) the appealing party was responsible for the filing fee and other arbitration costs, subject to the arbitrators' fair apportionment of costs);

[195] *See* Linda L. Rusch, *Multiple Documents, One Contract?*, 2 THE TRANSACTIONAL LAWYER 2 (June 2012); Stephen L. Sepinuck, *Binding Guarantors to Terms in the Note*, 1 THE TRANSACTIONAL LAWYER 1 (June 2011); Chelsey Thorne, *An Update on Binding Guarantors to a Forum-Selection Clause*, 4 THE TRANSACTIONAL LAWYER 4 (Feb. 2014). *But cf.* Unison Co. v. Juhl Energy Dev., Inc., 789 F.3d 816 (8th Cir. 2015) (a supply agreement's arbitration clause covered a dispute arising under the parties' contemporaneously executed financing agreement); Parker v. Schlumberger Tech. Corp., 475 S.W.3d 914 (Tex. Ct. App. 2015) (the arbitration clause in an asset purchase agreement, which covered claims arising "under or in connection with" the agreement, covered the buyer's claims against the seller's former employee, who had signed a separate agreement not to compete required for the asset purchase to close, even though the former employee was not a signatory to the asset purchase agreement and the agreement not to compete lacked an arbitration clause); Marwell Corp. v. Marwell Corp., 2015 WL 4393289 (D. Utah 2015) (a choice-of-forum clause in a security agreement applied to claims under the simultaneously executed promissory note and asset purchase agreement).

guarantees. Including an arbitration clause in one of those documents but not the others leaves it unclear whether a dispute under those other agreements must be arbitrated. An arbitration clause in one agreement and a choice of a judicial forum in another agreement might be even worse, making it difficult for the entire dispute to be resolved in a single place. Accordingly, the transactional lawyer should strongly consider harmonizing across the documents the clauses on such matters.

E. NOTIFICATION

Transactions that involve only a brief interaction between the parties and that are to be consummated shortly after the agreement is executed – for example, a sale of goods in one installment – might not contain any provision about how the parties are to communicate with each other.[196] On the other hand, agreements that create what the parties expect will be a long-term relationship often do require one party to communicate with the other in specified circumstances. In some agreements, communication is necessary to exercise a right. For example, communication is often needed to exercise an option to buy property, to renew a lease, or to accelerate a debt. Similarly, insurance contracts typically condition coverage on the insured's prompt notification of the insurer of any casualty or claim. In other agreements, communication might be needed to fulfill a duty, such as to inform the other party of an expected delay in performance or other event.

Regardless of the purpose of the communication, the agreement might contain a clause on how the communication is to be made. The following clause is a typical, albeit poorly drafted, example:

---

[196] Even in such a simple transaction, communication might be required by law in some circumstances. *See, e.g.*, U.C.C. § 2-607(3) (requiring a buyer who has accepted the goods to notify the seller of any breach within a reasonable time or be barred from any remedy).

> *Notification.*[197] Any notification required or permitted under this Agreement will be sufficient if sent by United States certified mail, return receipt requested, addressed as follows:
>
> | If to Part A | If to Party B |
> |---|---|
> | [Party A's address] | [Party B's Address] |
>
> Each party has the right from time to time to change the place notice is to be given under this paragraph by written notification thereof to the other party.

In Chapter Five, we will discuss a variation of this clause and you will be asked to identify and correct its problems. For the present, there is one thing to consider about this clause or any clause dealing with notification: should notifications be effective upon dispatch or receipt?

To answer this question, it is of course necessary to first identify every notification for which the agreement provides.

Exercise 4-19

The notification clause above appears in a draft commercial lease. The other provisions in the draft lease dealing with notification are:

Sender	*Purpose*
Tenant	To extend the lease term
Landlord	To change the place rent is due
Tenant	To terminate the lease after damage
Landlord	To notify Tenant of default (and have the right to terminate the lease 15 days thereafter if the default is not cured)

---

[197] Many boilerplate clauses on communication use the word "notice" rather than "notification." However, "notice" is a term that the law frequently uses to deal with a person's state of mind. That is, a person is deemed to have notice of a fact when the person knows or has reason to know of it. Many state real property recording statutes use the word "notice" in this manner. *See also* U.C.C. § 1-202(a). In short, "notice" sometimes refers to a communication and sometimes to a mental state, and hence is ambiguous "Notification," on the other hand, always refers to a communication, and is therefore a more appropriate word to use when referring to a communication.

Tenant   To notify Landlord of default (and have the right 15
              days thereafter to cure the default and deduct
              the cost thereof from the rent due)

You represent the landlord. Should notifications be effective upon dispatch
or receipt? Should the answer to this be the same for each notification?
Why or why not?

CHAPTER FIVE
DRAFTING WITH PRECISION

In Chapter Two, we explored the different types of contract terms. In so doing, we discussed the word or words that should be used to create each type of term. This chapter provides additional advice about the language to use in written agreements and additional guidance on drafting such agreements. This advice and guidance is not exhaustive. Many books on contract drafting contain additional suggestions that are worth following. This chapter focuses on those things that are likely to affect the meaning or interpretation of the agreement and which, in our experience, transactional attorneys are most likely to overlook.

A. UNDERSTAND THE AUDIENCE

Although a transactional lawyer might write an agreement *for* a client, it is wise to think of the document as written *to* a court. A lawyer might, on occasion, draft an agreement in part to explain a transaction or set of obligations to a client or the client's counterparty. In many cases, however, the client does not read the document carefully or completely. After all, the client understands what the deal is, or at least what it is supposed to be. From the client's perspective, the document exists only to make everything "legal" and to protect the client in the event something goes wrong and a dispute arises between the parties. When that occurs, a court will read and interpret the document.

B. UNDERSTAND THE APPLICABLE INTERPRETIVE PRINCIPLES

Courts use numerous principles to interpret agreements. These principles can affect the meaning of an agreement, even an agreement that on its face is clear. They are therefore relevant to understanding – and from the transactional lawyer's perspective, creating – the rights and obligations of the parties. What follows is a brief discussion of a few of the interpretive principles that are most relevant to the transactional lawyer's job.

1. Usage of Trade and Course of Dealing

Usage of trade is any meaning ascribed to words, or any practice or method of dealing, having such regularity of observation in a place, vocation, or trade as to justify an expectation that it will be observed with respect to a particular agreement or transaction.[1] Course of dealing is a sequence of previous conduct between the parties to an agreement that is fairly to be regarded as establishing a common basis for understanding or interpreting their expressions or conduct.[2] Put another way, usage of trade is like the lexicon of a trade or industry. Course of dealing is the parties' own gloss on, or addendum to, that lexicon. But they are more than a repository of definitions for words and phrases that appear in a written agreement. Together, they comprise unstated assumptions and understandings on which the parties' agreement is based.

Consequently, both usage of trade and course of dealing are relevant in interpreting a written agreement. They explain and supplement the written terms.[3] Although the express terms of an agreement take precedence over both usage of trade and course of dealing,[4] there is no requirement that the language of the agreement be ambiguous for evidence of usage of trade or course of dealing to be admissible,[5] and courts often bend over backwards to interpret express terms consistently with usage of trade and course of dealing, so as give effect to all of them.[6]

This presents a challenge for transactional lawyers, who often lack expertise in their clients' trades and businesses or knowledge of the clients' prior dealings. In spite of that, usage of trade or course of dealing might supplement or qualify any written agreement that the lawyer drafts. If the lawyer fails to expressly negate an unwanted trade usage, for example, the agreement might mean something very different from what the lawyer and the lawyer's client desired. In short, knowledge

---

[1]   *See* RESTATEMENT (SECOND) OF CONTRACTS § 222(1); U.C.C. § 1-303(c).

[2]   *See* RESTATEMENT (SECOND) OF CONTRACTS § 223(1); U.C.C. § 1-303(b).

[3]   *See* RESTATEMENT (SECOND) OF CONTRACTS §§ 222(3), 223(2); U.C.C. § 1-303(d).

[4]   *See* RESTATEMENT (SECOND) OF CONTRACTS § 203(b); U.C.C. § 1-303(e).

[5]   *See* RESTATEMENT (SECOND) OF CONTRACTS §§ 222 cmt. b, 223 cmt. b.

[6]   *See, e.g.*, Ragus Co. v. City of Chicago, 628 N.E.2d 999 (Ill. Ct. App. 1993) (written specifications for rodent traps calling for "24/case" of one size and "12/case" of another size meant 12 and 24 pairs, respectively, because such traps were regularly sold and packaged in pairs).

of applicable usage of trade and course of dealing is just as important to the transactional lawyer as knowledge of applicable law. The drafter of an agreement who lacks such knowledge – who operates in the dark, so to speak – might not merely stumble and fall, but might bump into something large and ferocious.

Although contracting parties have the right to override a specific usage of trade or course of dealing with express language,[7] some transactional attorneys attempt to negate *all* usage of trade and course of dealing on a wholesale basis by incorporating into their written agreements a clause such as the following:

> ***Interpretation.*** Neither usage of trade nor course of dealing is relevant to the interpretation or meaning of this Agreement.

The efficacy of such a clause is questionable.[8] Accordingly, a transactional lawyer should not rely solely on a clause such as this. Moreover, if the clause were effective, it is just as likely to exclude consideration of something beneficial to the lawyer's client as it is to exclude consideration of something contrary to the client's interests.

2. Avoid Forfeiture

Another important rule of construction deals with whether a term imposes a duty or a condition. Courts are somewhat hostile to conditions and, when the language used is susceptible to different interpretations, will prefer one that does

---

[7]   *See* RESTATEMENT (SECOND) OF CONTRACTS §§ 222(3), 223(2) (both beginning "[u]nless otherwise agreed"). *See also id.* § 203(b) (express terms "are given greater weight" than course of dealing and usage of trade); U.C.C. § 1-303(e)(1) (express terms "prevail over" course of dealing and usage of trade).

[8]   *See* Wells Fargo Bank v. Cherryland Mall Ltd. P'ship, 812 N.W.2d 799, 810 (Mich. Ct. App. 2011) (admitting usage of trade to explain an undefined technical term despite a clause in the parties' agreement stating in capital letters that "no trade practice . . . shall be used to contradict, vary, supplement or modify any term of this guaranty agreement"); U.C.C. § 2-202 cmt. 2 (indicating that usage of trade and course of dealing become an element of the meaning of the words used in the parties' agreement "[u]nless *carefully* negated") (emphasis added). Arguably, trying to negate the relevance of all usage of trade is like trying to disclaim the relevance of a dictionary to interpret the words used. Usage of trade includes the lexicon of a trade or profession.

not result in a forfeiture.[9] In other words, courts will, if at all possible, interpret an agreement so as to not absolve one party from all of its promises if the other party has performed all but a minor portion of its obligations. Perhaps the most well known example of this is Judge Cardozo's decision in *Jacob & Youngs, Inc. v. Kent*, a case reprinted in most contracts casebooks and which involved a contractor's failure to use "Reading" pipe in the construction of a home.[10] The issue also frequently arises in connection with insurance contracts, which typically purport to deny liability for a casualty if the insured does not notify the insurer within a specified period of time.[11]

Because of this hostility to forfeiting conditions, transactional lawyers need to use great care when drafting conditions, particularly conditions that might negate the benefit of the bargain for one party.

Exercise 5-1

You are an attorney who has been presented with a draft agreement for construction services between Contractor and Subcontractor. The draft provides that "Contractor shall pay Subcontractor within 10 days after receiving payment from Owner." You are uncertain what would happen if Owner fails to pay Contractor. Put another way, it is unclear to you whether the quoted language makes Owner's payment to Contractor a condition to Contractor's duty to pay Subcontractor or is merely a covenant with language about timing.

A. You represent Contractor. Redraft the language so that payment by Owner is clearly a condition to Contractor's duty to pay Subcontractor. In so doing, fix any other problems with the draft language.

B. You represent Subcontractor. Redraft the language so that payment by Owner is clearly not a condition to Contractor's duty to pay Subcontractor. In so doing, fix any other problems with the draft language.

---

[9]   *See* RESTATEMENT (SECOND) OF CONTRACTS § 227(1).

[10]   129 N.E. 889 (1921). The Restatement includes an illustration based on this case to support a slightly different rule: that the non-occurrence of a condition should be excused if failing to do so would cause a disproportionate forfeiture and the condition was not a material part of the agreed exchange. RESTATEMENT (SECOND) OF CONTRACTS § 229 & ill.1.

[11]   *See, e.g.*, Howard v. Federal Crop Ins. Corp., 540 F.2d 695 (4th Cir. 1976).

3.   *Expressio Unius* and *Ejusdem Generis*

Two common maxims of both statutory and contract interpretation are known by their expression in Latin: (i) *expressio unius est exclusio alterius* ("the expression of one thing excludes another"); and (ii) *ejusdem generis* ("of the same genus or class"). The first means that if an agreement expressly lists what is within its coverage, then it excludes that which is not mentioned. For example, if a sales agreement expressly authorized the seller to ship the goods by "Federal Express or United Parcel Service," a court would likely interpret it not to authorize shipment by the U.S. Postal Service.

Ejusdem generis is a somewhat related maxim. It applies when an agreement contains a specific enumeration of items followed by a general catchall phrase. In that context, the maxim calls for the catchall phrase to be interpreted to include only things of the same kind or with the same characteristics as the specific items listed.[12] For example, in a vehicle lease that prohibited the lessee from using the vehicle to "transport vegetables, dairy, fruit, or other products," the catchall phrase "or other products" might be interpreted to mean products of the same genus as "vegetables, dairy, [and] fruit."[13] Thus, the catchall phrase might refer to food products but not manufactured goods. Alternatively, the phrase might include non-manufactured goods that are not foods, such as fresh flowers or lumber. To determine the scope of this phrase – in other words, to determine the applicable genus – it is often important to know the purpose of the entire clause.[14]

---

[12]   For an interesting discussion of *ejusdem generis*, see Maxus Cap. Group, LLC v. Liberty Surplus Ins. Corp., 2014 WL 4809430 (N.D. Ohio 2014), in which the court ruled that the doctrine was not relevant to the interpretation of an insurance policy that defined "claim" to mean "receipt of a civil action, suit, proceeding or demand." According to the court, the interpretive principle applies only when a series of specific terms is followed by a general term but the word "demand" was not a general term. Moreover, the court noted, the general term must normally be linked to the specific terms, such as by the word "other" in the phrase "fishing rods, nets, hooks, bobbers, sinkers, and other equipment." In the definition at issue, there was no explicit link to demonstrate that the word "demand" was connected conceptually to the words that preceded it.

[13]   In this context, "genus" means a group with common attributes, not necessarily the taxonomic category below family and above species in the Linnaean classification system for living organisms. If it is helpful, think of "genus" as similar to "genre," a word that comes from the same root.

[14]   A somewhat related principle, referred to as *noscitur a sociis*, states that a word is known by the company it keeps. That is, a word will be given a more precise meaning by the

Exercise 5-2

A. An apartment lease provides that "Tenant may keep cats and dogs" in the leased apartment. May Tenant keep a gerbil there? Rewrite the clause so that is clearer but not restricted to cats and dogs.

B. A lease of farmland provides that "Tenant may keep sheep, cows, pigs, and other animals" on the leased property. May Tenant keep alpacas? What about ostriches? What about tigers? Rewrite the clause so that it is clearer while also consistent with the parties' likely intent.

4. Public Interest Preferred

Another well-recognized rule of construction is that, in interpreting an agreement that affects the public interest, a meaning that serves the public interest is to be preferred over one that does not.[15] This rule is probably applied most commonly when interpreting a covenant not to compete. Thus, for example, a court might interpret an employment agreement that prohibits the employee, after the employment period ends, from competing with the employer anywhere "within 50 miles" of the employer's office as referring to the shortest driving distance, not to a distance measured by air.[16] A better drafted agreement would avoid this interpretive problem.

5. *Contra Proferentem*

One age-old maxim of contract interpretation is *contra proferentem*, which requires that ambiguity in an agreement be interpreted against the party who proffered the ambiguous language.[17] Traditionally, *contra proferentem* was a rule of last resort, applicable only when all other interpretive devices fail to resolve the

---

neighboring words with which it is associated. *See, e.g.*, Yates v. United States, 135 S. Ct. 1074, 1085-86 (2015) (using this canon to interpret a statute).

[15] *See* RESTATEMENT (SECOND) OF CONTRACTS § 207.

[16] *See* Vantage Tech., LLC v. Cross, 17 S.W.3d 637 (Tenn. Ct. App. 1999).

[17] *See* RESTATEMENT (SECOND) OF CONTRACTS § 206; Cal. Civ. Code § 1654.

ambiguity.[18] However, the maxim is not expressly so limited in the Restatement (Second) of Contracts and the frequency and ardor with which some courts now resort to the maxim suggest that it might no longer be a rule of last resort, particularly with respect to a contract of adhesion.[19]

To head off application of the maxim, it is now common to find written agreements that contain a clause such as one of the following:

> ***Interpretation.*** Both parties drafted and reviewed this Agreement and share equal responsibility for its wording.

> ***Interpretation.*** Neither this Agreement nor any uncertainty or ambiguity herein is to be interpreted against the party that was the principal drafter of the Agreement or of any uncertain or ambiguous language in the Agreement. Instead, this Agreement is to be interpreted according to the ordinary meaning of the words used so as to accomplish fairly the purposes and intentions of the parties.

Unfortunately, no known court decision deals with the efficacy or effect of such a clause and it seems questionable that a court would abide by it. After all, the maxim is essentially an equitable rule that puts the burden of any ambiguity on the party responsible for it.[20] It might also be premised in part on the belief that the party that drafts the agreement or otherwise supplies the language at issue is likely to be the one with the greater bargaining power, and any effort to prevent application of the maxim might be viewed as overreaching.[21] For this reason,

---

[18] *See, e.g.,* Residential Mktg. Group, Inc. v. Granite Inv. Group, 933 F.2d 546, 549 (7th Cir. 1991); Cal. Civ. Code § 1654.

[19] Staffing Specifix, Inc. v. TempWorks Mgmt. Servs., Inc., 896 N.W.2d 115 (Minn. Ct. App. 2017); Neal v. State Farm Ins. Cos., 10 Cal. Rptr. 781 (Cal. Ct. App. 1961).

[20] Note that in a transaction involving sophisticated parties represented by counsel who review and mark up multiple drafts of an agreement, it might not be obvious which party should be regarded as the one who supplied the ambiguous language.

[21] One author has suggested that a clause that seeks to avoid application of *contra proferentem* might even lead to problematic results. For example, if the maxim truly is a rule of last resort, but a court is not to apply it, there might be no way for the court to resolve the interpretive problem. If the term at issue cannot readily be severed, the court might have no alternative to declaring the entire agreement void. *See* Scott J. Burnham, *Contracting Around* Contra Proferentem, 3 THE TRANSACTIONAL LAWYER 6 (June 2013).

transactional attorneys who draft written agreements are well advised to assume that, even if they include such a clause, the agreements will be interpreted against their clients. Thus, they should diligently try to make their agreements clear, complete, and correct. The remainder of this chapter contains advice on how to do that.

C. IN GENERAL, USE THE ACTIVE VOICE

Imagine the following covenant in a residential lease:

> The premises shall be kept in good repair.

Does this impose an obligation on the landlord or on the tenant? A judge could reasonably interpret it either way. Of course, context might provide guidance. If the clause were in a section of the lease delineating the tenant's duties, or under a heading identifying it as one of the tenant's duties, that placement would strongly suggest that the tenant is the party obligated by this statement. Usage of trade might also provide guidance. For example, if most residential leases put this obligation on the tenant, then perhaps this lease does so. In the absence of such context or usage of trade, however, there is really no reliable way to know who is obligated under this clause.[22]

Similarly, consider a real estate purchase agreement that purports to give the buyer an option to purchase adjoining tracts of land and further provides:

> If Buyer exercises said option to purchase, a fair and equitable price for said property will be established at a later date.

---

[22] The California Residential Purchase Agreement and Joint Escrow Instructions, a form document prepared by the California Association of Realtors, provides: "Within the time frame specified in paragraph 14, Buyer shall be provided a current preliminary title report." Inasmuch as the parties to the agreement are the buyer and the seller, it might be assumed that this term imposes an obligation on the seller. Apparently, however, that is not the industry understanding; instead, the obligation is performed by the escrow company (which receives instruction under the agreement, but which is not a party).

Because the price term is expressed in the passive voice, it is it unclear how the price is to be determined or by whom. As a result, a court presented with such language ruled that the entire option was unenforceable.[23]

Another example arose from a set of agreements in which: (i) the owner of a small business agreed to sell the assets of the business; (ii) the buyer promised to employ the seller for four years; and (iii) the seller covenanted not to engage in a competing business until one year after the termination of seller's employment with the buyer. However, the agreements further provided that the restriction on competition would cease to be binding if the seller's "employment with Buyer is terminated" less than two years after the sale for any reason other than cause. The day before the two-year period was to expire, the seller quit. The seller then brought an action seeking a declaratory judgment that the non-compete clause was no longer enforceable. The court agreed, concluding that the passive language indicated that termination could be by either party.[24] It seems very unlikely that the buyer, who had paid a lump sum up front for the covenant not to compete, intended the seller to be able to evade that covenant by simply resigning. In other words, the buyer no doubt intended the conditional language to apply only when "Buyer terminates Seller's employment." The passive voice obscured that intent.

On the other hand, consider the difference between the following two representations that might appear in an agreement for sale:

The car has been driven less than 60,000 miles.

The seller has driven the car less than 60,000 miles.

The former is passive but is certainly preferable from the buyer's standpoint because it is broader: it deals with how far the car has traveled, not merely how far the seller has driven it, and thus includes mileage racked up by former owners and others in the seller's household.[25]

---

[23] *See* Keltner v. Estate of Simpkins, 2016 WL 1247704 (Tenn. Ct. App. 2016).

[24] East Texas Copy Sys., Inc. v. Player, 528 S.W.3d 562 (Tex. Ct. App. 2016).

[25] *See* Rivers v. Revington Glen Inv., LLC, 2018 WL 3045784 (Ga. Ct. App. 2018) (a warranty that "Seller has at all times complied with" applicable environmental laws did not promise that all previous owners had complied with such laws or that the property was free from hidden environmental contamination, and thus the seller had no warranty liability for the acts of prior owners).

In short, the passive voice can on occasion be proper – particularly when the action, not the actor, is what matters or in the phrasing of a condition – but do not use it by accident. Especially in a covenant, using the passive voice can create ambiguity, which in turn can lead to litigation.[26]

D. USE THE PRESENT TENSE

In general, terms in an agreement – particularly declarations – should be drafted in the present tense. Consider the following:

> The law of the State of Washington **will** govern this Agreement.

This clause nicely avoids both the passive voice (*i.e.*, it is properly not phrased as "this agreement will be governed by the law of the State of Washington") and the false imperative (*i.e.,* it does not use "shall" in a term that is a declaration, rather than a covenant). However, it is in the future tense, not the present tense. One problem with the future tense is that it is indefinite: it does not indicate how far in the future it applies or becomes operative. Imagine that, a year after the parties entered into an agreement containing this clause, a dispute arises and the parties litigate. Does Washington law now govern? Presumably that is what the parties intended but the language of the choice-of-law clause indicates merely that Washington law will govern in the future, not that it does govern. Perhaps Washington law has not yet kicked in and will not apply for another year or two. The language used simply does not provide a sure basis for knowing.

---

[26] See Chemical Bank v. Long's Tri-County Mobile Homes, 2011 WL 521158 (Mich. Ct. App. 2011), in which one of the issues was whether a creditor that had loaned funds to a mobile home dealer had breached the loan agreement. The agreement included the statement: "Manufacturers [sic] buyback agreement required." Each party claimed that the other had the duty to obtain the buyback agreements. The court ruled for the debtor, concluding that the creditor had that duty, a conclusion likely to be contrary to normal commercial practices and expectations. *See also* In re Simoukdalay, 557 B.R. 597 (Bankr. E.D. Tenn. 2016) (an attorney's fees clause in a promissory note written in the passive voice and which did not specify who was responsible for the fees was unenforceable); Moniuszko v. Karuntzos, 2014 WL 4657134 (Ill. Ct. App. 2014) (language in a lease requiring the landlord to release its security interest in the tenant's equipment unless, prior to a specified date, the tenant "was found to be in default," required a judicial finding even though the security agreement permitted the landlord to declare a default in its sole discretion).

E. USE THE SINGULAR

When drafting a condition, describe the triggering event in the singular, not the plural. Using the plural implies that the event must happen multiple times for the condition to apply, and that is rarely what the parties intend. For example, consider the following:

> If the parties assign their **rights** under this Agreement, they shall notify the other party 30 days in advance.

> If any provisions of this Agreement are determined to be unenforceable, the other terms of this Agreement will remain in effect.

The first example is no doubt intended to apply if either party assigns its rights, and should be expressed in such terms. It should also probably cover an assignment of only a single right under the agreement, rather than multiple or all rights. The second example is intended to cover a situation in which a court declares a single provision unenforceable, but it arguably does not cover that situation.

F. USE CONSISTENT WORDING

Ralph Waldo Emerson famously observed that "[a] foolish consistency is the hobgoblin of little minds."[27] But for the drafter of written agreements, consistency is not foolish, it is essential. Lawyers and judges are trained to assume that the same word or phrase carries with it the same meaning throughout a single document.[28] An important corollary to this principle is that different words and phrases presumably mean different things. Accordingly, if you mean the same

---

[27] The line continues, "adored by little statesmen, philosophers and divines." Essays: First Series. *Self Reliance* (1841).

[28] *See, e.g.*, Eisen v. Capital One, 232 S.W.3d 309, 313 (Tex. Ct. App. 2007) ("When the testator uses the same words in different parts of the will with reference to the same subject matter, we presume he intended the words to have the same meaning unless the context indicates the testator used the words in a different sense."); Finest Invs. v. Security Trust Co. of Rochester, 468 N.Y.S.2d 256, 258 (N.Y. App. Div. 1984) ("We may presume that the same words used in different parts of a writing have the same meaning.").

thing, use the same words. Variation in language might make for appealing prose, but at the cost of creating ambiguity. In short, comply with the following two maxims:

Never change your wording unless you wish to change your meaning.[29]

Always change your wording if you wish to change your meaning.

Failure to follow these rules can lead to significant interpretive problems and cause a court to interpret the agreement in a way that the drafter did not intend.[30] For example, consider an agreement that contains the following two clauses:

> Except as otherwise provided in this Agreement, Shareholders may not **sell, transfer, assign, pledge, convey, or otherwise dispose of (by operation of law or otherwise)** shares of the Corporation.
>
> If a Shareholder proposes to **transfer** shares of the Corporation and dies prior to the closing of the transaction . . . .

Notice that the first clause uses six verbs (in blue), each with a slightly different meaning, while the second clause uses only one of them. This suggests that the second clause has a much more narrow scope than the first, yet that might not be what the parties meant.

Note, the need for consistency in language when the same meaning is intended applies across multiple documents that the parties execute in connection with the

---

[29] There is a rule of statutory construction that says that if different language is used in the same connection in different parts of a statute, presumably it has a different meaning and effect. *See* BFP v. Resolution Trust Corp., 511 U.S. 531, 537 (1994) (interpreting "value" in § 548 of the Bankruptcy Code not to mean "fair market value" in part because the latter phrase is used elsewhere in the Code, so the reference in § 548 presumptively means something different); Quarles v. St. Clair., 711 F.2d 691, 701 n.31 (5th Cir. 1983); In re Ramirez, 204 F.3d 595, 599 (5th Cir. 2000) (Benavides, J., concurring). Courts apply the same rule when interpreting agreements. *See, e.g.*, Moniuszko v. Karuntzos, 2014 WL 4657134 (Ill. Ct. App. 2014).

[30] *See, e.g.,* Middleton v. First Nat'l Bank, 399 S.W.3d 463 (Mo. Ct. App. 2013) (because Addendum A to a deposit agreement between a bank and its customers referred to both the Deposit Agreement and "this form," the latter reference was to Addendum A itself; because that reference indicated that the customers were not bound unless they signed "this form," and they had signed the Deposit Agreement but not Addendum A, they were not bound by Addendum A).

same transaction or related transactions.[31] It also applies to such mundane things as the use of the plural and singular. If more than one person has the same role in a transaction or in a transaction document – for example, if two or more joint owners are selling property to a single buyer or if a trust agreement is appointing two or more persons as trustees – inconsistent use of the singular and plural can cause interpretive problems.[32]

G. AVOID REPETITION

Using language consistently does not mean that the same idea should be repeated. Repetition is at best unnecessary and in many cases can cause a problem. You might recall from page 28 the simple scenario in which Buyer agreed to pay Seller $20,000 for a car, to be paid in two, equal installments. We discussed how that agreement could be expressed adequately in either of two ways: as a covenant (the first example below) or as a covenant accompanied by a declaration (the second example below):

> Buyer shall pay Seller $10,000 on June 1 and another $10,000 on July 1.

---

[31] For example, in one case, an individual entered into a contribution agreement with a newly formed limited liability company pursuant to which the individual contributed specified assets to the company, including "software programs and source codes." The company, in return, issued a $500,000 promissory note payable to the individual and executed a security agreement granting the individual a security interest in "software" to secure its obligation under the promissory note. The court ruled that while the term "software" might, in other contexts, include source code, the term did not do so in the security agreement because the parties had differentiated "software" from "source code" in the contribution agreement. *See* The Mostert Group, LLC v. Mostert, 2017 WL 4700343 (Ky. Ct. App. 2017). *See also* In re Albert G. Aaron Living Trust, 181 A.3d 703 (Md. 2018) (discussing whether the phrase "my wife" in a codicil meant the same thing as it did in the trust agreement that it modified, even though the decedent had since remarried); Orix Fin. Servs., Inc. v. Martin, 2011 WL 13257692 (S.D.N.Y. 2011) (involving a dispute about the meaning of a forum selection clause in a promissory note that was phrased slightly differently from the forum selection clause in the associated guaranty).

[32] *See, e.g.*, Estate of Lieurance, 2016 WL 5800007 (Cal. Ct. App. 2016) (interpreting a trust agreement that used the word "trustee" 162 times and the word "trustees" 5 times).

> Buyer shall pay Seller $20,000. $10,000 is due on June 1 and the remaining $10,000 is due on July 1.

But now consider the same term expressed as two covenants:

> Buyer shall pay Seller $20,000. Buyer shall pay $10,000 on June 1 and another $10,000 on July 1.

This repetition creates an interpretive problem: read literally it indicates that Buyer has duty to pay a total $40,000 instead of $20,000.[33]

Repetition is even more problematic when the statements are not phrased identically. One common canon of statutory construction is that words and phrases are to be construed so as to give meaning and effect to each word.[34] A similar principle applies to the interpretation of agreements.[35] While this interpretive principle is rather dubious at the level of individual words,[36] courts apply it

---

[33] Replacing the period with a comma or semi-colon might help alleviate the problem, but it is easier and better practice to simply avoid the duplication.

[34] *See, e.g.*, United States v. Menasche, 348 U.S. 528, 538-39 (1955) (quoting Montclair v. Ramsdell, 107 U.S. 147, 152 (1882)); Sultana Corp. v. Jewelers Mut. Ins. Co., 860 So. 2d 1112 (La. 2003). *See also* Uniform Statutory Construction Act § 13(2).

[35] *See* RESTATEMENT (SECOND) OF CONTRACTS § 203(a); Cal. Civ. Code § 1651. *See also, e.g.,* Wells Fargo Bank v. Cherryland Mall Ltd. P'ship, 812 N.W.2d 799 (Mich. Ct. App. 2011).

[36] The principle that each *word* have independent meaning might be a corruption of the canon requiring that no *part or provision* be inoperative or superfluous. *See, e.g.,* Yates v. United States, 135 S. Ct. 1074, 1085 (2015); Corley v. United States, 556 U.S. 303, 314 (2009). At that broader level, the canon probably makes sense. It is premised on the notion that drafters choose their language carefully (and when applied to a statute, reflects the courts' subservient role to the legislature). At the level of individual words, however, the principle flies in the face of common experience. Lawyers often include numerous nouns or verbs in a single clause to ensure that nothing intended to be covered is inadvertently omitted. Thus, it is common for lawyers to write "cease and desist," "null and void," "convey, transfer, and assign," and a whole host of similar phrases. This practice reflects a cautious approach to drafting even though one or more words in the list might be unnecessary (*i.e.,* not encompass anything not already covered by the other words in the list). To insist that each word have independent meaning is to presume that drafters never employ redundancy and the type of careful drafting it represents. It therefore presumes precisely what the canon is designed to reject: that drafters are sloppy and do not take great care in their work.

regularly.[37] As a result, repetition in a written agreement with any variation in language presents a problem: a court might labor to find a way to interpret the repeated phrases or clauses to express different things, so as to give each independent meaning. While this effort is not supposed to result in an unreasonable interpretation,[38] it might nevertheless lead to a result that is not consistent with the parties' intent.

One corollary to this deals with numbers. Legal documents often express numbers, particularly dollar amounts, in both words and numerals. This practice is ubiquitous in promissory notes but also common in mortgages, guarantees, and other written agreements. Thus, for example, a legal document might state the following (for reasons that are not apparent, it is common to use all capital letters when expressing dollar amounts in words, so that the text appears to shout at the reader):

> "ONE MILLION SEVEN THOUSAND AND NO/100
> ($1,700,000.00) DOLLARS."

Of course, if the amount expressed in words matches the amount expressed in numerals, then one of the expressions is unnecessary. If the amounts are different (as in the example above – did you notice?), the discrepancy presents a significant problem. In a case involving just such a discrepancy, a lender lost $693,000![39]

---

[37] *See, e.g.*, Maxus Cap. Group, LLC v. Liberty Surplus Ins. Corp., 2014 WL 4809430 (N.D. Ohio 2014); Ted Ruck Co. v. High Quality Plastics, Inc., 1991 WL 1559 (Ohio Ct. App. 1991) ("In construing a contract, a court must endeavor to give meaning to every paragraph, clause, phrase and word, omitting nothing as meaningless, or surplusage").

[38] *See* FCCD Ltd. v. State Street Bank & Trust, 2011 WL 519228 (S.D.N.Y. 2011) ("[a] small redundancy is preferable to an unreasonable result").

[39] *See* Charles R. Tips Family Trust v. PB Commercial LLC, 459 S.W.3d 147 (Tex. Ct. App. 2015) (a draft version of this decision is discussed in Charles Nichols, *The Danger of Writing Amounts in Both Words and Numerals*, 4 THE TRANSACTIONAL LAWYER 1 (Oct. 2014)). Because the words prevail over discrepant numerals – a rule presumably based on the assumption that it is easier to err when writing the numerals – numerals are, at best, surplusage.

H. PLACE MODIFIERS NEXT TO THE WORD OR PHRASE THEY MODIFY

Many competent writers are a bit too casual in their placement of words and phrases within a sentence. Consider the difference between the following two sentences:

Never include a provision in an agreement that you do not understand.

Never include in an agreement a provision that you do not understand.

These sentences mean very different things. In the former, it is an agreement that is not understood; in the latter, it is a provision. Admittedly, this particular example is unlikely to confuse anyone: a reader of either is likely to understand that the author meant what the second sentence actually states. That will not always be the case. Improper placement of words or phrases can sometimes create difficult interpretive problems.

Exercise 5-3

Employee quits and then claims severance benefits under an employment agreement that provides for such payments:

> . . . on termination of Employee's employment by Company.

Is Employee entitled to the benefits? Rewrite the clause without changing, subtracting or adding any words – merely by reordering the words used – to make it clear that benefits are not available in this situation. Then rewrite the original clause – by changing only one word and moving none – to make it clear that Employee is entitled to benefits on these facts.

To further illustrate the point about placing modifiers, study the chart below. It shows the different meanings that are created by inserting the word "only" into different places in a sentence.

Placement	*Effect / Meaning*
Only the attorney sent Pat the will yesterday.	No one else sent the will (*e.g.*, not the testator).
The *only* attorney sent Pat the will yesterday.	No other attorney was involved.
The attorney *only* sent Pat the will yesterday.	The attorney did nothing else (*e.g.*, call, deliver the will).
The attorney sent *only* Pat the will yesterday.	The attorney sent the will to nobody else.
The attorney sent Pat *only* the will yesterday.	The attorney sent nothing other than the will.
The attorney sent Pat the *only* will yesterday.	There were no other wills.
The attorney sent Pat the will *only* yesterday.	Emphasizes the timing, implying that the will should have been sent earlier.
The attorney sent Pat the will yesterday *only*.	Emphasizes the day, implying that the will was to be sent on multiple days.

Be very careful when using an adverb such as "only." It is a powerful word that can significantly change the meaning of a sentence when put in the wrong place.[40]

Exercise 5-4

How do the two sentences below, which might appear in a loan agreement, differ?

Only the interest is due on demand. | *The interest is due only on demand.*

Exercise 5-5

The following sentence, taken from a trademark license, has the word "only" in the wrong place. Where in the sentence should the word be placed and why?

> Licensee may only use the License in the Assigned Territory.

---

[40] *Cf.* In re Wages, 508 B.R. 161 (9th Cir. BAP 2014) (discussing whether 11 U.S.C. § 1123(b)(5) applies to claims secured *only* by real property used as the debtor's principal residence or to claims secured by real property used *only* as the debtor's principal residence).

Exercise 5-6

The following sentence, taken from a distributorship agreement, has the word "only" in the wrong place. Where in the sentence should the word be placed and why?

> Distributor agrees to only sell the Products to Approved Dealers.

I. CRAFT DEFINITIONS AND USE DEFINED TERMS WITH CARE

As noted in Chapter Two, using defined terms in a written agreement can save space, make the agreement more readable, and help prevent error by avoiding inconsistent phrasing. Those benefits come with a price, however. The drafter must be exceedingly careful in crafting the definition and then similarly careful wherever incorporating the defined term into the agreement. Every use of a defined term carries with it the *entire* definition. The following discussion explains this in more detail by identifying five errors that lawyers commonly make with respect to definitions and defined terms.

1. Error One – Making a Term Too Specific

Do not incorporate into a definition detail that will or might be contradicted later or elsewhere. For example, consider an agreement for the purchase and sale of equipment that the seller will manufacture specially for the buyer. The agreement contains detailed specifications for the equipment – specifications that will themselves become a defined term. The agreement then defines the "Equipment" to be purchased and sold as "goods manufactured pursuant to the Specifications." This definition of Equipment is likely to be problematic if, as is likely, the agreement contains a clause on what happens "if all or part of the Equipment does not conform to the Specifications."

The problem might be more readily apparent if you start by placing the definition beside the clause that uses the defined term:

Definition	*Body of Agreement*
"Equipment" means goods manufactured pursuant to the Specifications.	If all or any part of the Equipment does not conform to the Specifications . . . .

Then, where the defined term is used, replace the defined term with the full definition:

	Body of Agreement
	If all or any part of the *goods manufactured pursuant to the Specifications* does not conform to the Specifications . . . .

As you can see, the resulting language becomes somewhat contradictory and almost meaningless. Can goods be manufactured pursuant to the Specifications yet not conform to the Specifications? Possibly, but one has to struggle to make sense of it. Better drafting would avoid this problem.

2.   Error Two – Creating Redundancy

This error is very similar to the previous one and is attributable to the same basic point: that each use of a defined term carries with it the entire definition. Consider:

Definition	*Body of Agreement*
"VIN" means vehicle identification number.	Borrower shall provide Lender with the VIN number of each motor vehicle.

When the definition is substituted for the defined term in the body of the agreement, the agreement then nonsensically refers to the "vehicle identification number number." To avoid this problem, make the hypothetical substitution in each place the defined term is used and check to make sure that the result is appropriate.

3. Error Three – Using a Term in Its Definition

A good dictionary never uses a word in its own definition. To do so is to make the definition circular, confusing, and unhelpful.

Poor	*Better*
"**Purchased Receivables**" means the accounts and other **receivables** arising out of the invoices sold by Seller to Buyer.	"**Purchased Receivables**" means the accounts and other **rights to payment** arising out of the invoices sold by Seller to Buyer.

Transactional attorneys should follow the same principle.

4. Error Four – Inconsistent Capitalization

Most written agreements follow the convention of capitalizing the initial letter of each word in every defined term. This convention provides a very useful signal to the reader each time a defined term is used without excessively distracting the reader (as using all capital letters might). A problem or ambiguity arises, however, if the agreement ever uses a defined term without capitalizing the initial letter. Is that a use of the defined term or of something other than the defined term?[41] For example:

Definition	*Body of Agreement*
"Premises" means the land and structures at 123 Main Street, Spokane, Washington.	Tenant shall maintain casualty insurance on the **leased premises** for the full value thereof.

Does "leased premises" refer to the Premises, some portion thereof, or to something else entirely? The implication of the failure to capitalize the word "Premises" in the

---

[41] *See* CFIP Master Fund, Ltd. v. Citibank, 738 F. Supp. 2d 450, 463-64 (S.D.N.Y. 2010) (refusing to determine on a motion for summary judgment whether the uncapitalized word "subordination" was imbued with the definition of the capitalized term). *See also* Erie Indemnity Co. v. Estate of Harris, 99 N.E.3d 625 (Ind. 2018) (struggling to determine whether the phrase "others we protect" in an insurance policy meant the same thing as the defined term "OTHERS WE PROTECT"); Republic Bank of Chicago v. 1st Advantage Bank, 999 N.E.2d 9, 17 (Ill. Ct. App. 2013) (refusing to interpret the word "guaranty" as meaning what the capitalized term was defined to mean).

body of the agreement is that the parties mean something other than the defined term, but this is by no means certain. To avoid this problem, the drafter should: (i) always follow the capitalization convention whenever the intent is to use the defined term; and (ii) use a word or phrase other than the defined term when something different is intended.

5.   Error Five – Making a Term Too Broad

This error is the inverse of the first error. Sometimes a definition is drafted so broadly that it encompasses things that the drafter did not consider and does not want to be covered. Consider the following problem.

Exercise 5-7

Insurer issued an automobile insurance policy that insures against personal injury to any "occupant" of an insured motor vehicle. Pedestrian was struck by a car insured by Insurer and thrown onto the car's hood. Pedestrian suffered injuries both from the initial impact and while on the car's hood. In Pedestrian's action against Insurer for the latter injuries, the court ruled that Pedestrian was an "occupant" of the vehicle because the insurance policy defines "occupant" as "an individual in, on, entering or alighting from" the insured vehicle.[42]

A.   Why does the insurance policy include the preposition "on" in its definition of "occupant"? In other words, what is that word intended to cover?

B.   Redraft the definition of "occupant" so that it does not cover someone such as Pedestrian but does cover whatever you concluded in Part A the term was intended to cover.

Exercise 5-8

Municipality wishes to raise funds through the issuance of bonds to finance economic development in portions of the city. The bonds are to be secured by a specified portion of the hotel occupancy tax to which

---

[42]   *See* Bennett v. State Farm Mutual Auto. Ins. Co., 731 F.3d 584 (6th Cir. 2013).

Municipality becomes entitled during the life of the bonds. Those funds are to be deposited with Agent, which will represent the bondholders. The relevant documents for the transactions include the following definitions:

- "Collateral" means "all Revenues, and all rights of Agent to receive Revenues."
- "Revenues" means "[formula for computing the intended portion of the hotel occupancy taxes] received by Agent."

Why might these definitions not work as intended?

J. PUNCTUATE PROPERLY

Compare the two sentences below:

The assailant was a fat, armed man. | *The assailant was a fat-armed man.*

The one on the left refers to an overweight man with a weapon. The one on the right refers to a man with fat arms. Now compare these two sentences, made famous by a book title:

The panda eats shoots and leaves. | *The panda eats, shoots, and leaves.*

The sentence on the left identifies two things the animal eats. The sentence on the right refers to three things the animal does, one of which might involve a gun or a basketball.[43] Similarly, you might be familiar with the following two sentences, which appear on a humorous poster:

Let's eat Grandma! | *Let's eat, Grandma!*

---

[43] This huge difference in meaning is possible because the words "shoots" and "leaves" are both nouns and verbs. Specifically, they are nouns in the sentence at the left and verbs in the sentence at the right. Other examples of this phenomenon include:

Babies only eat poop and cry. / *Babies only eat, poop, and cry.*

The plaintiff owns trains and races horses. | *The plaintiff owns, trains, and races horses.*

The latter is derived from the statement of the facts in Brewer v. Peak Performance Nutrients Inc., 2012 WL 3861169 (Del Super. Ct. 2012).

The sentence on the left, lacking a comma, refers to something unpleasant you might do *to* your grandmother; the sentence on the right, with a comma, refers to something you might like to do *with* her.

Perhaps the most significant effect a single comma can produce is in the following sentence used to describe a video game:

> *Nothing happens slowly.* | *Nothing happens, slowly.*

The statement at the right, with the comma, evokes a sense of excruciating tedium. The statement at the left, lacking the comma, means almost the opposite; it suggests that everything happens quickly.

The problems of interpretation presented by improper punctuation are not always so humorous. Nor are they fanciful. Numerous cases, including at least one decided by the U.S. Supreme Court, have rested in whole or in part on the presence or absence of a single comma.[44] The most common problem involves a modifying clause or phrase that either was or was not set off by commas. For example, consider the following two sentences from a security agreement (an agreement that creates a lien on personal property to secure a debt). They differ only in the comma after the word "chemicals."

Buyer grants Seller a security interest in all Buyer's inventory, including all chemicals, that Seller sold to Buyer.	Buyer grants Seller a security interest in all Buyer's inventory, including all chemicals that Seller sold to Buyer.

---

[44] *See, e.g.,* United States v. Ron Pair Enters., Inc., 489 U.S. 235 (1989) (interpreting the Bankruptcy Code); O'Connor v. Oakhurst Dairy, 851 F.3d 69 (1st Cir. 2017) (interpreting a statute). American Int'l Group, Inc. v. Bank of Am., 712 F.3d 775 (2d Cir. 2013) (interpreting a statute); Shelby County State Bank v. Van Diest Supply Co., 303 F.3d 832 (7th Cir. 2002) (interpreting a security agreement); Berkshire Aircraft, Inc. v. AEC Leasing Co., 84 P.3d 608 (Kan. Ct. App. 2002) (interpreting a contract); Judson v. Associated Meats & Seafoods, 651 P.2d 222 (Wash. App. 1982) (interpreting a statute that had been amended to remove a comma); Reeves v. American Sec. & Trust Co., 115 F.2d 145, 146 (D.C. App. 1940) (interpreting a will). *But cf.* Overhauser v. United States, 45 F.3d 1085, 1087 (7th Cir. 1995) (expressing skepticism about the grammatical expertise of the drafters of legal documents, and therefore of the relevance of grammatical arguments).

After the First Circuit's decision in *Oakhurst Dairy*, the Maine legislature amended the statute by, among other things, replacing the commas with semi-colons. 2017 Me. Legis. Serv. Ch. 219.

The clause at the left is far more limited than the clause at the right. Specifically, the clause at the left grants a security interest only in inventory sold by Seller to Buyer, whereas the clause at the right grants a security interest in all of Buyer's inventory, regardless of from whom Buyer acquired it. Do you see why? It is because in the left sentence the final, limiting clause "that Seller Sold to Buyer" (in blue below) modifies the first clause, which contains the grant of the security interest. In other words, in the sentence at the left, the middle phrase "including all chemicals" is set off by a comma both before and after, with the result that the subsequent limiting clause modifies the opening clause (underlined below). In contrast, in the sentence at the right, the limiting clause "that Seller sold to Buyer" modifies the phrase closest to it: "including all chemicals." As a result, there is no limitation on the opening clause's grant of the security interest.

Buyer grants Seller a security interest in **all Buyer's inventory**, including all chemicals, **that Seller sold to Buyer**.	Buyer grants Seller a security interest in all Buyer's inventory, **including all chemicals** that **Seller sold to Buyer**.

The addition of a seemingly insignificant thing – a comma – drastically changes the meaning.[45]

Exercise 5-9

The following two sentences differ only in the comma after the word "terms." How do the two sentences differ in meaning?

The contract shall continue in force for a period of five years from the date it is made, and thereafter for successive five-year terms, unless and until terminated by one year prior notice in writing by either party.	The contract shall continue in force for a period of five years from the date it is made, and thereafter for successive five-year terms unless and until terminated by one year prior notice in writing by either party.

---

[45] This illustration is taken from Shelby County State Bank v. Van Diest Supply Co., 303 F.3d 832.

Exercise 5-10

Testator died leaving a valid will that bequeathed Testator's entire estate "in equal shares to Ann, Bob, Cathy and Dave." To what portion of the estate is Ann entitled?

K. PAY ATTENTION TO PREPOSITIONS

The difference between doing something *to* your grandmother and doing something *with* her – as suggested by the discussion on page 162 of a humorous poster – can be very significant. Consider also the following sentences, loosely taken from an episode of the television show *Community*:

I studied at Columbia.	*I studied in Columbia.*

That one change in preposition drastically changes the sentence, in part because it implies a different meaning for the noun "Columbia." In the sentence at the left, Columbia is an Ivy League university in New York. In the sentence at the right, Columbia is probably the capital of South Carolina.[46] Obviously, not every change in a preposition will imply a change in the noun to which it relates. Nevertheless, prepositions do make a difference. A payment due *to* a person is emphatically not the same as a payment due *from* that person. A clause requiring action *before* a specified event or time is very different from one requiring that action *at*, *after*, or *during* the same event or time. These differences are likely to be obvious to the drafter but occasionally the preposition chosen can be important in more subtle ways. For example, a clause authorizing a "regular associate *with* a law firm" to share compensation earned by the firm might be different from a clause authorizing "a regular associate *in* a law firm" to share compensation earned by the firm.[47] A written agreement referring to personal property "located *on* said land" might or might not include piping and other property located beneath the surface.[48] In short, pay close attention to every word, no matter how small.[49]

---

[46] Alternatively, it might be a location in any of 22 other U.S. states, each of which has a city, town, or other geographic division by that name.

[47] *See* In re Ferguson, 445 B.R. 744 (Bankr. N.D. Tex. 2011).

[48] Aaron Ferer & Sons v. Richfield Oil Corp., 150 F.2d 12 (9th Cir. 1945).

[49] *See* John F. Hilson, *Itsy Bitsy Its*, 6 THE TRANSACTIONAL LAWYER 1 (Oct. 2016).

Exercise 5-11

Cloud Computing, LLC approached Hedge Fund for a $5 million loan. In July 2017, before agreeing to provide the funds, Hedge Fund and Cloud Computing signed a term sheet that established the parties' contractual duties to each other during the loan approval process. Those duties included an obligation by Cloud Computing to pay a $500,000 fee "if, within 45 days from the Termination Date, Hedge Fund is prepared to make the Loan under substantially the same terms and conditions as set forth herein, but Cloud Computing fails to close with Hedge Fund due to the fact that the company has arranged any financing through another source." The term sheet defines Termination Date as November 15, 2017. What period of time does the phrase "within 45 days from the Termination Date" cover?

L. AVOID AMBIGUITY

Ambiguity exists when a word, phrase, clause, or entire provision can reasonably be interpreted in two or more mutually exclusive ways.[50] It is a matter of choice between or among different alternative meanings. Vagueness, in contrast, is a matter of degree, a shading of meaning.

For example, an offer to purchase "a red shirt" is vague. The requested color could fall along a wide spectrum from dark pink to crimson. An offer to purchase "a red pen" is similarly vague but is also ambiguous: it could mean a pen that is red in color or that contains red ink.

Vagueness is often acceptable, at least when one or both parties wants it. Thus, it is not uncommon to find in written agreements such phrases as "best efforts," "workmanlike manner," "good faith," "just cause," "material adverse change," "and "reasonable [fill in the blank]."[51] Proving that a vague standard has been satisfied or breached can be extremely difficult. Nevertheless, parties frequently outline their obligations and rights in such terms. Sometimes they rely on the prevailing practices in their trade or industry to provide context and meaning to a vague standard. Other times they simply prefer to trust each other rather than incur the

---

[50] Although not etymologically true, it might be helpful to think of the "bi" in "ambiguous" as meaning "two."

[51] Such vague standards are generally enforceable, although some courts require that they be accompanied by "objective criteria" or "clear guidelines." *See* Maestro West Chelsea SPE LLC v. Pradera Realty Inc., 954 N.Y.S.2d 819 (N.Y. Sup. Ct. 2012).

time and expense involved in trying to negotiate and draft something more specific.[52] Most often, they are prepared to allow the facts and circumstances to determine whether the standard has been satisfied.

Ambiguity, in contrast, is never acceptable.[53] It is the enemy of every drafter.[54] Unfortunately, it is also very common, perhaps because there are least three different types of ambiguity: semantic, contextual, and syntactic.

1. Semantic Ambiguity

Semantic ambiguity exists when a word or phrase has multiple meanings and more than one of those meanings could reasonably apply.[55] An agreement calling

---

[52] *See, e.g.*, B. Douglas Bernheim & Michael D. Whinston, *Incomplete Contracts and Strategic Ambiguity*, 88 AM. ECON. REV. 902, 903 (1998) (noting that transactions costs require many agreements to be somewhat incomplete).

[53] For a contrary view, see Christopher Honeyman, *In Defense of Ambiguity,* NEGOTIATION J. 81-86 (Jan. 1987), albeit the thrust of most of the argument made is in favor of vagueness, not ambiguity.

[54] One might be tempted to think that only unintentional ambiguity is a problem. But intentional ambiguity borders on deceit and can also cause problems for the drafter or the drafter's client. For an interesting decision showing why this is true, see United Rentals, Inc. v. RAM Holdings, Inc., 937 A.2d 810 (Del. Ch. Ct. 2007) (ruling that two clauses in an agreement were in conflict, and because one party knew during negotiations of the interpretation placed on them by the other party but said nothing, the forthright negotiator principle was applicable and the court would construe the contract to mean what the other party understood). One scholar has suggested that the underlying messages of the case are that lawyers might have a professional and ethical obligation to draft contracts clearly and that "conscious ambiguity" undermines those obligations. Gregory M. Duhl, *Conscious Ambiguity: Slaying Cerberus in the Interpretation of Contractual Inconsistencies,* 71 U. PITT. L. REV. 71 (2009). Note, the forthright negotiator principle is embodied in RESTATEMENT (SECOND) OF CONTRACTS §§ 20, 201, each of which uses a principle of comparative fault to deal with a misunderstanding or difference in meaning. If both parties are at equal fault (or neither is at fault), neither is bound by the meaning of the other, even if that means there is no contract. However, if one is more at fault than the other, the meaning of the other applies. For this purpose, fault includes having reason to know of the other's meaning.

[55] Semantic ambiguity can also arise from the use of what linguists refer to as "opaque" verbs. Opaque verbs typically deal with states of mind and the ambiguity they produce arises not from the meaning of the verb itself, but from the structure of the sentence in which they

for payment of 10,000 "dollars" could mean U.S. dollars, Canadian dollars, Australian dollars, or the similarly named currency of numerous other nations. The words "ounce" and "ton" – each commonly used in written agreements as a measure of goods to be bought and sold – also suffer from semantic ambiguity. The former might refer to an avoirdupois ounce (437.5 grains) or a troy ounce (480 grains). The latter might mean a long ton (2,240 lbs.), a short ton (2,000 lbs.), or a metric ton (2,204.6 lbs.).

Some very common words in the English language are semantically ambiguous. The word "since" is often used as a preposition denoting time or sequence but can also substitute for the conjunction "because," to suggest causation. In most situations, the intended meaning is clear. However, sometimes it is not, as in the following:

> I have felt better since I came home.

To avoid this problem, always use "because" – not "since" – to indicate causation and, when necessary to avoid confusion, use "after" or "ever since" to indicate chronological sequence:

> I felt better after I came home.

> I have been feeling better ever since I came home.

The word "may" is also syntactically ambiguous. It sometimes means "is permitted to" but in other uses is synonymous with "might" and indicates a possibility. In most cases, the author's meaning is obvious but occasionally either meaning would be a reasonable interpretation of what appears on the page. Consider the following:

---

are used. To illustrate, consider the following two sentences:
> Chris ate a cupcake.
> Chris wanted a cupcake.

The first, which linguists would label as "transparent," implies that a cupcake existed. The second, which is opaque, can be read two ways: (i) there was a particular cupcake and Chris wanted it; or (ii) Chris wanted something that falls within the category of things constituting a cupcake. Accordingly, the statement is ambiguous. Note, the more common reading is the latter, which does not imply the existence of a cupcake. *See* Jill C. Anderson, *Misreading Like a Lawyer: Cognitive Bias in Statutory Interpretation*, 127 HARV. L. REV. 1521 (2014).

> John may come home from school early today.

Transactional lawyers are well advised to use "might" – never "may" – to indicate possibility, and to use "may" or "is permitted to" to grant discretion authority.

The list continues. The word "bimonthly" traditionally meant every two months but has come to also mean twice per month (that is, to mean "semi-monthly"). An analogous fate has befallen the word "biweekly."[56] The word "day" can have a variety of meanings. In some situations it includes any day of the week; in others in encompasses only workdays, and therefore excludes weekend days and legal holidays. Beyond that, the word might mean a full 24-hour period, the daylight portion of a 24-hour period, or some small fraction thereof. As one court put it:

> Although "day" is a commonly used word, it has no fixed meaning. When we speak of a term of days, *e.g.*, the first hundred days of a presidential administration, we generally mean 24–hour days. Yet in other situations, *e.g.*, forty days and forty nights, we differentiate between days and nights. In terms of work or play – "I work five days a week" – people generally understand we are talking about increments of days. Sometimes days can embrace different fractions of days – "I went to the library every day this week" – and could mean ten minutes or 24–hours.[57]

For two reasons, ambiguity resulting from such semantically ambiguous words is a problem that a transactional lawyer can avoid. First, a lawyer will often be able to spot the ambiguity and either select a different word or add qualifying language to eliminate the confusion.[58] Second, usage of trade or context will often solve the problem.[59] For example, an agreement to buy and sell a specified number of ounces of a precious metal will almost assuredly mean troy ounces, because that is the usage in the precious metal trade. In the context of an agreement between two

---

[56]   *See* THE NEW SHORTER OXFORD ENGLISH DICTIONARY 228, 235 (1993).

[57]   *See* BSI Holdings, LLC. v. Arizona Dept. of Transp., 417 P.3d 782 (Ariz. 2018) (concluding that the word "day" in a statute was ambiguous).

[58]   There are also a few dozen English words that are contronyms: words with antonymous meanings. For example, the word "sanction" means both to punish and to approve. Other contronyms include "to cleave," "oversight" "to peruse," and "to weather." Unless context will remove all doubt, transactional lawyers should avoid these words as well.

[59]   *See* U.C.C. § 1-303(c), (d); RESTATEMENT (SECOND) OF CONTRACTS §§ 219–222.

domestic U.S. parties that calls for payment in "dollars" no doubt means payment in U.S. currency.[60]

Unfortunately, the semantic ambiguity of some other words and phrases is less obvious. One classic contracts case involved the semantic ambiguity of the word "chicken" in an agreement between a domestic seller and foreign buyer: did the word mean only young birds suitable for broiling and frying (as the foreign buyer thought) or also included older fowl best suited for stewing (as the domestic seller believed)?[61] Similarly, it might not occur to the parties or lawyers involved in documenting a transaction that there are multiple ways to measure distance on land (*i.e.*, by direct measure or by driving route).[62]

Semantic ambiguity can also result from a reference to something that might change over time. Such a reference might be intended to be static or dynamic. That is, it might mean the referent as it exists when the parties enter into the agreement or it might mean the referent at whatever later time is relevant. For example, a clause referring to "applicable law" might mean the law in effect when the agreement is signed or the law as it might later be amended.[63]

The problem of semantic ambiguity is probably most difficult to avoid when the ambiguity is latent: that is, when it arises from facts external to the transaction documents and unknown by the parties. A classic example of such a latent semantic ambiguity involved a contract for the sale of cotton to be transported from Bombay

---

[60] In contrast, if the agreement were between one party in Toronto and another in Detroit, the agreement would presumably require payment either in U.S. dollars or in Canadian dollars, but how are the parties – or a court – to know which is the correct currency?

[61] *See* Frigaliment Imp. Co. v. B.N.S. Int'l Sales Corp., 190 F. Supp. 116 (S.D.N.Y. 1960).

[62] *See* Vantage Tech. v. Cross, 17 S.W.3d 637 (Tenn. Ct. App. 1999). The case involved a covenant not to compete in an employment agreement. The court ruled that "because we are to construe covenants not to compete favorably to the employee," the 50-mile limit would be interpreted as the "shortest driving distance," not the radius. *Cf.* RESTATEMENT (SECOND) OF CONTRACTS § 207 (preferring interpretation that favors the public interest).

[63] *See, e.g.*, Kia Motors Am., Inc. v. Glassman Oldsmobile Saab Hyundai, Inc., 706 F.3d 733 (6th Cir. 2013). The case involved an automobile dealership agreement that permitted the manufacturer to establish new dealerships in the dealer's geographic area "only as permitted by applicable law." At the time the manufacturer and dealer executed the agreement, state law restricted a manufacturer's ability to establish new dealerships within six miles of an existing dealership. That law was later amended to expand the restricted area to nine miles. The court ruled that the agreement referred to the law in effect when the agreement was signed.

to Liverpool via the ship *Peerless*.[64] What the parties apparently did not know when they made their agreement was that two ships with that name existed and made that voyage, one departing in October and the other in December.

Exercise 5-12

The word "located" in the sentence below has semantic ambiguity: it could mean at least four different things. Identify those four possible meanings.

> Licensor shall not license the Software to any other business located in Idaho.

Exercise 5-13

The lease of commercial space in a shopping center to a supermarket contains the following clause.

> **Release.** Landlord shall not, without Tenant's prior written permission, permit any portion of the shopping center to be used for or occupied by any business that sells groceries. However, the use of up to **500 square feet of sales area** of any store within the shopping center for the sale of such items, incidental to the conduct of another business, is not a violation of this covenant.

Identify at least three different ways that "500 square feet of sales area" might be computed for the purposes of this clause.

Exercise 5-14

A guaranty agreement contains the following provision. Identify and explain why the provision is or might be ambiguous.

---

[64] Raffles v. Wichelhaus, 159 Eng. Rep. 375 (Ex. 1864).

> ***Choice of Law.*** This guaranty is governed by the laws of the State in which it is executed.

Exercise 5-15

A purchase and sale agreement contains the following provision. Identify and explain why this provision is ambiguous. Then rewrite the provision to remove the ambiguity.

> ***Setoff.*** Buyer has no right to withhold or setoff any amounts due hereunder except for and to the extent of any amounts owed by the Seller for Losses that may be suffered or incurred after the Closing Date.

Exercise 5-16

A bank's mortgage loan agreement with a developer of real property contains the following clause. Identify and explain all of the ways in which the provision is ambiguous. Then rewrite the provision to remove the ambiguity.

> ***Partial Release of Collateral.*** Borrower may, at any time, pay a pro-rata share of the outstanding indebtedness to obtain a corresponding, pro-rata release of the mortgaged property.

Exercise 5-17

Debtor borrows $100,000 from Bank and simultaneously executes a security agreement to provide collateral for the resulting debt. The security agreement defines the secured obligations as follows:

> "Secured Obligations" means Debtor's obligations on the promissory note of even date herewith and payable to Bank, along with all subsequent obligations of Debtor to Bank.

Explain how that language is or might become ambiguous.

2. Contextual Ambiguity

Contextual ambiguity can arise in three distinct ways. First, it is created when two or more statements or clauses in the same agreement or in related agreements are inconsistent. For example, consider an agreement that calls for "payment of $75,000 in six monthly installments of $15,000." Six payments of $15,000 total $90,000. So, does the agreement require payment of $75,000 or $90,000?

As with semantic ambiguity, contextual ambiguity can occasionally be latent. That is, the ambiguity might not be apparent on the face of the document and instead become evident only after reference to external facts. Consider a marital settlement agreement that requires the husband to pay alimony to the wife "until 2/20/20, Yasmine's 18th birthday." As it so happens, February 20, 2020 will be the 18th birthday of the couple's youngest daughter, Myriam. The couple's middle daughter, Yasmine, will turn 18 on August 1, 2015. So, which date controls? Put another way, did the couple err by misstating the date their daughter Yasmine would turn eighteen or did they err by confusing two of their daughters?[65]

Note, in both of the examples above, the conflicting statements were contained in a single sentence. More commonly, contextual ambiguity arises from the interaction of two different sentences. For example, a lease of office space might contain the following two provisions:

> Tenant shall maintain the Leased Premises.
>
> Landlord shall maintain the Building.

Assuming that the Leased Premises are within the Building, one might be tempted to conclude that Landlord is obligated to maintain only those portions of the Building not within the Leased Premises. Yet that is not what the second sentence actually says. So, how are these two statements to be reconciled?[66] Consider also

---

[65] *See* Hussein-Scott v. Scott, 298 P.3d 179 (Alaska 2013) (discussing various principles that could be used to resolve such an irreconcilable conflict between the two statements).

[66] A variety of interpretive rules can be used to resolve the conflict. A court might interpret the agreement against the drafter, *see* RESTATEMENT (SECOND) OF CONTRACTS § 206, or might prefer the more specific term over the more general, *id.* at § 203(c). Of course, it is not always easy to ascertain which term is more specific. Some jurisdictions give primacy to the provision that appears first in the writing. *See, e.g.*, DJ Mort., LLC v. Synovus Bank, 750 S.E.2d 797, 805 (Ga. Ct. App. 2013); Klever v. Klever, 52 N.W.2d 653, 658 (Mich. 1952). *See also* Helms v. LeMieux, 780 N.W.2d 878, 882 (Mich. Ct. App. 2009) (applying that rule to give to conflicting provisions in two different documents comprising a single agreement, and giving primacy to the document created first). *But cf.* In re Cook, 504 B.R.

this slightly simplified example from a loan agreement that prompted litigation:[67]

> ***Choice of Forum.*** All judicial proceedings arising out of or relating to this Agreement shall be brought in a court of competent jurisdiction in the District of Columbia. Nothing herein shall limit the right of Lender to bring proceedings against Borrower in the courts of any other jurisdiction.

Obviously, if the first sentence is, as it purports to be, a statement mandating a forum for the litigation of disputes, the second sentence is in conflict. A similar ambiguity arises if an agreement provides for arbitration of all disputes between the parties but also contains a clause on venue for some actions.[68] Are the parties permitted to litigate those specified actions in court?

To make matters worse, conflicting statements might not be in close proximity. Consider this other litigated example. A written agreement dated June 2014 between an insurance company and a broker, which provided for the broker to market and the insurance company to issue a new type of life insurance policy, contained the following terms:

> ***Term of Agreement.*** This Agreement will continue indefinitely, until terminated by either party upon thirty days written notification.
>
> ***Commitments.*** Insurer shall accept at least $100,000,000 of premiums for each twelve-month period from July 1, 2014 until June 30, 2017.

The first sentence purports to give either party the right to terminate at any time, upon thirty days notification. The latter purports to obligate the insurer for three

---

496 (8th Cir. 2014) (if terms in sequential agreements between the same parties conflict, the later agreement controls). *See also* Hussein-Scott v. Scott, 298 P.3d 179 (mentioning many of these principles).

An interpretive principle based on the placement of the conflicting terms in a writing is arbitrary and just as likely to yield a result contrary to the intentions or desires of the parties as it is to yield a result consistent with their intentions or desires. *See* ANTONIN SCALIA & BRYAN A. GARNER, READING LAW: THE INTERPRETATION OF LEGAL TEXTS 189 (2012) (criticizing this principle).

[67] KC Ravens LLC v. Nima Scrap, LLC, 2016 WL 1614174 (Kan. Ct. App. 2016).

[68] *See* Siljan, Inc. v. Filet Menu, Inc., 2007 WL 2429941(Cal. Ct. App. 2007).

years.   This conflict prevented summary judgment about what the contract requires.[69]

Exercise 5-18

The following provision in a guaranty agreement is ambiguous. Identify and explain what the ambiguity is. Then rewrite the provision to remove the ambiguity.

> *Arbitration.* Except as provided below, Lender and Guarantor shall arbitrate any Claim. "Claim" means any dispute, claim, or counterclaim, now or hereafter existing between Lender (including Lender's corporate parent, affiliates, subsidiaries, agents, employees, lawyers, officers, directors, successors, and assigns) and Borrower. A Claim includes, without limitation, anything arising out of, in connection with, or relating to this Agreement.

Exercise 5-19

Manufacturer entered into an agreement with Distributor pursuant to which Distributor became Manufacturer's exclusive sales representative for the States of Maine, New Hampshire, Vermont, Massachusetts, Connecticut, Rhode Island, and New York. The agreement, which refers to any such representative as "Agent," contains the following two clauses relating to commissions:

> Manufacturer shall pay Distributor, as full remuneration for Distributor's services and expenses, a 10% commission on all products sold by Distributor within the assigned territory

> When goods are sold by one Agent for delivery to a customer in another Agent's exclusive territory, the commission shall be divided and a 5% commission shall be paid to the Agent into whose territory the goods are shipped.

---

[69]   Life Plans, Inc. v. Security Life of Denver Ins. Co., 800 F.3d 343 (7th Cir. 2015).

Explain two ways in which these clauses create an ambiguity and then redraft one or both of them to remove the ambiguities.

The inconsistency that gives rise to contextual ambiguity need not be an actual conflict. In other words, the inconsistency need not be so stark that the two statements cannot both be true. It is sufficient to create contextual ambiguity if the language of one statement renders another statement superfluous or irrelevant, in seeming violation of the interpretive principle that each provision should have independent meaning.[70]

For example, one case involved loan documents that listed several different events that triggered a guarantor's liability. One event was the creation of any voluntary lien on the collateral. Another was any "transfer" of the collateral, a term defined in the agreement to include the creation of any lien, whether voluntarily or involuntarily. Obviously, the term regarding transfer seems to render the term regarding voluntary liens superfluous. The court concluded that the agreement therefore contained contextual ambiguity that prevented summary judgment on whether the imposition of mechanics' liens on the collateral – something that occurred involuntarily – was sufficient to trigger the guarantor's liability.[71]

The second way in which contextual ambiguity can be created is through a glaring omission. For example, if a sales agreement refers to property listed on an attached sheet and no sheet is attached, it might be unclear to which goods the agreement refers.

Finally, contextual ambiguity can be created through the juxtaposition of terms. Put simply, context matters. Courts have long recognized that the meaning of words and terms can be affected by those around them. Indeed, this recognition underlies the classic interpretive canons of *noscitur a sociis* and *ejusdem generis*.

The former, *noscitur a sociis*, states that a word is known by the company it keeps. That is, a word will be given a more precise meaning by the neighboring words with which it is associated. Thus, for example, a Master Sale and Purchase Agreement providing that the buyer assumed product liability claims caused by "accidents or incidents" after closing, had to be interpreted so that the words "accidents and "incidents" have different meanings, "but that these meanings should

---

[70]   *See* discussion about avoiding repetition, beginning *supra* page 153.

[71]   *See* CP III Rincon Towers, Inc. v. Cohen, 666 F. App'x 46 (2d Cir. 2016).

be conceptually related."[72] The latter, *ejusdem generis*, discussed above on page 145, applies when a specific enumeration of items is accompanied by a general catchall phrase. For example, a sales agreement might include a clause excusing the seller "in the event that a fire, flood, tornado, or other unanticipated event interferes with production." The canon calls for the catchall phrase – "other unanticipated event" – to be interpreted to include only things of the same genre or with the same characteristics as the specific items listed.

Unfortunately, the juxtaposition of terms can just as easily create ambiguity as it can help resolve it. Consider the following clause, which appears in the agreement between Uber and its drivers:

> ***Dispute Resolution.*** You and Company agree that any dispute, claim or controversy arising out of or relating to this Agreement will be settled by binding arbitration. You acknowledge and agree that you and Company are each waiving the right to a trial by jury or to participate as a plaintiff or class member in any purported class action or representative proceeding. Further, unless both you and Company otherwise agree in writing, the arbitrator may not consolidate more than one person's claims, and may not otherwise preside over any form of any class or representative proceeding.

In isolation, the middle sentence in blue appears to be a waiver of a right to bring or participate in a class action. However, because the clause was sandwiched between two sentences dealing with arbitration, a court ruled that the waiver was limited to arbitration proceedings and did not apply to actions as to which arbitration had been waived.[73]

Similarly, consider the following clause from a commercial lease:

---

[72] In re Motors Liquidation Co., 447 B.R. 142, 148 (Bankr. S.D.N.Y. 2011). For other recent cases applying this canon when interpreting a contract, see In re Meridian Sunrise Village, LLC, 2014 WL 909219 (W.D. Wash. 2014); Severstal Dearborn, LLC v. Praxair, Inc., 899 F. Supp. 2d 667 (E.D. Mich. 2012).

[73] Meyer v. Kalanick, 185 F. Supp. 3d 448 (S.D.N.Y. 2016).

> ***Alterations.*** After Tenant's Initial Build-Out, Tenant shall not make any alterations involving structural, weight bearing changes, changes which affect any building systems, or changes to the storefront . . . without securing Landlord 's written consent, which consent shall not be unreasonably withheld, conditioned or delayed. After Tenant's Initial Build-Out, Tenant may make all other alterations or additions, including, without limitation, non-weight bearing alterations to the Premises as Tenant may desire . . . without obtaining Landlord's written consent. **Any alterations or additions made by Tenant will be made in compliance with all applicable laws, in a good workmanlike manner without cost to Landlord.**

The third sentence (in blue) appears to refer to all alterations. However, the prior two sentences both refer to alterations made "after Tenant's Initial Build-Out." Accordingly, this created ambiguity as to whether the third sentence is similarly limited.[74]

Exercise 5-20

Determine how the following clause in a purchase agreement for genetically modified seed – in particular, the third sentence (in blue) – is contextually ambiguous.

> ***Warranties.*** Seller warrants that all products sold have been labeled as required under applicable state and federal seed laws and conform to the description on the label within standard tolerances or variations. No claim shall be asserted against Seller unless Buyer reports to Seller, promptly after discovery (not to exceed thirty days), any condition that might lead to a complaint. **All claims must be asserted within one year from the date of acceptance of the product.** Buyer's exclusive remedy for any claim or loss, including, without limitation, claims resulting from breach of warranty, breach of contract, tort, strict liability or negligence, shall be limited to repayment of the amount of the purchase price.

---

[74] Kinney Building Assocs., LLC v. 7-Eleven, Inc., 2016 WL 2855063 (D.N.J. 2016).

3. Syntactic Ambiguity

Syntactic ambiguity is probably the most common type of ambiguity, and transactional lawyers must be on constant vigil for it. It is a disease that infects all kinds of written agreements and, judging by its frequency, appears almost epidemic.

Generally speaking, syntactic ambiguity arises from sentence structure, that is, from the manner in which a word or phrase relates linguistically to the other words or phrases in the sentence. Although the precise causes of syntactic ambiguity are legion, the two most common culprits are probably conjunctions and modifiers.

The conjunction "and" can create ambiguity. Consider, for example, an offer to buy "ten black and white dresses." It could refer to: (i) ten bi-colored dresses (each both black and white); (ii) ten dresses, some of which are black and some of which are white; or even, albeit less likely, (iii) twenty dresses, ten of each color.

The conjunction "or" can also cause a problem. The word can be exclusive (either . . . or) or inclusive (and/or), and context does not always make it clear which is intended.[75] A phrase containing both "and" and "or" can be even more problematic. For example, a phrase in the structure of "if X and Y or Z" might mean "if (X and Y) or Z" or it might mean "if X and (Y or Z)." Often there is no way to discern what the author meant.

For example, one case involved a lease that contained the following clause:

> In the event that Lessor's building is damaged by fire or other casualty **and** Lessor elects not to restore such building, **or** Lessor elects to demolish the building, Lessor may terminate the Lease.

---

[75] That the ambiguity of "or" is heightened somewhat when it is part of a negative phrase (*e.g.*, "not x or y"). Consider the statement "ninety percent of students failed math or English." That statement is ambiguous because it could mean that: (i) 90% percent failed at least one of those courses; or (ii) 90% failed one and only one of those courses. Adding the word "either" suggests the latter meaning but does not fully remove the ambiguity.

Now consider the statement "ninety percent of students did not pass math or English." That could mean that: (i) 90% failed at least one of those courses; (ii) 90% failed both of those courses; or (iii) 90% failed one and only one of those courses. Moreover, adding the word "either" does not really remove the problem. The statement "ninety percent of students did not pass either math or English" is still ambiguous and could have any of the three meanings noted above.

Although no casualty occurred, the landlord decided to demolish the building and terminate the lease. A trial court's summary judgment for the landlord was reversed on appeal because the language is ambiguous.[76]

The misuse of modifiers is likely the most common cause of syntactic ambiguity. In general, a modifying word or phrase modifies whatever immediately follows it (or, if nothing follows it, whatever immediately precedes it). Consequently, the placement of a modifier affects the meaning of the sentence. For example, consider the following sentence, which contains a modifying phrase (in blue):

> The chief financial officer shall present a recommendation about payment of the funds **to the president.**

Does the sentence really, as its structure suggests, refer to a payment of funds to the president (a recommendation concerning which the CFO is to present to someone)? Perhaps the author intended to refer to a recommendation made to the president (concerning payment to someone). If so, the phrase "to the president" should have been positioned immediately after the verb it modifies:

> The chief financial officer shall present **to the president** a recommendation about payment of the funds.

When a modifying word or phrase follows a list of nouns or verbs, the resulting ambiguity is even more of a problem. In such a situation, it is often unclear whether each item in the list is modified or only the last. For example, a sales agreement might identify the property to be sold as:

> . . . all inventory, equipment, accounts, and general intangibles **used in or arising out of the operation of the Business.**

Does the blue phrase modify only "general intangibles" or also the other nouns? This could matter greatly if the seller had multiple lines of business, only one of which was being sold and fell within the agreement's definition of the capitalized term.

---

[76]   BL Partners Group, L.P. v. Interbroad, LLC, 2017 WL 2591473 (Pa. Super. Ct. 2017).

Exercise 5-21

The following provision is ambiguous in two ways. Identify and explain what the ambiguities are and how they arose. Then rewrite the provision to remove the ambiguities.

> **Bonus Eligibility.** Employer shall pay an annual bonus of $2,000 to supervisory and salaried employees.

Exercise 5-22

The following provision has an ambiguity. Identify and explain what the ambiguity is and how it arose. Then rewrite the provision to remove the ambiguity. For the purpose of this Exercise and those that follow, assume that any capitalized word is defined elsewhere in the agreement and that its meaning is not ambiguous.

> **Rights upon Default.** Upon default under this Agreement or under the Loan Agreement, Lender may sell the Collateral or seek payment of the Secured Obligation.

Exercise 5-23

Pursuant to a written agreement, Tenant has leased retail space in a mall that contains space for three anchor stores. The agreement contains the following term:

> **Termination.** Tenant may terminate this Lease if at least 100,000 square feet of Floor Area is not being operated on any one of the Anchor Store Areas.

Explain how the provision is ambiguous. Then rewrite the provision to remove the ambiguity.

Exercise 5-24

A settlement agreement provides, in part, as follows:

> ***Release.*** All claims for the avoidance or recovery of transfers in the amount of $59,999.99 or less are released.

Determine how the clause is ambiguous.

Exercise 5-25

The following provision has an ambiguity. Identify and explain what the ambiguity is and how it arose. Then rewrite the provision to remove the ambiguity.

> ***Use of Collateral.*** Borrower shall not sell, lease, license, or encumber, outside the ordinary course of business, all or any part of the Collateral.

Exercise 5-26

The following provision in a purchase agreement has an ambiguity. Identify and explain what the ambiguity is and how it arose. Then rewrite the provision to remove the ambiguity.

> ***Representations.*** Buyer acknowledges that Buyer has not relied upon any representations not set forth or incorporated in this agreement or previously made in writing.

Exercise 5-27

A guaranty contains the following provision. Identify and explain why this provision is ambiguous. Then rewrite the provision to remove the ambiguity.

> **Waiver of Subrogation.** Until the Obligations have been paid in full, Guarantor waives any right of subrogation, reimbursement, indemnification, and contribution, arising from the existence or performance of this Guaranty, and waives any benefit of, and any right to participate in, any security now or hereafter held by Lender.

Exercise 5-28

A loan agreement defines default, in part, as follows:

> **Default.** * * * the failure by the Borrower to pay any installment of principal, interest, or other payments required under the Note when due.

Determine how the clause is ambiguous and then redraft the clause to avoid the ambiguity.

Exercise 5-29

The following provision in an intercreditor agreement among two groups of lenders is ambiguous in two ways. Identify and explain what the ambiguities are and how they arose. Then rewrite the provision to remove the ambiguity.

> **Allocation of Expenses.** The expenses of the Collateral Agent shall be borne by the Senior Lenders and the Junior Lenders in equal shares.

Exercise 5-30

The following provision in a guaranty agreement is ambiguous in multiple ways. Identify and explain what the ambiguities are and how they arose. Then rewrite the provision to remove the ambiguity.

> ***Scope of Guaranty.*** Guarantor hereby guarantees payment of $500,000 of the principal balance of the Loan together with any and all accrued and unpaid interest thereon.

Exercise 5-31

The following provision has multiple ambiguities. Identify and explain what the ambiguities are and how they arose. Then rewrite the provision to remove them.

> ***Assignment.*** Tenant may assign its rights under this Lease to any Affiliate of Tenant that has a Net Worth of at least $1,000,000.

M. DOUBLE-CHECK ... EVERYTHING

1. Mathematical Formulas

Sometimes a contract term simply does not work the way it was intended. For example, a computational formula might simply be wrong in some way, with the result that it yields a result that neither party intended.[77] Consider a multi-year lease of office space that requires the tenant to pay the landlord Annual Rent and also provides:

> Base Rent is $120,000 per year. During the first year of this Agreement, Annual Rent is the Base Rent. On the first anniversary of the Agreement, and on each subsequent anniversary during the Lease Term, the Annual Rent will be the Base Rent times the percentage change in the Consumer Price Index for the previous year.

---

[77] For an example of a computational mistake that cost more than $10 million, see Marathon Funding, LLC v. Paramount Pictures Corp., 2013 WL 785915 (Cal. Ct. App. 2013) (studio's agreement with actor Tommy Lee Jones to make *No Country for Old Men,* which agreement was supposed to provide for bonuses if either the domestic box office receipts reached a certain level or worldwide box office receipts reached twice the domestic level, was mistakenly drafted to provide for bonuses if worldwide box office receipts, when multiplied by two, reached the levels prescribed for domestic box office bonuses).

There are at least five problems with this language. First, the rent adjustment should probably occur on the anniversary of the commencement of the Lease Term, not the anniversary of the Agreement. In other words, if the parties signed the lease on June 13 for occupancy beginning on August 1, the adjustment should occur in subsequent years on August 1, not June 13.

Second, the phrase "for the previous year" is ambiguous. It might mean the previous twelve months or the prior calendar year. For example, if the Lease Term begins on August 1, 2015, and rent is to be adjusted on August 1, 2016, the phrase might mean that the adjustment is to be based on the change in the Consumer Price Index from August 1, 2015 to July 31, 2016 or that the adjustment is to be based on the change in the Consumer Price Index for the calendar year 2015.

Third, there is more than one Consumer Price Index. In fact, the Bureau of Labor Statistics publishes hundreds of Consumer Price Indexes each month. Some of these indexes are for different population groups, some are for different geographic areas, and some are for different categories of products or services. For many of these indexes, the Bureau publishes both seasonally adjusted data and data that is not seasonally adjusted. Thus, the reference to "the Consumer Price Index" is ambiguous.

Fourth, the parties undoubtedly intended that the adjustment be based on the previous year's rent, not on the Base Rent. The significance of this can be seen over time.

	Change in CPI for previous year	Annual Rent Under Clause as Drafted	Annual Rent As Intended
Year 1		$120,000	$120,000
Year 2	4%	$124,800	$124,800
Year 3	3%	$123,600	$128,544
Year 4	5%	$126,000	$134,971
Year 5	3%	$123,600	$139,020
Year 6	5%	$126,000	$145,971
Year 7	4%	$124,800	$151,810

Fifth, instead of *increasing* the rent based on the change in the Consumer Price Index, the clause *sets* the rent based on the percentage change in the index. As a result, the rent would decrease drastically after the first year:

	Change in CPI for previous year	Annual Rent Under Clause as Drafted	Annual Rent As Intended
Year 1		$120,000	$120,000
Year 2	4%	$4,800	$124,800
Year 3	3%	$3,600	$128,544
Year 4	5%	$6,000	$134,971
Year 5	3%	$3,600	$139,020
Year 6	5%	$6,000	$145,971
Year 7	4%	$4,800	$151,810

A careful transactional lawyer must double-check computational formulas to make sure they produce the result intended. In other words, input data, follow the contractual language to generate an output, and then compare that output to what the parties intend. The difficulty in doing this is the same difficulty that confronts anyone trying to edit his or her own work: the writer knows what was intended and, unless careful, will read the words as saying the same thing. A careful drafter fights that tendency and reads the drafted language critically and with an open mind. One technique that often helps in this regard is to complete a draft, put it aside for a while, and then re-read it at a later time.

Exercise 5-32

Redraft the clause on page 184 so that it is correct.

Exercise 5-33

You are counsel to Bank, which is preparing to make an $8.7 million loan to Developer. Guarantor, one of the principal owners of Developer, will be guarantying half the debt. An initial draft of the guaranty agreement provides in part as follows:

> If Developer fails at any time to pay any part or all of the
> Liabilities when due, whether by acceleration or otherwise,
> Guarantor, upon written demand of Bank, shall pay or perform the
> Liabilities. Notwithstanding the foregoing, the obligations of
> Guarantor herein shall be limited to fifty percent of the outstanding
> balance of principal and accrued interest under the Note; provided,
> however, that any reduction of the Liabilities whether prior to or after
> the occurrence of an Event of Default shall be applied first to that
> portion of the Liabilities not guaranteed by Guarantor hereunder.

In reviewing this language, you realize there is a problem: the limiting language does not specify when or how often the computation is to be made. During the life of the loan, the "outstanding balance of principal and accrued interest" will change daily, as payments are made and interest accrues. Is the computation to be performed each day? If so, how does that square with the last clause of the second sentence? If not, when and how often is the computation to be performed? Redraft the language so that it is clear how the clause works.

2. Anticipating Future Events

A similar problem occurs when subsequent events are not what the drafter anticipated they would be and the language used does not contemplate the situation that has arisen. Yet this is precisely what lawyers are paid to do: to imagine what might occur and draft accordingly. Returning to the prior example, consider what might happen if, during the lease term, the Bureau of Labor Statistics stopped publishing the Consumer Price Indexes or replaced them with some other group of indexes. How would the rent escalator clause apply?[78] What if a loan agreement pegs the interest rate to the London Interbank Offered Rate (LIBOR), a benchmark

---

[78] One of us worked on a case in which a rent escalator clause was tied to changes in the Wholesale Price Index. This was problematic not only because there were numerous WPIs, but because during the lease term the Bureau replaced all of the WPIs with the Producer Price Indexes. The tenants argued that because the WPI was no longer computed, rent should no longer be adjusted.

commonly used in many commercial loan agreements, but that benchmark ceases to be published?[79] Now consider this example.

> Bank's deposit account agreement with Depositor provides that "[a]ny fees or expenses (including attorney's fees and expenses) the Bank incurs in responding to legal process may be charged against any account you maintain with the Bank." Bank responds to legal process, thereby incurring substantial attorney's fees. The fees incurred far exceed the balance credited to Depositor's deposit account. Does the clause limit Bank's recourse to the deposit account or is Depositor personally liable for the portion of the fees in excess of the deposit account balance? Put another way, did the lawyer who drafted the agreement consider the possibility that the deposit account might not have a balance sufficient to cover the fees incurred?[80]

---

[79] During the financial crisis that began in 2008, many questioned whether LIBOR reflected the rate at which banks were actually able to borrow in the London market. Indeed, there were indications that the rate was artificially depressed to mask the true financial condition of some of the member banks. As a result, the Financial Conduct Authority revealed in the summer of 2017 that LIBOR will be phased out by the end of 2021. Even before that announcement, financial regulators urged banks to revise their transaction documents to deal with the possibility that LIBOR becomes unavailable or impracticable. The following is representative language:

> In the event that any change in market conditions or any law, regulation, treaty, or directive, or any change therein or in the interpretation of application thereof, shall at any time after the date hereof, in the reasonable opinion of any Lender, make it unlawful or impractical for such Lender to fund or maintain LIBOR Rate Loans or to continue such funding or maintaining, or to determine or charge interest rates at the LIBOR Rate, such Lender shall give notice of such changed circumstances to Agent and Borrower and Agent promptly shall transmit the notice to each other Lender and (y) in the case of any LIBOR Rate Loans of such Lender that are outstanding, the date specified in such Lender's notice shall be deemed to be the last day of the Interest Period of such LIBOR Rate Loans, and interest upon the LIBOR Rate Loans of such Lender thereafter shall accrue interest at the rate then applicable to Base Rate Loans, and (z) Borrower shall not be entitled to elect the LIBOR Option until such Lender determines that it would no longer be unlawful or impractical to do so.

[80] *See* Gunderson v. Wells Fargo Bank, 2010 WL 2636162 (Tex. Ct. App. 2010).

Exercise 5-34

Lender's counsel drafts a $2.7 million promissory note for a prospective loan to Borrower. The note requires Borrower to pay monthly interest, at a rate of 6% per annum, for two years and then to make a final balloon payment of the entire principal balance on the second anniversary of the note. The note further provides:

> Upon any default in payment, Lender may accelerate the payments so that the entire debt becomes immediately due and payable. Thereafter, interest will accrue on all unpaid amounts at a rate of 18% per annum.

Why might this language not do what Lender's counsel intends?

Exercise 5-35

Attorney has a contingent-fee agreement with Client. The agreement requires Client to pay Attorney "30% of the recovered judgment awarded in Client's breach of contract action against Defendant." Identify at least two different reasons why this language might become problematic for Attorney.

Exercise 5-36

Author sold to Movie Studio the film rights to Author's trilogy of books. The sales agreement requires Movie Studio to pay Author "5% of the Gross Receipts of the first motion picture" based on each book. How might this language become problematic for Author?

Exercise 5-37

Pursuant to a written agreement, Supplier is to provide printers and copiers for Buyer's office for five years. The agreement, which requires Supplier to maintain the equipment and provide toner as needed, fixes a price of $0.008 for each black-and-white image processed and $0.04 for each color image processed. The agreement further provides as follows:

> Supplier may increase the Cost Per Image up to 10% annually for each year beyond the initial 12–month period.

Explain why the provision is or might become problematic.

Exercise 5-38

A purchase and sale agreement for the assets of an automobile manufacturer contains the following provision.

> ***Liabilities Assumed.*** Buyer hereby assumes all liabilities arising under express written warranties of Seller provided in connection with the sale of any motor vehicles or motor vehicle parts manufactured by Seller prior to the Closing. Buyer does not assume any liability arising out of, related to, or in connection with: (i) any implied warranty made in connection with the sale of any motor vehicle or motor vehicle parts manufactured by Seller prior to the Closing; (ii) any consumer protection statute that provides a consumer with remedies in addition to or different from those specified in Seller's express warranties; or (iii) any tort or products liability arising from the sale or manufacture of any motor vehicle or motor vehicle parts prior to the Closing.

How might the distinction drawn in this clause among different types of claims become problematic?

Exercise 5-39

A draft lease of commercial property for use as a drug store provides for monthly rental equal to $10,000 plus 2.75% of the "gross sales" of the business. The lease defines "gross sales" as "the aggregate of all retail sales of every kind, type, and description, and services performed for patrons made in, upon, or from the demised premises." How might this formula for computing rent be problematic for the tenant? Put another way, what might the tenant sell – either now or in the future – for which this formula would be inappropriate? What other interpretive problems might arise in applying this language?

Exercise 5-40

An agreement for the sale of a business requires the seller to use its best efforts to obtain consent to the transaction from third parties ("Third Party Consents"). It also includes the following express condition to the transaction:

> **Condition.** The obligations of the parties are conditioned upon receipt of all Third Party Consents prior to the Closing Date.

What is the problem with this clause? How should the clause be rewritten to remove the problem?

Exercise 5-41

A commercial lease contains the following provisions. Why might this clause not work as the landlord desires? Rewrite the provisions to remove the ambiguity.

> **Basic Rent.** The Basic Rent for the period January 1, 2015 through December 31, 2015 is $96,000, which Tenant shall pay in advance on or before January 1, 2015.
>
> **No Return of Basic Rent.** If this Lease is terminated prior to the Expiration Date for any reason other than pursuant to Article 7 (casualty), Tenant will not be entitled to the return of any Basic Rent paid in advance and covering a period beyond the date on which the Lease is terminated.

Exercise 5-42

Bank is planning to make a large loan to Developer to finance the acquisition and development of a new residential subdivision. The standard form deed of trust describes the collateral as follows:

> ***Conveyance and Grant.*** . . . all of Grantor's right, title, and interest
> in the following described real property, together with all existing or
> subsequently erected or affixed buildings, improvements and fixtures;
> all easements, rights of way, and appurtenances; all water, water
> rights, and ditch rights (including stock in utilities with ditch and
> irrigation rights); and all other rights, royalties, and profits relating to
> the real property, including without limitation all minerals, oil, gas,
> geothermal, and similar matters.

If Developer defaults prior to completion of the project, Bank wants to have
the right, if it is the high bidder at the trustee sale, to take over and
complete the project. What might this language fail to encumber, thereby
frustrating Bank's plans?

Exercise 5-43

Homeowner is suing Contractor and several subcontractors for damages
relating to the construction of Homeowner's house. To finance the
litigation, Friend loans $200,000 to Homeowner, who signs a promissory
note promising to repay the debt "by the earlier of: (i) three years from the
date hereof; or (ii) settlement of the lawsuit by and between Homeowner
and Contractor, et al." What is the problem with this language?

3. Cross-References

A more mundane thing that must be double-checked is each cross-reference in
the agreement. Consider the following clause in a sales agreement:

> Except as provided in § 3.2, Seller makes no warranty of any
> kind.

The drafter must verify that: (i) the exception to which the clause is supposed to
refer is, in fact, contained in section 3.2; and (ii) the agreement contains no other
exception that this clause should also reference. A drafter can avoid the need to
check cross-references, while simultaneously ensuring that no cross-reference is
inaccurate, by making them more vague. For example, the clause above could be
rephrased as follows:

> Except as provided below, Seller makes no warranty of any kind.

or

> Except as otherwise provided in this Agreement, Seller makes no warranty of any kind.

The trouble with both of these approaches is that they create room for one party to argue that any one or more of numerous clauses in fact create an exception.[81] In short, while imprecision can remove some problems it merely creates the potential for others. Do not follow this path . . . it leads to the dark side.

N. PUTTING IT ALL TOGETHER

Exercise 5-44

You are drafting a commercial lease on behalf of Landlord. The form that you begin with has the following clause:[82]

> *Notification.* Any notification required or permitted under this Agreement will be sufficient if sent by United States certified mail, return receipt requested, addressed as follows:
>
> | If to Landlord: | If to Tenant: |
> | --- | --- |
> | 110 Brookline Avenue | 3 Yawkey Way |
> | Boston, MA 02215 | Boston, MA 02215 |
> | landlord@gmail.com | tenant@comcast.net |
> | copy to Law Firm | copy to Attorney |
>
> Each party has the right from time to time to change the place notice is to be given under this paragraph by written notification thereof to the other party.

---

[81]   The first alternative, by distinguishing between what appears above and what appears below, might also present a problem if something intended as an exception is placed before the clause.

[82]   A notification clause very similar to this was the focus of Exercise 4-19.

Identify all the problems with this clause and then rewrite the clause to avoid those problems.

Exercise 5-45

You are preparing a trust agreement. The draft contains the following clause. Identify all the problems with the clause and then rewrite the clause to avoid those problems. The clause is available in electronic format on the web page for the book: www.transactionalskills.com.

Residue of Estate.
A. The residue of the Trust shall be distributed as follows:
    1. Russell Richardson shall receive a 20% share of the residue of the Trust if he survives settlor by forty-five days.
    2. Jesse E. Richardson shall receive a 20% share of the residue of the Trust if he survives settlor by forty-five days.
    3. Kevin Rhodes shall receive a 30% share of the residue of the Trust if he survives settlor by forty-five days.
    4. Kelly Rhodes shall receive a 30% share of the residue of the trust if she survives Settlor by forty-five days.
B. If any beneficiary of the residue of the settlor's trust fails to survive distribution of his/her share, the percentage of the residue that said beneficiary was to have received will be added to the other residuary beneficiaries' shares of the trust's residue in proportion to the then percentages applicable to all beneficiaries entitled to the residue at that time. This gift will therefore pass to the other beneficiaries of the residue of the trust in proportion to their other interests in the residue.

Exercise 5-46

Review sections 1, 2, 5, 9, 10, 12, 13, and 14 of the form commercial lease included in Exercise 3-1. Identify the problem or problems with each such section and then rewrite each section to avoid those problems.

Exercise 5-47

You represent a Client, which operates a small business. Client maintains a web site, which it uses primarily to attract customers (rather than to conduct transactions with customers). Client is contemplating hiring Marketing Consultant to redesign the web site. In connection with this work, Marketing Consultant will monitor the web site, collect data about those using it (*e.g.*, their IP addresses, how long they are on the site, what pages they examine), and then use that data to determine how to modify the web site to better appeal to and expand Client's customer base. Client is naturally concerned that Marketing Consultant not use the data collected to aid any business that competes with Client. However, because the agreement between Client and Marketing Consultant will be for only a short period of time and will represent a very small portion of Marketing Consultant's business, it is unrealistic to expect that the agreement will contain a clause prohibiting Marketing Consultant from entering into agreements with or performing services for a competitor of Client. Accordingly, Client wants the agreement to contain a confidentiality clause prohibiting Marketing Consultant from disclosing to anyone else the information it collects or otherwise obtains about Client or Client's customers.

Marketing Consultant's sales representative proposed the following language for incorporation into the agreement between Client and Marketing Consultant:

> Marketing Consultant uses the data it collects from client campaigns solely for the limited purpose of providing the services necessary to support and operationalize those campaigns for the advertiser, and for the operation, improvement, and quality control of our services generally. Marketing Consultant does not and will not sell or share any of the data it collects about Client's audience, customers, or website visitors with any other advertiser or third party.

A. Critique the proposed language. Determine what problems, it any, it has.

B. Redraft the language to remove all the problems identified in Part A.

Exercise 5-48

You are counsel to a bank that makes student loans. The form loan agreement that the bank currently uses provides that the loan payments are to commence "at the end of the ninth month following the month in which Student ceases to be matriculated." The agreement does not currently define what "matriculated" means. You are, of course, aware that some students: (i) take classes part time; (ii) take time off from school before completing their degree; and (iii) after receiving their degree, enroll in courses, which might or might not be in pursuit of another degree.
A. Determine under what circumstances loan payments should commence.
B. Draft for inclusion in the form agreement a definition of "matriculated" that will give efficacy to your answer to Part A.

Exercise 5-49

University, which is located in the United States, operates a summer abroad program in Italy. Students from University as well as from other domestic and international colleges attend the program. University has, until now, staffed the program with faculty who teach full time (*i.e.,* both fall and spring terms) at University's campus in the United States. University pays such faculty as adjuncts, on a per credit basis, for teaching in the Italy program and reimburses their expenses in traveling to and from and staying in Italy.

University has been negotiating with a small number of other domestic colleges to participate more fully in the Italy program, by allowing those who provide at least ten students to: (i) designate one of their own full-time faculty members to teach in the program the following year; and (ii) receive one-fifth of the profit from the program that is attributable to the portion of the students in the program that come from the college.

University's counsel has prepared a rough draft of a written agreement that could be used between University and any such other college (designated in the draft as "Home School"). An excerpt from that draft is reproduced below. Review the excerpt carefully (assume terms in initial capital letters are defined appropriately elsewhere in the draft). Identify all the problems with the excerpt, including: (i) the extent to which, if any, it is not consistent with the description provided above; and (ii) errors or ambiguities in the drafting. Then, rewrite the excerpt to eliminate those problems. The excerpt is available in electronic format on the web page for the book: www.transactionalskills.com.

ITALY PROGRAM PARTICIPATION AGREEMENT
(excerpt)

FACULTY EXCHANGE

As part of this affiliation, Home School faculty will be eligible to teach in the Italy Program. This eligibility will be based on Home School student enrollment. For each ten Home School students who participate in the Italy Program, Home School may designate a Home School faculty member to teach in the Italy program. The designated Home School faculty member will be eligible to teach in the next available Italy program session. This Home School faculty member will teach as an adjunct instructor, and University will provide the compensation and travel expenses that University faculty who teach in the Italy program receive.

Home School may designate only full-time faculty to teach in the Italy program. Furthermore, designated Home School faculty members, and their proposed courses, must be approved by the University faculty. Home School faculty members participating in the Italy program shall cooperate reasonably with the Italy Program Director and Academic Dean in preparing for and contributing to the Italy Program, and shall participate actively in all mandatory program activities.

TUITION RETURN:

Home School students will enroll in the Italy program as visiting students, and will pay Italy Program tuition directly to University. University and Home School agree, however, that subject to the following provisions, University will return a portion of Home School student tuition to Home School.

During each Italy Program session in which one or more Home School students participate, University will timely determine the amount of any tuition revenue that remains after all Italy program costs and expenses for that session are deducted. University will have exclusive authority to determine the costs and expenses of each Italy program. From any tuition revenue remaining after costs and expenses are deducted, University will return 20% of Home School student tuition. This amount will be prorated for the number of Home School students within total Italy enrollment. For example, if three Home School students participate in a Italy Program that has a total enrollment of thirty students, University will return 20%

of 3/30th of any tuition revenue that remains after program costs and expenses are deducted.

This tuition return provision does not guarantee that Italy program tuition revenue will exceed costs and expenses in any specific program session. This provision also will not apply to any Home School student who leaves the Italy program prior to its scheduled conclusion.

Exercise 5-50

You represent Retailer, which sells goods both in stores and online. Retailer has approached Web Analytics, LLC for assistance in redesigning Retailer's web site. To do this, Web Analytics will first analyze how Retailer's customers interact with Retailer's web site (*e.g.*, which pages they visit, for how long, how they navigate from page to page, and what they buy). Web Analytics will then propose changes to make the site more accessible to users and more likely to generate sales, particularly of items with the highest profit margins. The parties have negotiated a written agreement covering these services.

Retailer is concerned, however, that Web Analytics will, in the process of providing its services, learn information about Retailer's business which, if disclosed to competitors, could greatly damage Retailer. Accordingly, Retailer wants Web Analytics to agree not to disclosure confidential information acquired during the performance of the services agreement.

Web Analytics has sent the form Non-Disclosure Agreement below, which it has used with its other clients. Review the agreement. Identify all the problems with the agreement, including: (i) the extent to which, if any, it might fail to provide the protection that Retailer seeks; and (ii) errors or ambiguities in the drafting. Then, rewrite the agreement to eliminate those problems. The agreement is available in electronic format on the web page for the book: www.transactionalskills.com.

NON-DISCLOSURE AGREEMENT

This Non-disclosure Agreement (the "Agreement") is entered into by and between _____ ("Disclosing Party") and Web Analytics, LLC, 610 W. Main Street, Spokane, WA 99201 ("Receiving Party") for the purpose of preventing the unauthorized disclosure of Confidential Information as defined below. The parties agree to enter into a confidential relationship with respect to the disclosure of certain proprietary and confidential information ("Confidential Information").

1. For purposes of this Agreement, "Confidential Information" shall include all information or material in any form emanating, directly or indirectly, from Disclosing Party, concerning or relating to Disclosing Party or its business operations, which information has been imparted to Receiving Party by Disclosing Party. If Confidential Information is in written form, the Disclosing Party shall label or stamp the materials with the word "Confidential" or some similar warning. All information disclosed by Disclosing Party shall be presumed to constitute Confidential Information and will be so regarded by Disclosing Party. If Confidential Information is transmitted orally, the Disclosing Party shall promptly provide a writing indicating that such oral communication constituted Confidential Information.

2. Confidential Information does not include any information which is: (a) publicly known at the time of disclosure or subsequently becomes publicly known through no act or omission of or on behalf of the Receiving Party; (b) discovered or created by the Receiving Party before disclosure by Disclosing Party; or (c) learned by the Receiving Party through legitimate means other than from the Disclosing Party.

3. Receiving Party (which for the purposes of this agreement shall mean Receiving Party, its affiliates , their officers, stockholders, employees and agents) will hold and maintain the Confidential Information in strictest confidence for the sole and exclusive benefit of the Disclosing Party. Receiving Party shall carefully restrict access to Confidential Information to employees, contractors, and third parties as is reasonably required and shall require those persons to sign nondisclosure restrictions at least as protective as those in this Agreement. Receiving Party shall not, without prior written approval of Disclosing Party, use for Receiving Party's own benefit, publish, copy, or otherwise disclose to others, or permit the use by others for their benefit or to the detriment of Disclosing Party, any Confidential Information.

4. Receiving Party recognizes that unauthorized disclosure of the Confidential Information will give rise to irreparable injury to Disclosing Party, which injury cannot be wholly compensated for in damages. Accordingly, Disclosing Party may seek and obtain injunctive relief against the breach or threatened breach of the covenants and agreements contained herein, in addition to (and not in lieu of) any other remedies at law or in equity that may be available to Disclosing Party.

5. If Receiving Party is requested or required (by deposition, interrogatory, request for documents, subpoena, civil investigative demand or similar process) to disclose any of the Confidential Information, Receiving Party will notify Disclosing Party promptly so that Disclosing Party may seek an appropriate protective order and/or take any other action. In the event that such protective order is not obtained, or that Disclosing Party waives compliance with the provisions hereof, (i) Receiving Party may disclose to any tribunal or other person that portion of the Confidential Information which Receiving Party is advised by legal counsel in writing is legally required to be so disclosed and shall exercise best efforts to obtain assurance that confidential treatment will be accorded such Confidential Information and (ii) Receiving Party shall not be liable for such disclosure unless such disclosure to such tribunal or other person was caused by or resulted from a previous disclosure by Receiving Party not permitted by this agreement.

6. The nondisclosure provisions of this Agreement shall survive the termination of this Agreement and Receiving Party's duty to hold Confidential Information in confidence shall remain in effect until the Confidential Information no longer qualifies as a trade secret or until Disclosing Party sends Receiving Party written notice releasing Receiving Party from this Agreement, whichever occurs first.

7. This agreement contains the entire understanding between the parties hereto with respect to the subject matter contained herein and supersedes all prior written or oral communications, negotiations, understandings or agreements of any kind with respect to such subject matter. This agreement may not be modified or amended except in a writing signed by a duly authorized agent of the party to be charged with such modification or amendment and dated subsequent to the date hereof. This Agreement and the legal relations between the parties shall be construed and determined in accordance with the laws of the State of Washington without regard to conflict of laws principles. Any dispute under this agreement shall be decided in the federal or state courts with the State of Washington.

_____   **Web Analytics, LLC**

Company Name

By: _____   By: _____

Name:_____   Name:_____

Exercise 5-51

Molly Blanchette is a breeder and seller of miniature Australian Shepherd dogs. She has recently mated two of her dogs – Jackman and Kidman – and they produced a litter of four puppies three weeks ago. Sam Hemsworth, a resident of Yakima, is interested in buying one of the litter, a female puppy currently named *Watts*. Hemsworth wants to raise *Watts* and eventually to breed her with other Miniature Australian Shepherd dogs.

Blanchette normally charges $2,000 for each purebred dog she sells. She has agreed, however, to sell *Watts* to Hemsworth for $1,500 and the second pick of the first litter born to *Watts*.

Review the purchase agreement below, which is the standard form that Blanchette drafted and uses. Identify all the problems with the agreement, including: (i) which terms in the form are of questionable enforceability and why; and (ii) which terms in the draft agreement are not consistent with the deal points described above, and therefore need to be changed. Then, rewrite the agreement. The agreement is available in electronic format on the web page for the book: www.transactionalskills.com.

PURCHASE AGREEMENT FOR NON-BREEDING PUPPY

Molly Blanchette, d/b/a Columbia Aussies and hereinafter known as Breeder, in consideration of payment of $2,000 and the agreement of _____ hereinafter known as the Buyer, to abide by the terms of the agreement set forth below, the execution of which is acknowledged, hereby releases to the undersigned Buyer full responsibility and ownership subject to the reservation of rights set forth below for the Miniature Australian Shepherd dog described as:

Name:	Call Name:
Sex:	Date of Birth:
Color & Markings:	Eye Color: Left: Right:
Litter Registration: MASC #:	Registration Papers Marked: Not for Breeding
Sire:	Dam:

Terms of the Agreement:

I. HEALTH & GUARANTEES

A. The Breeder guarantees the Dog to be in good health when it leaves their kennel. If within 72 hours the Dog is found not to be in good health, the

Breeder agrees to refund the full purchase price of the Dog so long as a letter from the examining veterinarian accompanies the dog and the Dog is returned to the Breeder at the Buyer's expense within seven (7) days of leaving the Breeder.

B. The Breeder guarantees the Dog to be free from the clinical symptoms of hereditary eye defects other than those specified below until the age of 26 months. Verification of hereditary eye disease will require a non pass CERF evaluation by a veterinary ophthalmologist. The dog is guaranteed to be free of clinical symptoms of hip dysplasia, elbow dysplasia, patellar luxation, and inherited epilepsy until the age of 26 months. Verification of any of these diseases will require evaluation by a veterinarian in accordance with CERF & OFA protocols, including an OFA rating of dysplastic in the case of hip or elbow dysplasia.

C. Upon verification of genetic eye disease or hip dysplasia, elbow dysplasia, patellar luxation or inherited epilepsy within the specified time frames, the Breeder will either refund the full purchase price upon return of the dog to the Breeder or will contribute up to one-half the purchase price toward treatment, the choice to be the Buyer's. If the Buyer does not want to keep the dog, the dog must be returned to the Breeder according to the terms (See section III below).

D. To maintain good health, the Buyer agrees to have the Dog examined, vaccinated, and checked for internal parasites, including heartworm, annually by a licensed veterinarian. The Dog will be maintained on NON-IVERMECTIN HEARTWORM prevention as recommended for the area of residence, and will be treated as recommended by the vet and within reason for other problems. The Buyer will also strive to keep the Dog free of external parasites throughout its life.

E. The Buyer is encouraged to have the Dog's eyes checked annually by a veterinary ophthalmologist, and to have the Dog's hips and elbows radiographed and evaluated by (OFA) at 24 months. The Breeder would appreciate receiving copies of the evaluations to track the success of her breeding program. All expenses for such evaluations will be the responsibility of the Buyer.

F. Breeder does not guarantee that said puppy will be in the height range for miniature Australian Shepherds. Breeder makes no other guarantees regarding the Dog.

II. BASIC CARE AND HOUSING

A. To ensure the emotional well-being of the Dog, he/she will be housed indoors as a companion. The Buyer will provide food, water, medical care, socialization, training, and exercise appropriate to the age and condition of the Dog. The Dog will not be left unattended on a chain, rope, or other tie-out device. The Dog will not be allowed to run at large, and will be kept under leash or voice control at all times when not within a fenced area. If the Buyer fails to comply with these requirements for proper care and control, the Buyer agrees to return the dog to the Breeder upon demand with no financial or other compensation.

B. Non-breeding: The Dog is sold as a Pet and may not be used for breeding. The Buyer agrees to have the dog spayed or castrated between 6 and 9 months of age. Should the dog be allowed to breed and produce a litter, all guarantees herein are void, and the Breeder may take possession of the dog and all puppies with no compensation to the Buyer.

C. Name and Registration: At the time of proof of Spay/Neuter, the Breeder will provide Buyer with MASCA registration paper. The Dog's registered name will have the word "Columbia" as the first word of the dog's registered name. The Breeder may have the final say regarding the registered name of the Dog. The Dog will be registered with LIMITED PRIVILEGES, meaning that should the dog be used for breeding in spite of the terms of this agreement, its puppies will not be eligible for registration.

D. Licensing and Identification: The Dog will be licensed by the Buyer according to state and local laws, and will wear identification at all times. The Breeder urges the Buyer to have the dog micro-chipped or tattooed and to register the microchip or tattoo with an appropriate registry.

III. RETURNS

A. Right of First Refusal: If within three months after accepting delivery of the Dog, Buyer decides to not keep the Dog in their household, Breeder will be given first opportunity to take the Dog. Buyer shall not place the Dog in any animal shelter, pound, animal control facility, animal research facility, or any animal rescue organization, nor shall Buyer offer the Dog for free or otherwise to any third-party that has not been approved, in writing, by Seller.

B. Reservation of Rights: Breeder reserves the right to void the contract and repossess the Dog without any compensation to Buyer if Buyer neglects to provide proper food, water, shelter, grooming, necessary veterinary care, or is found to be otherwise neglecting the Dog. The foregoing determination of neglect and/or decision to repossess the Dog shall be made in Breeder's sole discretion. Breeder further reserves the right to follow up on any complaints and/or reports of improper treatment of the Dog in order to protect the welfare of the Dog.

C. Refunds will be made on the following basis, subject to the Dog's examination by the Breeder's veterinarian upon its return. Date of purchase is expressly understood to be the date of initial payment for the dog or date of actual possession of the dog by the Buyer, whichever comes earlier. Date of return is expressly understood to be the date on which the return becomes complete. A return is not complete until all of the following are returned to the Breeder: the dog; signed release of ownership statement; signed documents returning all registrations to the Breeder.

1-7 days after purchase (see section I-A. above): If the Dog is returned for reasons other than poor health, and it is accompanied by a veterinary certificate of good health no more than 48 hours prior to return, the Buyer will receive 100% of the purchase price. If no veterinary certificate of good health accompanies the Dog, the refund will be 100% of the purchase price minus fee for veterinary exam, isolation boarding if necessary, and treatment.

Between 8-28 days after purchase: 75% of the purchase price minus fee for veterinary exam and any necessary treatment, isolation boarding if necessary, and the fees for transferring MASCA registration to the Breeder.

More than 28 days after purchase: 50% of the resale price minus fee for veterinary exam and any necessary treatment including isolation boarding if necessary plus additional expenses pending resale. Should the Dog be deemed unfit for resale within 30 days for any reason no money shall be refunded. Fitness for resale shall be determined solely by the Breeder.

All costs associated with the return of the Dog and the transfer of ownership to Breeder shall be borne entirely by Buyer unless otherwise agreed in writing

IV. REMEDIES

A. Equitable Relief. Buyer agrees that a breach of any provision of this Agreement by Buyer will cause immediate and irreparable damage and injury to Breeder. Buyer confirms that damages at law will be an inadequate remedy for breach or threatened breach of any such provision. Buyer agrees that in such event Breeder shall be entitled by right to an injunction restraining Buyer from violating any of such provisions. The parties hereto acknowledge that a violation of any of the provisions of this Agreement is material and important and Breeder shall be entitled, in addition to all other rights and remedies available under this Agreement, at law or otherwise, to a temporary restraining order and an injunction to be issued by any court of competent jurisdiction enjoining and restraining Buyer from committing any violation of such provisions of this Agreement, and Buyer shall consent to the issuance of such injunction. Buyer acknowledges that the remedies provided for in this Agreement do not injure or violate any public interest or policy, and will not create a hardship greater than is necessary to protect the interest of Breeder.

B. Liquidated Damages. If, for any reason, Buyer shall fail, neglect or refuse to perform any of the conditions herein according to the terms specified herein, or shall otherwise fail to comply with any provision of this Agreement, Buyer shall, if Breeder so elects and demands, forfeit and pay to Breeder, in lieu of the enforcement of this Agreement, as liquidated damages, a sum equal to Twenty Nine Thousand Five Hundred and No/100 Dollars ($29,500), plus those costs and expenses set forth in subsection (C) of this Section. This sum is agreed upon as liquidated damages and not as a penalty. The parties hereto have computed, estimated and agreed upon the sum as an attempt to make a reasonable forecast of probable actual loss because of the difficulty of estimating with exactness the damages which will result from Buyer's breach hereof.

C. Costs and Attorneys' Fees. It is agreed that should any legal action result from Buyer's breach of this Agreement, Buyer shall bear all legal costs, attorney's fees and expert witness fees incurred by Breeder in enforcing the Agreement.

D. Venue: This agreement is mutually stipulated to have been entered into in Whatcom County, Washington regardless of the place where it is signed. The Buyer and the Breeder agree that venue for any legal action taken to enforce the terms and conditions of this agreement shall be in the county of Breeder's residence and that this agreement shall be interpreted in accordance with the laws of the State of Washington. In the event that legal action is taken to enforce the terms of this agreement, the prevailing party shall be entitled to an award of attorney's fees and costs.

F. Columbia Aussies are registered with MASCA only. They will not be registered with any other registry or as another breed, other than an Australian Shepherd of the miniature variety. If a Columbia Aussie is ever registered with AKC as a Miniature American Shepherd (MAS), litigation and/or seizure of said dog will result.

Buyer:_____   Date:_____

Breeder:_____   Date:_____

Exercise 5-52

Samuel Beacon and Cindy Kline are professors who are in the process of completing the manuscript for a new book and the accompanying teacher's manual. The editors at Professional Publications, Inc. have tentatively agreed to publish the book and the teacher's manual. They have further agreed that the authors will submit the book in camera-ready pages via an electronic file in pdf format. However, because the book is designed for use both by professionals and by students, and Professional Publications does not typically sell to the academic market – and thus does not have a network for distributing either a teacher's manual or a complimentary copy to teachers who might require students to purchase the book – Professional Publications is in the process of negotiating an agreement for Academic Press – which does have such a network – to serve as co-publisher.

Review the publication agreement below, which is the standard form publication agreement used by Professional Publications with the names of the authors and title of the book filled in. Identify all the problems with the agreement, including all significant omissions. Rewrite what should be revised and draft a suitable provision for each significant, omitted term. The agreement is available in electronic format on the web page for the book: www.transactionalskills.com.

PUBLICATION AGREEMENT

This Agreement is made between Professional Publications, Inc., located at 401 E. Pratt Street, Baltimore, Maryland 21202 ("Publisher") and Samuel L. Beacon, of Olympia University, and Cindy F. Kline, of Excelsior College ("Author(s)").

1. DESCRIPTION OF THE WORK

Authors agree to create and deliver to the Publisher the complete and final version of a work tentatively entitled The Social Scientist's Guide to Empirical Research (the "Work") consisting of approximately 250 printed pages.

2. RIGHTS

2.1 *Grant of Rights.* The Authors hereby grant to the Publisher, for the full term of copyright and all extensions thereof, the exclusive copyright in the Work and all revisions thereof, throughout the World, in all languages, and in all formats, including but not limited to all electronic, digital, and computer-based formats, and in all media now known or hereafter developed, except as provided herein.

2.2 *Third-Party Licenses.* The Publisher has the exclusive right to grant or license any part of or all of these rights to third parties, and all rights to the title of the Work.

2.3 *Formatting, Style, and Costs.* Publisher has the right to publish the Work in the format and style it deems appropriate. The Publisher is responsible for all costs related to the publication, promotion, distribution, sale, licensing, or other disposition of the Work.

3. COPYRIGHT

3.1 *Copyright Registration.* The Publisher will register in the Publisher's name, the copyright and in any renewals or extensions thereof, in and to all editions of the Work published in the United States and elsewhere. Authors hereby irrevocably appoint the Publisher, its successors and assigns, as each Author's attorney in fact with power of substitution in the name of the Publisher to execute on each Author's behalf any and all documents necessary to protect the rights granted to the Publisher under this Agreement. Each Author agrees to execute any document that the Publisher may deem necessary to assure or perfect the rights granted hereunder.

3.2 *Out of Print.* If at any time the Work is out of print during the term of this Agreement, Author may terminate the Agreement by written request to the Publisher. For this purpose, "out of print" means not available in the United States through the Publisher's web store in an English language edition (including print, print-on-demand, or digital format) or listed in the Publisher's marketing catalog for six months or more. Within sixty (60) days of receipt of the request, the Publisher will return all rights in the Work to Author, subject to any prior grants of rights authorized by Publisher or Authors and the continuing right to retain Publisher's share of any future proceeds from those grants.

4. DELIVERY

4.1 *Delivery of Manuscript.* Authors will deliver the manuscript of the Work (the "Manuscript) to the Publisher no later than ___August 20__, cleared of all necessary permissions and acceptable to Publisher in its sole judgment and discretion. The Manuscript, inclusive of all tables, charts, photographs, and other illustrative materials (if applicable),will be delivered to the Publisher in form and content appropriate for the market for which the Work is intended, satisfactory to the Publisher, suitable for use by a compositor, and in typed or electronic format as specified by the Publisher.

4.2 *Failure to Deliver.* If the Authors fail to deliver the Manuscript in length, form, or content satisfactory to the Publisher by such date, then the Publisher may terminate this Agreement.

4.3 *Related Expenses.* All expenses for preparation and delivery of the Manuscript are Authors' responsibility.

5. PREPARATION OF THE WORK; CORRECTIONS

5.1 *Galleys and Proofs.* Authors agree to read and correct all galley and page proofs or electronic prototypes of the Work and all revisions thereof, and return them with all necessary corrections within ten (10) days of receipt. If Author fails or is unable to comply with these requirements, the Publisher may have the proofs or prototypes reviewed and corrected by others, and charge the cost, if any, to Authors.

5.2 *Changes in or Additions to Work.* The Publisher is authorized to make such editorial changes in the Work as it deems necessary or desirable, and it will give Author such opportunity to review these changes as is permissible within the publication schedule established by the Publisher.

5.3 *Costs of Alterations.* If the cost of alterations to the galleys, page proofs, or electronic prototypes exceeds 10% of the cost of the original composition, then Author will pay the excess cost within 30 days after receiving a statement from the Publisher.

6. PAYMENT

6.1 *Royalties.* If Authors have delivered the Manuscript of the Work in accordance with Section 4 and the Publisher has deemed the manuscript acceptable, the Publisher will pay Authors the following royalties from all sales of the Work published by the Publisher less returns, credits, taxes, and bookkeeping adjustments that are necessary to accurately reflect the amount of gross revenues:

     a. __% of gross revenues on all copies sold in print form;

     b. __% of gross revenues on all copies sold in digital/electronic form;

6.2 *No Royalties Due.* Notwithstanding the above, the Publisher may distribute free copies for review or promotion and may license others to publish selections from the Work for appropriate purposes to benefit its sale, with no payment of royalties to Author. No royalties will be due on copies of the Work furnished without charge, damaged copies, copies supplied to or purchased by Authors at author's discount rate, copies donated by the Publisher, copies returned after sale, or copies sold at less than the Publisher's cost of production.

6.3 *Royalty Splits.* If applicable all amounts payable under this Section 6 will be divided between the Authors as follows:
     Samuel L. Beacon – 50%
     Cindy F. Kline – 50%

7. ACCOUNTING STATEMENTS

7.1 *Annual Accounting.* The Publisher will account to Authors annually, on or before December 31 for the fiscal year ending August 31. The Publisher will be entitled to withhold from all payments of royalties a reasonable reserve for estimated returns of the Work. The reserve will be adjusted by the Publisher from time to time as appropriate in view of historical returns experience.

7.2 Any amounts due to the Publisher under this or any other agreement (as a result, for example, of an overpayment) may be deducted by the Publisher from any sums due to the Authors under this or any other agreement.

8. AUTHOR COPIES

Free and Discounted Copies. Publisher will present each Author with 10 free copies of the Work upon publication. Authors may purchase copies of the Work for personal use and not for resale at a discount of forty percent (40%) from the suggested retail price, plus shipping and handling charges.

9. DESIGNATION AS AUTHOR

Use of Name and Likeness. The Publisher has the right to use each Author's name and likeness in connection with the marketing, advertising, and promotion of the Work, the Publisher, and any other Publisher publications in any media throughout the world. The Publisher also has the right to grant these rights in connection with the license of any subsidiary rights in the Work. Publisher, in its sole discretion, will determine all marketing and promotions related to the sale and promotion of the Work.

10. DESIGNATION AS PUBLISHER

The Publisher may, in its discretion, designate Academic Press as a co-publisher of the Work.

11. REVISIONS, SUPPLEMENTS, AND NEW EDITIONS

11.1 *Request for Revision.* If Publisher determines that a revision, supplement, or new edition (collectively, a "Revision") of the Work is desirable, Publisher will invite the Author(s) to participate in a Revision in accordance with a reasonable schedule proposed by the Publisher.

11.2 *Author's Non-participation in Revision.* If any Author does not respond to Publisher's invitation by the deadline indicated in the invitation, then Publisher may: (i) select one or more competent third parties to participate in a Revision, and to charge the cost for those participants against any amounts which are or become payable to the Author; or (ii) terminate this Agreement. In the event of termination, the Publisher would retain its rights to any copyright in the Work.

11.3 *Subsequent Revisions.* If, for any reason or no reason, any Author does not participate in the preparation of a Revision, the Publisher will have no obligation to invite such person, nor will such person have a right to participate, in any subsequent Revision of the Work and such person will not receive any royalties for any Revision.

11.4 *Author's Credit.* The Publisher may, but is not obligated to, list as an "author" of a Revision the name of any person comprising the Author even if such person did not participate in revising the Work.

11.5 *Applicability of Other Provisions.* Except where the context indicates otherwise, all sections of this Agreement apply to Revisions requested by the Publisher and prepared by Author, and the Work will include all Revisions.

12. WARRANTY

12.1 *Authority; Originality; Permissions.* Each Author represents and warrants that he has the full power and authority to enter into this Agreement and grant the rights herein; that the Work is original, except for material in the public domain or material from other works included with the written permission of the rights owners; that no part of the Work has been previously published; and that the Work does not contain any matter that is libelous, obscene, injurious, violates any right of copyright, trademark, privacy, or any other right of any person or entity, or violates any law or regulation.

12.2 *Indemnification.* Author(s) will indemnify and hold the Publisher, its licensees, customers, affiliates, and assigns, harmless from all damages, costs, and expenses (including counsel fees) arising out of any claim concerning material(s) contained in or omitted from the Work, or otherwise inconsistent with any of the above warranties, representations, and covenants. Until any claim or suit is resolved, the Publisher may withhold any sums due to Author(s) under this or any other agreement between Author(s) and the Publisher.

12.3 *Consents and Rights.* Each Author represents and warrants that he has obtained in writing all necessary consents and rights under the same terms and conditions and to the same extent granted from Author to the Publisher herein, from any third parties whose materials are included in the Work. Author is solely responsible for paying any compensation due to third-party contributors. Upon written request from Author, the Publisher will include credits or acknowledgments or both for third-party contributors in the Work, as Publisher and Author deem appropriate under the circumstances.

12.4 *Survival After Termination.* The representations and warranties of this section 11 survive the termination of this Agreement and extend to the Publisher's licensees, successors, and assigns.

13. INFRINGEMENT

If the copyright in the Work is infringed, the Publisher has the right, but not the obligation, to pursue legal action in such manner as it deems appropriate. If Publisher does so, the Publisher will recoup the expenses incurred from any recovery, and the balance of the proceeds, if any, shall be divided equally between the Author and the Publisher. If the Publisher does not pursue such a claim after the Author's request to do so, the Author, at the Author's expense, will have the right to pursue legal action, and any recovery will belong solely to the Author.

14. OTHER PUBLICATIONS BY THE AUTHOR

No Conflicting Publications. During the term of this Agreement, Authors will not publish any other material written or edited in whole or in part by him that would be detrimental to the sale of the Work, unless he obtains Publisher's written consent.

15. GENERAL

15.1 *Assignment.* This Agreement is binding on and inures to the benefit of the Publisher and its successors and assigns, and is binding on and inures to the benefit of Author, his heirs, legal representatives, executors, administrators, and assigns. Author cannot assign the rights or delegate the duties created by this Agreement to any person or entity without the express written consent of Publisher.

15.2 *Governing Law; Venue.* This Agreement will be interpreted under the laws of the State of Maryland. Any dispute related to this Agreement must be resolved in the appropriate state or federal court in Maryland. The parties waive any objection they may have to the personal jurisdiction of these courts.

15.3 *Entire Agreement.* This is the entire agreement and understanding of the parties. It supersedes any prior Agreements between the Publisher and Authors. No provision of the Agreement can be waived or modified unless made in a writing signed by both parties. A party may waive the other party's breach or default of a provision of this Agreement, but that waiver will not extend to any other breach or default. If a court holds any provision of this Agreement invalid, the remaining provisions will not be affected.

IN WITNESS WHEREOF the parties hereto have signed this Agreement on the _____ day of _____, 20__ .

CHAPTER SIX
DEAL DESIGN

In Chapter Five, Section M, we discussed the importance of anticipating future events and checking to ensure that the language of the agreement properly covers them. Anticipating future events also plays a role in deal design. That is, even before evaluating draft language, the transactional lawyer needs to identify the risks associated with the parties' planned transaction and then ascertain how, if at all, the agreement should deal with each risk.

A. IDENTIFYING RISKS INHERENT IN THE DEAL

When parties are contemplating or negotiating a transaction – whether it is to buy and sell goods or real estate, provide services, loan money, or almost anything else – they tend to focus on the main terms: price, quality, quantity, duration. They usually assume that the other party intends to fulfill its end of the bargain and either assume or determine after some investigation that the other party is able to perform.

Unfortunately, in their zeal to deal, clients sometimes are too generous in their assumptions about the good faith or abilities of those with whom they are about to contract. More important, things can change between the time the parties reach agreement and the time they are to perform. Individuals and businesses have second thoughts. They suffer financial reversals. Prevailing prices rise or fall. Laws change. People die. Wars break out. You get the idea. In extreme cases, contract law might provide relief to a party whose performance has become impracticable or impossible,[1] but what happens in less extreme cases is a matter normally left to the agreement of the parties.

One of the jobs of the transactional lawyer is to determine what contingencies are sufficiently likely and important that they should be expressly addressed in the parties' agreement or affect how the transaction is structured. In many cases, this must be done in consultation with the client. The lawyer identifies a risk and explains it to the client. The client will then decide whether the risk is something that the transaction documents should cover, given the time constraints on the deal, the cost in legal fees, and the possibility that negotiations over how to handle the

---

[1] *See* RESTATEMENT (SECOND) OF CONTRACTS §§ 261–271.

risk might jeopardize the deal. But regardless of whether the lawyer or the client is the one who determines whether to address a particular risk, the fact remains that it is the lawyer's job to identify legal risks in the first place.

Some risks are fairly obvious. For example, if a lender is providing funds to a borrower to remodel a nightclub, and the deal is for the borrower to begin repaying the loan thirty days after the nightclub opens, the lender's lawyer should immediately consider the possibility that the nightclub might never open.[2] More generally, any time a contract calls for a buyer or borrower to pay later for property acquired or funds loaned at the closing, there is the risk that the buyer or borrower will not have the ability to make payment when due. In other words, while creditworthiness can be evaluated at the time the agreement is entered into, subsequent events might dramatically impair the likelihood of payment. An individual might become sick and lose income. A business might flounder due to an economic recession, poor management, or increased competition. There might be little or nothing that a lawyer can put into an agreement to completely avoid these risks, but sometimes authorizing the seller or lender to sever relations at the first sign of a problem can mitigate the risk, and avoid transforming a small loss into a large one.

Exercise 6-1

You represent Jefferson Properties, Inc., the owner of an office building in a metropolitan area. Jefferson Properties is negotiating a seven-year lease of the building to a four-person law firm that specializes in consumer bankruptcy and foreclosure defense. The firm also represents plaintiffs in small tort cases. Identify all the things that, in preparing the first draft of the lease, you should consider including as a default by the law firm. In other words, what events or actions should trigger the landlord's right to use its default remedies (whatever those remedies might be)?

Identifying obvious risks – such as the risk of nonpayment – is comparatively easy. Even the most novice lawyer is likely to understand that a borrower or tenant might fail to pay when payment is due. Other risks are less obvious and require more thought to identify. There are at least three things transactional lawyers can do to help identify less obvious risks.

---

[2]   *See* Hunt v. Kadlick, 2013 WL 4659772 (D. Md. 2013).

First, the lawyer can confer with the client about the problems the client has encountered in the past or is worried about in connection with the deal to be documented. Clients know their own businesses much better than their lawyers do and should be able to alert the lawyer to most trade-specific risks, at least if the lawyer is savvy enough to ask and to listen.

Second, the lawyer can review forms or agreements used previously in similar transactions. Even if those forms or agreements are poorly drafted, they might nevertheless include language designed to deal with a risk that the lawyer had not considered.

Finally, the transactional lawyer can make daily, weekly, monthly, and yearly time lines for the parties' performances under the agreement. In other words, map out what the parties must, may, and might do – in the order those things are likely to occur – and then consider what might interfere with each of those things.

B. DEALING WITH RISKS INHERENT IN THE DEAL

When the parties do not contemplate an ongoing relationship and the transaction between them is fairly simple – such as a single-lot sale of goods for cash – most of the risks inherent in the transaction can and should be evaluated and dealt with either before the agreement is reached or, at a minimum, before the transaction is consummated. For example, the buyer would want to be sure the seller owns the goods to be sold and that the goods conform to whatever description the seller has provided. Although the buyer's lawyer might wish to draft warranties to deal with these issues, greater protection is normally obtained through inspection of the goods and other aspects of the due diligence investigation that we will explore in Chapter Seven.

For other transactions, the lawyer is often expected to recommend one or more ways to minimize an identified risk. Consider, for example, a lawyer who represents the buyer of a small business, such as a bakery, dentistry practice, or accounting practice. The prospective buyer typically plans to provide goods or services to the existing clients of the business and expects the seller not to interfere with that plan. If, however, the seller opens up a competing business in a nearby location shortly after the sale, the buyer might well lose much or all of the value of the business for which the buyer has paid. To deal with this, the buyer's lawyer will often include in the sales agreement a provision by which the seller promises not to compete with the buyer for a specified period of time. Many common transactions involve risks that might not be immediately obvious but which the careful lawyer should attempt to uncover.

Exercise 6-2

You represent Better Buy, a national retailer of consumer electronics. What should you consider putting in your client's agreements with its suppliers to protect your client from being stuck with goods that either cannot be sold at all or sold only at a loss because more advanced competing goods soon come on the market. Does the answer to this depend on whether the supplier is also the manufacturer of the now antiquated goods? Does it depend on whether the supplier is also the manufacturer or seller of the more advanced competing goods?

The most common way to deal with a risk inherent in a deal is to allocate that risk by agreement. This is frequently accomplished by including one or more warranties, covenants, or conditions in the parties' agreement. For the most part, this approach is effective. However, a transactional lawyer should be aware of six traps that lie along this path.

First, warranties and covenants are types of promises but not every promise is kept. The promisor might be unwilling or unable to perform. Indeed, the law itself might interfere with the enforcement of a covenant. For example, a covenant not to compete might be unenforceable if it is unreasonably broad in duration or geographic scope.[3] A promise to refrain from conducting business with others might violate antitrust law or laws against discrimination, or be an unenforceable restraint on alienation.

Second, while an unexcused breach of an enforceable warranty or covenant gives rise to a claim for damages, the right to damages might be limited. In general, contract damages are recoverable only if and to the extent that: (i) they were reasonably foreseeable at the time of contracting,[4] (ii) they cannot be mitigated by reasonable actions,[5] (iii) the aggrieved party is able to prove the damages with

---

[3] We dealt with covenants not to compete in Exercises 4-4 and 4-5. Because such clauses reduce competition – and thus are not in the public interest – they are subject to various legal limitations. *See* RESTATEMENT (SECOND) OF CONTRACTS § 188. The lawyer must therefore be familiar with the scope and application of those limitations under the law applicable to the transaction.

[4] *See, e.g.*, RESTATEMENT (SECOND) OF CONTRACTS § 351; Hadley v. Baxendale, 156 Eng. Rep. 145 (1854).

[5] *See, e.g.*, RESTATEMENT (SECOND) OF CONTRACTS § 350; Rockingham Cty .v. Luten Bridge Co., 35 F.2d 201 (4th Cir. 1929).

reasonable certainty,[6] and (iv) the statute of limitations on the claim for damages has not expired before the aggrieved party learns of the breach and commences a legal action. A transactional lawyer needs to be aware of these limitations and consider how they might apply to the transaction at hand. Consider the following illustration.

Illustration

Your client, Art Collector, is contemplating the purchase of a Renoir painting from Seller, a reputable art dealer. Seller obtained the painting from the estate of another collector, who purchased the painting 30 years ago. Both you and Art Collector are cognizant of the risk that the painting might, more than 30 years ago, have been stolen. For example, it might have been looted by Nazis during World War II. If so, the rightful owner might be able to assert a valid claim to the painting, even after all this time. The statute of limitations does not begin to run on the rightful owner's claim for conversion against the current possessor until the owner knows or has reason to know who has possession.[7]

You take some solace in the fact that the law will impute a warranty of title into Art Collector's transaction with Seller.[8] Thus, Seller will be warrantying that Art Collector will receive good title to the painting. However, the warranty will be breached, if at all, at the time the painting is delivered to Art Collector; this is true regardless of whether you or Art Collector is aware of the breach at that time.[9] The statute of limitations on any claim for breach of warranty is four years.[10] Thus, there is a risk that,

---

[6] *See, e.g.*, RESTATEMENT (SECOND) OF CONTRACTS § 352; Freund v. Washington Square Press, Inc., 314 N.E.2d 419 (N.Y. 1974).

[7] *See* O'Keeffe v. Snyder, 416 A.2d 862 (N.J. 1980). *See also* Solomon R. Guggenheim Found. v. Lubell, 569 N.E.2d 426 (N.Y. 1991) (cause of action for replevin against the good-faith purchaser of a stolen chattel accrues when the true owner makes demand for return of the chattel and the person in possession of the chattel refuses to return it).

[8] *See* U.C.C. § 2-312.

[9] *See* U.C.C. § 2-725(2).

[10] *See* U.C.C. § 2-725(1); Doss, Inc. v. Christie's Inc., 2009 WL 3053713 (S.D.N.Y. 2009) (also dealing with misrepresentation claims).

In some states, the limitations period a claim for misrepresentation does not begin to run until the buyer discovers or should discover all of the elements of the claim. *E.g.*, Ranes &

if the painting was stolen long ago, the rightful owner might be able to recover the painting from Art Collector long after Art Collector's warranty claim against Seller has expired.

Exercise 6-3

What should you add to the sales agreement between Art Collector and Seller to reduce or eliminate the risk to Art Collector depicted by the illustration above?

Third, a promisor might lack the ability to pay damages for breach of a warranty or covenant. The goal in allocating risk is not merely to create contract liability – that is, to allocate the risk on paper – but to truly protect the client by allocating the risk in reality. A promise from an insolvent party is often meaningless.

Fourth, the breach of a warranty or covenant does not normally permit the aggrieved party to rescind the contract. While a breach – if material – might give rise to a right to cancel the contract or to suspend performance,[11] the right to suspend performance will not be helpful if the aggrieved party has already fully performed. Thus, a transactional attorney needs to consider the sequence of the conduct contemplated by the parties' agreement.

Fifth, a condition to a duty or to a right might similarly not be triggered at an opportune time. Consider, for example, an agreement to buy and sell a small business. The agreement conditions the buyer's duty to close the transaction on the accuracy and completeness of the financial statements that the seller previously provided to the buyer.[12] If the buyer is unlikely to learn of any problem with the financial statements before consummating the purchase and taking control of the business, the condition will not serve its purpose. In short, carefully consider both when a condition will be triggered and when the parties are likely to acquire knowledge of that fact before relying on a condition to allocate risk.

Shine, LLC v. MacDonald Miller Alaska, Inc., 355 P.3d 503 (Alaska 2015). However, if at the time of the sale Seller had no knowledge or reason to know of the rightful owner's claim to the painting, Art Collector will not have a cognizable claim for misrepresentation.

[11]   *See* RESTATEMENT (SECOND) OF CONTRACTS § 237.

[12]   This example is taken from Exercise 2-3(a).

Finally, while conditions can be an extremely effective way to allocate risk,[13] courts are reluctant to enforce a condition if doing so would result in disproportionate forfeiture: that is, if it would excuse one party from providing the bargained-for exchange and even though the other party has already substantially performed.[14] Accordingly, courts will often engage in some analytical gymnastics to interpret the language of a forfeiting condition as something else.[15]

C. AVOIDING RISKY INCENTIVES

A secondary but sometimes equally important task for the transactional lawyer is to make sure that the agreement itself does not provide an incentive or remove a disincentive to engage in behavior that might be costly to the client. This is a bit like game theory, which looks at strategic decision making and studies how one person's actions might affect another person's actions.

Consider, for example, a typical homeowner's insurance policy. It will provide coverage for damage from specified perils, including fire or lightning, windstorm or hail, explosion, impact from aircraft or vehicles, smoke, vandalism or malicious mischief, and theft. The policy will also identify other risks for which it provides no coverage for resulting damage. For the most part, these exclusions fall into two categories. One category – sometimes referred to as correlated risks – consists of those risks that are likely to affect a large group of policy holders at a time and thus potentially subject an insurer to more claims than it has the ability to pay. These include damage resulting from floods, earthquakes, or war.[16]

A second category of risks – sometimes referred to as moral hazards – is quite different. These risks arise from behavior that an insured might take because, absent the exclusion, any resulting loss would be borne by the insurer. Thus, for example, the policy might generally cover loss resulting from the sudden and accidental discharge or overflow of water from within a plumbing system but

---

[13] For example, a condition to a duty can excuse a party regardless of materiality, and thus avoid the doctrine of substantial performance. *See, e.g.,* In re Griffin, 509 B.R. 864, 897-98 (Bankr. W.D. Ark. 2014).

[14] *See* RESTATEMENT (SECOND) OF CONTRACTS § 229.

[15] *See, e.g.,* Jacob & Youngs, Inc. v. Kent, 129 N.E. 889 (N.Y. 1921).

[16] Insurers do sell insurance for these risks, but they usually require additional premiums for this coverage and they often protect themselves from the correlated risk by purchasing reinsurance.

exclude from coverage any loss attributable to deterioration, corrosion, or rust resulting from seepage or leakage of water over a period of time. The rationale for the exception is that the policyholder should have repaired a slow leak before it became a big problem and that the policy itself should not give the policy holder the incentive to forego routine maintenance.

Exercise 6-4

A. A homeowner's insurance policy generally covers losses resulting from falling objects but excludes from this coverage "loss to property contained in a building unless the roof or an exterior wall of the building is first damaged by a falling object." What is the moral hazard that explains this exception?

B. You are drafting a homeowner's insurance policy for Insurer. Insurer wishes to generally cover losses caused by animals. Identify at least two moral hazards potentially associated with this coverage and draft appropriate language to exclude them.

Exercise 6-5

Splinter Technologies, LLC is in the business of modifying vehicles for alternative fuels and has an excellent reputation in the field. Last month, Splinter was awarded a five-year contract from a major vehicle manufacturer to convert gasoline-powered cargo vans to compressed natural gas. The contract is a requirements contract in which the forecasted quantities are non-binding estimates, but it is expected to generate annual revenue of $20-25 million for Splinter.

Boomer Holdings, Inc., which is somewhat new to the vehicle conversion business, was an unsuccessful bidder for that contract. In response to losing out on the contract, Boomer decided to buy Splinter's assets and the parties have reached a tentative agreement on a purchase price of $10 million in cash, plus an "earn-out" payment of $10 million in Boomer common stock if annual revenue for the twelve months after the sale equals or exceeds $45 million.

You represent Splinter. What might Boomer do to avoid the earn-out payment? What should you include in the purchase and sale agreement to deal with this risk?

D. ASSESSING & DEALING WITH LEGAL RISKS

The most important aspect of deal design – because it is the aspect most likely to fall under the responsibility of the transactional lawyer – is assessing and dealing with legal risks. Clients typically understand the business risks associated with a transaction. In fact, they probably have a greater understanding of the *business* risks than do their attorneys. What clients most rely on their attorneys to do is to identify *legal* risks and to develop strategies for eliminating or reducing those risks.

To perform each of these tasks competently, the transactional lawyer must be familiar with the applicable law, whether rooted in statute, regulations, or judicial decisions. The lawyer must also review the transaction from at least three different vantage points. That is because a problem – or its solution – might relate to a single clause, an entire document, or the structure of the transaction.

1. Legal Risks Relating to an Individual Clause

We begin at the micro level. In each of the following three exercises, both the legal risk and its solution relate to a small portion of the parties' agreement.

Exercise 6-6

You are drafting a commercial lease on behalf of the landlord. The term of the lease is ten years, with an option for ten additional years. Should the option be phrased as a right to "renew" or a right to "extend," and why? In considering that question, assume that the initial draft of the option, phrased as a right to renew, is as follows:

> Tenant may renew the Lease for an additional term of ten years by giving written notification to Landlord not less than 90 days prior to expiration of the Lease Term.

Exercise 6-7

Diamond Retail, Inc. owns and operates a small chain of grocery stores. The business is fundamentally sound but Diamond Retail recently suffered a large uninsured loss and is in desperate need of cash. State Bank has tentatively agreed to provide Diamond retail with a $2.5 million loan. State

Bank would like Diamond Retail's largest current creditor – County Bank – to subordinate the debt Diamond Retail owes it to the new loan from State Bank. Unfortunately, there is insufficient time to obtain that agreement before State Bank's loan to Diamond Retail must close. Accordingly, instead of making receipt of the subordination agreement a condition to closing, the loan agreement provides as follows:

> Borrower shall use commercially reasonable efforts to obtain, within one month after the Closing Date, a subordination agreement from County Bank in form and substance reasonably satisfactory to Lender.

Assuming that State Bank is willing to accept the risk that Diamond Retail might not be able to obtain the subordination agreement but that State Bank wants any subordination that is obtained to be enforceable – in other words, assuming that County Bank executes a satisfactory subordination agreement after the loan closes – what legal problem might arise? How should the loan agreement be modified to solve that legal problem?

Exercise 6-8

Your client, a small printing business cannot afford to hire a full-time accountant and is therefore considering using a payroll processing company to calculate wages and withholdings for each employee, invoice the client for the total due, and then issue payment to the employees. Read *Lonely Maiden Productions, LLC v. Goldentree Asset Mgmt. LP*, 135 Cal. Rptr. 3d 69 (Cal. Ct. App. 2011). What risk does the use of such a payroll processor present and what do you recommend be included in the agreement with the payroll processor to minimize the risk?

Exercise 6-9

Plaintiff sued Defendant in tort and sought $5 million in damages. The parties have reached a tentative agreement to settle for payment of $1.3 million. Defendant does not have the liquid assets to pay that amount upon signing the agreement, so the tentative agreement provides for Defendant to make and deliver a promissory note calling for payment over time plus interest, and a security agreement to secure that obligation. Because

Plaintiff is adamant about actually getting paid, Plaintiff insists and Defendant has agreed that, if there is a default, Defendant must pay an additional $600,000.

Why might the term calling for the additional $600,000 payment not be enforceable? If you represented Plaintiff, how would you draft the settlement agreement to reduce the risk?

2.   Larger-Scale Problems and Solutions

Sometimes, a legal problem either relates to an entire document or can be solved through the creation of one or more additional documents.

Exercise 6-10

Owner has agreed to convey some real property near Safeco Field in Seattle to Buyer. However, if the Seattle Mariners ever lose more than 90 games in a regular season, ownership of the property is to go automatically to Nephew or Nephew's heirs. You have been asked to draft the document or documents necessary to effectuate the transfer. In preparing to do so, you conclude that the transaction as described presents a Rule Against Perpetuities problem. That is, Nephew's interest is not sure to vest or lapse within the applicable perpetuities period (21 years after some life in being at the creation of the interest). How can you structure the transaction to avoid this problem without altering the substance of the deal?

Exercise 6-11

Your client, Smith Company, is both a supplier to and customer of Jones Company. Each company regularly sells goods and services to the other on open account, with payment due within 30 days after delivery or performance. The accountants for each company have a practice of conferring at the end of each month, determining which company is a net obligor to the other, and arranging for a single payment of the net amount due.

Smith recently received from Factor a notification stating that Factor has acquired a security interest in all of the accounts receivable of Jones.

Read U.C.C. § 9-404(a).[17] You want to make sure that Smith is not required to pay Jones for the goods and services it purchases from Jones if Jones fails to pay for what it buys from Smith. In other words, you want to ensure that Smith retains the ability to setoff its obligations to Jones against the amounts that Jones owes to Smith. What do you recommend?

Exercise 6-12

Lender has tentatively agreed to lend $1.5 billion to Borrower, a manufacturer of cell phones. Most of Borrower's phones are produced and assembled abroad by suppliers and subcontractors. Thus, Borrower owns little manufacturing equipment that could serve as collateral for the loan. Borrower's major assets are its patents and trademarks, and Borrower has taken steps to protect its intellectual property around the world by filing the necessary registration documents in the appropriate public office of each major country.

The preliminary draft of the loan agreement between Lender and Borrower contains language granting Lender a security interest in all of Borrower's intellectual property. You have already determined what steps are needed to perfect that security interest in every country in which Borrower does business. You have further determined that, in the event Borrower defaults, the U.S. Patent and Trademark Office will permit Lender to transfer record ownership of Borrower's patents and trademarks. Thus, Lender will, after default, not only have the legal right to sell Borrower's U.S. intellectual property, but will have the practicable ability to do so as well. Unfortunately, you are not sure that other countries will be so accommodating. Some might require Borrower's signature on a document of transfer but you cannot be sure that, after default, Borrower will cooperate by signing the necessary documents. What do you recommend to solve this problem?

---

[17] Note that a security interest is a type of "assignment" within the meaning of U.C.C. § 9-404(a). The term "account debtor" is defined in U.C.C. § 9-102(a)(3).

3. Structural Issues

In the foregoing discussion, the lawyer's role in deal design related to minor – although also critical – aspects of the transaction. In other cases, however, the lawyer's role is more akin to that of an architect: affecting not only the interior design of the deal but also the transaction's underlying structure. In those instances, the role of a lawyer includes: (i) identifying different ways in which a transaction might proceed and the legal risks associated with each; (ii) advising the client as to the alternative structures that a transaction might take; and (iii) negotiating the alternative structures with the lawyer for the other side. There are several common examples of this large-scale planning:

- Determining whether a client's purchase of a business should be a stock acquisition (*i.e.*, the purchase of the ownership interests in a business entity) or an asset acquisition (*i.e.*, the purchase of the tangible and intangible assets of a business entity). The decision will often be affected by numerous factors, including the tax consequences to each party.

- Determining whether a transfer of equipment in return for periodic payments over time should be structured as a sale (with a retained security interest) or as a lease. This decision too will have important tax and accounting consequences for the parties. It will also affect the remedies available after default, particularly if the transferee files for bankruptcy protection.

- Determining whether a transfer of technology should be via a sale or a license and, if by license, whether the license should be exclusive or non-exclusive. The decision can affect which party will be responsible for protecting the technology from infringement (*i.e.*, which party has standing to bring a claim for infringement against a third party) and which party can grant permission for others to exploit the technology.

- Determining whether a transfer of receivables should be structured as a true sale or a secured loan. This will affect not only the level of recourse the transferee has (*i.e.*, the buyer/lender's ability to go after the seller/borrower in the event the amount collected is less than amount provided) – a matter than can be adjusted by agreement regardless of the structure – but also how the receivables are reported on the parties' financial statements.

One legal risk that commands a great deal of attention from transactional attorneys, particularly those engaged in a finance practice, and which often requires a fair amount of creativity to manage, is the risk that a transfer of property or incursion of debt might be avoidable – that is, subject to rescission – as a fraudulent transaction.

A bit of explanation about the law governing such transactions is in order. In 1918, the National Conference of Commissioners on Uniform State Laws (now referred to as the Uniform Law Commission) promulgated the Uniform Fraudulent Conveyance Act ("UFCA"), later adopted by more than half of the states, to provide uniform rules on what constitutes a fraudulent transaction. In 1984, the Commission approved a new Uniform Fraudulent Transfer Act ("UFTA") to replace the UFCA. About two-thirds of the states enacted the UFTA. In 2014, the Commission adopted some minor amendments to the UFTA and re-titled it the Uniform Voidable Transactions Act ("UVTA"). In most states, one of these acts is in effect. Each of the remaining states has a similar, nonuniform statute.[18]

All three uniform acts, as well as the few nonuniform statutes, allow a creditor of one party to a fraudulent transaction, among other remedies, to sue the counterparty to rescind the transaction. There are two principal types of fraudulent transactions: those that are intentionally fraudulent and those that are constructively fraudulent.

An intentionally fraudulent transfer occurs when a debtor transfers property in an effort to hinder, delay, or defraud one or more creditors.[19] Such a transfer might be designed to conceal the asset transferred or remove it from the jurisdiction. Thus, for example, a debtor who has a house or car re-titled in the name of a family member to hinder or prevent a judgment creditor from seizing the property has probably made an intentionally fraudulent transfer.[20]

---

[18]   The Bankruptcy Code also contains analogous rules. *See* 11 U.S.C. § 548.

[19]   Note, it is not the *transferee* whom the debtor must intend to hinder, delay, or defraud, it is the *debtor's creditors* who are the intended victims. Note also, that intent to defraud is not required; intent to hinder or delay will suffice. *See, e.g.,* Kenneth C. Kettering, *The Uniform Voidable Transactions Act; or, the 2014 Amendments to the Uniform Fraudulent Transfer Act*, 70 BUS. LAW. 777, 806-07 (2015). Finally, note that it is the transferor's intent that matters, not the transferee's intent. *But cf.* UVTA § 8(a) (providing a defense to avoidance if the transferee took in good faith for reasonably equivalent value).

[20]   *See, e.g.*, In re Wiggains, 2015 WL 1954438 (Bankr. N.D. Tex. 2015) (debtor who, one hour before filing a bankruptcy petition, partitioned the homestead he held as community property with his wife into separate property, with each owning an undivided one-half interest, acted with the intent to hinder or delay creditors within the meaning of § 548 of the

A constructively fraudulent transfer is premised on an oft-quoted maxim of the law that "a debtor must be just before being generous." This maxim expresses the principle that, before a debtor gives away property, the debtor should pay or at least be prepared to pay the debtor's rightful creditors. Because an insolvent debtor by definition cannot pay all creditors, insolvent debtors should not be permitted to make gifts while leaving their creditors without recourse. Thus, for example a dividend paid by an insolvent corporation to holders of common stock is a fraudulent transfer.[21] A corporation receives no value in exchange for the dividends it pays.

However, because a gift can easily be structured or disguised as a sale – for example, the sale of a $10,000 diamond ring to a relative for $10 is, in effect, a gift of $9,990 – constructively fraudulent transfers are not limited to gifts. Any transfer by an insolvent debtor for less than reasonably equivalent value is an avoidable fraudulent transfer.

Incurring debt can also be an avoidable fraudulent transaction if done either with intent to hinder, delay, or defraud or if done while insolvent for less than reasonable equivalent value. For example, consider a parent who, while insolvent and shortly before filing for bankruptcy protection, guaranteed a child's outstanding student loans in the hope that some of the assets of the parent's bankruptcy estate would be distributed to the student loan creditors. The parent received nothing in exchange for that guaranty yet the parent's other creditors are injured by it: with more claims to share in an unchanged amount of assets, each claim holder will recover less.

Fraudulent transfer law greatly affects how many commercial transactions are planned and structured. It is of paramount concern with leveraged buyouts but is also an important consideration in many transactions involving related business entities.

Exercise 6-13

Owner is the sole member of Construction Company, a limited liability company that operates a small construction business. Owner now wants to start a second business to perform landscaping work and needs a loan from Bank to get that new business running. Bank is insisting on collateral.

Bankruptcy Code).

[21] *Cf.* Boyer v. Crown Stock Distribution, Inc., 587 F.3d 787 (7th Cir. 2009); In re Structurlite Plastics Corp., 224 B.R. 27 (6th Cir. BAP 1998).

Owner is willing to have Construction Company grant Bank a security interest in its construction equipment to secure Bank's loan (whether made to Owner or to a new landscaping entity). If Construction Company is insolvent or the transaction leaves Construction Company with inadequate capital to conduct its operations, Construction Company's grant of a security interest to Bank might be an avoidable fraudulent transfer. How do you recommend restructuring the deal to reduce the fraudulent transfer risk?

Exercise 6-14

Home Improvement Center is known to the public as a single business that manufactures, distributes, and sells materials for repairing and improving homes. In fact, the business is operated by four related corporate entities with the following ownership structure:

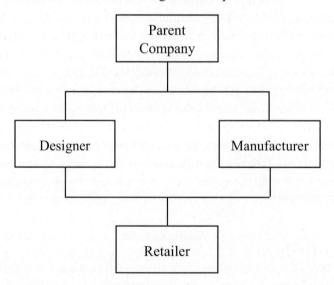

The business is in need of financing and you represent Bank, which is considering making a $400 million loan to one of the entities. The other three entities will guaranty the debt. Putting aside other considerations that might apply, to which entity should the loan be made to minimize the risk that the guarantees will be avoidable fraudulent transactions? How might Bank require that the organizational structure be changed to further minimize the fraudulent transfer risk?

We will return to deal design issues in Chapter Eight, in which we explore the tactics and ethics of negotiation.

E. PROVIDING FOR REMEDIES

Another aspect of deal design is deciding what, if anything, to include in the agreement with respect to remedies for breach. Allocating some risks through a warranty or a covenant often addresses the risk adequately. However, a transactional lawyer also needs to confront the possibility that the client's counterparty will breach in some way. The question then becomes whether the client's rights will be adequately protected.

For example, counsel for a lender or landlord should contemplate that the borrower or tenant might not pay on time and consider suggesting that the borrower or tenant provide adequate collateral, obtain a guaranty from a credit-worthy backer, or have a bank issue a letter of credit.[22] Each of these types of credit protection is, essentially, a way to deal with a potential breach. That is, each is a way to supplement the remedies that the law would otherwise provide. In short, while much of deal design is about defining the deal, another part is about enforcing the deal. The line between these two things is thin,[23] but the fact remains that a transactional lawyer needs to be concerned with end-game issues.

Contracting parties occasionally include in their written agreement provisions that simply restate a remedy for breach the law already provides. For example, it is not unusual for a security agreement to authorize the secured party to repossess and sell the collateral after default, rights that the Uniform Commercial Code expressly grants.[24] While superfluity alone is not a reason to omit or excise such provisions from written agreements, there are reasons to avoid this practice. Expressly providing for remedies obviously available under the law lengthens the written agreement. More important, it creates a negative implication that other remedies not mentioned in the agreement, but which the law would normally additionally or alternatively provide, are not to be available.

---

[22] The lawyer would then, of course, be expected to draft or review the documents needed for the type of credit protection that the parties chose.

[23] The grant of a security interest or provision of a guaranty is in one sense part of defining the deal and is in another sense about enhancing the remedies available for breach.

[24] *See* U.C.C. §§ 9-609(a)(1), 9-610(a).

So, when should an agreement expressly provide for a remedy for breach? When any of the following five reasons applies.[25]

1.   To Comply with the Law

Some transactions, particularly those involving a consumer, require that a remedy be expressly stated to be available. If so, then obviously the agreement should expressly provide for the remedy if that remedy is part of the deal.

2.   To Create or Expand a Remedy

Some statutory remedies are expressly made available only in limited situations but the law allows parties to make those remedies available in other situations. Article 9 of the Uniform Commercial Code, for example, gives a secured party certain basic remedies after a debtor's default but permits the parties to provide for additional remedies.[26] As a result, a security agreement might provide for various additional remedies, depending on the type of collateral involved.[27] Similarly, parties are sometimes permitted to waive in advance certain defenses to enforcement that the law otherwise provides. For example, most suretyship

---

[25]   *See* Stephen L. Sepinuck, *When to Contract for Remedies*, 3 THE TRANSACTIONAL LAWYER 3 (June 2013), *reprinted in* Stephen L. Sepinuck, *When to Contract for Remedies*, BUS. LAW TODAY (July 2014).

A potential sixth reason is to preserve a remedy the law might eliminate. However, it seems remarkably unlikely that the law will change so as to: (i) eliminate a remedy currently available; but (ii) permit parties to contract around that change by agreement. Accordingly, this reason is not a sufficient justification for expressly including in the parties' agreement a remedy that the law currently makes available.

[26]   *See* U.C.C. § 9-601(a).

[27]   These might include: (i) the right to disable collateral other than equipment, *cf.* U.C.C. § 9-609(a)(2); (ii) the right to vote collateralized stock, partnership interests, and LLC interests; (iii) the right to enter the debtor's premises, *cf.* U.C.C. § 9-609(a)(1); (iv) the right to sell stock or other securities in a manner that avoids application of federal securities laws regarding registration; or (v) the right to retain a surplus following a foreclosure sale to cover unliquidated or contingent secured obligations, *cf.* U.C.C. § 9-615(a), (d). For a more complete discussion of these remedies and possible limits on them, see Stephen L. Sepinuck, *When to Contract for Remedies, supra* n.25.

defenses can be waived at the outset of a transaction.[28] Accordingly, most guaranty agreements waive these defenses, thereby enhancing the remedial rights of the creditor. Most negotiable promissory notes waive presentment and notice of dishonor,[29] thereby making it easier to enforce those notes. In an agreement for many types of transactions, a liquidated damages clause can be a way to provide for monetary damages – particularly consequential damages – that the common law might otherwise limit through the requirements that damages be reasonably certain, foreseeable, and not susceptible to mitigation.[30] Alternatively, even a simple statement about the types of damages that a party is likely to suffer can be effective to make consequential damages foreseeable, and therefore more likely to be recoverable.[31]

3. To Enhance Availability of a Remedy

Some remedies, particularly equitable remedies, are within a court's discretion. For example, the appointment of a receiver to manage collateral before final judgment is subject to a variety of factors, the most critical of which are whether the creditor is undersecured and whether the debtor is insolvent.[32] To enhance the likelihood that a court will appoint a receiver, the mortgage or security agreement might provide for such an appointment upon the lender's application therefor after the borrower's default. Courts will not be bound by such a contractual provision, but the provision might help. It may also permit such an appointment to occur on an ex parte basis.[33]

---

[28] *See* RESTATEMENT (THIRD) OF SURETYSHIP AND GUARANTY § 48.

[29] U.C.C. § 3-502 cmt. 2.

[30] *See* RESTATEMENT (SECOND) OF CONTRACTS §§ 350–352. *See also* CitiMortgage, Inc. v. Chicago Bancorp, Inc., 808 F.3d 747 (8th Cir. 2015) (a repurchase obligation for breached warranties, which is essentially a liquidated damages clause, was not subject to the damages-limiting doctrines of foreseeability and mitigation; indeed, the damages under the clause were not unforeseeable; they were explicitly bargained for)

[31] *See* RESTATEMENT (SECOND) OF CONTRACTS § 356 cmt. d ("A mere recital of the harm that may occur as a result of a breach of contract . . . may increase damages by making that harm foreseeable under the rule stated § 351.").

[32] *See, e.g.,* Canada Life Assurance Co. v. LaPeter, 563 F.3d 837 (9th Cir. 2009).

[33] *See, e.g.,* U.S. Bank v. Gotham King Fee Owner, LLC, 2013 WL 2149992 (Ohio Ct.

Similarly, an award of specific performance is subject to judicial discretion and will not be ordered if, among other reasons, an award of damages would be adequate or the remedy would be unfair.[34] Because courts regularly regard equitable relief as jurisdictional and beyond the competence of private contracting parties, they are unlikely to treat a clause expressly declaring damages to be inadequate or expressly authorizing specific performance as binding or even as relevant. This certainly appears to be the approach taken by federal courts.[35] Nevertheless, a contractual clause declaring damages in certain instances to be inadequate - such as for breach of a covenant not to compete - might enhance the prospect that a court would conclude similarly. Moreover, in some states, courts regard a clause stipulating to the existence of irreparable harm in the event of breach as binding.[36] A clause declaring goods to be sold as "unique" or indicating that the buyer will not be able to cover quickly enough to avoid irreparable injury might also be helpful.[37]

Another set of remedies is available only following a material breach. Under modern contract law, the contracting parties' main promises to each other are regarded as dependent – rather than independent – covenants. As a result, one condition to a party's duty to perform is that there be no uncured material failure by the other party to perform.[38] In short, any breach gives rise to a claim for damages but only a material breach excuses the non-breaching party from the duty to perform.

Unfortunately, it is not always clear what constitutes a material breach. As a result, after a dispute arises, a game of chicken might ensue. For example, a

---

App. 2013); Fortress Credit Corp. v. Alarm One, Inc., 511 F. Supp. 2d 367 (S.D.N.Y. 2007). *Cf.* Comerica Bank v. State Petroleum Distribs., Inc., 2008 WL 2550553 (M.D. Pa. 2008) (secured creditor was not entitled to appointment of receiver in part because the security agreement did not provide for such remedy)

[34] *See* RESTATEMENT (SECOND) OF CONTRACTS §§ 357(a), 359(1), 364(1).

[35] *See, e.g.*, Dominion Video Satellite, Inc. v. Echostar Satellite Corp., 356 F.3d 1256, 1266 (10th Cir. 2004); Smith, Bucklin & Assocs., Inc. v. Sonntag, 83 F.3d 476, 481 (D.C. Cir. 1996); Riverside Publ'g Co. v. Mercer Publ'g LLC, 2011 WL 3420421 (W.D. Wash. 2011).

[36] *See* Martin Marietta Materials, Inc. v. Vulcan Materials Co., 2012 WL 2783101 (Del. 2012).

[37] *Cf.* U.C.C. § 2-716(1) (authorizing specific performance when the goods are unique or in other proper circumstances).

[38] *See* RESTATEMENT (SECOND) OF CONTRACTS § 237.

contractor renovating a home might, in violation of its agreement with the owners, leave them without running water for several days. The owners might respond by withholding the next installment payment. The contractor might then walk off the job. Who wins in the resulting lawsuit will depend on who was the first to materially breach. If the contractor's initial breach was material, the owners were permitted to withhold payment. If that breach was not material, the owners had a duty to pay. If their failure to pay the installment was a material breach, then the contractor was justified in refusing to complete the work. If their failure to pay was not material, then the contractor's refusal to finish was a further breach, and no doubt a material one. Needless to say, it is difficult to predict in advance how a court or jury will rule.[39]

To clarify the parties' rights, the agreement might expressly provide under what circumstances a breach by one party will excuse the other. To be clear, however, such a clause need not – and probably should not – be exhaustive. That is, it should not purport to identify all of the breaches that suspend the other party's duty to perform, unless the drafter is confident that nothing else should so qualify.[40]

4. To Negate or Limit a Remedy

Contracting parties often wish to make unavailable a remedy to which one or both of them would otherwise be entitled or limit the extent or duration of a remedy that will remain available. Common examples of this are disclaimers of consequential damages, liquidated damages clauses,[41] limits on the time or grounds

---

[39] *See, e.g.*, K & G Constr. Co. v. Harris, 164 A.2d 451 (Md. 1960) (involving a dispute between a general contractor and a subcontractor).

[40] One caveat is in order. Some written agreements purport to do this by simply declaring a particular type of breach to be "material." For example, one standard purchase agreement for the sale of grapes from a vineyard to a winery provides "[b]uyer's failure to make payment within sixty (60) days of due dates constitutes material breach of this agreement." There are at least two problems with this clause. First, outside of Louisiana, the contract would be governed by U.C.C. Article 2, which does not use the phrase "material breach." Thus, it is not clear what purpose such a declaration would serve in an agreement of this type. Second, payment by the buyer was the last act called for under the agreement; the seller would necessarily have shipped the grapes months before and have no duties remaining. As a result, the seller would have no performance to suspend if the buyer failed to pay, and the declaration of materiality would be meaningless.

[41] Note, a liquidated damages clause can be used to restrict damages or, as discussed above,

for rejecting tendered goods, clauses shortening the applicable limitations period, and terms conditioning a right to recovery on prompt notice of the claim. Secured lending on a nonrecourse basis can also be viewed as a negation of personal liability for any deficiency. Any intention to negate or limit a remedy must be stated in the parties' agreement. Even when clearly stated, however, a limitation may be ineffective if it fails to comply with applicable law.[42]

5. To Set Standards

Some remedies are subject to vague standards that the parties cannot waive or disclaim but which they can help clarify. For example, the Uniform Commercial Code requires that every aspect of a disposition of collateral be commercially reasonable.[43] The parties cannot by agreement alter this requirement,[44] but they can set the standards for what is reasonable, as long as those standards are not themselves "manifestly" unreasonable.[45] Accordingly, a security agreement might contain a clause on how the secured party may dispose of the collateral. Such a clause is particularly important when the parties anticipate no ready market for the collateral,[46] such as closely held stock.[47]

---

to enhance them. A liquidated damages clause that sets damages unreasonably high can be invalidated as a penalty. *See* RESTATEMENT (SECOND) OF CONTRACTS § 356(1). In contrast, a liquidated damages clause that sets damages at an unreasonably small amount is invalid only if unconscionable. *See id.* cmt. d.

[42] *See, e.g.*, U.C.C. §§ 2-719(2)

[43] *See* U.C.C. § 9-610(b).

[44] *See* U.C.C. § 9-602(7).

[45] *See* U.C.C. §§ 1-302(b), 9-603(a).

[46] *See, e.g.*, Gulf Coast Farms, LLC v. Fifth Third Bank, 2013 WL 1688458 (Ky. Ct. App. 2013) (because the security agreement covering equine collateral expressly provided that "any disposition of Collateral at a regularly scheduled auction where similar Collateral is ordinarily sold (e.g. Keeneland or Fasig-Tipton sales) with or without reserve . . . is per se commercially reasonable," the bank's sale of the collateral at a Keeneland sale was commercially reasonable and the debtors could not argue, even through expert testimony, that the disposition was commercially unreasonable); Financial Fed. Credit Inc. v. Boss Transp., Inc., 456 F. Supp. 2d 1367 (M.D. Ga. 2006) (upholding standards for notification and disposition set forth in the parties' security agreement).

[47] The agreement could: (i) disclaim any obligation by the secured party to engage in a

Exercise 6-15

Review sections 2, 4, 6, 7, 8, 13, and 14 of the form commercial lease included in Exercise 3-1. What remedies for breach, if any, should be added to the agreement to protect Tenant? What remedies for breach, if any, should be added to the agreement to protect Landlord?

Exercise 6-16

A loan agreement to Real Property Developer contains the following clause:

> **Remedies.** Upon the occurrence and during the continuance of an Event of Default, Lender shall have the right to an immediate writ of possession without notice or a hearing. Lender shall have the right to the appointment of a receiver for the Property, and Developer hereby consents to such appointment and hereby waives the right to have Lender post a bond or other security.

Drawing on the principles of good drafting discussed in Chapter Five, how should the clause be revised?

---

public offering of privately held securities; (ii) provide that any sale may be conducted by means of a private placement, restricting bidders to those who represent that they are purchasing for their own account and not with the intent to distribute; (iii) provide that the secured party may solicit offers from a limited number of prospective purchasers willing to represent that they are institutional investors or, possibly, accredited investors, and (iv) provide that any sale made by or in conformity with the practices of a broker that makes a market in similar securities is commercially reasonable.

CHAPTER SEVEN
DUE DILIGENCE

Both deal design, discussed in Chapter Six, and due diligence, which is the subject of this chapter, are about identifying and assessing risk. They differ, however, about the nature of the risk. Deal design is largely about external factors and future events that might impact one or both parties, their relationship, or the subject matter of the transaction. Due diligence, on the other hand, typically concerns facts – often facts existing when the parties enter into their transaction – about one of the parties or about the property that is the subject of the transaction.

In an ideal world, perhaps, due diligence would precede deal design. Often, however, because of the time and expense involved, parties do not wish to undertake due diligence until after they have reached a tentative agreement about the nature, structure, and price of a deal.

Due diligence is a term of art that first came into common use as a result of the Securities Act of 1933. That Act included a defense for broker-dealers of securities when accused of inadequate disclosure to investors of material information about the securities. So long as broker-dealers conducted a "reasonable investigation" into the company whose securities they were selling, and disclosed to the investor every material thing they found, they would not be liable for the failure to disclosure other information.[1] The entire broker-dealer community quickly institutionalized, as standard practice, the conduct of a due diligence investigation before any public stock offering in which a broker-dealer was involved.

Originally, the term was limited to public offerings of equity investments and focused on the legal obligations of the sellers and their agents. Over time it has come to be associated with almost any investigation conducted before a transaction is consummated. Such an investigation might be broad in scope, so as to uncover any potential problem. Alternatively, the investigation might focus on one or more specific areas of concern, such as liability for environmental pollution, infringement of copyright, the validity of a patent, tax liability, or the likelihood of future labor disputes. The list can be almost endless but it starts with the identification of one or more issues of concern.

Such issues might relate to the property at issue in the contemplated transaction. For example, it might involve a risk that what the investigating party is to receive

---

[1] 15 U.S.C. § 77k(b)(3).

might not be worth what the party expects or that someone else will have superior rights in it. Alternatively, due diligence can also involve checking into the other party to the planned transaction. For example, if the contemplated contract involves the provision of services rather than a transfer of property, a due diligence investigation might involve checking into the background of either the service provider,[2] or the service recipient.[3]

Due diligence might be motivated by a sincere desire to identify and assess the risks of the transaction. Alternatively, it might be undertaken merely to fall within some protection that the law affords to those who conduct a proper investigation. For example, an action for misrepresentation typically requires reasonable reliance. Thus, a person to whom a representation is made usually needs to conduct some due diligence to have a cognizable claim if the representation later proves to be untrue.[4] Similarly, a statute or common-law doctrine might offer protection only to those who act in good faith, which in turn might require an investigation of any red flags.[5]

---

[2]   *See, e.g.*, The Florida Bar v. Gilbert, 2018 WL 1417440 (Fla. 2018) (a lawyer's "failure to exercise even a modicum of due diligence" with respect to the hiring of a convicted embezzler to serve as the firm's bookkeeper and later as the law firm's chief financial officer, coupled with the lawyer's failure to properly supervise him, warranted disbarment after the individual embezzled nearly $5 million from the firm's trust account).

[3]   *See, e.g.*, FTC v. WV Universal Mgmt., LLC, 877 F.3d 1234 (11th Cir. 2017) (the entity that provided credit card processing services to a fraudulent telemarketer, and which was liable for assisting the telemarketer because it failed to conduct a proper investigation, was liable for the entire unjust enrichment that the telemarketer received, not merely for the much smaller amount that the processor received).

[4]   It might be possible, however, to dispense with the requirement that reliance be reasonable by including in the agreement a declaration that reliance on representations is expected without any due diligence. *See* Wise v. SR Dallas, LLC, 436 S.W.3d 402 (Tex. Ct. App. 2014). *See also* DDJ Mgt., LLC v. Rhone Group LLC, 931 N.E.2d 87 (N.Y. 2010) (when a party has insisted that the other party provide a written representation that facts are true, it will often be justified in accepting the representation without further inquiry)

[5]   For example, the Uniform Commercial Code provides several protections for someone who qualifies as a buyer in ordinary course of business. *See* U.C.C. §§ 2-403(2); 9-320(a). *See also* § 1-201(b)(9) (defining "buyer in ordinary course of business"). To so qualify, a buyer might need to conduct due diligence, particularly if there are facts known to the buyer that suggest that the seller might be doing something improper. *See, e.g.*, Chen v. New Trend Apparel, Inc., 8 F. Supp. 3d 406 (S.D.N.Y. 2014); Davis v. Carroll, 937 F. Supp. 2d 390 (S.D.N.Y. 2013).

Similarly, to be insulated from liability for some fraudulent transfers, a transferee needs to act in good faith. *See* Uniform Fraudulent Transfer Act § 8(a). *See also* 11 U.S.C.

Let us consider a simple example. You buy and sell sports memorabilia. A person you do not know offers to sell you an autographed Ted Williams 1955 baseball card. What sort of due diligence will you need to conduct? First, you will want to investigate the card to determine that it is what it purports to be. In other words, that the card is authentic and that the signature is genuine.[6] Second, you will want to ascertain that the person offering to sell the card is the rightful owner of the card and that no one else has an interest in or claim to the card. This second line of inquiry might be more difficult because there is no central registry to document ownership of most personal property, including baseball cards.

Exercise 7-1

What would you do to determine whether the prospective seller of the baseball card above is the only owner of the card?

If, instead of buying a baseball card, you were contemplating the acquisition of an expensive piece of equipment, your due diligence might include making sure:

1. The seller owns the equipment to be sold;
2. No one other than the seller has an ownership interest in the equipment or, if someone does, that interest will be transferred to you as part of the purchase transaction;
3. There are no liens on the equipment or, if there are any liens, they will be discharged as part of the purchase transaction;

---

§§ 548(c), 550(b)(2), (e)(1) (providing analogous Bankruptcy Code protections to good faith transferees of a fraudulent transfer). On occasion, this requires completion of adequate due diligence. SEC v. Helms, 2015 WL 1040443 (W.D. Tex. 2015) (attorney of Ponzi scheme investor failed to conduct adequate due diligence, preventing the investor from qualifying as a good faith transferee).

With respect to the common law, see Boresek v. U.S. Dept. of Agriculture, 109 F. Supp. 3d 1338 (D. Or. 2015) (refusing to allow a lender that paid off a first lien to be subrogated to the first lien creditor's rights because the lender failed to conduct adequate due diligence and the second lien creditor would be prejudiced by equitable subrogation); In re Ajax Integrated, LLC, 2016 WL 1178350 (Bankr. N.D.N.Y. 2016) (ruling that a secured party was not entitled to a constructive trust in part because it failed to take basic precautions and exercise due diligence when it made the loan without having the debtor sign the notice of lien forms).

[6]   The television show *Pawn Stars* features of a lot of this type of due diligence.

4. If the seller is a business entity, the person acting for the seller has the authority to bind the seller;

5. The equipment is in good working order;

6. You will have or the seller will provide whatever expertise is needed to operate the equipment;

7. If the equipment is under warranty from someone other than the seller, you will acquire the seller's rights under the warranty;

8. If the seller will be warrantying the equipment, that the seller has sufficient financial stability to make the warranty meaningful (*i.e.,* that the seller is expected to remain in business and have the resources to compensate you for any breach of the warranty); and

9. If no one will be warrantying the equipment (and perhaps even if the seller will be), that you will have access to suitable repair services if the equipment malfunctions, so that the equipment can be repaired in a reasonable time and at a reasonable price

In a more complex transaction, such as the acquisition of a business, due diligence would be much more extensive and would almost certainly include a review of all of the material agreements of the business and an evaluation of each to determine whether it can be validly assigned and whether either party is in breach.[7]

As you can see, due diligence can be a massive and time-consuming endeavor. Unfortunately, business pressures often necessitate that the due diligence investigation be conducted in some haste. Fortunately, some aspects will typically be performed by the client or the client's business advisors, leaving only a discrete portion to the lawyers. No matter what the situation, though, the transactional lawyer should have a clear understanding – preferably in writing – of which aspects of the due diligence investigation the lawyer is responsible for conducting. The lawyer does not want the client coming back years later, after a problem surfaces, falsely claiming that it was the lawyer's responsibility to uncover the problem.

The discussion of due diligence so far has focused on an investigation designed to protect the client. In what might prove to be a very important pronouncement, the New York State Bar issued an opinion indicating that a lawyer who has reason

---

[7] The movie *Working Girl* (1988) provides an example of due diligence. The lead character, played by Melanie Griffith, recommended that a client of her financial consulting firm acquire a particular radio broadcaster. At a later critical point in the movie, she counseled a colleague to make sure that the broadcaster's contract with its star DJ be reviewed because the value of the broadcasting company would be significantly reduced if the DJ would not continue to be employed by the broadcaster.

to be suspicious of the lawyer's own client has an obligation to conduct a due diligence investigation of the client, so as to be sure that the lawyer is not assisting in fraud or criminal activity.[8] The opinion purports to interpret Rule of Professional Conduct 1.2(d), which prohibits a lawyer from assisting a client in conduct that the lawyer *knows* to be criminal or fraudulent. The opinion then borrows the criminal law standard of "conscious avoidance," and concludes that a lawyer may be deemed to have knowledge that the client is engaged in a criminal or fraudulent transaction if the lawyer "is aware of serious questions about the legality of the transaction." In short, the lawyer cannot ignore red flags relating to the client's conduct or plans. The opinion adds:

> What constitutes a suspicion sufficient to trigger inquiry will depend on the circumstances. . . . For example, . . . the lawyer may have a duty to inquire of the client as to the reasons for a purchase of a business at a higher-than-market price and for running the funds through a bank in a secrecy jurisdiction to determine whether the transaction is being used to launder money, to avoid legitimate taxes, or for some other criminal or fraudulent purpose.[9]

Finally, the opinion notes that a lawyer who has a duty to conduct such an investigation is not relieved of the obligation merely because the client refuses to pay for the lawyer's time involved in it.

Exercise 7-2

Dwight and Rose Kettle, a married couple, have grown wheat and corn in Kansas for more than 20 years. Six years ago, on the advice of a tax consultant, they formed Sunflower Farms, LLC to operate their farm. Higher seed and fuel costs in the last few years, coupled with lower crop prices, have left the Kettles in need of a loan to finance production this year. They have approached Jayhawk State Bank for a $400,000 loan. All of the equipment used in the farming operation and all the crops to be produced are to serve as collateral for the loan. You are counsel for the bank and have been tasked with conducting the requisite due diligence for the loan.

A. Identify every individual or entity that might own all or part of the collateral.

---

[8] *See* N.Y. Bar Ethics Opinion 2018-04.

[9] *Id.*

B. For each piece of collateral, how will you determine who the actual owner or owners are? What documents will you examine?

C. How useful would it be if the loan and security agreement, which is to be executed on behalf of Sunflower Farms, LLC, contained the following:

Representations.

1. Borrower represents that Borrower is the sole owner of the Collateral and that none of the Collateral is encumbered by any lien.

2. Borrower represents that it has right and authority to enter into this agreement and to grant Lender a security interest in the Collateral.

D. What do you recommend to ensure that the bank does in fact acquire a security interest in the collateral?

Exercise 7-3

You represent Dentist, who has a private dental practice in Metropolis, the largest city in the State of Columbia. Dentist employs full-time three dental hygienists, one receptionist, and one office manager who does the required accounting, pays bills, bills insurers, and collects accounts. The lease on Dentist's current office space is expiring and Dentist has been negotiating with Jefferson Properties, Inc. to rent office space in its building. The premises will require a significant amount of money to renovate and reconfigure for a dental practice. Jefferson Properties will treat 50% of the renovation costs as a credit toward the rent due, but Dentist will be responsible for the remainder. Accordingly, Dentist wants to make sure that nothing will interfere with Dentist's plans or practice if Dentist rents from Landlord and incurs the expense to renovate.

Another attorney in your office will be reviewing all the applicable zoning, environmental, and public health ordinances to make sure that they will be satisfied. You have been asked to review the preliminary title report to: (i) determine which documents referenced in the report require further investigation; (ii) review each of those documents and determine which require further action; and (iii) for each document that requires further action, determine what action is necessary.

In the event that they are relevant to your assigned task, several state statutes are reproduced below. The preliminary title report for the property and all the underlying documents referenced in that report follow.

State of Columbia
General Statutes – Title 11, Part 22, Division 3

§ 11.22.301. Definitions

(1) The term "real property" as used in Sections 11.22.300 through 11.22.303 includes lands, tenements and hereditaments and chattels real and mortgage liens thereon except a leasehold for a term not exceeding two years.

(2) The term "purchaser" includes every person to whom any estate or interest in real property is conveyed for a valuable consideration and every assignee of a mortgage, lease or other conditional estate.

(3) The term "conveyance" includes every written instrument by which any estate or interest in real property is created, transferred, mortgaged or assigned or by which the title to any real property may be affected, including an instrument in execution of a power, although the power be one of revocation only, and an instrument releasing in whole or in part, postponing or subordinating a mortgage or other lien; except a will, a lease for a term of not exceeding two years, and an instrument granting a power to convey real property as the agent or attorney for the owner of the property. "To convey" is to execute a "conveyance" as defined in this subdivision.

(4) The term "recording officer" means the county clerk.

§ 11.22.302. Recording of Conveyances

A conveyance of real property, when acknowledged by the person executing the same (the acknowledgment being certified as required by law), may be recorded in the office of the recording officer of the county where the property is situated. Every such conveyance not so recorded is void as against any subsequent purchaser or mortgagee in good faith and for a valuable consideration from the same vendor, his heirs or devisees, of the same real property or any portion thereof whose conveyance is first duly recorded. An instrument is deemed recorded the minute it is filed for record.

§ 11.22.303. Lis Pendens

At any time after an action affecting title to real property has been commenced, or after a writ of attachment with respect to real property has been issued in an action, the plaintiff or the defendant may file with the recording officer of each county in which the property is situated a notice of the pendency of the action, containing the names of the parties, the object of the action, and a description of the real property in that county affected thereby. From the time of the filing only shall the pendency of the action be constructive notice to a purchaser or encumbrancer of the property affected thereby, and every person whose conveyance or encumbrance is subsequently executed or subsequently recorded shall be deemed a subsequent purchaser or encumbrancer, and shall be bound by all proceedings taken after the filing of such notice to the same extent as if he or she were a party to the action. The court in which the said action was commenced may, at its discretion, at any time after the action shall be settled, discontinued or abated, on application of any person aggrieved and on good cause shown and on such notice as shall be directed or approved by the court, order the notice authorized in this section to be canceled of record, in whole or in part, by the recording officer of any county in which the same may have been filed or recorded, and such cancellation shall be evidenced by the recording of the court order.

Excelsior Title Insurance Company
National Commercial Services
345 Main Street
Metropolis, Columbia

September 24, 2018
Abigail Adams, Esq.
Adams & Revere
1776 Lafayette Avenue
Metropolis, Columbia

Title Officer:	John Hancock
Phone:	201-111-3333
Fax No.:	201-111-4444
E-Mail:	jhancock@atic.com

Owner: Jefferson Properties, Inc.

PRELIMINARY REPORT

In response to the above referenced application for a policy of title insurance, this company hereby reports that it is prepared to issue, or cause to be issued, as of the date hereof, a Policy or Policies of Title Insurance describing the land and the estate or interest therein hereinafter set forth, insuring against loss which may be sustained by reason of any defect, lien, or encumbrance not shown or referred to as an Exception below or not excluded from coverage pursuant to the printed Schedules, Conditions, and Stipulations of said Policy forms.

The printed Exceptions and Exclusions from the coverage and Limitations on Covered Risks of said policy or policies are set forth in Exhibit A attached. Copies of the policy forms should be read. They are available from the office which issued the report.

Please read the exceptions shown or referred to below and the exceptions and exclusions set forth in Exhibit A of this report carefully. The exceptions and exclusions are meant to provide you with notice of matters which are not covered under the terms of the title insurance policy and should be carefully considered.

It is important to note that this preliminary report is not a written representation as to the condition of title and might not list all liens, defects, and encumbrances affecting title to the land.

This report (and any supplements or amendments hereto) is issued solely for the purpose of facilitating the issuance of a policy of title insurance and no liability is assumed hereby. If it is desired that liability be assumed prior to the issuance of a policy of title insurance, a Binder or Commitment should be requested.

Date as of August 31, 2018 at 7:30 A.M.

The form of Policy of title insurance contemplated by this report is:

    ALTA Standard Owner's Policy 2006

A specific request should be made if another form or additional coverage is denied.

Title to said estate or interest at the date hereof is vested in:

    Jefferson Properties, Inc., a Columbia corporation

The estate or interest in the land hereinafter described or referred to covered by this Report is:

    A fee.

The Land referred to herein is described as follows:

    Lots 13 through 18, Block 2, as shown on the map of the Monroe Addition to Metropolis, Columbia, as recorded in Volume E of Plats at page 77, Records of Washington County, Columbia.

At the date hereof exceptions to coverage in addition to the printed Exceptions and Exclusions in said policy form would be as follows:

1.   General and specific taxes and assessments for the 2018 year, a lien not yet due or payable.

2.   General and special taxes and assessments for the 2018 year.
      First Installment: $3,021.29, PAID
      Penalty: $0.00
      Second Installment: $3,021.28, PAYABLE
      Penalty: $0.00

3.   The lien of supplemental taxes, if any, assessed pursuant to Chapter 3.5 commencing with Section 75 of the Columbia Revenue and Taxation Code.

4.   Water rights, claims to title to water, whether or not shown by the public records.

5.   Rights of the public in and to that portion of the land lying within any road, street, or highway.

6.   An easement for electricity and gas lines and incidental purposes, recorded March 10, 1971 in Book 10204, Page 220 of Washington County, Columbia, Official Records.
      In Favor of: Columbia Power Company, Inc., a corporation
      Affects: As described therein

7.   Rights, reservations, and exceptions contained in that certain Quitclaim Deed dated April 18, 1981, recorded May 12, 1981 in book 11223, Page 101, aforesaid Official Records.

8. Covenants, conditions, and restrictions contained in Quitclaim Deed dated May 29, 2007, recorded May 30, 2007, as Instrument No. 07-123456789, aforesaid Official Records, but deleting any covenant, condition, or restriction indicating a preference, limitation, or discrimination based on race, color, religion, sex, handicap, familial status, national origin, sexual orientation, marital status, ancestry, source of income or disability, to the extent such covenants, conditions, and restrictions violate Title 42, Section 3054(c), of the United States Code or Section 12955 of the Columbia Government Code. Lawful restrictions under state and federal law on the age of occupants in senior housing or housing for older persons shall not be constructed as restrictions based on familial status.

9. A mortgage, to secure an original principal indebtedness of $625,000.00, and any other amounts or obligations secured thereby, recorded July 6, 2007, as Instrument No. 07 1234567, aforesaid Official records.

      Dated: July 5, 2007
      Mortgagor: Jefferson Properties, Inc., a Columbia corporation
      Mortgagee: First State Bank, a Columbia state banking corporation

10. Notice of pendency of action recorded April 16, 2018, as Instrument No. 18-0069268, aforesaid Official Records.

      Court: Superior Court of Columbia, County of Washington
      Case No.:   18-00389
      Plaintiff: Burr Realty Investors, LLC
      Defendant: Jefferson Properties, Inc.
      Purpose: Specific performance under real estate contract and sale agreement

11. Any facts, rights, interests, or claims which would be disclosed by a correct ALTA/ACSM Land Title Survey.

12. Rights of parties in possession.

EXHIBIT A
LIST OF PRINTED EXCEPTIONS AND EXCLUSIONS

EXCEPTIONS FROM COVERAGE

This policy does not insure against loss or damage (and the Company will not pay costs, attorney's fees, or expenses) which arise by reason of:

1.   Taxes or assessments which are not shown as existing liens by the records of any taxing authority that levies taxes or assessments on real property or by the public records. Proceedings by a public agency which may result in taxes or assessments, or notice of such proceedings, whether or not shown by the records of such agency or by the public records.

2.   Any facts, rights, interests, or claims which are not shown by the public records but which could be ascertained by an inspection of the land or which may be asserted by persons in possession thereof.

3.   Easements, liens, or encumbrances, or claims thereof, which are not shown by the public records.

4.   Discrepancies, conflicts in boundary lines, shortage in area, encroachments, or any other facts which a correct survey would disclose, and which are not shown by the public records.

5.   (a) Unpatented mining claims; (b) reservations or exceptions in patents or in Acts authorizing the issuance thereof; (c) water rights, claims, or title to water, whether or not the matters excepted under (a), (b), or (c) are shown by the public records.

EXCLUSIONS FROM COVERAGE

The following matters are expressly excluded from the coverage of this policy and the Company will not pay loss or damage, costs, attorney's fees, or expenses which arise by reason of:

1.   (a) Any law, ordinance, or governmental regulation (including but not limited to building and zoning laws, ordinances, or regulations) restricting, regulating, prohibiting, or relating to (i) the occupancy, use, or enjoyment of the land; (ii) the character, dimensions, or location of any improvement now or hereafter erected on the land; (iii) a separation in ownership or a change in the dimensions or area of the land or any parcel of which the land is or was a part; or (iv) environmental protection, or the effect of any violation of these laws, ordinances, or governmental regulations, except to the extent that a notice of the enforcement thereof or a notice of a defect, lien, or encumbrance resulting from a violation or alleged violation affecting the land has been recorded in the public records at Date of Policy.

         (b) Any governmental police power not excluded by (a) above, except to the extent that a notice of the exercise thereof or a notice of a defect, lien, or encumbrance resulting from a violation or alleged violation affecting the land has been recorded in the public records at date of Policy.

2.   Rights of eminent domain unless notice of the exercise thereof has been recorded in the public records at Date of Policy, but not excluding from coverage any taking which has occurred prior to Date of Policy which would be binding on the rights of a purchaser from value without knowledge.

3. Defects, liens, encumbrances, adverse claims, or other matters:

   (a) whether or not recorded in the public records at Date of Policy, but created, suffered, assumed, or agreed to by the insured claimant;

   (b) not known to the Company, not recorded in the public records at Date of Policy, but known to the insured claimant and not disclosed in writing to the Company by the insured claimant prior to the date the insured claimant became an insured under this policy;

   (c) resulting in no loss or damage to the insured claimant;

   (d) attaching or created subsequent to Date of Policy; or

   (e) resulting in loss or damage which would not have been sustained if the insured claimant had paid value for the insured mortgage or for the estate or interest insured by this policy.

4. Unenforceability of the lien of the insured mortgage because of the inability or failure of the insured at Date of Policy, or the inability or failure of any subsequent owner of the indebtedness, to comply with applicable "doing business" laws of the state in which the land is situated.

5. Invalidity or unenforceability of the lien of the insured mortgage, or claim thereof, which arises out of the transaction evidenced by the insured mortgage and is based upon usury or any consumer credit protection or truth-in-lending law.

6. Any lien, or right to a lien, for services, labor, or material theretofore or hereafter furnished, imposed by law and not shown by the public records.

7. Any claim, which arises out of the transaction vesting in the insured the estate or interest insured by this policy, by reason of the operation of federal bankruptcy, state insolvency, or similar creditors' rights laws, that is based on:

   (i) The transaction creating the estate or interest insured by this policy being deemed a fraudulent conveyance or fraudulent transfer; or

   (ii) The transaction creating the estate or interest insured by this policy being deemed a preferential transfer except where the preferential transfer results from the failure;

      (a) To timely record the instrument of transfer; or

      (b) Of such recordation to impart notice to a purchaser for value or a judgment or lien creditor.

8. The failure of the residential structure, or any portion of it, to have been constructed before, on, or after Date of Policy in accordance with applicable building codes.

UTILITY EASEMENT
Washington County, State of Columbia

GRANTOR, Martha Franklin, for and in consideration of Ten Dollars ($10.00) and other consideration, receipt of which is hereby acknowledged, hereby conveys and quitclaims to Columbia Power Company, Inc., GRANTEE, whose address is P.O. Box 10000, Metropolis, Columbia, its successors and assigns, an easement, together with the rights of ingress and egress for the installation, improvement, operation, and maintenance of electricity and gas lines over, on, and through the following described real property located in Washington County, Columbia, more particularly described as follows (the "Property"):

The northernmost six (6) feet of Lots 13 through 18, Block 2, as shown on the map of the Monroe Addition to Metropolis, Columbia, as recorded in Volume E of Plats, at page 77, Records of Washington County, Columbia.

The Grantor agrees to keep the easement clear of all buildings, structures, and other obstructions. The Grantor further agrees that all facilities installed on or underground the Property by Grantee, its successors and assigns, shall remain the property of Grantee, its successors and assigns, and may be removed at the option of the Grantee, its successors and assigns.

Should it be necessary for the Grantee, its successors or assigns to remove fencing, pavement, or any other obstruction to exercise its rights herein granted, Grantor shall promptly pay Grantee for the costs so incurred and Grantor shall be responsible for restoring the property to its original condition.

This transfer shall be binding on Grantor and Grantor's heirs, assigns, and successors in interest, and shall be deemed covenants running with the land.

Dated this 4th day of February, 1971.

Martha

_____
Martha Franklin

Franklin

STATE OF COLUMBIA)
) ss
County of Washington)

On this 8th day of March, 1971, before me, the undersigned, a Notary Public in and for the State of Columbia, duly commissioned and sworn, personally appeared Martha Franklin, known to me to be the person who executed the foregoing instrument, and acknowledged the instrument to be the free and voluntary act and deed of said Martha Franklin, for the uses and purposes therein mentioned.

GIVEN under my hand and official seal this 8th day of March, 1971.

Patrick Henry

_____
Print Name: Patrick Henry

QUITCLAIM DEED
Washington County, State of Columbia

GRANTOR, Martha Franklin, for and in consideration of Ten Dollars ($10.00) and other consideration, receipt of which is hereby acknowledged, hereby conveys and quitclaims to Alex Hamilton, whose address is 880 W. Center Street, Metropolis, Columbia, GRANTEE, all of her right, title, and interest in and to the real property located in Washington County, Columbia, more particularly described as follows (the "Property"):

Lots 13 through 18, Block 2, as shown on the map of the Monroe Addition to Metropolis, Columbia, as recorded in Volume E of Plats, at page 77, Records of Washington County, Columbia,

subject to the following reservation: Grantor hereby expressly saves, excepts, and reserves out of the grant hereby made, unto herself and her heirs and assigns forever, all oils, gases, coals, ores, minerals, and fossils of every name, kind, or description, and which may be in or upon said lands above described, or any part thereof, and the right to explore the same for such oils, gases, coal, ores, minerals, and fossils; and also hereby expressly saves and reserves out of the grant hereby made, unto herself and her heirs and assigns forever, the right to enter by individually or through agents, attorneys, and servants upon said lands, or any part or parts thereof, at any and all times, for the purposes of opening, developing, and working mines thereon, and taking out and removing therefrom all such oils, gases, coal, ores, minerals, and fossils, and to that end further expressly reserves out of the grant hereby made, unto herself, her heirs and assigns, forever, the right individually or through agents, servants, and attorneys at any and all times to erect, construct, maintain, and use all such buildings, machinery, roads, and railroads, sink such shafts, remove such soil, and to remain on said lands or any part thereof for the business of mining and to occupy as much of said lands as may be necessary or convenient for the successful prosecution of such mining business, hereby expressly reserving to herself and her successors and assigns, as aforesaid, generally, all rights and powers in, to, and over said land, whether herein expressed or not, reasonably necessary or convenient to render beneficial and efficient the complete enjoyment of the property and the rights hereby expressly reserved.

No rights shall be exercised under the foregoing reservation, by the Grantor or her heirs or assigns, until provision has been made by the Grantor or her heirs or assigns, to pay to the owner of the land upon which the rights reserved herein to the Grantor or her heirs or assigns, are sought to be exercised, full payment for all damages sustained by said owner, by reason of entering upon the land. PROVIDED, that if said owner from any cause whatever refuses or neglects to settle said damages, then the Grantor or her heirs or assigns, shall have the right to institute such legal proceedings in the superior court of the county wherein the land is situate to determine the damages which said owner of said land may suffer.

Dated this 18th day of April, 1981.

Martha

QUITCLAIM DEED
Washington County, State of Columbia

GRANTOR, Alex Hamilton, for and in consideration of Ten Dollars ($10.00) and other consideration, receipt of which is hereby acknowledged, hereby conveys and quitclaims to Jefferson Properties, Inc., whose address is P.O. Box 54625, Metropolis, Columbia, GRANTEE, all of his right, title, and interest in and to the real property located in Washington County, Columbia, more particularly described as follows (the "Property"):

Lots 13 through 18, Block 2, as shown on the map of the Monroe Addition to Metropolis, Columbia, as recorded in Volume E of Plats, at page 77, Records of Washington County, Columbia,

subject to the following restriction and condition: Grantee hereby agrees and covenants that no part of the Property will be used to operate an accountancy business or to provide accounting services for a period of ten (10) years from the date hereof. If any part of the Property is used to operate an accountancy business or to provide accounting services for a period of ten (10) years from the date hereof, Grantor or his heirs may reenter and terminate the Grantee's estate.

Dated this 29th day of May, 2007.

Alex Hamilton
_____
Alex Hamilton

STATE OF COLUMBIA)
) ss
County of Washington   )

On this 29th day of May, 2007 before me, the undersigned, a Notary Public in and for the State of Columbia, duly commissioned and sworn, personally appeared Alex Hamilton, known to me to be the person who executed the foregoing instrument, and acknowledged the instrument to be the free and voluntary act and deed of said Alex Hamilton, for the uses and purposes therein mentioned.

GIVEN under my hand and official seal this 29th day of May, 2007.

Mercy Warren
_____
Print Name: Mercy Warren
Notary Public in and for the State of Columbia
My Appointment Expires: May 12, 2009

REAL ESTATE MORTGAGE

FOR VALUE RECEIVED, Jefferson Properties, Inc., a Columbia corporation, (the "Mortgagor"), whose address is P.O. Box 54625, Metropolis, Columbia, does hereby grant, bargain, sell, and convey unto First State Bank, a Columbia state banking corporation, (the "Mortgagee"), whose address is 15404 East Main Street, Metropolis, Columbia, that certain real property, improvements, and appurtenances, located in Washington County, Columbia, more particularly described as follows (the "Property"):

Lots 13 through 18, Block 2, as shown on the map of the Monroe Addition to Metropolis, Columbia, as recorded in Volume E of Plats, at page 77, Records of Washington County, Columbia,

To have and to hold the Property, with its appurtenances thereon or thereto and rents therefrom, unto the Mortgagee, and its successors and assigns forever.

This conveyance is intended as a Mortgage to secure each agreement of Mortgagor herein contained and the payment of the sum of Six Hundred Twenty-Five Thousand and No/100ths Dollars ($625,000.00) with interest (together with any further advances made by Mortgagee to Mortgagor, or expended by Mortgagee to protect the Property or Mortgagee's interest therein), in accordance with the terms of a Promissory Note from Mortgagor of even date herewith, in such amount (the "Note"), payable to the order of Mortgagee, with final payment due on or before July 31, 2027, and providing for acceleration of the due date of the principal for default in the payment of interest or any installment of principal.

Mortgagor hereby represents that Mortgagor is the owner in fee simple of the above-described Property and that the Property is free from all encumbrances other than those encumbering the Property as of the date of this Mortgage;

To protect the security of this Mortgage, Mortgagor covenants and agrees:

1.   To keep the Property in good condition and repair; to permit no waste thereof; to complete any building, structure, or improvement being built or about to be built thereon; to restore promptly any building, structure, or improvement thereon which may be damaged or destroyed; and to comply with all laws, ordinances, regulations, covenants, conditions, and restrictions affecting the Property.

2.   To pay before delinquent all lawful taxes and assessments upon the Property; to keep the Property free and clear of all other charges, liens, or encumbrances impairing the security of this Mortgage.

3.   To keep all buildings now or hereafter erected on the Property described herein continuously insured against loss by fire or other hazards in an amount not less than the total debt secured by this Mortgage. All policies shall be held by the Mortgagee, and be in such companies as the Mortgagee may approve and have loss payable first to the Mortgagee, as its interest may appear, and then to the Mortgagor. The amount collected under any insurance policy may be applied upon any indebtedness hereby secured in such order as the Mortgagee shall determine. Such application by the Mortgagee

shall not cause discontinuance of any proceedings to foreclose this Mortgage. In the event of foreclosure, all rights of the Mortgagor in insurance policies then in force shall pass to the purchaser at the foreclosure sale.

4.   To defend any action or proceeding purporting to affect the security hereof or the rights or powers of the Mortgagee, and to pay all costs and expenses, including cost of title search and attorneys' fees in a reasonable amount, in any such action or proceeding, and in any suit brought by Mortgagee to foreclose this Mortgage.

5.   To pay all costs, fees, and expenses, including without limitation, reasonable attorneys' fees, in connection with this Mortgage, including the expenses of the Mortgagee incurred in enforcing the obligation secured hereby whether or not any action or proceeding is commenced, and including all appeals and bankruptcy matters.

6.   Should Mortgagor fail to pay when due any taxes, assessments, insurance premiums, liens, encumbrances, or other charges against the Property hereinabove described, Mortgagee may pay the same, and the amount so paid, with interest at the rate set forth in the Note secured hereby, shall be added to and become a part of the debt secured in this Mortgage.

IT IS MUTUALLY AGREED THAT:

1.1. In the event any portion of the Property is taken or damaged in an eminent domain proceeding, the entire amount of the award or such portion as may be necessary to fully satisfy the obligation secured hereby, shall be paid to Mortgagee to be applied to said obligation.

1.2. By accepting payment of any sum secured hereby after its due date, Mortgagee does not waive its right to require prompt payment when due of all other sums so secured or to declare default for failure to so pay.

1.3. The Mortgagee shall release this Mortgage upon satisfaction of the obligation secured.

1.4. Upon default by Mortgagor or Borrower in the payment of any indebtedness secured hereby or in the performance of any agreement contained herein, all sums secured hereby shall immediately become due and payable at the option of the Mortgagee. In such event, Mortgagee may foreclose this Mortgage and cause the Property to be sold in the manner provided by law. Out of the monies arising from such sale, Mortgagee may retain all principal, interest, and late charges, together with any sums advanced as provided herein, with interest as set forth in the Note, together with the costs and charges of such foreclosure suit and sale, including such sum as the court may adjudge reasonable as attorneys' fees to be allowed to Mortgagee.

1.5. This Mortgage applies to, inures to the benefit of, and is binding not only on the parties hereto, but on his/her/their heirs, devisees, legatees, administrators, executors, and assigns. The term Mortgagee shall mean the holder and owner of the Note secured hereby, whether or not named as Mortgagee herein.

1.6. All notices, requests, and demands hereunder will be in writing and (i) made to the address set forth above, or to such other address as either party may designate by written notice to the other in accordance with this provision, and (ii) deemed to have been given or made: if delivered in person, immediately upon delivery; if by facsimile immediately upon sending and upon confirmation of receipt; if by nationally recognized overnight courier service with instructions to deliver the next business day, one (1) business day after sending; and if by certified mail, return receipt requested, five (5) days after mailing.

Dated this 5th day of July, 2007.

Mortgagor: Jefferson Properties, Inc.

                                         Abigail Adams
                                         _____
                                         By: Abigail Adams, President

STATE OF COLUMBIA)
) ss
County of Washington)

   On this 5th day of July, 2007 before me, the undersigned, a Notary Public in and for the State of Columbia, duly commissioned and sworn, personally appeared Abigail Adams, known to me to be the person who executed the foregoing instrument, and acknowledged the instrument to be the free and voluntary act and deed of said Abigail Adams, for the uses and purposes therein mentioned.

   GIVEN under my hand and official seal this 5th day of July, 2007.

                                         Nathan Hale
                                         _____
                                         Print Name: Nathan Hale
                                         Notary Public in and for the State of Columbia
                                         My Appointment Expires: March 14, 2015

IN THE SUPERIOR COURT OF THE

STATE OF COLUMBIA, IN AND FOR THE COUNTY OF WASHINGTON

BURR REALTY INVESTORS, LLC,	)))	Case No. 18-00389
Plaintiff,	))	
vs.	))	LIS PENDENS
JEFFERSON PROPERTIES, INC.,	)))	
Defendant.	)))	

NOTICE IS HEREBY GIVEN that Burr Realty Investors, LLC, as Plaintiff has commenced an action in the Superior Court of the State of Columbia, in and for the County of Washington, against Jefferson Properties, Inc., as Defendant therein, designated as Case No. 16-00389 in which action the Plaintiff seeks an order of said court for specific performance under a real estate purchase and sale agreement as to the following described real property, to wit:

Lots 13 through 18, Block 2, as shown on the map of the Monroe Addition to Metropolis, Columbia, as recorded in Volume E of Plats, at page 77, Records of Washington County, Columbia.

Dated this 16th day of April, 2018.

KLIMA & KIMBROUGH, PLLC

Paul Revere

Paul Revere,
Attorneys for Plaintiff

CHAPTER EIGHT
THE TACTICS AND ETHICS OF NEGOTIATION

A. NEGOTIATING LEGAL ISSUES

Most scholarship and books on negotiation strategy focus on what is probably the principal goal of most negotiations: reaching agreement on the main terms of the deal.[1] In the context of a purchase and sale of goods, that might mean determining the price, the quantity, and possibly the warranties or date for delivery. For a loan, that might mean the principal amount, the interest rate, the due date, and what collateral will be provided. In settling a dispute, it might mean the size of the payment and scope of the release from liability.

Transactional attorneys do occasionally negotiate such issues. More commonly, however, the parties have resolved the principal deal points before they bring in the lawyers to "paper the deal." The transactional attorneys are expected to accurately incorporate the deal points into a written agreement and to flesh out the other terms necessary to protect their clients' rights. This task might require negotiation, but a type of negotiation that requires knowledge of the applicable law and the principles of contract drafting discussed in the preceding chapters. Consider the following illustration.[2]

Illustration – Part One

Art Collector, is contemplating the purchase of a Renoir painting from Seller, a reputable art dealer. Art Collector and Seller have agreed to a purchase price of $15 million. They have also agreed that the transaction is to be conditioned on authentication of the painting by an expert selected by Art Collector. The parties then turned the matter over to their lawyers to finalize the deal and draft the agreement. During their discussion, the lawyers have the following exchange:

---

[1] *See infra* note 13.

[2] This illustration was inspired by Tina L. Stark, *Contract Drafting: A Prerequisite to Teaching Transactional Negotiation*, 12 TRANSACTIONS 162-69 (2011).

Art Collector's Lawyer: That brings us to the matter of title. In a brokered transaction, the broker typically disclaims any warranty of title, but this is not a brokered transaction, is it? In other words, Seller is the owner of the painting, right?

Seller's Lawyer: Right. Seller obtained the painting about nine months ago from the estate of a collector, who purchased the painting 30 years ago. We showed you the provenance documents a few weeks ago in connection with your due diligence investigation.

Art Collector's Lawyer: I remember, and yes, that was very helpful. But we need something more – something in the agreement. First, we'll want a representation and warranty that the documents you provided are authentic

Seller's Lawyer: That should not be a problem.

Art Collector's Lawyer: Second, we expect Seller to be warranting that the title conveyed to Art Collector is good, the transfer is rightful, and that the painting is not encumbered by any lien.

Seller's Lawyer: Doesn't § 2-312 already imply that? Why does the agreement need to cover it?

Art Collector's Lawyer: Section 2-312 normally does imply such a warranty, but it also states that the warranty can be excluded or modified by circumstances. We want to avoid any question about that and make it clear that Seller is warranting good title.

Seller's Lawyer: Okay, that should not be a problem. Are we done?

Art Collector's Lawyer: Not quite. As I am sure you know, the painting's provenance dates back only 30 years. The painting is much older. Given all the press attention in recent years about artwork plundered by the Nazis, we are concerned that a former owner might surface and try to reclaim the painting.

Seller's Lawyer: Do you want attorney's fees for the defense? Would not the warranty of title cover that?

Art Collector's Lawyer: It might, but our concern goes beyond attorney's fees. As I understand it, the statute of limitations does not begin to run on a rightful owner's claim for conversion against the current possessor until the owner knows or has reason to know who has possession. In contrast, the warranty is breached, if at all, at the time the painting is delivered, even if neither party is aware of the breach at that time. Thus, the statute of limitations on a claim for breach of warranty might expire long before a former owner surfaces and seeks the painting.

Seller's Lawyer: Okay, I see your point. So, what do you want?

Art Collector's Lawyer: We need an indemnity agreement. Such an agreement cannot be breached until the request to indemnify is made; hence, it has the effect of extending Seller's responsibility for any defect in title.

Seller's Lawyer: That seems reasonable. How long do you want the indemnification obligation to last?

Art Collector's Lawyer: For as long as my client either owns the painting or is potentially liable to someone further down the chain of title.

Seller's Lawyer: I don't know; that could be forever. Seller will want some finality to this transaction. I will have to confer with my client and get back to you.

There are several things worth noting about a negotiation of this type. First, the parties agreed to the essential business terms and then turned to the lawyers to memorialize it. But that is not the job of a mere scribe. The lawyers need to understand the legal implications of the business deal – that is, appreciate the legal risks associated with the transaction – and then supplement the agreement with additional terms designed to provide their client with appropriate rights and effective remedies. Second, to do this, the lawyers need to know how each type of contract term works and what the applicable law is. It also helps to have some creativity in problem solving. Third, on some matters, the transactional lawyer will simply accede and on others the lawyer will seek guidance from the client. For example, in the dialogue above, Seller's attorney pretty much agreed to include a representation and warranty that the provenance documents are authentic and to add an express warranty of title, although the agreement on both points was no doubt tentative and subject to Seller's approval. In contrast, Seller's attorney balked at the idea of an eternal duty to indemnify. Knowing when to agree and when to push back can be difficult and will depend on a variety of factors, including the importance of the issue, the risk it poses to the client, and how much trust the client has placed in, and how much authority the client has delegated, to the attorney.

Finally, this type of negotiation encompasses more than the general substance of the terms needed to flesh out the deal. It also involves haggling over the language of the agreement. It therefore implicates every aspect of contract drafting covered in the previous chapters of this book. Consider the following extension of the illustration.

Illustration – Part Two

After conferring with Seller, Seller's lawyer sent Art Collector's lawyer an initial draft of the purchase and sale agreement. The draft includes the following indemnification clause:

> ### *Indemnification.*
>
> Seller shall, for [x] years from the date hereof, indemnify, defend, and hold Art Collector harmless from any loss, cost, expense, or liability, including reasonable attorney's fees, arising out of any breach of the warranty of title with respect to the Painting.

The lawyers then had another conversation:

Art Collector's Lawyer: I looked over the draft and have a few things to discuss. Chief among them is the indemnification clause. We appreciate Seller's willingness to include such a promise – recognizing that the length of the promise has not yet been determined – but have two concerns about the phrase "arising out of any breach of the warranty of title with respect to the Painting."

Seller's Lawyer: Okay, what are they?

Art Collector's Lawyer: First, I realize that expiration of the statute of limitations does not negate a breach, it merely makes the breach not actionable. Nevertheless, I'd prefer to tie the indemnification duty not to a breach of the warranty of title. The whole point of this clause is to avoid the statute of limitations on a warranty claim and I don't want the clause to implicitly bring the statute of limitations back in.

Seller's Lawyer: Well, I don't share the concern but I have no problem with an appropriate change. What if we rephrased "arising out of any breach of the warranty of title" to "arising out of any defect in the title"?

Art Collector's Lawyer: That suggestion brings me to my second concern. In both the written draft and the suggestion you just made, the scope of the indemnification clause is limited to situations in which there is a real defect in title. The clause would therefore not cover the cost of defending title if the defense is successful. I suggest that the clause be phrased to cover "any loss, cost, expense or liability, including reasonable attorney's fees, arising out of any claim of an ownership interest in the Painting."

Seller's Lawyer: Well I have two reactions to that. First, that would cover claims based on facts occurring at any time, even after the sale. That's not appropriate. Such a claim could be based on something Art Collector does years from now. At a minimum, the clause would need to be restricted to a claim of an ownership interest based on facts or events that predate our clients' transaction.

Art Collector's Lawyer: That makes sense, fine.

Seller's Lawyer: Second, I am not sure my client will agree to covering the cost of a successful defense. It's one thing to agree to indemnify Art Collector for a loss of the painting, it's quite another to bear the costs of defending against frivolous or baseless claims. That's just a risk associated with owning anything and is therefore a risk that Art Collection should be assuming. But let me talk with my client and get back to you.

Art Collector's Lawyer: That will be fine. Thanks.

Notice that, in this second conversation, even though the conversation focused on the language of the written agreement, the lawyers again agreed to compromise on some points while deferring agreement on other matters until they conferred with their clients. That is not uncommon.

One often critical portion of a negotiation such as this is knowing when not to raise an issue. For example, one thing that might have occurred to Art Collector's lawyer when reviewing the draft indemnification clause in the illustration above is that the indemnification clause does not explain the extent of Seller's liability. For example, if five years after the sale, a rightful owner of the painting appeared and successfully reclaimed the painting, which in turn prompted Art Collector to seek indemnification from Seller, for what amount would Seller be liable: (i) the purchase price that Art Collector paid to Seller; or (ii) the value of the painting at the time the rightful owner reclaimed it?[3] If the painting appreciates in value, which is presumably a very real possibility, the difference between these two amounts could be substantial.

However, raising the issue in the negotiation with Seller's lawyer is probably not in Art Collector's interest. That is because Seller and Seller's attorney would almost assuredly insist that Seller's liability be limited to the purchase price paid (plus the costs incurred in defending against the rightful owner's claim). So, from the perspective of Art Collector's lawyer, the choice is between: (i) raising the issue and, in all likelihood, having the written agreement clarified in a way that suits Seller; or (ii) not raising the issue and thus leaving the document ambiguous, so that a court might interpret it favorably to Art Collector.

This kind of tactical silence might make some uncomfortable or seem deceitful. Such feelings are natural and appropriate. Attorneys engaged in transactional work, like their counterparts who litigate, must abide by the applicable rules of professional conduct. That means, among other things, that they must be diligent, be honest, and not disclose confidential information. Read the following nine excerpts from the ABA Model Rules of Professional Conduct, which expand upon these basic ethical precepts. Most states have adopted rules based on the ABA model. Then consider the problems that follow. In doing so, bear in mind that determining what the rules require and permit in a particular situation is not the end of the analysis. Being ethical sometimes means more than merely conforming one's behavior to the minimum standards mandated by the applicable licensing board. Also bear in mind that professional misconduct can lead to tort liability, not merely to the client but also to those with whom the client contracts.[4] Thus, a transactional attorney might need to be aware of, and conform to, ethical norms outside the rules that can lead to disciplinary sanctions.

---

[3] Put another way, the purchase price is a reliance measure of Art Collector's "loss"; the value at the time of reclamation is an expectancy measure of Art Collector's "loss."

[4] *See. e.g.,* Raicevic v. Lopez, 2015 WL 301936 (Cal. Ct. App. 2015) (law firm could be liable for misrepresentation in its letter transmitting a draft agreement to a party that contracted with the firm's client).

ABA Model Rules of Professional Conduct

Rule 1.2　Scope of Representation and Allocation of Authority Between Client and Lawyer

* * *

(d) A lawyer shall not counsel a client to engage, or assist a client, in conduct that the lawyer knows is criminal or fraudulent, but a lawyer may discuss the legal consequences of any proposed course of conduct with a client and may counsel or assist a client to make a good faith effort to determine the validity, scope, meaning or application of the law.

Rule 1.3　Diligence

A lawyer shall act with reasonable diligence and promptness in representing a client.

Rule 1.4　Communication

(a) A lawyer shall:

(1) promptly inform the client of any decision or circumstance with respect to which the client's informed consent, as defined in Rule 1.0(e), is required by these Rules;

(2) reasonably consult with the client about the means by which the client's objectives are to be accomplished;

(3) keep the client reasonably informed about the status of the matter;

(4) promptly comply with reasonable requests for information; and

(5) consult with the client about any relevant limitation on the lawyer's conduct when the lawyer knows that the client expects assistance not permitted by the Rules of Professional Conduct or other law.

(b) A lawyer shall explain a matter to the extent reasonably necessary to permit the client to make informed decisions regarding the representation.

Rule 1.6　Confidentiality of Information

(a) A lawyer shall not reveal information relating to the representation of a client unless the client gives informed consent, the disclosure is impliedly authorized in order to carry out the representation or the disclosure is permitted by paragraph (b).

(b) A lawyer may reveal information relating to the representation of a client to the extent the lawyer reasonably believes necessary:

(1) to prevent reasonably certain death or substantial bodily harm;

(2) to prevent the client from committing a crime or fraud that is reasonably certain to result in substantial injury to the financial interests or property of another and in furtherance of which the client has used or is using the lawyer's services;

(3) to prevent, mitigate or rectify substantial injury to the financial interests or property of another that is reasonably certain to result or has resulted from the client's commission of a crime or fraud in furtherance of which the client has used the lawyer's services;

(4) to secure legal advice about the lawyer's compliance with these Rules;

(5) to establish a claim or defense on behalf of the lawyer in a controversy between the lawyer and the client, to establish a defense to a criminal charge or civil claim against the lawyer based upon conduct in which the client was involved, or to respond to allegations in any proceeding concerning the lawyer's representation of the client; or

(6) to comply with other law or a court order.

Rule 1.16 Declining or Terminating Representation

(a) Except as stated in paragraph (c), a lawyer shall not represent a client or, where representation has commenced, shall withdraw from the representation of a client if:

(1) the representation will result in violation of the rules of professional conduct or other law;

(2) the lawyer's physical or mental condition materially impairs the lawyer's ability to represent the client; or

(3) the lawyer is discharged.

(b) Except as stated in paragraph (c), a lawyer may withdraw from representing a client if:

(1) withdrawal can be accomplished without material adverse effect on the interests of the client;

(2) the client persists in a course of action involving the lawyer's services that the lawyer reasonably believes is criminal or fraudulent;

(3) the client has used the lawyer's services to perpetrate a crime or fraud;

(4) the client insists upon taking action that the lawyer considers repugnant or with which the lawyer has a fundamental disagreement;

(5) the client fails substantially to fulfill an obligation to the lawyer regarding the lawyer's services and has been given reasonable warning that the lawyer will withdraw unless the obligation is fulfilled;

(6) the representation will result in an unreasonable financial burden on the lawyer or has been rendered unreasonably difficult by the client; or

(7) other good cause for withdrawal exists.

(c) A lawyer must comply with applicable law requiring notice to or permission of a tribunal when terminating a representation. When ordered to do so by a tribunal, a lawyer shall continue representation notwithstanding good cause for terminating the representation.

(d) Upon termination of representation, a lawyer shall take steps to the extent reasonably practicable to protect a client's interests, such as giving reasonable notice to the client, allowing time for employment of other counsel, surrendering papers and property to which the client is entitled and refunding any advance payment of fee or expense that has not been earned or incurred. The lawyer may retain papers relating to the client to the extent permitted by other law.

Rule 4.1 Truthfulness in Statements to Others

In the course of representing a client a lawyer shall not knowingly:

(a) make a false statement of material fact or law to a third person; or

(b) fail to disclose a material fact to a third person when disclosure is necessary to avoid assisting a criminal or fraudulent act by a client, unless disclosure is prohibited by Rule 1.6.

Comment:

Misrepresentation. A lawyer is required to be truthful when dealing with others on a client's behalf, but generally has no affirmative duty to inform an opposing party of relevant facts. A misrepresentation can occur if the lawyer incorporates or affirms a statement of another person that the lawyer knows is false. Misrepresentations can also occur by partially true but misleading statements or omissions that are the equivalent of affirmative false statements. For dishonest conduct that does not amount to a false statement or for misrepresentations by a lawyer other than in the course of representing a client, see Rule 8.4

Statements of Fact. This Rule refers to statements of fact. Whether a particular statement should be regarded as one of fact can depend on the circumstances. Under generally accepted conventions in negotiation, certain types of statements ordinarily are not taken as statements of material fact. Estimates of price or value placed on the subject of a transaction and a party's intentions as to an acceptable settlement of a claim are ordinarily in this category, and so is the existence of an undisclosed principal except where nondisclosure of the principal would constitute fraud. Lawyers should be mindful of their obligations under applicable law to avoid criminal and tortious misrepresentation. [*See also* Formal Opinion 06-439 (2006).]

Rule 4.2 Communication with Person Represented by Counsel

In representing a client, a lawyer shall not communicate about the subject of the representation with a person the lawyer knows to be represented by another lawyer in the matter, unless the lawyer has the consent of the other lawyer or is authorized to do so by law or a court order.

Rule 4.3 Dealing with Unrepresented Person

In dealing on behalf of a client with a person who is not represented by counsel, a lawyer shall not state or imply that the lawyer is disinterested. When the lawyer knows or reasonably should know that the unrepresented person misunderstands the lawyer's role in the matter, the lawyer shall make reasonable efforts to correct the misunderstanding. The lawyer shall not give legal advice to an unrepresented person, other than the advice to secure counsel, if the lawyer knows or reasonably should know that the interests of such a person are or have a reasonable possibility of being in conflict with the interests of the client.

Rule 4.4 Respect for Rights of Third Persons

(a) In representing a client, a lawyer shall not use means that have no substantial purpose other than to embarrass, delay, or burden a third person, or use methods of obtaining evidence that violate the legal rights of such a person.

(b) A lawyer who receives a document relating to the representation of the lawyer's client and knows or reasonably should know that the document was inadvertently sent shall promptly notify the sender.

Rule 8.4   Misconduct

It is professional misconduct for a lawyer to:

(a) violate or attempt to violate the Rules of Professional Conduct, knowingly assist or induce another to do so, or do so through the acts of another;

(b) commit a criminal act that reflects adversely on the lawyer's honesty, trustworthiness or fitness as a lawyer in other respects;

(c) engage in conduct involving dishonesty, fraud, deceit or misrepresentation;

(d) engage in conduct that is prejudicial to the administration of justice;

(e) state or imply an ability to influence improperly a government agency or official or to achieve results by means that violate the Rules of Professional Conduct or other law; or

(f) knowingly assist a judge or judicial officer in conduct that is a violation of applicable rules of judicial conduct or other law.

Exercise 8-1

Yastrzemski and Williams are attorneys negotiating a settlement on behalf of their clients. In each of the following situations, which of the ABA Model Rules of Professional Conduct, if any, has Yastrzemski violated?

A. Yastrzemski's client has informed Yastrzemski that the client hopes to receive $3,000 in the settlement. Yastrzemski told Williams that "my client wants $5,000."

B. Yastrzemski's client has informed Yastrzemski that the client will not accept less than $3,000 in the settlement. Yastrzemski told Williams that "my client will not accept less than $5,000." *See* ABA Formal Op. 93-370; ABA Formal Op. 06-439.

Exercise 8-2

Foxx and Rice are attorneys negotiating a commercial lease on behalf of their clients. After they have exchanged several drafts and reached apparent agreement on most of the language, Foxx and Rice discuss and resolve the last few issues. Foxx promises to send a revised draft reflecting their discussions in the next few days. In each of the following situations, which of the ABA Model Rules of Professional Conduct, if any, has Foxx violated?

A. Foxx electronically transmitted to Rice a word-processing file containing a revised draft that changed the last terms agreed to in subtle but significant ways from those that Foxx and Rice discussed.

B. Foxx electronically transmitted to Rice a word-processing file containing a revised draft that accurately reflected the changes to which they last agreed but also changed some other terms in the document in subtle but significant ways. In a message accompanying the file, Foxx wrote only the following: "Here is the revised document. It incorporates the changes to which we have agreed."

C. If you were Rice, how would you be sure to discover Foxx's changes, particularly in Part B? Is there an efficient way to do so without laboriously comparing every word in the draft sent by Foxx to the previous draft?

Exercise 8-3

Lawyer represents Ortiz in connection with Ortiz's upcoming sale of a business to Fisk. The transaction is scheduled to close next week. The representations that Ortiz made in the purchase and sale agreement regarding the financial condition of the business were truthful when Ortiz signed the agreement two months ago. Since then, however, the business experienced a significant downturn in sales. As a result, Ortiz has informed Lawyer that Ortiz cannot truthfully represent at the time of the closing, as the agreement requires, that the statements remain correct. Nevertheless, Ortiz wants to make the representations and close the deal. Which, if any, of the following may Lawyer do without violating the ABA Model Rules of Professional Conduct?[5]

A. Continue to represent Ortiz in connection with the transaction and say nothing to Fisk or Fisk's lawyer about the falsity of Ortiz's representations.

B. Continue to represent Ortiz in connection with the transaction and, over Ortiz's objection, inform Fisk or Fisk's lawyer about the falsity of Ortiz's representations.

C. Withdraw from representing Ortiz in connection with the transaction and say nothing to Fisk or Fisk's lawyer about the falsity of Ortiz's representations.

D. Withdraw from representing Ortiz in connection with the transaction and, over Ortiz's objection, inform Fisk or Fisk's lawyer about the falsity of Ortiz's representations.

Exercise 8-4

You are general counsel to Bank and are currently reviewing its form automobile loan agreement. The agreement contains a clause specifying that, upon default, Bank may repossess and sell the vehicle without notification to the borrower. You agree that no notification is needed before repossessing the vehicle after a default but conclude that the law requires notification before a sale. *See* U.C.C. § 9-611(b), (c)(1), (d). Of course, most borrowers will not be aware of the law's requirements and the

---

[5]   *See* Gregory M. Duhl, *The Ethics of Contract Drafting*, 14 LEWIS & CLARK L. REV. 989, 999-1000 (2010).

presence of the clause might have an *in terrorem* effect: impel some borrowers not to assert their legal rights if Bank fails to provide notification or if a notification it does provide is untimely or contains errors. Must you remove or revise the clause? Should you? Why or why not? *See* N.Y. Ethics Op. 584 (1987); Alaska Ethics Op. 84-4.

Exercise 8-5

Petrocelli and Doerr are attorneys negotiating a complex intercreditor agreement on behalf of their clients, both of whom have made sizeable loans to the same borrower. Under the terms of the agreement, the debt owed to Doerr's client will be subordinated to the debt owed to Petrocelli's client. After they have exchanged several drafts and reached apparent agreement on most of the language, Doerr realizes that the last draft supplied by Petrocelli (and all the previous drafts) fails to include a term vital to Petrocelli's client. Without that term, the agreement will treat the debt owed to both clients equally (and thus significantly benefit Doerr's client). What must Doerr do, what must Doerr not do, and what may Doerr do? In answering these questions, consider the three ethics opinions that follow.

ABA Informal Op. 86-1518
Notice to Opposing Counsel of Inadvertent Omission of Contract Provision
February 9, 1986

Where the lawyer for A has received for signature from the lawyer for B the final transcription of a contract from which an important provision previously agreed upon has been inadvertently omitted by the lawyer for B, the lawyer for A, unintentionally advantaged, should contact the lawyer for B to correct the error and need not consult A about the error.

A and B, with the assistance of their lawyers, have negotiated a commercial contract. After deliberation with counsel, A ultimately acquiesced in the final provision insisted upon by B, previously in dispute between the parties and without which B would have refused to come to overall agreement. However, A's lawyer discovered that the final draft of the contract typed in the office of B's lawyer did not contain the provision which had been in dispute. The Committee has been asked to give its opinion as to the ethical duty of A's lawyer in that circumstance.

The Committee considers this situation to involve merely a scrivener's error, not an intentional change in position by the other party. A meeting of the minds has already occurred. The Committee concludes that the error is appropriate for correction between the lawyers without client consultation.[6]

___A's lawyer does not have a duty to advise A of the error pursuant to any obligation of communication under Rule 1.4 of the ABA Model Rules of Professional Conduct (1983). "The guiding principle is that the lawyer should fulfill reasonable client expectations for information consistent with the duty to act in the client's best interests and the client's overall requirements as to the character of representation." Comment to Rule 1.4. In this circumstance there is no "informed decision," in the language of Rule 1.4, that A needs to make; the decision on the contract has already been made by the client. Furthermore, the Comment to Rule 1.2 points out that the lawyer may decide the "technical" means to be employed to carry out the objective of the representation, without consultation with the client.

The client does not have a right to take unfair advantage of the error. The client's right pursuant to Rule 1.2 to expect committed and dedicated representation is not unlimited. Indeed, for A's lawyer to suggest that A has an opportunity to capitalize on the clerical error, unrecognized by B and B's lawyer, might raise a serious question of the violation of the duty of A's lawyer under Rule 1.2(d) not to counsel the client to engage in, or assist the client in, conduct the lawyer knows is fraudulent. In addition, Rule 4.1(b) admonishes the lawyer not knowingly to fail to disclose a material fact to a third person when disclosure is necessary to avoid assisting a fraudulent act by a client, and Rule 8.4(c) prohibits the lawyer from engaging in conduct involving dishonesty, fraud, deceit, or misrepresentation.

The result would be the same under the predecessor ABA Model Code of Professional Responsibility (1969, revised 1980). While EC 7-8 teaches that a lawyer should use best efforts to ensure that the client's decisions are made after the client has been informed of relevant considerations, and EC 9-2 charges the lawyer with fully and promptly informing the client of material developments, the scrivener's error is neither a relevant consideration nor a material development and

---

[6] Assuming for purposes of discussion that the error is "information relating to [the] representation," under Rule 1.6 disclosure would be "impliedly authorized in order to carry out the representation." The Comment to Rule 1.6 points out that a lawyer has implied authority to make "a disclosure that facilitates a satisfactory conclusion" – in this case completing the commercial contract already agreed upon and left to the lawyers to memorialize. We do not here reach the issue of the lawyer's duty if the client wishes to exploit the error.

therefore does not establish an opportunity for a client's decision.[7] The duty of zealous representation in DR 7-101 is limited to lawful objectives. *See* DR 7-102. Rule 1.2 evolved from DR 7-102(A)(7), which prohibits a lawyer from counseling or assisting the client in conduct known to be fraudulent. See also DR 1-102(A)(4), the precursor of Rule 8.4(c), prohibiting the lawyer from engaging in conduct involving dishonesty, fraud, deceit, or misrepresentation.

Md. Ethics Opinion 89-44
Communication with and/or Attorney Adversary

Your letter consists of four pages describing a very complex and detailed factual summary of various transactions, which I will not attempt to summarize in this Opinion. However, the Committee will attempt to present the issue in such a way as to be responsive to your inquiry as well as to be of some guidance to others facing similar problems. The issue which you raise is basically as follows: what duty of disclosure, if any, does a lawyer have in negotiating a transaction when the other party's counsel has drafted contracts which fail to set forth all of the terms which you believe have been agreed to, and where the omission results in favor of your client? It is assumed in the foregoing question, based on the facts set forth in your letter, that neither you nor your client in any way induced the other lawyer and his client to omit the material terms, and, indeed, throughout the negotiations, you and your client conducted yourselves in a way which implicitly should have caused the other lawyer to include the material terms. Finally, the foregoing question assumes, based on the facts set forth in your letter, that your client has instructed you not to disclose the omission to the other attorney.

The Committee believes that the answer to the foregoing question is governed by Rule 4.1 of the Maryland Rules of Professional Conduct, which provides as follows:

Rule 4.1 Truthfulness in Statements to others
(a) In the course of representing a client a lawyer shall not knowingly:
   (1) Make a false statement of material fact or law to a third person; or

---

[7]   The delivery of the erroneous document is not a "material development" of which the client should be informed under EC 9-2 of the Model Code of Professional Responsibility, but the omission of the provision from the document is a "material fact" which under Rule 4.1(b) of the Model Rules of Professional Conduct must be disclosed to B's lawyer.

(2) Fail to disclose a material fact to a third person when disclosure is necessary to avoid assisting a criminal or fraudulent act by a client.

(b) The duties stated in this Rule apply even if compliance requires disclosure of information otherwise protected by Rule 1.6

Based on the facts set forth in your letter, the Committee is of the opinion that you are under no obligation to reveal to the other counsel his omission of a material term in the transaction. Based on the facts set forth in your letter, it does not appear that you or your client have made any false statement of material fact or law to the other side at any time during the negotiations, and, furthermore, the omission in no way is attributable to a fraudulent act committed by you or your client. To the contrary, it appears that the omission was made by the other counsel either negligently or, conceivably, because they do not believe that the terms were part of the transaction. In either case, Rule 4.1(a), based on these facts, does not require you to bring the omission to the other side's attention.

We must point out that if the omission had been because of a false statement made by you or your client or because of a false statement made by you or your client or as a result of a fraudulent act by your client, then Rule 4.1(b) would have required you to bring this omission to the attention for the other side notwithstanding the confidentiality requirements set forth in Rule 1.6. However, as stated above, Rule 4.1(a) does not require disclosure based on the facts set forth in your letter. Accordingly, the confidentiality requirements of Rule 1.6 govern your conduct in this situation. In your letter you state that your client has specifically instructed you not to bring the omission to the attention of the other lawyer or his client. Rule 1.6 obligates you to obey this instruction in your letter.

Another Rule implicated by your inquiry is Rule 1.4(b), which requires a lawyer to explain matters to the client to an extent reasonably necessary to permit the client to make informed decisions. In the context of your inquiry, the Committee believes that you should explain to your client, if you have not already done so, what legal action might be commenced by the other party to reform the contracts, the likelihood of success of such an action, the expense of defending such an action, and any other matters which might impact on your client's decision as to whether to bring the omission to the attention of the other party or his counsel. If, after such a consultation, your client still instructs you not to reveal the omission, you are bound to adhere to this instruction pursuant to Rule 1.6.

STATE BAR OF CALIFORNIA
STANDING COMMITTEE ON PROFESSIONAL RESPONSIBILITY AND CONDUCT
FORMAL OPINION NO. 2013-189

STATEMENT OF FACTS

Buyer and Seller have been in discussions regarding the sale of the Company from Seller to Buyer, and have agreed in concept to some of the material terms, including total consideration of $5 million to be paid by Buyer and Buyer's requirement that Seller enter into a covenant not to compete with the Company following the sale. Buyer's Attorney and Seller's Attorney are tasked with preparing a Purchase and Sale Agreement to reflect the agreement of the parties.

Buyer's Attorney prepares an initial draft of the Purchase and Sale Agreement. One section towards the back of the 50-page draft agreement contains the terms of an enforceable covenant not to compete, and includes a provision that Buyer's sole and exclusive remedy for a breach by Seller of its covenant not to compete is the return of that portion of the total consideration which has been allocated in the Purchase and Sale Agreement for the covenant not to compete. Another section in the front of the draft agreement provides that, of the $5 million to be paid by Buyer, $3 million is to be allocated to the purchase price for the Company and $2 million is to be allocated as consideration for the covenant not to compete.

Scenario A

After soliciting input on the initial draft from Seller and Seller's tax advisor, Seller's Attorney provides Buyer's Attorney with comments on the initial draft, including the observation from Seller's tax advisor that payments received by Seller with respect to the covenant not to compete are not as favorable, from a tax perspective, as payments with respect to the purchase price for the Company.

Buyer's Attorney then prepares a revised version of the Purchase and Sale Agreement which, apparently in response to the comments of Seller's Attorney, provides for an allocation of only $1 as consideration for the covenant not to compete with $4,999,999 allocated to the purchase price for the Company. In reviewing the changes made in the revised version, Seller's Attorney recognizes that the allocation of only $1 as consideration for the covenant not to compete essentially renders the covenant meaningless, because Buyer's sole and exclusive remedy for breach by Seller of the covenant would be the return by Seller of $1 of the total consideration. Seller's Attorney notifies Seller about the apparent error with respect to the consequences of the change made by Buyer's Attorney. Seller instructs Seller's Attorney to not inform Buyer's Attorney of this apparent error. Seller's Attorney says nothing to Buyer's Attorney and allows the Purchase and Sale Agreement to be entered into by the parties in that form.

Scenario B

After receiving the initial draft from Buyer's Attorney, Seller's Attorney prepares a revised version of the Purchase and Sale Agreement which provides for an allocation of only $1 as consideration for the covenant not to compete, with the intent of essentially rendering the covenant not to compete meaningless. Although Seller's Attorney had no intention of keeping this change secret from Buyer's Attorney, Seller's Attorney generates a "redline" of the draft that unintentionally failed to highlight the change, and then tenders the revised version to Buyer's Attorney. Subsequently, Seller's Attorney discovers the unintended defect in the "redline" and notifies Seller about the change, including the failure to highlight the change, in the revised version. Seller instructs Seller's Attorney to not inform Buyer's Attorney of the change. Seller's Attorney says nothing to Buyer's Attorney and allows the Purchase and Sale Agreement to be entered into by the parties in that form.

Under either Scenario, has Seller's Attorney violated any ethical duties?

DISCUSSION

Following Client's Instruction to Not Disclose

Attorneys generally must follow the instructions of their clients. *See* ABA Model Rule 1.2(a).[8] However, if the client insists on certain unethical conduct, the attorney may have an obligation to withdraw from the representation. Rule 3-700(B)(2) provides "[a] member representing a client . . . shall withdraw from employment, if: . . . [t]he member knows or should know that continued employment will result in violation of these rules or of the State Bar Act." Such an obligation, for example, may arise if the unethical conduct in question involves a fraudulent failure to make a disclosure. * * *

---

[8] The ABA Model Rules are not binding in California but may be used for guidance by lawyers where there is no direct California authority and the ABA Model Rules do not conflict with California policy.

Under either Scenario A or Scenario B of our Statement of Facts, once Seller's Attorney has informed Seller of the development,[9] Seller's Attorney must abide by the instruction of Seller to not disclose. If, however, failure to make such disclosure constitutes an ethical violation by Seller's Attorney, then Seller's Attorney may have an obligation to withdraw from the representation under such circumstances.

Failure to Alert Opposing Counsel

Attorneys are held to a high standard, and may be subject to general obligations of professionalism. For example, attorneys have been held to have a duty to respect the legitimate interests of opposing counsel. "An attorney has an obligation not only to protect his client's interests but also to respect the legitimate interests of fellow members of the bar, the judiciary, and the administration of justice." *Kirsch v. Duryea*, 146 Cal. Rptr. 218 (Cal. 1978). Further, this Committee has previously concluded that attorneys should treat opposing counsel with candor and fairness. *See* Cal. State Bar Formal Opn. No. 1967-11. *See also* ABA Model Rule 3.4.

Any duty of professionalism, however, is secondary to the duties owed by attorneys to their own clients. There is no general duty to protect the interests of nonclients. Furthermore, a duty to nonclients would damage the attorney-client relationship.

Attorneys generally owe no duties to opposing counsel nor do they have any obligation to correct the mistakes of opposing counsel. There is no liability for conscious nondisclosure absent a duty of disclosure. There is also no duty to

---

[9]   Attorneys have an obligation to keep their clients reasonably informed about significant developments relating to the matter for which they have been employed. Rule 3-500 and Bus. & Prof. Code § 6068(m). Both the apparent error made by Buyer's Attorney in Scenario A and the intentional change made by Seller's Attorney in Scenario B would constitute a "significant development," which would require that Seller be informed of the potential for added costs and burdens of enforcement, including litigation and the likelihood that Buyer may seek reformation of the Purchase and Sale Agreement. On the other hand, if Seller's Attorney intends to inform Buyer's Attorney of the apparent error, Seller's Attorney need not inform Seller of the apparent error. Where a client has already agreed to a contract provision which is inadequately reflected in the draft contract prepared by opposing counsel, the inadvertent error by opposing counsel by itself (i.e., unless left uncorrected in the final executed version) does not constitute a significant development, and the client's attorney may correct the drafting error and need not inform the client. *See* ABA Informal Opn. No. 86-1518.

correct erroneous assumptions of opposing counsel. *See* ABA Formal Opn. No. 94-387 (no duty to disclose to opposing party that statute of limitations has run).[10]

On the other hand, it is unlawful (and a violation of an attorney's ethical obligations) for an attorney to commit any act of moral turpitude, dishonesty, or corruption. Bus. & Prof. Code § 6106. It is similarly inappropriate for an attorney to engage in deceit or active concealment, or make a false statement of a material fact to a nonclient. Bus. & Prof. Code § 6128(a). Also, an attorney may not knowingly assist his or her client in any criminal or fraudulent conduct. *See* rule 3-210; Bus. & Prof. Code § 6068(a); ABA Model Rule 1.2(d).

As a result, an attorney may have an obligation to inform opposing counsel of his or her error if and to the extent that failure to do so would constitute fraud, a material misstatement, or engaging in misleading or deceitful conduct. Even when no duty of disclosure would otherwise exist, "where one does speak he must speak the whole truth to the end that he does not conceal any facts which materially qualify those stated. One who is asked for or volunteers information must be truthful, and the telling of a half-truth calculated to deceive is fraud." *Cicone v. URS Corp.*, 131 Cal. Rptr. 2d 777 (Cal. Ct. App. 1986).

Scenario A

In Scenario A of our Statement of Facts, although the Purchase and Sale Agreement contains a covenant not to compete, the apparent error of Buyer's Attorney limits the effectiveness of the covenant because the penalty for breach results in payment by Seller of only $1. However, Seller's Attorney has engaged in no conduct or activity that induced the apparent error. Further, under our Statement of Facts, there had been no agreement on the allocation of the purchase price to the covenant, and the Purchase and Sale Agreement does in fact contain a covenant not to compete the terms of which are consistent with the parties' mutual understanding. Under these circumstances, where Seller's Attorney has not engaged in deceit, active concealment or fraud, we conclude that Seller's Attorney does not have an affirmative duty to disclose the apparent error to Buyer's Attorney.

---

[10] This opinion does not address a scrivener's error. *See* ABA Informal Opn. No. 86-1518. *See also* In re Conduct of Gallagher, 26 P.3d 131 (Or. 2001) (attorney who was aware of opposing counsel's mistake regarding settlement checks – settlement amount had been wrongly calculated – had a duty to correct such mistake). *But see* Md. State Bar Ass'n, Comm. on Ethics Opn. No. 89-44 (1989) (opining that there is no obligation to reveal the omission of a material term in a contract).

Scenario B

Had Seller's Attorney intentionally created a defective "redline" to surreptitiously conceal the change to the covenant not to compete, his conduct would constitute deceit, active concealment and possibly fraud, in violation of Seller's Attorney's ethical obligations. However, in Scenario B of our Statement of Facts, Seller's Attorney intentionally made the change which essentially renders the covenant not to compete meaningless, but unintentionally provided a defective "redline" that failed to highlight for Buyer's Attorney that the change had been made. Under these circumstances, and prior to discovery of the unintentional defect, Seller's Attorney has engaged in no such unethical conduct. But once Seller's Attorney realizes his own error, we conclude that the failure to correct that error and advise Buyer's Attorney of the change might be conduct that constitutes deceit, active concealment and/or fraud, with any such determination to be based on the relevant facts and circumstances.[11] If Seller instructs Seller's Attorney to not advise Buyer's Attorney of the change, where failure to do so would be a violation of his ethical obligations, Seller's Attorney may have to consider withdrawing.[12]

CONCLUSION

Where an attorney has engaged in no conduct or activity that induced an apparent material error by opposing counsel, the attorney has no obligation to alert the opposing counsel of the apparent error. However, where the attorney has made a material change in contract language in such a manner that his conduct constitutes deceit, active concealment, or fraud, the failure of the attorney to alert opposing counsel of the change would be a violation of his ethical obligations.

Exercise 8-6

Burelson and Conigliaro are lawyers negotiating a commercial lease on behalf of the prospective landlord and tenant, respectively. The main

---

[11] Any such determination – which may depend, for example, on whether the changed provision is further negotiated and revised (thereby effectively calling Buyer's Attorney's attention to the changed language) – is beyond the scope of this opinion.

[12] Subject to any ethical obligations regarding withdrawal from representation. *See, e.g.,* Rule 3-700.

remaining issues on which they are attempting to reach agreement are the scope of the rent escalation clause (that is, to what extent the rent will increase during the term of the lease) and the amount of any allowance for the tenant's cost of customizing the space to tenant's business. During the discussion, taking place in a conference room at Conigliaro's office, Conigliaro makes an offer on both issues. Burelson leaves the room to confer with the prospective landlord by phone, leaving behind Burelson's confidential notes about the prospective landlord's desires and bottom line. Conigliaro reviews the notes during Burelson's absence. Upon Burelson's return, the lawyers reach an agreement very close to the prospective landlord's bottom line. What ethical duties, if any, has each lawyer violated?

Exercise 8-7

Pesky is a lawyer in New Jersey who represents the potential buyer in a leveraged buyout transaction. Martinez is a lawyer in California who represents the prospective lender. While discussing via email a non-disclosure agreement for their clients to sign – something that the buyer needs before it releases any details to the lender about the prospective transaction – Pesky sends Martinez some financial projections relating to the target's business, along with a promise to send a draft of the non-disclosure agreement soon. Whom, if anyone, should Martinez notify of the disclosure of the financial projections. With respect to the financial projections themselves, what may Martinez do, what must Martinez do, and what must Martinez not do?

B. NEGOTIATING THE DEAL

Transactional lawyers often engage in substantive negotiations not merely about legal issues but about the nature or structure of a proposed transaction. Before doing this, a lawyer needs to realize that the parties are likely to have different objectives and that some of those objectives might be patent while others will be latent. The lawyer's task will be to uncover as many of those objectives as possible and determine the best method by which to negotiate a structure that accomplishes the client's most important objectives.

Modern negotiation theory[13] holds that interests and positions are a large part of negotiations. In the seminal work, *Getting to Yes*, the authors urge negotiators to focus on interests, not positions.[14] By positions, the authors mean the statements of a position that each party has articulated. By interests, they mean the underlying interests that motivate the parties. A successful negotiation almost invariably means some compromise by each side. But to reach an optimal result – one that is likely to yield to greatest happiness or value for the parties combined – the negotiators need to understand and appreciate each side's interests, not merely their stated positions. Consider the following illustration:

Illustration

Husband and Wife are recently purchased a new house. Neither likes the color of the walls in the living room and they are discussing what color to repaint the room. Husband suggests blue and Wife suggests yellow. They could compromise by mixing the paint colors to produce green, but that might be far less desirable from each party's standpoint than simply acceding to the other's preference. Choosing stripes of blue and yellow is likely to be worse.

If, however, the parties articulated their underlying motivations, perhaps they could reach a reasoned and mutually desired resolution. For example, perhaps Husband is chiefly concerned that the color go with the carpet, which he does not want to replace, while Wife is concerned that the

---

[13] A partial bibliography of modern negotiation literature includes the following:
CHARLES B. CRAVER, EFFECTIVE LEGAL NEGOTIATION AND SETTLEMENT (7th ed. 2012);
ROGER FISHER, WILLIAM URY, AND BRUCE PATTON, GETTING TO YES (3d. ed. 2011);
RUSSELL KOROBKIN, NEGOTIATION THEORY AND STRATEGY (3d ed. 2014);
DAVID A. LAX AND JAMES K. SEBENIUS, 3-D NEGOTIATION: POWERFUL TOOLS TO CHANGE THE GAME IN YOUR MOST IMPORTANT DEALS (2006);
ROBERT MNOOKIN, BARGAINING WITH THE DEVIL: WHEN TO NEGOTIATE, WHEN TO FIGHT (2010);
ROBERT H. MNOOKIN, SCOTT R. PEPPET, AND ANDREW S. TULUMELLO, BEYOND WINNING: NEGOTIATING TO CREATE VALUE IN DEALS AND DISPUTES (2000);
MICHAEL WHEELER, THE ART OF NEGOTIATION: HOW TO IMPROVISE AGREEMENT IN A CHAOTIC WORLD (2013); and
WILLIAM URY, GETTING PAST NO: NEGOTIATING YOUR WAY FROM CONFRONTATION TO COOPERATION (1991).

[14] *See* FISHER, URY, AND PATTON, *supra* note 13. The approach is often referred to as integrative bargaining. *See also* CRAVER, *supra* note 13.

color go with the upholstered furniture that they plan to place in the room and to which she has great attachment. Knowing this, the parties might be able to agree on a color that achieves both objectives.

It is frequently difficult for a party or an attorney to discern the other side's underlying interests. Moreover, sometimes a party states a position – either to the other side or to the party's own lawyer – without fully knowing or appreciating the interests that the party desired to achieve. Nonetheless, it is critical for a lawyer to determine the client's interests and the interests of the other side. That is because there can be significant asymmetries with respect to parties' interests and a skillful negotiator will be able to exploit the asymmetries for mutual gain. The illustration above is one simple example. Another example might involve a defendant, who highly values its reputation and has deep pockets, negotiating with a plaintiff who seeks damages but is not motivated by a desire to expose the defendant's wrongdoing. In such a scenario, there is an opportunity to settle the dispute for a higher amount if the settlement agreement contains no admission of wrongdoing and includes a robust set of non-disclosure provisions.

Once the lawyer has identified the client's interests and attempted to determine the interests of the other side, the lawyer needs to prioritize both sets of interests. A useful way in which to do so is to categorize the interests as either: (i) essential, (ii) important, or (iii) desirable. While there might be some uncertainty as to the category in which a particular interest falls, the process of discussing the issues with the client should clarify the degree of importance that the client ascribes to a particular interest. In most situations, it will be more difficult to correctly prioritize the other side's interests, but a lawyer should attempt to do so and should revisit the prioritization from time to time as more information is revealed by the other side.

Having prioritized the client's interests and those of the other side, the lawyer should then attempt to determine which interests are: (i) common; (ii) independent; or (iii) conflicting. Such an assessment should also include an overlay of the priority of those interests. Thus, the lawyer might determine that the client and the other side have a common interest in concluding the transaction before year end, but that her client's interest is merely an important interest whereas for the other side that timing is an essential interest.

Finally, the lawyer should determine, in consultation with the client, the client's best alternative to a negotiated agreement ("BATNA"). The concept is easy to describe but is not nearly as easy to implement. Essentially, the analysis here is to contrast the deal that the other side is offering with the client's realistic alternatives if the client fails to reach agreement with the other side. For example, if a seller of goods is having difficulty reaching an acceptable deal with a prospective buyer, the seller should assess the current proposal against its alternatives. The fundamental premise is that the client should not accept the other side's current proposal if it can obtain a better result elsewhere.

A few words about alternatives are, however, in order. First, to be meaningful, the alternatives must be realistically achievable, not merely unexplored or theoretical options. Thus, a seller of goods who has a firm offer from an alternative buyer has an achievable alternative; a seller that believes it can go to the market and find a better deal does not. Second, the variables that are likely inherent in each alternative will often make comparing one to another quite difficult. For example, one buyer might be offering to pay more but asking for extended payment terms for a portion of the purchase price. Whether that offer is preferable will depend in part on the creditworthiness of the buyer and what security can be provided to reduce the risk of nonpayment. Similarly, one offer might be subject to one or more conditions precedent. Evaluating such an offer involves assessing the likelihood that the condition will be satisfied.

Once the lawyer has outlined the client's BATNA, the lawyer should also attempt to determine what the other side's BATNA is. This might be difficult but the mere attempt will be useful in assessing the level of commitment to the negotiations that the other party might have.

Exercise 8-8

Morgan Frank is the majority owner and chief executive officer of Wizard Technology, LLC ("Wizard"), a Delaware limited liability company. The purpose of Wizard is to develop game-changing technology. Up until recently, most of Wizard's inventions have had limited commercial success and mediocre prospects.

For the past few years, however, Wizard has been working on an exciting new technology for smart phones: a proprietary miniature solar device that can be inserted into a phone and will recharge the phone's battery any time that the phone is exposed to any meaningful amount of light, whether that light be sunlight or artificial light (including incandescent, fluorescent, neon, and halogen sources). In testing that has been performed by Wizard's engineers, the results have been impressive. Much like a self-winding watch, the engineers report that a phone used exclusively outside will – assuming 12 hours of sunlight – work continuously without needing a charge and a phone used exclusively indoors will operate for 24 hours continuously without the need for a charge.   Wizard has not, however, had the technology tested by independent laboratories.

Rumors of Wizard's breakthrough have started to swirl in various circles. Among the market participants that would like to get their hands on this technology are phone manufacturers, technology companies, and battery manufacturers. In particular, Emerald Batteries, Inc. ("Emerald") has been especially focused on the technology's possibilities. Emerald is a market leader in the development and manufacture of miniature batteries for cell phones and laptops.

Emerald's newest offering, the Cyclone, was introduced in the last twelve months after many years and millions of dollars of research and development costs. The Cyclone has quickly become the gold standard in the market because of its light weight and ability to retain a charge. Currently, an average user of a smartphone that utilizes the Cyclone can get up to eight hours of continuous usage without needing to recharge. This performance eclipses the other market alternatives by up to three hours. As a result, Emerald currently has a 40 percent market share of the worldwide market for cell phone batteries and the future looks bright.

Emerald is concerned about Wizard's new technology. In particular, Emerald wants to capitalize on its investment in the Cyclone and does not want another technology to render its batteries obsolete. As a result, the president of Emerald, Maggie Hamilton, asked Emerald's investment bankers at Tinmann, Hayman & Lyon, Inc. ("THL"), to arrange a meeting with Mr. Frank to explore strategic alternatives. That meeting occurred recently and both parties regard it as positive and wish to explore a possible transaction.

At the meeting, however, Mr. Frank indicated to Ms. Hamilton that while he recognized Wizard's limitations when it came to commercializing its technology, he clearly wanted the technology to be commercialized. He indicated that he was concerned that Emerald's motives might not be to develop Wizard's technology, but instead might be to "bury" the technology.   Mr. Frank made clear that such an outcome would be completely unacceptable to Wizard. Ms. Hamilton indicated that she had public shareholders to answer to and they would not be happy with her if she made a major investment and then failed to capitalize on the investment.

Mr. Frank has indicated to Wizard's lawyers that the people at Wizard are engineers, not entrepreneurs, and that they do not know the best way to structure a potential business deal between Wizard and Emerald. He has also instructed the lawyers to look out for his interests as much as possible. As an example, he instructed them to insist that he receive a lucrative, long-term employment agreement and that the technology is marketed as the Frank Solar Device. Finally, Mr. Frank told the lawyers that he is not certain that Ms. Hamilton can be trusted. As a result, he has instructed the lawyers to be creative in structuring the transaction in such a way that Wizard can be assured that the technology is fully developed and commercialized.

Ms. Hamilton has told Emerald's lawyers that neither Emerald nor THL has a clear view as to the best way to structure a proposed deal. She has instructed Emerald's lawyers to get Mr. Frank less focused on the commercialization issue by offering him (but not the other members of Wizard) a package of financial incentives, including an employment agreement. She has also indicated that, as part of any deal, she wants the lawyers to insist that she receive a new employment agreement with robust financial incentives.

While neither side has committed to do a deal with the other, both Mr. Frank and Ms. Hamilton have indicated that it is time to "bring in the lawyers" to figure out the best structure for a possible deal.

A. Identify Wizard's interests in entering into a transaction with Emerald. Once you have done so, categorize them as essential, important, or desirable. Note, from the stated facts, you know Mr. Frank's individual interests, but his interests and Wizard's interests might not be perfectly aligned.

B. Identify Emerald's interests in entering into a transaction with Wizard. Once you have done so, categorize them as essential, important, or desirable. Note, from the stated facts, you know Ms. Hamilton's individual interests, but her interests and Emerald's interests might not be perfectly aligned.

C. Identify the different ways in which a proposed business transaction might be structured. After you have done so, determine: (i) which structure best addresses the essential interests of Wizard that you identified in Part A, and why; and (ii) which structure best addresses the interests of Emerald that you identified in Part B. Finally, for each transaction structure you have identified, determine whether it satisfies the essential and important interests of each party.

D. The instructor will divide the class into two groups, one of which will represent Wizard and the other of which will represent Emerald. The instructor might provide either or both sides with additional, confidential information. Prepare a memorandum to your client explaining your strategy for your upcoming negotiations with the other side concerning the structure of a transaction between Wizard and Emerald. The memorandum should be based upon, but should not repeat, Parts A through C of this exercise. The memorandum should detail what you think your client's BATNA is and what you think the BATNA of the other side is. The memorandum should include a clear recommendation about what structure or structures will best serve your client's interests while adequately addressing the most important interests of the other side. That recommendation must be firm and thoughtful, not something that equivocates or ignores the interests of the other side.

Part Two – Simulations

CHAPTER NINE
SIMULATION ONE – NIGHT CLUB LICENSE

———————

Facts

Red Light Lounge and Nightclub, LLC ("Red Light") operates a nightclub called Innuendo in downtown Boston most Tuesdays through Sundays. On most weekday nights (Tuesdays through Thursdays), Red Light employs a disc jockey to play music for the nightclub's patrons. On such nights, Red Light earns revenue primarily through the sale of alcoholic beverages. On most weekend nights (Fridays through Sundays), Red Light hires performers to play music and, in addition to selling alcoholic beverages, charges patrons a $10 cover charge (*i.e.*, an entry fee).

Occasionally, Red Light allows individuals and organizations to use its facilities to host an event. For these events, Red Light might charge an up-front fee, require the event sponsor to guaranty that a specified number of people will attend, or both. The decision about what to charge is based on what night of the week the event will occur, the number of people expected to attend, and the projected consumption of alcohol.

The Middlesex Public Service Society (MPSS) is a recognized student group at Middlesex University School of Law. MPSS's mission is to promote and facilitate public service both by members of the law school community and by others. As part of this effort, MPSS issues awards for exceptional public service. MPSS is run by student volunteers and operates with a meager budget. To raise additional funds to finance some of its activities, MPSS wishes to host an event at Red Light. The event will include the announcement of public service awards, an auction, and a karaoke challenge in which one or more patrons will make a donation to get one or other patrons to sing on stage.

The president of MPSS and the manager of Red Light have tentatively worked out the following outline of the deal: The event will be held two months from now on a Friday evening. MPSS will provide whatever music it wants and a karaoke machine. Red Light is to receive $2,000 for use of the night club for the evening, in addition to whatever revenue it generates from its sale of beverages and food. MPSS will sell tickets to the event, probably for $25 each, but wants to provide tickets for no charge to some people (such as the award recipients). Only people with tickets will be admitted.

Part One – Due Diligence Memorandum

You represent either Red Light or MPSS in connection with the negotiation and drafting of an agreement between them for use of the nightclub (your instructor will specify which party you represent). On the pages that follow is an agreement that Red Light used in a similar transaction in the past and which you might use as a resource in drafting the agreement between Red Light and MPSS. Begin by preparing a due diligence memorandum that explains:

(i) the issues the proposed transaction raises and about which one or both of the parties should be concerned and which the agreement should cover (paying particular attention to things not covered in the attached agreement);

(ii) the information each party will need before entering into the transaction; and

(iii) the documents each party will need to examine before entering into the transaction.

For (ii) and (iii), explain the basis for the need.

Part Two – Draft Agreement

Draft the agreement, making sure that it accurately reflects the deal points discussed above. The agreement used in the prior transaction is available in electronic format on the web page for the book: www.transactionalskills.com.

Part Three – Final Agreement

Your instructor will match you with counsel for the other party. Review the other party's draft agreement and prepare a detailed analysis of how it differs from your draft. Then, with counsel for the other party, negotiate and redraft the agreement. Submit a single, redrafted agreement.

EVENT AND VENUE AGREEMENT

This Agreement ("Agreement") is made this _____ day of _____, by and between Red Light Lounge and Nightclub, LLC, a limited liability company, (hereafter "Red Light"), located at 98 Warrenton Street, Boston, MA 02216, and the BU-Public Interest Research Group, a Boston University School of Law student organization contracting independently and not as an agent of the University, (hereafter "BU-PIRG") (Red Light and BU-PIRG each a "Party" and collectively the "Parties").

WHEREAS, Red Light owns certain facilities described in this Agreement which, from time to time, are available for rent, and

WHEREAS, BU-PIRG wishes to use Red Light's Venue to hold its annual fundraiser benefitting the Boston Legal Services Network (the "Event").

In consideration of the mutual promises and covenants contained herein, the Parties agree as follows:

1. *Venue Use*. Red Light hereby grants to BU-PIRG a limited and revocable license (the "License") to use the venue located at 98 Warrenton Street, Boston, MA 02216 (the "Venue"). The License permits BU-PIRG to use the Venue only on the Event Date, during the hours specified below, and only for the purposes set forth in this Agreement.

2. *Event Date*. The Event shall be held on March 7, 2015 (the "Event Date"), between the hours of 7:00pm and 10:00pm. BU-PIRG, including its volunteers and performers, shall have access to the Venue between 5:30pm and 11:00pm on the Event Date to set up and clean up before and after the Event.

3. *Cancellations*. A cancellation of the Event by either party must be submitted in writing pursuant to Section 14 at least 30 calendar days before the Event Date.

4. *Condition of the Venue*. Red Light shall provide the following specifications:
   A. Before the Event Date:
   > (1) Minimum of twenty (20) hours of rehearsal time at Venue. Hours of availability for rehearsal are to be scheduled and coordinated between the Parties.
   > (2) Fully functioning sound system, including microphone and speakers, for all rehearsals at Venue.
   B. On the Event Date:
   > (1) Adequate tables and chairs to accommodate at least one hundred thirty (130) people;

(2) fully functioning Sound System, including microphone and speakers;

(3) at least two qualified bartenders, currently employed by Red Light, and at least one qualified Bar Back, currently employed by Red Light;

(4) at least one bar, fully stocked with all appropriate bar items, including, but not limited to, liquor, mixers, water, and beer;

(5) one person at the door to check minimum age requirements based on proper identification; and

(6) space for the student performers to prepare and dress for the Event.

C. In the event that less than two hundred (200) tickets to the Event are sold prior to the Event Date, BU-PIRG will be responsible for the cost of providing a door person under this Section 4(B)(5).

D. Aside from the specifications set forth above, the Venue shall be provided as-is, and Red Light makes no warranty to BU-PIRG regarding the suitability of the Venue for BU-PIRG's intended use.

E. BU-PIRG shall leave the Venue in the same or similar condition as when BU-PIRG entered.

F. BU-PIRG shall be responsible for any extraordinary damage, caused by its volunteers only, and not the guests, to the Venue beyond ordinary wear and tear, and shall be required to arrange for such repair at its own expense.

5. *Costs, Proceeds, and Profits*. BU-PIRG shall be responsible for all of its own costs and expenses related to advertising and performance of the Event. BU-PIRG is entitled to all profits earned from ticket sales for the Event. Red Light shall be responsible for all of its own costs and expenses related to its normal day-to-day operations. Red Light shall be entitled to all profits earned from the sale of liquor, beer, food, or any other normal operating earnings on the Event Date.

6. *Indemnification*. Red Light hereby indemnifies and holds harmless BU-PIRG from any and all damages, actions, suits, claims, or other costs (including reasonable attorney fees) arising out of or in connection with this Agreement, including but not limited to any damage to the Venue or any injury caused to any person (including death) caused by BU-PIRG's use of the Venue. BU-PIRG shall immediately notify Red Light of any damage or injury of which they have knowledge in, to, or near the Venue, regardless of the cause of such damage or injury.

7. *Permitted Use*. BU-PIRG is authorized pursuant to the License to use the Venue to hold the Event, and for no other purpose, unless Red Light gives BU-PIRG prior written authorization for additional permitted uses.

8. *Compliance with Laws*. The parties shall not use the Venue in any manner that would violate any local, state, or federal laws or regulations.

9. *Alternate Event Date*. In the event that Red Light is unable, for reasons beyond its control, to make the Venue available to BU-PIRG on the Event Date for the purposes as set forth in this Agreement, it must notify BU-PIRG at least fifteen (15) days before the Event Date. BU-PIRG shall have the option of choosing an alternate date to hold the Event (the "Alternate Event Date"). If BU-PIRG selects an Alternate Event Date that is reasonably acceptable to Red Light, then the Alternate Event Date shall replace the Event Date for the purposes of this Agreement, and all obligations, rights, duties, and privileges as set forth in this Agreement shall remain binding on the Parties. If BU-PIRG and Red Light cannot agree upon an Alternate Event Date within 30 days of the original Event Date, then Red Light shall refund to BU-PIRG the full amount of any costs or fees in association with advertising the Event. In neither case shall Red Light be liable for any additional costs or damages suffered by BU-PIRG (over and above the advertising costs) arising out of rescheduling or cancellation of the Event pursuant to this Section 9.

10. *Assignment*. Neither Party may assign or transfer their respective rights or obligations under this Agreement without prior written consent from the other Party. Except that if the assignment or transfer is pursuant to a sale of all or substantially all of a Party's assets, or is pursuant to a sale of a Party's Venue, then no consent shall be required. In the event that an assignment or transfer is made pursuant to either a sale of all or substantially all of the Party's assets or pursuant to a sale of the Venue then written notice must be given of such transfer within 10 days of such assignment or transfer.

11. *Governing Law*. This Agreement shall be construed in accordance with, and governed in all respects by, the laws of the Commonwealth of Massachusetts.

12. *Counterparts*. This Agreement may be executed in several counterparts, each of which shall constitute an original and all of which, when taken together, shall constitute one agreement.

13. *Severability*. If any part of this Agreement shall be held unenforceable for any reason, the remainder of this Agreement shall continue in full force and effect. If any provision of this Agreement is deemed invalid or unenforceable by any court of competent jurisdiction, and if limiting such provision would make the provision valid, then such provision shall be deemed to be construed as so limited.

14. *Notification*. Any notification required or otherwise given pursuant to this Agreement shall be in writing by e-mail, a response confirming receipt requested, and addressed as follows:

– 3 –

If to the BU-PIRG:
    To: _____
    cc: _____

If to Red Light:
    To: _____
    Cc:_____

15. ***Headings***. The headings for sections herein are for convenience only and shall not affect the meaning of the provisions of this Agreement.

16. ***Entire Agreement***. This Agreement constitutes the entire agreement between BU-PIRG and Red Light, and supersedes any prior understanding or representation of any kind preceding the date of this Agreement. There are no other promises, conditions, understandings or other agreements, whether oral or written, relating to the subject matter of this Agreement.

IN WITNESS WHEREOF, the parties have caused this Agreement to be executed this ___ day of 20__.

Red Light Lounge and Nightclub, LLC

_____
Name of Authorized Person
_____
Title
_____
Signature

BU-PIRG

_____
Name of Authorized Person
_____
Title
_____
Signature

CHAPTER TEN
SIMULATION TWO – ENTITY FORMATION

Facts

Doug and Wendy Stravecchio are successful investment bankers who live and work in New York City. For years, they have been oenophiles; they have collected fine wines from all over the world and made numerous trips to wineries in France, Italy, and Napa Valley, California. They have now decided to pursue their passion for wine on a full-time basis. They have quit their jobs, sold their cooperative apartment, and decided to enter the winery business.

To shield themselves from personal liability for the obligations of the winery business (whether arising in contract or tort), the Stravecchios have decided that the winery should be owned and operated by a Delaware limited liability company ("LLC") to be named Stravecchio Winery, LLC.

After some initial investigation, the Stravecchios have identified a winery that they would like the LLC to purchase. Preliminary negotiations with the current owner of the winery indicate that the purchase price will be $6-8 million. The Stravecchios have amassed $4.2 million of their own funds to invest in this endeavor. They will contribute those funds to the LLC in exchange for a 70% interest in the LLC. Three of their former colleagues will each provide $600,000 in exchange for a 10% interest in the LLC.

Part One – Deal Design Memorandum

You represent either the Stravecchios or their three colleagues in connection with the negotiation and drafting of the LLC agreement (your instructor will specify which party you represent).[1] Prepare a memorandum in two parts. In the first part,

---

[1]   While one lawyer may represent all the parties desiring to form a limited liability company if each gives *informed consent* to such representation, Model Rule of Prof. Conduct 1.7(b) – and clients often desire this as a way to save legal expenses – such representation is fraught with problems. One authority recommends that lawyers avoid this type of engagement because of the difficulty and complexity of obtaining informed consent "and the risk of post-formation malpractice claims by irate clients (which may come years after the formation)." JOHN M. CUNNINGHAM & VERNON R. PROCTOR, DRAFTING LIMITED LIABILITY COMPANY OPERATING AGREEMENTS § 8.10(b) (3d ed. 2013).

detail the principal issues that need to be resolved and, for each issue, suggest a reasonable resolution that would serve your clients' interests. For this purpose, you might wish to consult: (i) John M. Cunningham & Vernon R. Proctor, *Drafting Limited Liability Company Operating Agreements* (3d ed. 2013); and (ii) Tarik J. Haskins, *Exit Stage Left: Getting out of Your Limited Liability Company*, Business Law Today (July 2013). For the second part, explain how the identified issues and your proposed resolution of them interrelate. For example, some issues might go hand in hand, so that if you give in on one issue, another issue becomes immaterial. Alternatively, some issues might be inversely related, so that giving in on one makes the desired resolution of another all the more important.

Part Two – Negotiation Exercise

Your instructor will match you with counsel for the other parties. Provide to opposing counsel a copy of the first part of the memorandum you prepared in Part One and review the first part of the memorandum provided to you by opposing counsel. Prepare a detailed analysis of how the suggestions made in the memoranda differ. Then, with counsel for the other parties, negotiate a resolution of these differences and prepare and submit a single term sheet that identifies how the LLC agreement will resolve each issue.

Part Three – Agreement

Prepare the LLC agreement, making sure that it accurately reflects the term sheet prepared in Part Two.

CHAPTER ELEVEN
SIMULATION THREE – ASSET ACQUISITION

———————

Facts

Doug and Wendy Stravecchio are successful investment bankers who live and work in New York City. For years, they have been oenophiles; they have collected fine wines from all over the world and made numerous trips to wineries in France, Italy, and Napa Valley, California. They have now decided to pursue their passion for wine on a full-time basis. They have quit their jobs, sold their cooperative apartment, and decided to enter the winery business.[1] For this purpose, they have formed a new Delaware limited liability company, Stravecchio Winery, LLC, and provided it with the funds needed to purchase a winery.

Ron Fine owns and operates two businesses. The first, Fine Vines, Inc., is a Delaware corporation that operates a vineyard in St. Helena, California. Fine Vines owns all of its acreage and produces grapes for sale to multiple wineries. The second business is Fine Wines, Inc., a California corporation and a so-called micro-winery.

Fine Wines is located in Yountville, California on leased real property that includes a wine tasting room, a retail store, a building where the crush and fermentation occur, and an underground, temperature-controlled chamber where the casks and bottles are stored. Fine Wines purchases grapes from several local vineyards (including Fine Vines), crushes the grapes, conducts the fermentation process, and ages the fermented wine in casks and bottles. For its best wines – those that sell for the highest price and have the highest profit margin – Fine Wines purchases grapes from Rosemary Farm pursuant to a block-acreage agreement that entitles Fine Wines to all of the grapes harvested from a specific portion of Rosemary Farm's vineyard and gives Fine Wines input into the viticultural practices used in that portion.

Ron loves cultivating and harvesting grapes, but no longer enjoys the winery business. Accordingly, he has tentatively agreed to sell the winery to Stravecchio Winery. Ron intends to use the proceeds to buy and operate a second vineyard.

---

[1] There is an old adage that the easiest way to make a small fortune in the winery business is to start with a large one.

Part One – Deal Design Memorandum

The parties have tentatively agreed to a purchase price of $7 million. The parties have not yet determined whether the transaction should be structured as:

(i) a purchase and sale of Ron Fine's shares of stock of Fine Wines, Inc.;

(ii) a purchase and sale of the assets of Fine Wines, Inc., consisting of, and to be allocated among, its leasehold estate, equipment, inventory, accounts receivable, and general intangibles (including trade secrets and rights under contractual arrangements), other than deposit accounts, investment property, and the name "Fine Wines" or any derivations thereof; or

(iii) a merger of Fine Wines, Inc. with Stravecchio Winery, LLC.

Your law firm is counsel to Stravecchio Winery, LLC. Other lawyers in your firm are preparing memoranda about the tax and licensing[2] aspects of the purchase, and how each of them impacts the decision on how to structure the transaction. You are tasked with preparing a memorandum detailing the other principal differences among the three possible structures for the transaction.

Specifically, your memorandum should also address the risks and benefits of the three alternative structures for the transaction. In doing so, bear in mind that the Stravecchios are concerned about liabilities. Ron Fine has provided a list of Fine Wines' creditors, but that list might not be complete; there might be additional trade creditors or other creditors of the winery. Accordingly, your memorandum should address how the structure of the transaction will or might make Stravecchio Winery liable for those debts. Be sure to cover the possibility of successor liability and whether compliance with the provisions of Article 6 of the applicable Uniform Commercial Code (governing bulk sales) would be required. Note that even though the agreement will select New York law to govern the transaction, that choice might not be effective with respect to the issue of successor liability, the application of bulk transfer law, or both.

Your memorandum should include a definitive recommendation about how the transaction should be structured.

---

[2]   The production and sale of wine is subject to extensive licensing rules at both the state and federal level.

Part Two – Due Diligence Memorandum

After due consideration of all of the issues, the parties have settled on an asset acquisition agreement. It is now time for the buyer and its counsel to conduct due diligence. Other members of your firm are reviewing the employment agreement that Fine Wines, Inc. has with its master vintner and the contracts it has with viticultural consultants, to ensure that those personnel will be permitted to work for Stravecchio Winery after the transaction. The client has hired a consultant to check for environmental problems with the real property. Your task is to closely review the documents that follow and then prepare a memorandum detailing:

(i) what steps (legal, business, or otherwise) you or your client can take to determine that Fine Wines has good title to the assets that it proposes to sell, that the assets are unencumbered (other than by the security interest of Sonoma Bank), and that Stravecchio Winery can acquire the assets free and clear of liens; and

(ii) any issue or problem arising from or related to the documents that follow and how you propose to deal with each issue or problem identified.

BLOCK-ACREAGE GRAPE PURCHASE AGREEMENT

This agreement is made by and between Rosemary Farms, LLP, a California limited partnership growing wine grapes in the Napa Valley, CA ("Grower") and Fine Wines, Inc., located in Yountville, California ("Buyer")

Whereas, both parties desire to grow the highest quality grapes possible to provide the winemaker the starting point needed to produce superior wine; and

Whereas, precision farming techniques and rigorous viticultural practices will be applied within select blocks of Grower's vineyard to attain this goal,

Now, therefore, the parties agree as follows.

1. *Purchase and Sale.* Grower shall sell and deliver, and Buyer shall purchase upon the terms and conditions set forth in this Agreement, all the grapes which meet the standards set forth herein, harvested from

Blocks 308 & 309 = 3.0 acres.

of Grower's vineyard commonly known as "Rosemary Farms" ("Property"). Notwithstanding anything in this Agreement to the contrary, the relationship of the parties hereto is that of independent contractors; nothing herein is intended to create or imply any partnership, joint venture, employment, agency, or any other relationship between the parties.

2. *Price.* Pricing is fixed at $5,000 per acre, regardless of yield, so long as yield does not vary from four tons/acre by more than 20%. If yield exceeds target by more than 20%, Buyer will receive a 10% reduction in pricing. If yield falls short of target by more than 20%, Buyer shall pay the fixed price plus 20%. Payment is due by December 15 of the harvest year.

3. *Grape Quality.*

(a) Grower shall, at Grower's expense, do the acts customary or necessary to the production of the grapes in the manner customarily considered best suited to production of premium quality grapes. Buyer reserves the right to advise Grower as to the time and method of harvest as provided herein, but any such advice shall not be binding in any way upon Grower, nor shall such advice subject Buyer to liability for any harm or damage caused thereby nor shall it constitute acceptance of the grapes or waiver of any standards or warranties hereunder. Grower will cooperate with Buyer and Buyer's vineyardists and viticultural representatives with respect to production and harvest of the grapes, and will, without limiting the generality of the foregoing, permit such reasonable inspections, sampling, and testing, and provide such information as Buyer may request to evaluate the grapes and the viticultural practices of Grower.

(b) As harvest approaches, Grower will regularly monitor, sample, and test for sugar, acid, and pH levels; monitor flavor development and seed maturity; and report results to Buyer via e-mail. Buyer is responsible for determining when grapes are ready for harvest, and is encouraged to visit the vineyards to make Buyer's own observations. Buyer and Grower will collaborate to schedule harvest on a mutually amenable date and time.

(c) Grower warrants that the grapes sold hereunder shall be, at the point and time of delivery: (1) whole, sound, fully-matured wine grapes of the stated variety, that have been grown by Grower upon the blocks identified herein in accordance with the best viticultural practices for premium wine grapes, conforming in all respects to the specifications set forth herein; (2) in good and merchantable condition, free from commercial defects, and suitable for the production of premium wine, (3) in compliance with all applicable federal and state laws and regulations, (4) not adulterated or misbranded within the meaning of the Federal Food, Drug, and Cosmetic Act ("FDCA"); and (5) free of pesticide residues prohibited, or in excess of tolerances established, for human consumption by the FDCA or other applicable law or regulation.

4. *Rejection of Defective Grapes.*

(a) Buyer may reject any and all grapes delivered or tendered which contain in excess of 3 percent defects by weight. Defects include, but are not limited to, decomposition or decay induced by fungi or bacteria, damage caused by exposure to subfreezing temperatures, grapes not of the stated varietal, sunburn, raisining, water stress, and breaks in the skin not caused by mechanical harvesting.

(b) Buyer may reject any container of grapes, otherwise acceptable, containing more than 3 percent material other than grapes ("MOG") by weight.

(c) Notice of Defects and MOG. Inspection for defects and MOG shall take place at Buyer's designated point of delivery. Buyer will give verbal notice of rejection due to defects or MOG within eight hours of delivery and written confirmation of rejection within ten days. Grower may remove rejected grapes from Buyer upon Buyer's verbal notice of rejection. Failure of Buyer to give at least verbal notice of rejection for excess MOG within eight hours of delivery waives Buyer's right to reject grapes for excess MOG.

5. *Term.* The term of this agreement is ten harvest years, beginning January 1, 2016, and expiring December 31, 2026, with the first delivery of grapes beginning in harvest year 2016.

6. *Governing Law.* This Agreement, and all matters or issues collateral hereto shall be governed by and construed and interpreted in accordance with the laws of the State of California.

– 2 –

7. *Successor and Assigns.* Buyer may not assign this Agreement or any rights hereunder without the prior, written consent of Grower. Any attempted assignment without such prior, written consent is void.

8. *Integration.* This Agreement constitutes the entire understanding between the parties with respect to the subject matter of this Agreement and supersedes all previous understandings, oral or written.

    IN WITNESS WHEREOF, the undersigned have executed this Agreement on October 12, 2015.

Grower

By: _____*Rose M. Keller*_____
       Rose Mary Keller, President

Buyer:

By: _____*Ron Fine*_____
       Ron Fine, President

PROMISSORY NOTE AND SECURITY AGREEMENT

For value received, the undersigned Fine Wines, Inc. (the "Borrower"), at 200 Imperial Road, Yountville, California 94599, promises to pay to the order of Sonoma Bank (the "Lender"), at 1600 Mendocino Avenue, Santa Rosa, California, 95401 (or at such other place as the Lender may designate in writing), the sum of $1,750,000.00 with interest on all amounts unpaid at the rate of 6% per annum.

I. TERMS OF REPAYMENT

A. Payments. Unpaid principal after the Due Date shown below shall accrue interest at a rate of 9% annually until paid. The unpaid principal and accrued interest shall be payable in monthly installments of $15,000, beginning on May 1, 2017, and continuing until May 1, 2022, (the "Due Date"), at which time the remaining unpaid principal and interest shall be due in full.

B. Application of Payments. All payments on this promissory note and security agreement (this "Note") shall be applied first in payment of accrued interest and any remainder in payment of principal.

C. Late Fee. The Borrower promises to pay a late charge of $100.00 for each installment that remains unpaid more than ten day(s) after its Due Date. This late charge shall be paid as liquidated damages in lieu of actual damages, and not as a penalty. Payment of such late charge shall, under no circumstances, be construed to cure any default arising from or relating to such late payment.

II. SECURITY

The Borrower hereby grants Lender a security interest in all of the Borrower's existing and after-acquired inventory, equipment, farm products, accounts, instruments, chattel paper, documents, and general intangibles to secure all obligations of Borrower to Lender whether now existing or hereafter arising.

III. PREPAYMENT

The Borrower may prepay this Note, in whole or in part, prior to the Due Date with no prepayment penalty or charge.

IV. COLLECTION COSTS

If any payment obligation under this Note is not paid when due, the Borrower promises to pay all costs of collection, including reasonable attorney fees, whether or not a lawsuit is commenced as part of the collection process.

V. DEFAULT

If any of the following events of default occur, this Note and any other obligations of the Borrower to the Lender shall become due immediately, at the option of the Lender:

    (1) the failure of the Borrower to pay any principal or interest when due;

    (2) the liquidation or dissolution of the Borrower;

    (3) the filing of a bankruptcy proceeding involving the Borrower as a debtor;

    (4) the application for the appointment of a receiver for the Borrower;

    (5) the making of a general assignment for the benefit of the Borrower's creditors;

    (6) the insolvency of the Borrower;

    (7) a misrepresentation by the Borrower to the Lender for the purpose of obtaining or extending credit; or

    (8) the sale of a material portion of the business or assets of the Borrower.

In addition, the Borrower shall be in default if there is a sale, transfer, assignment, or any other disposition of any assets pledged as security for the payment of this Note, or if there is a default in any security agreement which secures this Note.

VI. SEVERABILITY OF PROVISIONS

If any one or more of the provisions of this Note are determined to be unenforceable, in whole or in part, the remaining provisions shall remain fully operative.

VII. MISCELLANEOUS

A. Waiver by Borrower. The Borrower waives presentment for payment, protest, and notice of protest and demand of this Note.

B. No Waiver by Lender. No delay in enforcing any right of the Lender under this Note, or assignment by Lender of this Note, or failure to accelerate the debt evidenced hereby by reason of default in the payment of a monthly installment or the acceptance of a past-due installment shall be construed as a waiver of the right of Lender to thereafter insist upon strict compliance with the terms of this Note without notice being given to Borrower. All rights of the Lender under this Note are cumulative and may be exercised concurrently or consecutively at the Lender's option.

C. Amendment. This Note may not be amended without the written approval of the holder.

VIII. GOVERNING LAW

This Note shall be construed in accordance with the laws of the State of California.

IX. ENTIRE AGREEMENT.

This Note constitutes the entire understanding between the parties with respect to the subject matter hereof; there are no other understandings, conditions or terms.

The Borrower:

By: _____*Ron Fine*_____

      Ron Fine, President

Date: March 28, 2017

UCC FINANCING STATEMENT
FOLLOW INSTRUCTIONS

A. NAME & PHONE OF CONTACT AT FILER (optional)

B. E-MAIL CONTACT AT FILER (optional)

C. SEND ACKNOWLEDGMENT TO: (Name and Address)

File No. 17-65134

April 3, 2017

THE ABOVE SPACE IS FOR FILING OFFICE USE ONLY

1. DEBTOR'S NAME: Provide only one Debtor name (1a or 1b) (use exact, full name; do not omit, modify, or abbreviate any part of the Debtor's name); if any part of the Individual Debtor's name will not fit in line 1b, leave all of item 1 blank, check here ☐ and provide the Individual Debtor information in item 10 of the Financing Statement Addendum (Form UCC1Ad)

1a. ORGANIZATION'S NAME
Fine Wines, Inc.

OR | 1b. INDIVIDUAL'S SURNAME | FIRST PERSONAL NAME | ADDITIONAL NAME(S)/INITIAL(S) | SUFFIX

1c. MAILING ADDRESS	CITY	STATE	POSTAL CODE	COUNTRY
200 Imperial Road	**Yountville**	**CA**	**94599**	**USA**

2. DEBTOR'S NAME: Provide only one Debtor name (2a or 2b) (use exact, full name; do not omit, modify, or abbreviate any part of the Individual Debtor's name will not fit in line 2b, leave all of item 2 blank, check here ☐ and provide the Individual Debtor information in item 10 of the Financing Statement Addendum (Form UCC1Ad)

2a. ORGANIZATION'S NAME

OR | 2b. INDIVIDUAL'S SURNAME | FIRST PERSONAL NAME | ADDITIONAL NAME(S)/INITIAL(S) | SUFFIX

| 2c. MAILING ADDRESS | CITY | STATE | POSTAL CODE | COUNTRY |

3. SECURED PARTY'S NAME (or NAME of ASSIGNEE of ASSIGNOR SECURED PARTY): Provide only one Secured Party name (3a or 3b)

3a. ORGANIZATION'S NAME
Sonoma Bank

OR | 3b. INDIVIDUAL'S SURNAME | FIRST PERSONAL NAME | ADDITIONAL NAME(S)/INITIAL(S) | SUFFIX

3c. MAILING ADDRESS	CITY	STATE	POSTAL CODE	COUNTRY
1600 Mendocino Avenue	**Santa Rosa**	**CA**	**95401**	**USA**

4. COLLATERAL: This financing statement covers the following collateral:

All of the Debtor's existing and after-acquired inventory, equipment, farm products, accounts, instruments, chattel paper, documents, and general intangibles.

5. Check only if applicable and check only one box: Collateral is ☐ held in a Trust (see UCC1Ad, item 17 and Instructions) ☐ being administered by a Decedent's Personal Representative

6a. Check only if applicable and check only one box:
☐ Public-Finance Transaction ☐ Manufactured-Home Transaction ☐ A Debtor is a Transmitting Utility

6b. Check only if applicable and check only one box:
☐ Agricultural Lien ☐ Non-UCC Filing

7. ALTERNATIVE DESIGNATION (if applicable): ☐ Lessee/Lessor ☐ Consignee/Consignor ☐ Seller/Buyer ☐ Bailee/Bailor ☐ Licensee/Licensor

8. OPTIONAL FILER REFERENCE DATA:

International Association of Commercial Administrators (IACA)

WINERY LEASE AGREEMENT

This Winery Lease Agreement ("Lease") is made and effective March 11, 2004, by and between Big Bad Wolf, LLC ("Landlord") and Fine Wines, Inc. ("Tenant").

WHEREAS, Landlord owns approximately 12 acres of land located in Yountville, California and identified on Exhibit A hereto ("Land") and the buildings and equipment affixed to the Land, including, without limitation, a building that contains a wine tasting room and a retail store, a building and equipment that is suited to the crush and fermentation of grapes, and an underground chamber that is suited to the storage of casks and bottles of wine ("Fixtures");

WHEREAS, Landlord desires to lease the Land and Fixtures ("Leased Premises") to Tenant, and Tenant desires to lease the Leased Premises from Landlord on the terms and conditions herein set forth.

THEREFORE, in consideration of the mutual promises herein contained and other good and valuable consideration, it is agreed:

1. Term.

A. Landlord hereby leases the Leased Premises to Tenant, and Tenant hereby leases the same from Landlord, for an initial term beginning April 1, 2004 and ending March 31, 2034 ("Initial Term").

B. Tenant may extend the term of this Lease once for a period of 10 years ("Extended Term"). Tenant shall exercise such renewal option, if at all, by giving written notice to Landlord not less than 180 days prior to the expiration of the Initial Term. The Extended Term shall be upon the same covenants, conditions and provisions as provided in this Lease.

2. Rental.

A. Tenant shall pay to Landlord during the Initial Term rent as follows:

(i) for the period of April 1, 2004 through March 31, 2009, rent of $5,000 per month,

(ii) for the period of April 1, 2009 through March 31, 2014, rent of $5,500 per month,

(iii) for the period of April 1, 2014 through March 31, 2019, rent of $6,050 per month,

(iv) for the period of April 1, 2019 through March 31, 2024, rent of $6,655 per month,

(v) for the period of April 1, 2024 through March 31, 2029, rent of $7,320.50 per month, and

(iv) for the period of April 1, 2029 through March 31, 2034, rent of $8,052.55 per month.

B. If Tenant exercises its option to extend the term of this Lease, Tenant shall pay to Landlord during the Extended Term rent as follows:

(i) for the period of April 1, 2034 through March 31, 2039, rent of $8,857.81 per month, and

(ii) for the period of April 1, 2039 through March 31, 2044, rent of $9,743.59 per month.

Each installment payment shall be due in advance on the first day of each calendar month during the lease term to Landlord at P.O. Box 321 St. Helena, California 94574 or at such other place designated by written notice from Landlord or Tenant. The rental payment amount for any partial calendar month included in the lease term shall be prorated on a daily basis. Tenant shall also pay to Landlord a security deposit prior to the commencement of the Initial Term in the amount of $5,000 ("Security Deposit").

3. Use.

The Leased Premises are leased to Tenant for the purpose of operating a winery facility and for all such other uses as are reasonably incident thereto and as allowed by and in conformance with applicable laws. Allowed uses shall include, without limitation, all winery and winemaking related activities, including but not limited to crushing, fermenting, bulk wine storage, bottling, case goods storage, operating a tasting room, and maintaining administrative offices. Tenant shall not convert the Leased Premises to any other use without the written consent of the Landlord.

Notwithstanding the foregoing, Tenant shall not bring or permit any animals to be located on the Leased Premises, shall not produce or permit to be stored any hazardous material (including any mold or fungus) on the Leased Premises, and shall not use the Leased Premises for the purposes of storing, manufacturing, or selling any inherently dangerous substance, chemical, thing, or device.

4. Sublease and Assignment.

Tenant shall have the right without Landlord's consent, to assign this Lease to a corporation with which Tenant may merge or consolidate, to any subsidiary of Tenant, to any corporation under common control with Tenant, or to a purchaser of all of Tenant's assets. Except as set forth above, Tenant shall not sublease all or any part of the Leased Premises, or assign this Lease in whole or in part without Landlord's consent.

5. Repairs.

During the Lease term, Tenant shall make, at Tenant's expense, all necessary repairs to the Leased Premises. Repairs shall include such items as routine repairs of floors, walls, ceilings, and other parts of the Leased Premises damaged or worn through normal use or occupancy, except for major mechanical systems or the roof, subject to the obligations of the parties otherwise set forth in this Lease.

6. Alterations and Improvements.

Tenant, at Tenant's expense, shall have the right following Landlord's consent to remodel, redecorate, and make additions, improvements, and replacements of and to all or any part of the Leased Premises from time to time as Tenant may deem desirable, provided the same are made in a workmanlike manner and utilizing good quality materials. Tenant shall have the right to place and install personal property, trade fixtures, equipment, and other temporary installations in and upon the Leased Premises, and fasten the same to the premises. All personal property, equipment, machinery, trade fixtures, and temporary installations, whether acquired by Tenant at the commencement of the term of the Lease or placed or installed on the Leased Premises by Tenant thereafter, shall remain Tenant's property free and clear of any claim by Landlord. Tenant shall have the right to remove the same at any time during the term of this Lease provided that all damage to the Leased Premises caused by such removal shall be repaired by Tenant at Tenant's expense.

7. Property Taxes.

Landlord shall pay, prior to delinquency, all general real estate taxes and installments of special assessments coming due during the Lease term on the Leased Premises, and all personal property taxes with respect to Landlord's personal property, if any, on the Leased Premises. Tenant shall be responsible for paying all personal property taxes with respect to Tenant's personal property at the Leased Premises.

8. Insurance.

A. If the Leased Premises or any part thereof is damaged by fire or other casualty resulting from any act or negligence of Tenant or any of Tenant's agents, employees, or invitees, rent shall not be diminished or abated while such damages are under repair, and Tenant shall be responsible for the costs of repair not covered by insurance.

B. Landlord shall maintain fire and extended coverage insurance on the Leased Premises in such amounts as Landlord shall deem appropriate. Tenant shall be responsible, at its expense, for fire and extended coverage insurance on all of its personal property, including removable trade fixtures, located in the Leased Premises.

C. Tenant and Landlord shall, each at its own expense, maintain a policy or policies of comprehensive general liability insurance with respect to the respective activities of each in the Leased Premises with the premiums thereon fully paid on or before the due date, issued by and binding upon some insurance company approved by Landlord, such insurance to afford minimum protection of not less than $1,000,000 combined single limit coverage of bodily injury, property damage, or combination thereof. Landlord shall be listed as an additional insured on Tenant's policy or policies of comprehensive general liability insurance, and Tenant shall provide Landlord with current Certificates of Insurance evidencing Tenant's compliance with this Paragraph. Tenant shall obtain the agreement of Tenant's insurers to notify Landlord that a policy is due to expire at least 10 days prior to such expiration. Landlord shall not be required to maintain insurance against thefts within the Leased Premises.

9. Utilities.

Tenant shall pay all charges for water, sewer, gas, electricity, telephone, and other services and utilities used by Tenant on the Leased Premises during the term of this Lease unless otherwise expressly agreed in writing by Landlord.

10. Signs.

Following Landlord's consent, Tenant shall have the right to place on the Leased Premises, at locations selected by Tenant, any signs which are permitted by applicable zoning ordinances and private restrictions. Landlord may refuse consent to any proposed signage that is in Landlord's opinion too large, deceptive, unattractive, or otherwise inconsistent with the Leased Premises. Landlord shall assist and cooperate with Tenant in obtaining any necessary permission from governmental authorities or adjoining owners and occupants for Tenant to place or construct the foregoing signs. Tenant shall repair all damage to the Leased Premises resulting from the removal of signs installed by Tenant.

11. Entry.

Landlord shall have the right to enter upon the Leased Premises at reasonable hours to inspect the same, provided Landlord shall not thereby unreasonably interfere with Tenant's business on the Leased Premises.

12. Damage and Destruction.

Subject to Section 8 A. above, if the Leased Premises or any part thereof or any appurtenance thereto is so damaged by fire, casualty, or structural defects that the same cannot be used for Tenant's purposes, then Tenant shall have the right within 180 days following damage to elect by notice to Landlord to terminate this Lease as of the date of such damage. In the event of minor damage to any part of the Leased Premises, and if such damage does not render the Leased Premises unusable for Tenant's purposes, Landlord shall promptly repair such damage at the cost of the Landlord. In making the repairs called for in this paragraph, Landlord shall not be liable for any delays resulting from strikes, governmental restrictions, inability to obtain necessary materials or labor, or other matters which are beyond the reasonable control of Landlord. Tenant shall be relieved from paying rent during any portion of the Lease term that the Leased Premises are inoperable or unfit for occupancy, or use, in whole or in part, for Tenant's purposes. Rentals paid in advance for any such periods shall be credited on the next ensuing payments, if any, but if no further payments are to be made, any such advance payments shall be refunded to Tenant. The provisions of this paragraph extend not only to the matters aforesaid, but also to any occurrence which is beyond Tenant's reasonable control and which renders the Leased Premises, or any appurtenance thereto, inoperable or unfit for occupancy or use, in whole or in part, for Tenant's purposes.

13. Default.

If default shall at any time be made by Tenant in the payment of rent when due to Landlord as herein provided, and if said default shall continue for 15 days after written notice thereof shall have been given to Tenant by Landlord, or if default shall be made in any of the other covenants or conditions to be kept, observed, and performed by Tenant, and such default shall continue for 30 days after notice thereof in writing to Tenant by Landlord without correction thereof then having been commenced and thereafter diligently prosecuted, Landlord may declare the term of this Lease ended and terminated by giving Tenant written notice of such intention, and if possession of the Leased Premises is not surrendered, Landlord may reenter said premises. Landlord shall have, in addition to the remedy above provided, any other right or remedy available to Landlord on account of any Tenant default, either in law or equity. Landlord shall use reasonable efforts to mitigate its damages.

14. Quiet Possession.

Landlord covenants and warrants that upon performance by Tenant of its obligations hereunder, Landlord will keep and maintain Tenant in exclusive, quiet, peaceable, and undisturbed and uninterrupted possession of the Leased Premises during the term of this Lease.

5

15. Condemnation.

If any legally constituted authority condemns the Leased Premises or such part thereof which shall make the Leased Premises unsuitable for use by Tenant, this Lease shall cease when the public authority takes possession, and Landlord and Tenant shall account for rental as of that date. Such termination shall be without prejudice to the rights of either party to recover compensation from the condemning authority for any loss or damage caused by the condemnation. Neither party shall have any rights in or to any award made to the other by the condemning authority.

16. Subordination.

Tenant accepts this Lease subject and subordinate to any mortgage, deed of trust, or other lien currently existing or hereafter arising upon the Leased Premises and to any renewals, refinancing, and extensions thereof. Landlord is hereby irrevocably vested with full power and authority to subordinate this Lease to any mortgage, deed of trust, or other lien now existing or hereafter placed upon the Leased Premises and Tenant agrees upon demand to execute such further instruments subordinating this Lease or attorning to the holder of any such liens as Landlord may request. In the event that Tenant should fail to execute any instrument of subordination herein required to be executed by Tenant promptly as requested, Tenant hereby irrevocably constitutes Landlord as its attorney-in-fact to execute such instrument in Tenant's name, place, and stead, it being agreed that such power is one coupled with an interest. Tenant agrees that it will from time to time upon request by Landlord execute and deliver to such persons as Landlord shall request a statement in recordable form certifying that this Lease is unmodified and in full force and effect (or if there have been modifications, that the same is in full force and effect as so modified), stating the dates to which rent and other charges payable under this Lease have been paid, stating that Landlord is not in default hereunder (or if Tenant alleges a default stating the nature of such alleged default), and further stating such other matters as Landlord shall reasonably require.

17. Security Deposit.

The Security Deposit shall be held by Landlord without liability for interest and as security for the performance by Tenant of Tenant's covenants and obligations under this Lease, it being expressly understood that the Security Deposit shall not be considered an advance payment of rental or a measure of Landlord's damages in case of default by Tenant. Unless otherwise provided by mandatory non-waivable law or regulation, Landlord may commingle the Security Deposit with Landlord's other funds. Landlord may, from time to time, without prejudice to any other remedy, use the Security Deposit to the extent necessary to make good any arrearages of rent or to satisfy any other covenant or obligation of Tenant hereunder. Following any such application of the

Security Deposit, Tenant shall pay to Landlord on demand the amount so applied in order to restore the Security Deposit to its original amount. If Tenant is not in default at the termination of this Lease, the balance of the Security Deposit remaining after any such application shall be returned by Landlord to Tenant. If Landlord transfers its interest in the Premises during the term of this Lease, Landlord may assign the Security Deposit to the transferee and thereafter shall have no further liability for the return of such Security Deposit.

18. Notice.
Any notice required or permitted under this Lease shall be deemed sufficiently given or served if sent by United States certified mail, return receipt requested, addressed as follows:

If to Landlord to:
    Big Bad Wolf
    P.O. Box 321
    St. Helena, California 94574
    bigbadwolf@gmail.com

If to Tenant to:
    Fine Wines, Inc.
    P.O. Box 122
    Napa, California 94558
    finewinesandvines@gmail.com

Landlord and Tenant shall each have the right from time to time to change the place notice is to be given under this paragraph by written notice thereof to the other party.

19. Waiver.
No waiver of any default of Landlord or Tenant hereunder shall be implied from any omission to take any action on account of such default if such default persists or is repeated, and no express waiver shall affect any default other than the default specified in the express waiver and that only for the time and to the extent therein stated. One or more waivers by Landlord or Tenant shall not be construed as a waiver of a subsequent breach of the same covenant, term, or condition.

20. Memorandum of Lease.
The parties hereto contemplate that this Lease should not and shall not be filed for record, but in lieu thereof, at the request of either party, Landlord and Tenant shall execute a Memorandum of Lease to be recorded for the purpose of giving record notice of the appropriate provisions of this Lease.

21. Headings.
The headings used in this Lease are for convenience of the parties only and shall not be considered in interpreting the meaning of any provision of this Lease.

7 –

22. Successors.

The provisions of this Lease shall extend to and be binding upon Landlord and Tenant and their respective legal representatives, successors, and assigns.

23. Performance.

If there is a default with respect to any of Landlord's covenants, warranties, or representations under this Lease, and if the default continues more than 15 days after notice in writing from Tenant to Landlord specifying the default, Tenant may, at its option and without affecting any other remedy hereunder, cure such default and deduct the cost thereof from the next accruing installment or installments of rent payable hereunder until Tenant shall have been fully reimbursed for such expenditures, together with interest thereon at a rate equal to the lesser of 12% per annum or the then highest lawful rate. If this Lease terminates prior to Tenant's receiving full reimbursement, Landlord shall pay the unreimbursed balance plus accrued interest to Tenant on demand.

24. Compliance with Law.

Tenant shall comply with all laws, orders, ordinances, and other public requirements now or hereafter pertaining to Tenant's use of the Leased Premises. Landlord shall comply with all laws, orders, ordinances, and other public requirements now or hereafter affecting the Leased Premises.

25. Final Agreement.

This Agreement terminates and supersedes all prior understandings or agreements on the subject matter hereof. This Agreement may be modified only by a further writing that is duly executed by both parties.

26. Governing Law.

This Agreement shall be governed, construed, and interpreted by, through, and under the Laws of the State of California.

IN WITNESS WHEREOF, the parties have executed this Lease as of the day and year first above written.

Big Bad Wolf, LLC   Fine Wines, Inc.

by:___*Goldie Wolf*___   by:___*Ron Fine*___
    Manager   President

Part Three – Draft Agreement

You represent either Fine Wines, Inc. or Stravecchio Winery, LLC in connection with the negotiation and drafting of the purchase and sale agreement between them (your instructor will specify which party you represent). Prepare an initial draft of the agreement, making sure that it accurately reflects the deal points on the term sheet that follows. You might wish to use or refer to the ABA Model Asset Purchase Agreement (with commentary) (2001).

TERM SHEET FOR ASSET PURCHASE & LICENSE TRANSACTION
FINE WINES, INC. ("SELLER") AND STRAVECCHIO WINERY, LLC ("BUYER")

TRANSACTION	Pursuant to an Asset Purchase Agreement, Seller will transfer to Buyer certain assets and liabilities of Seller in consideration for the payment by Buyer to Seller of the Purchase Consideration (as defined below).
ASSETS AND LIABILITIES	Purchased Assets: Seller will transfer to Buyer all assets of Seller (including, without limitation, equipment, inventory, accounts receivable, and general intangibles (including trade secrets and rights under contractual arrangements)), other than deposit accounts, investment property, and the name "Fine Wines" or any derivations thereof. Assumed Liabilities: Seller will assign to Buyer the Lease dated March 11, 2004 between Seller and Big Bad Wolf, LLC ("Lease"). Buyer will not assume any other liabilities of Seller.
CONSIDERATION	1. The assumption by Buyer of the obligations of Seller under the Lease; and 2. The payment of $7,000,000 by Buyer to Seller on the date of the Closing.

WORLDWIDE EXCLUSIVE LICENSE	Seller and Buyer will enter into a worldwide License Agreement whereby Seller will grant Buyer a worldwide exclusive royalty-free license for a period of one year to use the name "Fine Wines" in connection with the display, distribution, and sale of wine or other goods purchased by Buyer from Seller pursuant to the Asset Purchase Agreement.
CONDITIONS PRECEDENT	1. Completion of due diligence by Buyer to its satisfaction; 2. Execution and delivery of the Asset Purchase Agreement and the License Agreement; 3. Receipt of a pay-off letter from Sonoma Bank indicating that the amount necessary to repay, in full, all of the obligations of Seller and obtain a release of all of Sonoma Bank's liens is not greater than $2,800,000; 4. A consent to the assignment of the Lease by Seller to Buyer executed by Big Bad Wolf; 5. Consents to the assignment of all or substantially all of Seller's grape purchase agreements; 6. No material adverse change occurs with respect to the business or assets of Seller prior to Closing; 7. Compliance with all legal requirements necessary or desirable to insure that Buyer acquires all of the Purchased Assets free and clear of liens or claims of creditors of Seller; and 8. Such other conditions as are customary for transactions of this type. With respect to conditions 3 and 4 above, Seller agrees to use its best efforts to obtain all relevant consents from any third parties to consummate the transactions described in this Term Sheet and all ancillary and related matters.
WARRANTIES	Customary representations and warranties to be provided by Seller under the Asset Purchase Agreement and the License Agreement.

COVENANTS	Customary covenants relative to the operation of the business to be provided by Seller under the Asset Purchase Agreement and the License Agreement.
INDEMNIFICATION	Customary indemnification provisions to be included in the Asset Purchase Agreement and the License Agreement.
CONFIDENTIALITY	This term sheet is confidential and none of its provisions or terms shall be disclosed by either party other than to its officers, directors, or other representatives on a "need to know" basis for the purpose of consummating the transactions described herein, or except as required by law or regulation.
TRANSACTION FEES	Each party will be responsible for its own fees in relation to the negotiation and consummation of the transactions described in this Term Sheet.
GOVERNING LAW & FORUM SELECTION	This Term Sheet, the Asset Purchase Agreement, and the License Agreement will be governed by the laws of the State of New York and all disputes hereunder or thereunder shall be subject to the exclusive jurisdiction of the state or federal courts located in New York.
MISCELLANEOUS	This Term Sheet is non-binding on the parties hereto except with respect to Conditions Precedent, Confidentiality, Transaction Fees, and Governing Law/Jurisdiction (which provisions are intended to be legally binding between the parties).

Part Four – Final Agreement

Your instructor will match you with counsel for the other party. Review the other party's draft agreement and prepare a detailed analysis of how it differs from your draft. Then, with counsel for the other party, negotiate and redraft the agreement. Submit a single, redrafted agreement.

CHAPTER TWELVE
SIMULATION FOUR – COMMERCIAL LOAN

Facts

Steve's Surfboards, Inc., a Delaware corporation, is located in Huntington Beach, California and designs, manufactures, and sells surfboards to various surf shops. Steve's has been in business for approximately 15 years having been started in a basement by its owner, Steve Sharky. During that time, the business has enjoyed steady growth as the reputation of its boards for durability and stability has increased. Today, Steve's is one of the top three brands for high-performance boards and its future looks bright.

The domestic surfboard market, however, is highly cyclical. This puts a significant strain on Steve's finances. To begin with, Steve's builds inventory in the off-season by manufacturing its boards during the fall and winter months. During the time when it is building inventory, which Steve's stores at locations in California, Florida, and Hawaii, Steve's needs to pay all of the costs of the manufacturing process, which include the costs of the blanks and other raw materials, rent for the manufacturing and storage facilities, employees' salaries, and insurance. All of these costs occur at a time when Steve's has virtually no sales and, therefore, no revenue. To add to the strain on its finances, in the early spring, after it has built the required amount of inventory, Steve's begins to deliver the boards to its customers and those delivery costs can be substantial. Finally, many of the customers have negotiated payment terms that do not require payment until 60 days after the date on which the boards are delivered to them. After the deferred payment terms expire, however, each of the customers begins to make payment and money comes in waves to Steve's for about two months.

This cycle repeats itself each year. The net result of this cycle is that Steve's receives approximately 85% of its annual revenue over a two-month period but struggles through the remaining ten months of the year, when it incurs approximately 85% of its expenses. Accordingly, Steve's needs a loan of working capital because it, like most business in this country, lacks the ability to cover its expenses when its cash flow is insufficient to do so.

A few weeks ago, Steve met with Alex Flores, a senior vice-president of Surf City Bank, and explained to Alex that while the business is quite profitable, the trickle of cash flow for most of the year makes it very difficult for the business to operate. Steve sought Alex's assistance in arranging for a revolving credit facility[1] that would provide the business with sufficient liquidity to pay its bills during the dry months. Steve indicated that, based upon the company's projections, a revolver[2] of $5 million should be sufficient. Steve also indicated that the cost of the financing (*i.e.*, the interest rate and origination fees), while not unimportant, is less significant than the amount of the financing. After reviewing some recent financial statements, Alex indicated that the bank might be able to help Steve's. Alex indicated that the seasonal nature of the business does pose significant credit issues, but that with proper pricing, structure, and collateral protection (including a borrowing base[3]), Alex should be able to devise a loan arrangement that will address Steve's issues while providing the bank with a safe investment. Alex promised to speak with the bank's credit committee and, if the committee agrees to finance Steve's business, send Steve's a letter of intent outlining the proposed financing.

Before ending their meeting, Steve asked Alex about the possibility of obtaining separate financing for Steve's to purchase real property to serve as Steve's manufacturing facility (Steve's currently leases space that is a bit cramped), remodel the property, replace some worn-out equipment, and buy some new equipment. Steve indicated that the owner of the real property recently approached him to see whether Steve's had an interest in acquiring the property and that the discussion advanced to where they agreed upon a potential purchase price. Steve also indicated that he has obtained price quotations for the desired equipment and that it would make sense to have that equipment shipped to, and installed in, the new property if the business is going to move. Finally, Steve indicated that the total required financing for the real property and equipment will be approximately $2.5 million, with $1.6 million for the real property and $900,000 for the equipment.

---

[1]   A revolving credit facility is a line of credit pursuant to which the borrower may borrow, pay back, and then borrow again – repeatedly – at any time prior to maturity.

[2]   In this context, "revolver," is short for a revolving credit facility.

[3]   The term "borrowing base" is used in asset-based lending, where it limits the amount that may be borrowed under a revolving credit facility. The borrowing based is typically an amount equal to the value of eligible collateral (*e.g.*, inventory and accounts receivable) that will secure the debt, multiplied by a discount factor, and subject to a cap. For example, a lender or group of lenders might agree to advance funds equal to the total of 80% of the face amount of eligible accounts receivable and 70% of the value of eligible inventory, up to a maximum amount of $50 million.

Alex indicated that the bank does not typically provide this type of financing but that it might be willing to provide a portion of it and arrange for the balance to be provided by another lender. Steve responded that he is indifferent as to whether Surf City Bank provides or arranges the financing, so he asked Alex to proceed to obtain approval for the working capital financing and to arrange the fixed asset financing.

Not long afterwards, Alex met with, and made a presentation to, the bank's credit committee regarding the proposed financing. The committee was excited about the opportunity and the meeting ended with the committee indicating that it is favorably inclined to approve providing 100% of the working-capital financing based upon an outline of terms submitted to the committee by Alex. It is also favorably inclined to provide 20% of the fixed-asset financing[4] based upon the outline of terms, but that the balance of the fixed-asset financing would need to be arranged and, because the revolver and the fixed-asset financing will have different priority with respect to different items of collateral, a satisfactory intercreditor agreement needs to be negotiated.

Alex then called Kelly Moore, a banker in the real estate department of Inland Bank to see if Inland Bank would be willing to provide the remainder of the fixed-asset financing. After an exchange of information and documents, Kelly informed Alex that Inland Bank is interested in providing $2 million of the proposed fixed-asset financing based upon the outline of terms prepared by Alex, but that a satisfactory intercreditor agreement would need to be negotiated. Alex then prepared and sent to Steve the following letter of intent:

---

[4]   In other words, the loan to the purchase of the real estate and equipment.

October 15, 2018

Mr. Steve Sharky
Steve's Surfboards, Inc.
100 Ocean Drive
Huntington Beach, CA 90266

LETTER OF INTENT

Dear Steve:

As we, Surf City Bank, N.A. ("Bank"), understand, Steve's Surfboards, Inc. (the "Company"), is interested in obtaining financing in order to: (a) acquire formerly identified real property (the "Real Property") and manufacturing equipment (the "Equipment") (collectively, the "Acquisition Transaction"), and (b) provide for the ongoing working capital needs of the Company. This letter establishes terms under which we propose to provide to the Company a $7,500,000 senior secured credit facility (the "Facility"). Based upon information known to us today concerning the Company and the Transaction, we are pleased to provide you with this proposal, as further described in Attachment A. This letter is a proposal, to be used as a basis for continued discussions, and does not constitute a commitment of Bank, or an agreement to deliver such a commitment.

Costs and Expenses

In consideration of the Bank's proposal and recognizing that, in connection herewith, Bank is incurring costs and expenses, the Company hereby agrees to pay, or reimburse Bank for all such costs and expenses, regardless of whether any of the transactions contemplated hereby is consummated. The Company also agrees to pay all costs and expenses of Bank (including, without limitation, attorney's fees) incurred in connection with the enforcement of any of its rights and remedies hereunder.

Confidentiality

By accepting this proposal letter, the Company agrees that this proposal letter (including Attachment A) is for its confidential use only and that neither its existence nor the terms hereof will be disclosed by Company to any person other than its officers, directors, employees, accountants, attorneys and other advisors, and then only on a "need-to-know" basis in connection with the transactions contemplated hereby and on a confidential basis. The foregoing notwithstanding, following the Company's acceptance of the provisions hereof as provided below and its return of this proposal letter to Bank, the Company (i) may file a copy of this letter in any public record in which it is required by law to be filed, and (ii) may make such other public disclosures of the terms and conditions hereto as it is required by law, in the opinion of its counsel, to make.

Governing Law, Etc.

This proposal letter is be governed by, and construed in accordance with, the law of the State of California. This proposal letter sets forth the entire agreement between the parties with respect to the matters addressed herein and supersedes all prior communications, written or oral, with respect hereto. The Company's obligations under the paragraphs captioned "Costs and Expenses," and "Confidentiality" will survive the expiration or termination of this letter.

Waiver of Jury Trial

Each party hereto irrevocably waives all right to trial by jury in any action, proceeding or counterclaim (whether based on contract, tort or otherwise) arising out of or relating to letter or the transactions contemplated by this letter or the actions of Bank or any of its affiliates in the negotiation, performance, or enforcement of this letter.

Please indicate the Company's acceptance of the provisions hereof by signing the enclosed copy of this letter and returning it to Alex Flores, Surf City Bank, N.A., 3100 North Sepulveda Boulevard, Manhattan Beach, California 90266 at or before 5:00 p.m. on October 30, 2018.

Very truly yours,
SURF CITY BANK, N.A.

Alex Flores

By:_____
Alex Flores
Senior Vice President

ACCEPTED AND AGREED TO
this _____ day of October, 2018

Steve's Surfboards, Inc.

By: _____

Name:_____

Title:_____

ATTACHMENT A
Proposed Terms and Conditions
Senior Secured Credit Facility

Borrower: Steve's Surfboards, Inc. (the "Company")

Agent: Surf City Bank, N.A. will act as the agent for the Revolving Lenders ("Revolver Agent") and for the Term Lenders ("Term Loan Agent") (collectively, "Agent").

Lenders: (a) As to the Revolver, Surf City Bank, N.A. and any other financial institutions arranged by and satisfactory to Agent ("Revolver Lenders"), and
(b) As to the Term Loan, Surf City Bank, N.A. (as to $500,000) and Inland Bank, N.A. (as to $2,000,000), together with any other financial institutions arranged by and satisfactory to Agent ("Term Lenders").

Facility: A senior secured credit facility with a maximum credit amount ("Maximum Credit Amount") of $7,500,000. Under the Facility, Borrower would be provided with a Revolver and a Term Loan.

Revolver: Advances under the Revolver would be available up to a maximum aggregate amount outstanding not to exceed $5,000,000.

Borrowing Base: The sum of:
(a) 85% of the amount of Borrower's eligible accounts (to be defined), plus
(b) the lowest of
    (i) $1,500,000,
    (ii) 65% of the value (calculated at the lower of cost or market) of Borrower's eligible inventory (to be defined),
    (iii) 85% times the most recently determined net liquidation percentage (to be defined) times the value (calculated at the lower of cost or market) of Borrower's inventory.

Term Loan: Borrower would be provided with a Term Loan in an amount equal to $2,500,000.

Interest Rates: Advances outstanding under the Revolver and the Term Loan would bear interest at the Base Rate plus the Applicable Margin.

The "*Base Rate*" means the greater of (a) the prime lending rate as publicly announced from time to time by Surf City Bank, N.A., and (b) 3% per annum.

"***Applicable Margin***" means (i) 2.25% in the case of Base Rate loans under the Revolver and 3.25% in the case of LIBOR Rate loans under the Revolver, and (ii) 3.75% in the case of Base Rate Loans under the Term Loan and 4.75% in the case of LIBOR Rate Loans under the Term Loan.

All interest would be calculated based upon a year of 360 days for actual days elapsed. All interest be payable monthly in arrears in cash.

Closing Fee:	A fee in an amount equal to 1.5% of the Maximum Credit Amount would be payable in full to the Agent on the closing date.
Unused Revolver Fee:	A fee in an amount equal to 0.50% per annum times the unused portion of the Revolver shall be due and payable monthly in arrears.
Use of Proceeds:	To (i) acquire the Real Property and the Equipment, (ii) fund certain fees and expenses associated with the Facility, and (iii) finance the ongoing working capital needs of Borrower.
Term:	5 years from the closing date ("Maturity Date").
Collateral:	The Revolver would be secured by a first priority perfected security interest in all of Borrower's now owned or later acquired accounts receivable and inventory as well as the deposit accounts to which the proceeds thereof are deposited (the "Revolver Priority Collateral") and would be secured by a second priority perfected security interest in the Term Loan Priority Collateral.
	The Term Loan would be secured by a first priority perfected lien and security interest in the Real Property and all of Borrower's now owned or later acquired equipment (the "Term Loan Priority Collateral") and would be secured by a second priority perfected security interest in the Revolver Priority Collateral.
Depositary Relationship:	Borrower shall establish and maintain its primary depositary and treasury management relationships with Surf City Bank, N.A.
Financial Covenants:	Borrower would be required to maintain minimum levels of EBITDA, maximum leverage, and would be subject to a limitation on annual capital expenditures.
Financial Reporting:	Customary for Agent's loans of this type and those additional deemed appropriate by Agent for this transaction including quarterly financial statements and annual audited financial statements and projections.

– 2 –

Conditions Precedent to Closing:	Customary for Agent's loans of this type and those additional deemed appropriate by Agent for this transaction, including the following:

(a) Completion of Agent's business, legal, and collateral due diligence, including but not limited to, a review of Borrower's books and records, the results of which are satisfactory to Agent,

(b) Execution and delivery of an intercreditor agreement between Revolver Agent and Term Loan Agent, on terms and conditions satisfactory to Agent,

(c) UCC, tax lien, and litigation searches, the results of which are satisfactory to Agent,

(d) Customary individual background checks, the results of which are satisfactory to Agent,

(e) Receipt of a commitment from Inland Bank to provide not less than $2,000,000 of the Term Loan,

(f) Legal documentation regarding the Facility, including a loan agreement, security agreements, control agreements, intercreditor agreements, and financing statements, in each case, satisfactory to Agent,

(g) No material adverse change in the financial condition, business, results of operations, assets or liabilities of the Borrower, and

(h) Surf City Bank's receipt of final credit approval for its portion of the financing.

Scheduled Closing Date:	Closing Date to occur on or before December 31, 2018.

– 3 –

Part One – Due Diligence Memorandum

You are counsel to Surf City Bank in its role as Agent with respect to the proposed loans to Steve's Surfboards, Inc.

A. In response to your request for an official search for financing statements filed against "Steve's Surfboards, Inc.," the Delaware Secretary of State's office has disclosed the following:

(i) a financing statement filed by Cowabunga Finance, LLC, that identifies the debtor as "Steve's Surfboards, Inc.," lists the debtor's address as "100 Ocean Drive, Huntington Beach, CA 90266," and describes the collateral as "CNC shaping machines together with all accounts receivable, deposit accounts, chattel paper, and payment intangibles arising from or resulting from such machines"; and

(ii) a financing statement filed by Awesome Lending, LLC, that identifies the debtor as "Steve's SurfNboards, Inc.," lists the debtor's address as "600 Ocean Drive, Manhattan Beach, CA 90266," and describes the collateral as "all accounts, inventory, deposit accounts, and equipment."

Prepare a memorandum that, for each disclosed financing statement, analyzes: (i) whether it presents a problem; and (ii) if it does present a problem, whether that problem is major or minor, and why. Include in your memorandum a recommendation to your client as to whether and how to deal with each of these financing statements.

B. You have received and reviewed a copy of the lease agreement between Steve's and Tsunami Properties, LLC, pursuant to which Steve's leases its current manufacturing facility. The lease provides that "to secure all of Tenant's obligations to Lessor under this lease, Tenant grants Lessor a security interest in all of its now owned and hereafter acquired equipment located on the Leased Premises. No financing statement has been filed by or on behalf of Tsunami Properties. Prepare a memorandum that analyzes whether the language of the lease presents a problem for the proposed financing, assuming that Steve's will buy and relocate to a new facility financed with the loan proceeds. If the language in the lease does present a problem, indicate whether this is a major or minor problem and why, and provide a recommendation to your client as to whether and how to deal with this language in the lease.

Part Two – Deal Design Memorandum

You are counsel to Surf City Bank in its role as Agent with respect to the proposed loans to Steve's Surfboards, Inc. Review the ABA Model First Lien/Second Lien Intercreditor Agreement.[5] Without doing the actual drafting, prepare a written memorandum explaining how you would modify the model

---

[5]   *See* The Committee on Commercial Finance, *Report of the Model First Lien/second Lien Intercreditor Agreement Task Force*, 65 BUS. LAW. 809 (2010)

agreement from a first lien/second lien intercreditor agreement to a so-called split collateral intercreditor agreement, pursuant to which: (i) the Revolver Agent has a first priority security interest as to the Revolver Priority Collateral and the Term Loan Agent has a second priority security interest in that collateral; and (ii) the Term Loan Agent has a first priority security interest as to the Term Loan Priority Collateral and the Revolver Agent has a second priority security interest in that collateral.

Part Three – Negotiation Issue

You are counsel to Steve's Surfboards, Inc. Read *In re Denver Merchandise Mart, Inc.*, 740 F.3d 1052 (5th Cir. 2014). Having reviewed Surf City Bank's letter of intent, you recognize that the prepayment language, as currently written, does not appear to cover a payment made after acceleration of the Term Loan. Steve has asked that you "keep mum" about this issue, believing that the language might provide leverage later on. What are your ethical obligations and options with respect to this matter?

Part Four – Loan Agreement

You are counsel to Surf City Bank. Review the bank's form loan agreement for a revolving loan (which follows these instructions and an electronic version of which is available on the web page for the book: www.transactionalskills.com). Revise and adapt the form to the proposed revolving loan to Steve's Surfboards, Inc., making sure that it accurately reflects the terms of the letter of intent. In doing so, omit the borrower's representations and warranties, the borrowers' affirmative, negative, and financial covenants, the events of default, and the remedies upon default, as another lawyer is preparing those portions of the agreement. In preparing the conditions precedent to the initial extension of credit, you may omit standard conditions relating to the borrower's good standing, authorization to contract, and similar matters, but should include other appropriate conditions applicable to the planned transaction. To the extent that the loan agreement references or calls for a certificate or other document, you need not draft that certificate or other document.

Loan Agreement

THIS LOAN AGREEMENT (this "Agreement"), is entered into as of _____, by and between **SURF CITY BANK, N.A.**, a national banking association ("Bank") and _____, a _____ ("Borrower").

The parties agree as follows:

1. DEFINITIONS AND CONSTRUCTION.

1.1   Definitions. As used in this Agreement, the following terms shall have the following definitions:

"Account Advance Rate" means _____ %.

"Affiliate" means, as applied to any Person, any other Person who, directly or indirectly through one or more intermediaries, controls, is controlled by, or is under common control with, such Person. For purposes of this definition, "control" means the possession, directly or indirectly through one or more intermediaries, of the power to direct the management and policies of a Person, whether through the ownership of Equity Interest, by contract, or otherwise.

"Applicable Prepayment Premium" means, as of any date of determination, an amount equal to (a) during first year following the Closing Date, the then applicable Prepayment Premium Percentage *times* the Maximum Revolver Amount on the date immediately prior to the date of determination, (b) during the second year following the Closing Date, the then applicable Prepayment Premium Percentage *times* the Maximum Revolver Amount on the date immediately prior to the date of determination, (c) during the third year following the Closing Date, the then applicable Prepayment Premium Percentage *times* the Maximum Revolver Amount on the date immediately prior to the date of determination, and (d) from and after the date that is the third anniversary of the Closing Date, 0%.

"Applicable Rate" means, as of any date of determination, and with respect to Base Rate Loans or the Unused Line Fee, as applicable, the applicable rate set forth below:

Level	Average Availability	Applicable Rate Relative to Loans	Applicable Rate Relative to Unused Line Fee
I	≥ $_____	_._ percentage points	____ percentage points
II	< $_____ and ≥ $_____	_._ percentage points	____ percentage points
III	< $_____	_._ percentage points	____ percentage points

"Application Event" means the occurrence of (a) a failure by Borrower to repay all of the Obligations in full on the Maturity Date, or (b) an Event of Default and the election by Bank to require that payments and proceeds of Collateral be applied pursuant to Section 2.3(b)(ii) of this Agreement.

"Authorized Person" means any officer or employee of Borrower.

"Availability" means, as of any date of determination, the amount that Borrower is entitled to borrow as Revolving Loans hereunder (after giving effect to all then outstanding Revolving Loans or Letter of Credit Obligations).

"Bank's Account" means _____.

"Bank Expenses" means all (a) costs or expenses required to be paid by Borrower under any of the Loan Documents that are paid, advanced, or incurred by Bank, (b) fees or charges paid or incurred by Bank in connection with Bank's transactions with Borrower, including, filing, recording, publication, and appraisal fees, the costs of real estate surveys, real estate title policies and endorsements, and environmental audits, (c) costs and expenses incurred by Bank in the disbursement of funds to Borrower, (d) reasonable costs and expenses paid or incurred by Bank to correct any default or enforce any provision of the Loan Documents, or in gaining possession of, maintaining, handling, preserving, storing, shipping, selling, preparing for sale, or advertising to sell the Collateral, or any portion thereof, irrespective of whether a sale is consummated, (e) audit fees and expenses of Bank related to audit examinations of the books and records of Borrower, (f) Bank's reasonable costs and expenses (including attorney's fees) incurred in advising, structuring, drafting, reviewing, administering, syndicating, or amending the Loan Documents, and (h) Bank's reasonable costs and expenses (including attorneys, accountants, consultants, and other advisors fees and expenses) incurred in terminating, enforcing (including attorneys, accountants, consultants, and other advisors fees and expenses incurred in connection with a "workout," a "restructuring," or an Insolvency Proceeding concerning Borrower or in exercising rights or remedies under the Loan Documents), or defending the Loan Documents, irrespective of whether suit is brought, or in taking any Remedial Action concerning the Collateral.

"Bank's Liens" means the Liens granted by Borrower to Bank under the Loan Documents.

"Bank-Related Person" means Bank, together with Bank's Affiliates, officers, directors, employees, attorneys, and agents.

"Base Rate" means, the rate of interest announced, from time to time, by Bank at its principal office as its "prime rate", with the understanding that the "prime rate" is one of Bank's base rates and serves as the basis upon which effective rates of interest are calculated for those loans making reference thereto.

"Borrowing" means a borrowing hereunder consisting of Revolving Loans.

"Borrowing Base" means, as of any date of determination, the result of:

> (a) the Account Advance Rate multiplied by the amount of Eligible Accounts, *less* the amount, if any, of the Dilution Reserve, and

> (b) *the lowest of*

>> (i) $_____,

>> (ii)   the Inventory Advance Rate multiplied by the value of Eligible Inventory,

(iii)   the NOLV Advance Rate multiplied by the Net Orderly Liquidation Value Percentage times the book value of Borrower's Eligible Inventory, and

(iv)   ___% of the amount of credit availability created by <u>clause (a)</u> above, *minus*

(c) the aggregate amount of reserves, if any, established by Bank under <u>Section 2.1(b)</u>.

"<u>Borrowing Base Certificate</u>" means a certificate in the form of <u>Exhibit B-1</u>.

"<u>Business Day</u>" means any day that is not a Saturday, Sunday, or other day on which banks are authorized or required to close in the state of California.

"<u>Closing Date</u>" means the date of the making of the initial Loans (or other extension of credit) hereunder.

"<u>Code</u>" means the California Uniform Commercial Code.

"<u>Collateral</u>" means any and all property or assets of Borrower that either now or hereafter are subject to a Lien in favor of Bank.

"<u>Control Agreement</u>" means a control agreement, in form and substance satisfactory to Bank, executed and delivered by Borrower, Bank, and the applicable securities intermediary (with respect to a securities account), commodities intermediary (with respect to a commodities account), or bank (with respect to a deposit account).

"<u>Daily Balance</u>" means, as of any date of determination and with respect to any Obligation, the amount of such Obligation owed at the end of such day.

"<u>Default</u>" means an event, condition, or default that, with the giving of notice, the passage of time, or both, would be an Event of Default.

"<u>Designated Account</u>" means the Deposit Account of Borrower identified on <u>Schedule D-1</u>.

"<u>Designated Account Bank</u>" has the meaning ascribed thereto on <u>Schedule D-1</u>.

"<u>Dilution</u>" means, as of any date of determination, a percentage, based upon the experience of the immediately prior 90 day period, that is the result of dividing the Dollar amount of (a) bad debt write-downs, discounts, advertising allowances, credits, or other dilutive items with respect to Borrower's Accounts during such period, by (b) Borrower's billings with respect to Accounts during such period.

"<u>Dilution Reserve</u>" means, as of any date of determination, an amount sufficient to reduce the advance rate against Eligible Accounts by 1 percentage point for each percentage point by which Dilution is in excess of 5%.

"<u>Dollars</u>" or "<u>$</u>" means United States dollars.

"<u>Eligible Accounts</u>" means those Accounts created by Borrower in the ordinary course of its business, that arise out of Borrower's sale of goods or rendition of services, that comply with each of the representations and warranties respecting Eligible Accounts made in the

Loan Documents, and that are not excluded as ineligible by virtue of one or more of the excluding criteria set forth below; provided, however, that such criteria may be revised from time to time by Bank in Bank's Permitted Discretion to address the results of any audit performed by Bank from time to time after the Closing Date. In determining the amount to be included, Eligible Accounts shall be calculated net of customer deposits, unapplied cash, taxes, finance charges, penalties, late fees, discounts, credits, allowances, and rebates. Eligible Accounts shall not include the following:

(a) Accounts that the Account Debtor has failed to pay within 45 days of original invoice date, or Accounts with selling terms of more than 45 days,

(b) Accounts owed by an Account Debtor (or its Affiliates) if 50% or more of all Accounts owed by that Account Debtor (or its Affiliates) are deemed ineligible under clause (a) above,

(c) Accounts with respect to which the Account Debtor is an Affiliate of Borrower or an employee or agent of Borrower,

(d) Accounts arising in a transaction wherein goods are placed on consignment or are sold pursuant to a guaranteed sale, a sale or return, a sale on approval, a bill and hold, or any other terms by reason of which the payment by the Account Debtor may be conditional,

(e) Accounts that are not payable in Dollars,

(f) Accounts with respect to which the Account Debtor either (i) does not maintain its chief executive office in the United States, or (ii) is not organized under the laws of the United States or any state thereof, or (iii) is the government of any foreign country or sovereign state, or of any state, province, municipality, or other political subdivision thereof, or of any department, agency, public corporation, or other instrumentality thereof, unless (y) the Account is supported by an irrevocable letter of credit satisfactory to Bank (as to form, substance, and issuer or domestic confirming bank) that has been delivered to Bank and is directly drawable by Bank, or (z) the Account is covered by credit insurance in form, substance, and amount, and by an insurer, satisfactory to Bank,

(g) Accounts with respect to which the Account Debtor is either (i) the United States or any department, agency, or instrumentality of the United States (exclusive, however, of Accounts with respect to which Borrower has complied, to the reasonable satisfaction of Bank, with the Assignment of Claims Act, 31 USC § 3727), or (ii) any state of the United States,

(h) Accounts with respect to which the Account Debtor is a creditor of Borrower, has or has asserted a right of setoff, or has disputed its obligation to pay all or any portion of the Account, to the extent of such claim, right of setoff, or dispute.

(i) Accounts with respect to an Account Debtor whose total obligations owing to Borrower exceed 10% (such percentage, as applied to a particular Account Debtor, being subject to reduction by Bank in its Permitted Discretion if the creditworthiness of such Account Debtor deteriorates) of all Eligible Accounts, to the extent of the obligations owing by such Account Debtor in excess of such percentage;

(j) Accounts with respect to which the Account Debtor is subject to an Insolvency Proceeding, is not Solvent, has gone out of business, or as to which Borrower has received notice of an imminent Insolvency Proceeding or a material impairment of the financial condition of such Account Debtor,

(k) Accounts, the collection of which, Bank, in its Permitted Discretion, believes to be doubtful by reason of the Account Debtor's financial condition,

(l) Accounts that are not subject to a valid and perfected first priority Bank's Lien,

(m) Accounts with respect to which (i) the goods giving rise to such Account have not been shipped and billed to the Account Debtor, or (ii) the services giving rise to such Account have not been performed and billed to the Account Debtor, or

(n) Accounts that represent the right to receive progress payments or other advance billings that are due prior to the completion of performance by Borrower of the subject contract for goods or services.

"Eligible Inventory" means Inventory consisting of first quality (i) finished goods held for sale in the ordinary course of Borrower's business, and (ii) raw materials, in each case, that complies with each of the representations and warranties respecting Eligible Inventory made in the Loan Documents, and that is not excluded as ineligible by virtue of one or more of the excluding criteria set forth below. Eligible Inventory shall be valued at the lower of cost or market on a basis consistent with Borrower's historical accounting practices. An item of Inventory shall not be included in Eligible Inventory if:

(a) Borrower does not have good, valid, and marketable title thereto,

(b) it is not located in the continental United States,

(c) it is located on real property leased by Borrower or in a contract warehouse, in each case, unless it is subject to a Collateral Access Agreement executed by the lessor or warehouseman, as the case may be, and unless it is segregated or otherwise separately identifiable from goods of others, if any, stored on the premises,

(d) it is not subject to a valid and perfected first priority Bank's Lien,

(e) it consists of goods returned or rejected by Borrower's customers,

(b) it consists of goods that are obsolete or slow moving, restrictive or custom items, work-in-process, or goods that constitute spare parts, packaging and shipping materials, supplies used or consumed in Borrower's business, bill and hold goods, defective goods, "seconds," or Inventory acquired on consignment,

(f) Borrower does not have actual and exclusive possession thereof (either directly or through a bailee or agent of Borrower),

(g) it is the subject of a document of title,

(h) it is located at a location where the aggregate value of Eligible Inventory at such location is $_____ or less;

(i) it is, in Bank's Permitted Discretion, not readily saleable in the ordinary course of business, or

(j) it is subject to third party trademark, licensing or other proprietary rights, unless Bank is satisfied that such Inventory can be freely sold by Bank on and after the occurrence of an Event of a Default despite such third party rights.

"Event of Default" has the meaning set forth in Section 8.

"Extraordinary Loan" has the meaning set forth in Section 2.3(c)(ii).

"Funding Date" means the date on which a Borrowing occurs.

"Governmental Authority" means the government of any nation or any political subdivision thereof, whether at the national, state, territorial, provincial, municipal or any other level, and any agency, authority, instrumentality, regulatory body, court, central bank or other entity exercising executive, legislative, judicial, taxing, regulatory or administrative powers or functions of, or pertaining to, government (including any supra-national bodies such as the European Union or the European Central Bank).

"Insolvency Proceeding" means any proceeding commenced by or against any Person under any provision of the Bankruptcy Code or under any other state or federal bankruptcy or insolvency law, assignments for the benefit of creditors, formal or informal moratoria, compositions, extensions generally with creditors, or proceedings seeking reorganization, arrangement, or other similar relief.

"Inventory Advance Rate" means ___%.

"Issuer Document" means, with respect to any Letter of Credit, a letter of credit application, a letter of credit agreement, or any other document, agreement or instrument entered into (or to be entered into) by Borrower in favor of Bank relating to such Letter of Credit.

"Letter of Credit" has the meaning set forth in Section 2.11(a).

"Letter of Credit Amount" means $_____.

"Letter of Credit Collateralization" means either (a) providing cash collateral (pursuant to documentation reasonably satisfactory to Bank, including provisions that specify that the Letter of Credit Fees and all fees, charges and commissions provided for in Section 2.11(c) of this Agreement (including any fronting fees) will continue to accrue while the Letters of Credit are outstanding) to be held by Bank in an amount equal to 102% of the then existing Letter of Credit Usage, (b) delivering to Bank documentation executed by all beneficiaries under the Letters of Credit, in form and substance reasonably satisfactory to Bank, terminating all of such beneficiaries' rights under the Letters of Credit, or (c) providing Bank with a standby letter of credit, in form and substance reasonably satisfactory to Bank, from a commercial bank acceptable to Bank (in its sole discretion) in an amount equal to 102% of the then existing Letter of Credit Usage (it being understood that the Letter of Credit Fee and all fronting fees set forth in this Agreement will continue to accrue while the Letters of Credit are outstanding and that any such fees that accrue must be an amount that can be drawn under any such standby letter of credit).

"Letter of Credit Disbursement" means a payment made by Bank pursuant to a Letter of Credit.

"Letter of Credit Usage" means, as of any date of determination, the aggregate undrawn amount of all outstanding Letters of Credit.

"Lien" means any mortgage, deed of trust, pledge, hypothecation, assignment, charge, deposit arrangement, encumbrance, easement, lien (statutory or other), security interest, or other security arrangement.

"Loan" shall mean any Revolving Loan or Extraordinary Loan made (or to be made) hereunder.

"Loan Account" has the meaning set forth in Section 2.9.

"Loan Documents" means this Agreement, the Control Agreements, any Issuer Documents, the Letters of Credit, the Security Agreement, any note or notes executed by Borrower in connection with this Agreement and payable to Bank, and any other agreement (including any mortgage or deed of trust) entered into, now or in the future, by Borrower and Bank in connection with this Agreement.

"Maturity Date" means _____, 20___.

"Maximum Revolver Amount" means $_____.

"Net Orderly Liquidation Value Percentage" means the percentage of the book value of Borrower's Inventory that is estimated to be recoverable in an orderly liquidation of such Inventory net of all associated costs and expenses of such liquidation, such percentage to be as determined from time to time by a qualified appraisal company selected by Bank.

"NOLV Advance Rate" means _____%.

"Obligations" means all loans (including the Loans (inclusive of Extraordinary Loans), debts, principal, interest (including any interest that accrues after the commencement of an Insolvency Proceeding, regardless of whether allowed or allowable in whole or in part as a claim in any such Insolvency Proceeding), reimbursement or indemnification obligations with respect to Letters of Credit (irrespective of whether contingent), premiums, liabilities (including all amounts charged to the Loan Account pursuant to this Agreement), obligations (including indemnification obligations), fees, Bank Expenses (including any fees or expenses that accrue after the commencement of an Insolvency Proceeding, regardless of whether allowed or allowable in whole or in part as a claim in any such Insolvency Proceeding), guaranties, and all covenants and duties of any other kind and description owing by Borrower arising out of, under, pursuant to, in connection with, or evidenced by this Agreement or any of the other Loan Documents and irrespective of whether for the payment of money, whether direct or indirect, absolute or contingent, due or to become due, now existing or hereafter arising, and including all interest not paid when due and all other expenses or other amounts that Borrower is required to pay or reimburse by the Loan Documents or by law or otherwise in connection with the Loan Documents. Without limiting the generality of the foregoing, the Obligations of Borrower under the Loan Documents include the obligation to pay (i) the principal of the Loans, (ii) interest accrued on the Loans, (iii) the amount necessary to reimburse Bank for amounts paid or payable pursuant to Letters of Credit, (iv) Letter of Credit commissions, charges, expenses, and fees, (v) Bank Expenses, (vi) fees payable under this Agreement or any of the other Loan Documents, and (vii) indemnities and other amounts payable by Borrower under any Loan Document. Any reference in this Agreement or in the Loan Documents to the Obligations shall include all or any portion thereof and any extensions, modifications, renewals, or alterations thereof, both prior and subsequent to any Insolvency Proceeding.

"Overadvance" means, as of any date of determination, that the Revolver Usage is greater than the amount of Revolving Loans available to Borrower after giving effect to the limitations set forth in Section 2.1.

"Permitted Discretion" means a determination made in the exercise of reasonable business judgment.

"Person" means natural persons, corporations, limited liability companies, limited partnerships, general partnerships, limited liability partnerships, joint ventures, trusts, land trusts, business trusts, or other organizations, irrespective of whether they are legal entities, and governments and agencies and political subdivisions thereof.

"Prepayment Premium Percentage" means, with respect to any period, the percentage set forth in the following table for the applicable period set forth opposite thereto:

Applicable Period	Prepayment Premium Percentage
First Year	__%
Second Year	__%
Third Year	__%
Thereafter	0%

"Revolver Commitment" means $_____.

"Revolver Usage" means, as of any date of determination, the sum of (a) the amount of outstanding Revolving Loans, *plus* (b) the amount of the Letter of Credit Usage.

"Revolving Loans" has the meaning set forth in Section 2.1(a).

"Security Agreement" means a Security Agreement, in form and substance satisfactory to Bank, executed and delivered by Borrower to Bank.

"United States" means the United States of America.

1.2   Additional Definitions. The definitions contained in the Security Agreement are incorporated herein as if fully set forth herein.

1.3   Code. Any term used in this Agreement that are defined in the Code has the meaning set forth in the Code unless otherwise defined herein; provided, however, that to the extent that the Code is used to define any term herein and such term is defined differently in Article 9 and in one or more other Articles of the Code, the definition of such term contained in Article 9 governs.

1.4   Construction. Unless the context of this Agreement or any other Loan Document clearly requires otherwise, references to the plural include the singular, references to the singular include the plural, the terms "includes" and "including" are not limiting, and the term "or" has, except where otherwise indicated, the inclusive meaning represented by the phrase "and/or." The words "hereof," "herein," "hereby," "hereunder," and similar terms in this Agreement or any other Loan Document refer to this Agreement or such other Loan Document, as the case may be, as a whole and not to any particular provision of this Agreement or such other Loan Document, as the case may be. Section, subsection, clause, schedule, and exhibit references herein are to this Agreement unless otherwise specified. Any reference in this Agreement or in any other Loan Document to any agreement, instrument, or document includes all alterations, amendments, changes, extensions, modifications, renewals, replacements, substitutions, joinders, and supplements, thereto and thereof, as applicable (subject to any restrictions on such alterations, amendments, changes, extensions, modifications, renewals, replacements, substitutions, joinders, and supplements set forth herein). The words "asset" and "property" shall be construed to have the same meaning and effect and to refer to any and all tangible and intangible assets and properties. Any reference herein or in any other Loan Document to the satisfaction, repayment, or payment in full of the Obligations means (a) the payment or repayment in full in immediately available funds of (i) the principal amount of, and interest accrued and unpaid with respect to, all outstanding Loans, together with the payment of any premium applicable to the repayment of the Loans, (ii) all Bank Expenses that have accrued and are unpaid regardless of whether demand has been made therefor, (iii) all fees or charges that have accrued hereunder or under any other Loan Document (including the Letter of Credit Fee and the Unused Line Fee) and are unpaid, (b) in the case of contingent reimbursement obligations with respect to Letters of Credit, providing Letter of Credit Collateralization, (c) the receipt by Bank of cash collateral in order to secure any other contingent Obligations for which a claim or demand for payment has been made on or prior to such time or in respect of matters or circumstances known to Bank at such time that are reasonably expected to result in any loss, cost, damage, or expense (including attorney's fees and legal expenses), such cash collateral to be in such amount as Bank reasonably determines is appropriate to secure such contingent Obligations, and (d) the termination of all of the commitments of Bank hereunder and under the other Loan Documents. Any reference herein to any Person includes such Person's successors and assigns. Any requirement of a writing contained herein or in any other Loan Document may be satisfied by the transmission of a record.

1.5   Schedules and Exhibits. All of the schedules and exhibits attached to this Agreement are incorporated herein by reference and any reference to this Agreement includes such schedules and exhibits.

2. LOANS AND TERMS OF PAYMENT.

2.1   Revolver Revolving Loans.

(a) Subject to the terms and conditions of this Agreement, and during the term of this Agreement, Bank agrees to make advances ("Revolving Loans") to Borrower in an amount at any one time outstanding not to exceed an amount equal to the *lesser of* (i) the Maximum Revolver Amount *less* the Letter of Credit Usage, or (ii) the Borrowing Base *less* the Letter of Credit Usage.

(b) Bank shall have the right to establish reserves in such amounts, and with respect to such matters, as Bank in its Permitted Discretion shall deem necessary or appropriate, against the Borrowing Base, including reserves with respect to (i) sums that Borrower have failed to pay and are required to pay under any section of this Agreement or any other Loan Document, and (ii) amounts owing by Borrower to any Person to the extent secured by a Lien on, or trust over, any of the Collateral, which Lien or trust, in the Permitted Discretion of Bank likely would have a priority superior to Bank's Liens in and to such item of Collateral.

(c) Amounts borrowed pursuant to this Section 2.1 may be repaid and, subject to the terms and conditions of this Agreement, reborrowed at any time during the term of this Agreement.

2.2   Borrowing Procedures and Settlements.

(a) **Procedure for Borrowing.** Each Borrowing shall be made by a written request by an Authorized Person delivered to Bank and received by Bank no later than 10:00 a.m. (California time) on the Business Day that is 1 Business Day prior to the requested Funding Date, specifying (A) the amount of such Borrowing, and (B) the requested Funding Date (which shall be a Business Day). At Bank's election, in lieu of delivering the above-described written request, any Authorized Person may give Bank telephonic notice of such request by the required time. In such circumstances, Borrower agrees that any such telephonic notice will be confirmed in writing within 24 hours of the giving of such telephonic notice, but the failure to provide such written confirmation shall not affect the validity of the request.

(b) **Making of Loans.** If Bank has received a timely request for a Borrowing in accordance with the provisions hereof, and subject to the satisfaction of the applicable terms and conditions in this Agreement, Bank agrees to make the proceeds of such Loan available to Borrower on the applicable Funding Date by transferring available funds equal to such proceeds to Borrower's Designated Account.

(a) **Protective Loans and Optional Overadvances.**

(i) Any contrary provision of this Agreement or any other Loan Document notwithstanding, at any time (A) after the occurrence and during the continuance of a Default or an Event of Default, or (B) that any of the other applicable conditions precedent set forth in Section 3 are not satisfied, Bank may, in Bank's sole discretion, make Revolving Loans to, or for the benefit of, Borrower, that Bank, in its Permitted Discretion, deems necessary or desirable (1) to preserve or protect the Collateral, or any portion thereof, or (2) to enhance the likelihood of repayment of the Obligations (the Revolving Loans described in this Section 2.2(c)(i) being referred to as "Protective Loans").

(ii) Any contrary provision of this Agreement or any other Loan Document notwithstanding, Bank may, but is not obligated to, knowingly and intentionally, continue to make Revolving Loans to Borrower notwithstanding that an Overadvance exists or would be created thereby.

(iii) Each Protective Loan and each Overadvance (each, an "Extraordinary Loan") shall be deemed to be a Revolving Loan hereunder. The Extraordinary Loans shall be repayable on demand, secured by Bank's Liens, constitute Obligations hereunder, and bear interest at the rate applicable from time to time to Revolving Loans.

2.3   Payments.

(a) **Payments by Borrower.** Except as otherwise expressly provided herein, all payments by Borrower shall be made to Bank's Account for the account of Bank and shall be made in immediately available funds, no later than 11:00 a.m. (California time) on the date specified herein. Any payment received by Bank later than 11:00 a.m. (California time) will be deemed to have been received on the following Business Day and any applicable interest or fee will continue to accrue until such following Business Day.

(b) **Apportionment and Application.**

(i) All payments to be made hereunder by Borrower shall be remitted to Bank and all such payments, and all proceeds of Collateral received by Bank, shall be applied, so long as no Application Event has occurred and is continuing, to reduce the balance of the Revolving Loans outstanding and, thereafter, remitted to Borrower (to be wired to the Designated Account) or such other Person entitled thereto under applicable law.

(ii) At any time that an Application Event has occurred and is continuing, all payments remitted to Bank, and all proceeds of Collateral received by Bank, shall be applied first, to pay any Bank Expenses (including cost or expense reimbursements) or indemnities then due to Bank under the Loan Documents, until paid in full, second, to pay any fees or premiums then due to Bank under the Loan Documents until paid in full, third, to pay interest due in respect of all Extraordinary Loans until paid in full, fourth, to pay the principal of all Extraordinary Loans until paid in full, fifth, to pay interest accrued in respect of Loans (other than Extraordinary Loans) until paid in full, sixth, ratably (i) to pay the principal of all Loans (other than Extraordinary Loans) until paid in full, and (ii) to Bank, as cash collateral in an amount up to 102% of the Letter of Credit Usage (to the extent permitted by applicable law, such cash collateral shall be applied to the reimbursement of any Letter of Credit Disbursement as and when such disbursement occurs and, if a Letter of Credit expires undrawn, the cash collateral held by Bank in respect of such Letter of Credit shall, to the extent permitted by applicable law, be reapplied pursuant to this Section 2.3(b)(ii), beginning with the "first" tier hereof), seventh, to pay any other Obligations, and eighth, to Borrower (to be wired to the Designated Account) or such other Person entitled thereto under applicable law.

(iii) For purposes of the foregoing, "paid in full" of a type of Obligation means payment in cash or immediately available funds of all amounts owing on account of such type of Obligation, including interest accrued after the commencement of any Insolvency Proceeding, default interest, interest on interest, and expense reimbursements, irrespective of whether any of the foregoing would be or is allowed or disallowed in whole or in part in any Insolvency Proceeding.

(c) **Optional Prepayments**. Borrower may prepay the principal of any Revolving Loan at any time in whole or in part, without premium or penalty.

(d) **Mandatory Prepayments.** If, at any time, the outstanding principal balance of the Revolving Loans on such date exceeds the *lesser of* (A) the Maximum Revolver Amount *less* the Letter of Credit Usage, or (B) the Borrowing Base *less* the Letter of Credit Usage, then Borrower shall immediately prepay the Obligations in an amount equal to the amount of such excess.

(e) **Application of Payments.** Each prepayment pursuant to Section 2.3(d) above shall (i) so long as no Application Event shall have occurred and be continuing, be applied first, to the outstanding principal amount of the Revolving Loans, until paid in full, and, second, to cash collateralize the Letters of Credit in an amount equal to 102% of the then outstanding Letter of Credit Usage and (ii) if an Application Event shall have occurred and be continuing, be applied in the manner set forth in Section 2.3(b)(ii).

2.4   Promise to Pay. Borrower agrees to pay Bank Expenses on the earlier of (a) the first day of the month following the date on which the applicable Bank Expenses were first incurred or (b) the date on which demand therefor is made by Bank (it being acknowledged and agreed that any charging of such costs, expenses or Bank Expenses to the Loan Account pursuant to the provisions of Section 2.5(d) shall be deemed to constitute a demand for payment thereof for the purposes of this subclause (b)). Borrower promises to pay all of the Obligations (including principal, interest, premiums, if any, fees, costs, and expenses (including Bank Expenses)) in full on the Maturity Date or, if earlier, on the date on which the Obligations become due and payable pursuant to the terms of this Agreement. Borrower agrees that its obligations contained in the first sentence of this Section 2.4 shall survive payment or satisfaction in full of all other Obligations. Bank may request that any portion of the Loans made by it be evidenced by one or more promissory notes. In such event, Borrower shall execute and deliver to Bank the requested promissory notes payable to the order of Bank in a form furnished by Bank and reasonably satisfactory to Borrower.

2.5   Interest Rates and Letter of Credit Fee: Rates, Payments, and Calculations.

(a) **Interest Rates.** Except as provided in clause (c) below, all Obligations (except for undrawn Letters of Credit) that have been charged to the Loan Account pursuant to the terms hereof shall bear interest on the Daily Balance thereof at a per annum rate equal to the Base Rate plus the Applicable Rate applicable to Loans.

(b) **Letter of Credit Fee.** Borrower shall pay Bank a Letter of Credit fee (in addition to the charges, commissions, fees, and costs set forth in Section 2.10) which shall accrue at a rate equal to the Base Rate per annum *times* the Daily Balance of the undrawn amount of all outstanding Letters of Credit.

(c) **Default Rate.** Upon the occurrence and during the continuation of an Event of Default,

(i) all Obligations (except for undrawn Letters of Credit) that have been charged to the Loan Account pursuant to the terms hereof shall bear interest on the Daily Balance thereof at a per annum rate equal to 2 percentage points above the per annum rate otherwise applicable hereunder, and

(ii) the Letter of Credit fee provided for above shall be increased to 2 percentage points above the per annum rate otherwise applicable hereunder.

(d) **Payment**. Except to the extent provided to the contrary in Section 2.9 or Section 2.10, (i) all interest, all Letter of Credit Fees, and all other fees payable hereunder or under any of the other Loan Documents shall be due and payable, in arrears, on the first day of each month, and (ii) all costs and expenses payable hereunder or under any of the other Loan Documents and all Bank Expenses shall be due and payable on the date on which demand therefor is made by Bank. Borrower hereby authorizes Bank, from time to time without prior notice to Borrower, to charge to the Loan Account (A) on the first day of each month, all interest accrued during the prior month on the Loans hereunder, (B) on the first day of each month, all Letter of Credit Fees accrued or chargeable hereunder during the prior month, (C) on the first day of each month, the Unused Line Fee accrued during the prior month, (D) as and when incurred or accrued, all audit, appraisal, valuation, or other charges or fees payable hereunder, (E) as and when due and payable, all other fees payable hereunder or under any of the other Loan Documents, (F) as and when incurred or accrued, all fees, charges, commissions, and costs provided for in Section 2.9 or Section 2.10, (G) as and when incurred or accrued, all fees and costs provided for in Section 2.8, (H) as and when incurred or accrued, all other Bank Expenses, and (I) as and when due and payable all other payment obligations payable under any Loan Document (including the amounts due and payable with respect to any term loan). All amounts charged to the Loan Account shall thereupon constitute Revolving Loans hereunder, shall constitute Obligations hereunder, and shall accrue interest at the rate then applicable to Revolving Loans.

(e) **Computation.** All interest and fees chargeable under the Loan Documents shall be computed on the basis of a 360 day year for the actual number of days elapsed. In the event the Base Rate is changed from time to time hereafter, the rates of interest hereunder based upon the Base Rate automatically and immediately shall be increased or decreased by an amount equal to such change in the Base Rate.

(f) **Intent to Limit Charges to Maximum Lawful Rate.** In no event shall the interest rate or rates payable under this Agreement, plus any other amounts paid in connection herewith, exceed the highest rate permissible under any law that a court of competent jurisdiction shall, in a final determination, deem applicable. Borrower and

Bank, in executing and delivering this Agreement, intend legally to agree upon the rate or rates of interest and manner of payment stated within it; provided, however, that, if said rate or rates of interest or manner of payment exceeds the maximum allowable under applicable law, then, *ipso facto*, as of the date of this Agreement, Borrower is and shall be liable only for the payment of such maximum as allowed by law, and payment received from Borrower in excess of such legal maximum, whenever received, shall be applied to reduce the principal balance of the Obligations to the extent of such excess.

2.6   **Crediting Payments.** The receipt of any payment item by Bank shall not be considered a payment on account unless such payment item is a wire transfer of immediately available federal funds made to the Bank's Account or unless and until such payment item is honored when presented for payment. Should any payment item not be honored when presented for payment, then Borrower shall be deemed not to have made such payment and interest shall be calculated accordingly. Anything to the contrary contained herein notwithstanding, any payment item shall be deemed received by Bank only if it is received into the Bank's Account on a Business Day on or before 11:00 a.m. (California time). If any payment item is received into the Bank's Account on a non-Business Day or after 11:00 a.m. (California time) on a Business Day, it shall be deemed to have been received by Bank as of the opening of business on the immediately following Business Day.

2.7   **Designated Account.** Bank is authorized to make the Loans, and Bank is authorized to issue the Letters of Credit, under this Agreement based upon telephonic or other instructions received from anyone purporting to be an Authorized Person or, without instructions, if pursuant to Section 2.5(d). Borrower agrees to establish and maintain the Designated Account with the Designated Account Bank for the purpose of receiving the proceeds of the Loans requested by Borrower and made by Bank hereunder. Unless otherwise agreed by Bank and Borrower, any Loan requested by Borrower and made by Bank hereunder shall be made to the Designated Account.

2.8   **Maintenance of Loan Account; Statements of Obligations.** Bank shall maintain an account on its books in the name of Borrower (the "Loan Account") on which Borrower will be charged with all Loans made by Bank to Borrower or for Borrower's account, the Letters of Credit issued by Bank for Borrower's account, and with all other payment Obligations hereunder or under the other Loan Documents, including, accrued interest, fees and expenses, and Bank Expenses. In accordance with Section 2.6, the Loan Account will be credited with all payments received by Bank from Borrower or for Borrower's account. Bank shall make available to Borrower monthly statements regarding the Loan Account, including principal, interest, fees, and including an itemization of all charges and expenses constituting Bank Expenses owing, and such statements, absent manifest error, shall be conclusively presumed to be correct and accurate and constitute an account stated between Borrower and Bank unless, within 30 days after receipt thereof by Borrower, Borrower shall deliver to Bank written objection thereto describing the error or errors contained in any such statements.

2.9   **Fees.** Borrower shall pay to Bank the following fees and charges, which fees and charges shall be non-refundable when paid:

(a) **Unused Line Fee.** On the first day of each month during the term of this Agreement, an unused line fee (the "Unused Line Fee") in an amount equal to the Applicable Rate for the Unused Line Fee per annum times the result of (i) the Maximum Revolver Amount, less (ii) the sum of (A) the average Daily Balance of Revolving Loans that were outstanding during the immediately preceding month, plus (B) the average Daily Balance of the Letter of Credit Usage during the immediately preceding month, and

(b) **Closing Fee.** On the Closing Date, $_____.

2.10   Letters of Credit.

(a) Subject to the terms and conditions of this Agreement, Bank agrees to issue letters of credit for the account of Borrower (each, a "Letter of Credit"). Each request for the issuance of a Letter of Credit, or the amendment, renewal, or extension of any outstanding Letter of Credit, shall be made in writing by an Authorized Person and delivered to Bank via hand delivery, telefacsimile, or other electronic method of transmission reasonably in advance of the requested date of issuance, amendment, renewal, or extension. Each such request shall be in form and substance satisfactory to Bank and shall (i) specify (A) the amount of such Letter of Credit, (B) the date of issuance, amendment, renewal, or extension of such Letter of Credit, (C) the expiration date of such Letter of Credit, (D) the name and address of the beneficiary thereof, and (E) such other information (including, in the case of an amendment, renewal, or extension, identification of the outstanding Letter of Credit to be so amended, renewed, or extended) as shall be necessary to prepare, amend, renew, or extend such Letter of Credit and (ii) be accompanied by such Issuer Documents as Bank may request or require. Bank shall have no obligation to issue a Letter of Credit if any of the following would result after giving effect to the issuance of such requested Letter of Credit:

(i) the Letter of Credit Usage would exceed the Letter of Credit Amount,

(ii) the Letter of Credit Usage would exceed the Maximum Revolver Amount *less* the outstanding amount of Revolving Loans, or

(iii) the Letter of Credit Usage would exceed the Borrowing Base *less* the outstanding amount of Revolving Loans.

Additionally, Bank shall have no obligation to issue a Letter of Credit if any order, judgment, or decree of any Governmental Authority or arbitrator shall, by its terms, purport to enjoin or restrain Bank from issuing such Letter of Credit, or any law applicable to Bank or any request or directive (whether or not having the force of law) from any Governmental Authority with jurisdiction over Bank shall prohibit or request that Bank refrain from the issuance of letters of credit generally or such Letter of Credit in particular.

Each Letter of Credit shall be in form and substance acceptable to Bank, including that (i) Bank shall only be obligated to issue standby letters of credit, not commercial letters of credit, (ii) it shall be issued for a period of 365 days or less, (iii) it shall have an expiry date that is earlier than the Maturity Date, (iv) it shall be in Bank's discretion whether to include a provision providing for an "automatic amendment" to extend the expiration date of such Letter of Credit unless Bank notifies the beneficiary of such Credit or any advising bank of nonrenewal (an "<u>Evergreen Letter of Credit</u>") (it being understood and agreed that if Bank does issue an Evergreen Letter of Credit then Bank shall be entitled to send a notice of nonrenewal with respect thereto for any reason and for no reason at all), (v) all amounts payable thereunder must be payable in Dollars. If Bank is obligated to advance funds under a Letter of Credit, Borrower immediately shall reimburse such Letter of Credit Disbursement to Bank by paying an amount equal to such Letter of Credit Disbursement not later than 11:00 a.m., California time, on the date that such Letter of Credit Disbursement is made, if Borrower shall have received written or telephonic notice of such Letter of Credit Disbursement prior to 10:00 a.m., California time, on such date, or, if such notice has not been received by Borrower prior to such time on such date, then not later than 11:00 a.m., California time, on the Business Day that Borrower receives such notice, if such notice is received prior to 10:00 a.m., California time, on the date of receipt, and, in the absence of such reimbursement, the Letter of Credit Disbursement immediately and automatically shall be deemed to be a Revolving Loan hereunder and, thereafter, shall bear interest at the rate then applicable to Revolving Loans under <u>Section 2.5</u>. To the extent a Letter of Credit Disbursement is deemed to be a Revolving Loan hereunder, Borrower's obligation to reimburse such Letter of Credit Disbursement shall be discharged and replaced by the resulting Revolving Loan.

(b) Borrower hereby agrees to indemnify, save, defend, and hold Bank and each Bank-Related Person harmless from and against any claim, demand, suit, action, damages, investigation, audit, proceeding, loss, cost, expense, fine, penalty or liability, and all reasonable fees and disbursements of attorneys, experts and consultants incurred by Bank and such Bank-Related Person, and all other costs and expenses incurred by Bank and such Bank-Related Person in connection therewith or in connection with the enforcement of this indemnification, arising out of or in connection with any Letter of Credit and any Issuer Document. This indemnification provision shall survive the termination of this Agreement and all Issuer Documents, and the expiration or termination of all Letters of Credit. Borrower agrees to be bound by Bank's regulations and interpretations of any Letter of Credit issued by Bank to or for Borrower's account, even though this interpretation may be different from Borrower's own, and Borrower understands and agrees that neither Bank nor any Bank-Related Person shall be liable for any error, negligence, or mistake, whether of omission or commission, in following Borrower's instructions or those contained in the Letter of Credit, the related Issuer Document or any modifications, amendments, or supplements thereto. Borrower hereby acknowledges and agrees that neither Bank nor any Bank-Related Person shall be responsible for delays, errors, or omissions resulting from the malfunction of equipment in connection with any Letter of Credit.

(c) Borrower acknowledges and agrees that any and all charges, commissions, fees, and costs charged by Bank relating to Letters of Credit, upon the issuance of any Letter of Credit, upon the payment or negotiation of any drawing under any Letter of Credit, or upon the occurrence of any other activity with respect to any Letter of Credit (including the transfer, amendment, or cancellation of any Letter of Credit), together with any and all fronting fees in effect from time to time related to Letters of Credit, shall be Bank Expenses for purposes of this Agreement and immediately shall be reimbursable by Borrower to Bank for the account of Bank; it being acknowledged and agreed by Borrower that, as of the Closing Date, the issuance charge imposed by Bank is ___% per annum times the face amount of each Letter of Credit, that such issuance charge may be changed from time to time, and that Bank also imposes a schedule of charges for amendments, extensions, drawings, and renewals.

(d) If by reason of (i) any change after the Closing Date in any applicable law, treaty, rule, or regulation or any change in the interpretation or application thereof by any Governmental Authority, or (ii) compliance by Bank with any direction, request, or requirement (irrespective of whether having the force of law) of any Governmental Authority or monetary authority including, Regulation D of the Federal Reserve Board as from time to time in effect (and any successor thereto): (A) any reserve, deposit, or similar requirement is or shall be imposed or modified in respect of any Letter of Credit issued hereunder, or (B) there shall be imposed on Bank any other condition regarding any Letter of Credit issued pursuant hereto, and (C) the result of the foregoing is to increase, directly or indirectly, the cost to Bank of issuing, making, guaranteeing, or maintaining any Letter of Credit or to reduce the amount receivable in respect thereof by Bank, then, and in any such case, Bank may, at any time within a reasonable period after the additional cost is incurred or the amount received is reduced, notify Borrower, and Borrower shall pay on demand such amounts as Bank may specify to be necessary to compensate Bank for such additional cost or reduced receipt, together with interest on such amount from the date of such demand until payment in full thereof at the rate then applicable under Section 2.5. The determination by Bank of any amount due pursuant to this Section, as set forth in a certificate setting forth the calculation thereof in reasonable detail, shall, in the absence of manifest or demonstrable error, be final and conclusive and binding on all of the parties hereto.

(e) Bank and Borrower agree that, in paying any drawing under a Letter of Credit, neither Bank nor any Bank-Related Person shall have any responsibility to obtain any document (other than any sight draft, certificates and documents expressly required by the Letter of Credit) or to ascertain or inquire as to the validity or accuracy of any such document or the authority of the Person executing or delivering any such document. Neither Bank nor any Bank-Related Person shall be liable to Borrower or any Affiliate thereof for (i) any action taken or omitted in connection herewith at the request or with the approval of the Borrower; (ii) any action taken or omitted in the absence of gross negligence or willful misconduct; (iii) any error, omission, interruption, loss or delay in transmission or delivery of any draft, notice or other communication under or relating to any Letter of Credit or any error in interpretation of technical terms; or (iv) the due execution, effectiveness, validity or enforceability of any document or instrument related to any Letter of Credit or Issuer Document. Borrower hereby assumes all risks of the acts or omissions of any beneficiary or transferee with respect to its use of any Letter of Credit; provided, that this assumption is not intended to, and shall not, preclude Borrower from pursuing such rights and remedies as it may have against the beneficiary or transferee at law or under any other agreement. None of Bank or any of the Bank-Related

Persons shall be liable or responsible for any of the matters described in clauses (i) through (viii) of Section 2.10(f) or for any action, neglect or omission under or in connection with any Letter of Credit or Issuer Document, including in connection with the issuance or any amendment of any Letter of Credit, the failure to issue or amend any Letter of Credit, the honoring or dishonoring of any demand under any Letter of Credit, or the following of Borrower's instructions or those contained in the Letter of Credit or any Issuer Document or any modifications, amendments, or supplements thereto, and such action or neglect or omission will bind Borrower, and Borrower's obligations to reimburse Bank for each presentation honored under any such Letter of Credit shall not be impaired in any way. In furtherance and not in limitation of the foregoing, Bank may accept documents that appear on their face to be in order, without responsibility for further investigation, regardless of any notice or information to the contrary (or Bank may refuse to accept and make payment upon such documents if such documents are not in strict compliance with the terms of such Letter of Credit and may disregard any requirement in a Letter of Credit that notice of dishonor be given in a particular manner and any requirement that presentation be made at a particular place or by a particular time of day), and Bank shall not be responsible for the validity or sufficiency of any instrument transferring or assigning or purporting to transfer or assign a Letter of Credit or the rights or benefits thereunder or proceeds thereof, in whole or in part, which may prove to be invalid or ineffective for any reason. Bank shall not be responsible for the wording of any Letter of Credit (including any drawing conditions or any terms or conditions that are ineffective, ambiguous, inconsistent, unduly complicated or reasonably impossible to satisfy), notwithstanding any assistance Bank may provide to Borrower with drafting or recommending text for any letter of credit application or with the structuring of any transaction related to any Letter of Credit, and Borrower hereby acknowledges and agrees that any such assistance will not constitute legal or other advice by Bank or any representation or warranty by Bank that any such wording or such Letter of Credit will be effective. Without limiting the foregoing, Bank may, as it deems appropriate, use in any Letter of Credit any portion of the language prepared by Borrower and contained in the letter of credit application relative to drawings under such Letter of Credit. To the fullest extent permitted by applicable law, in no event shall Bank or any Bank-Related Person shall be liable to Borrower, or any Affiliate of Borrower, for any indirect, consequential, special, exemplary or punitive damages suffered or otherwise incurred arising out of, related to, or in connection with, any Letter of Credit.

(f) The obligation of Borrower to reimburse Bank for each drawing under each Letter of Credit shall be absolute, unconditional and irrevocable, and shall be paid strictly in accordance with the terms of this Agreement under all circumstances, including the following: (i) any lack of validity or enforceability of such Letter of Credit, this Agreement, or any other Loan Document, (ii) the existence of any claim, counterclaim, setoff, defense or other right that Borrower or any Affiliate of Borrower may have at any time against any beneficiary of such Letter of Credit, any transferee of such Letter of Credit or any assignee of proceeds of such Letter of Credit (or any Person for whom any such beneficiary, any such transferee or any such assignee may be acting), Bank or any other Person, whether in connection with this Agreement, the transactions contemplated hereby or by such Letter of Credit or any agreement or instrument relating thereto, or any unrelated transaction, (iii) any draft, demand, certificate or other document presented under such Letter of Credit proving to be forged, fraudulent, invalid or insufficient in any respect or any statement therein being untrue or inaccurate in any respect, or any loss or delay in the transmission or otherwise of any document required in order to make a drawing under such Letter of Credit, (iv) any payment or other honoring by Bank under such Letter of Credit against presentation of a draft or certificate that does not comply in whole or in part with the terms of such Letter of Credit (including, without limitation, any requirement that presentation be made at a particular place or by a particular time of day, or that presentation must strictly or substantially comply with the terms of such Letter of Credit), or any payment made or other honor of a presentation by Bank under such Letter of Credit to or for the benefit any Person purporting to be a trustee in bankruptcy, debtor-in-possession, assignee for the benefit of creditors, liquidator, or other representative of or successor to any beneficiary or any transferee of such Letter of Credit (including any Person purporting to be the beneficiary under such Letter of Credit under a new name), (v) any payment or other honoring by Bank under such Letter of Credit against a drawing up to the amount available under such Letter of Credit, even if such drawing demands an amount in excess of the amount then available under such Letter of Credit, (vi) any honoring by Bank of any presentation under such Letter of Credit that is subsequently determined to have been honored in violation of international, federal, state or local restrictions on the transaction of business with certain prohibited Persons, (vii) any other circumstance or happening whatsoever, whether or not similar to any of the foregoing, including any other circumstance that might otherwise constitute a defense available to, or discharge of, Borrower or any Affiliate of Borrower, or (viii) the fact that any Default or Event of Default shall have occurred and be continuing.

(g) Unless otherwise expressly agreed by Bank and Borrower when a Letter of Credit is issued, (i) the rules of the International Standby Practices 1998 (International Chamber of Commerce Publication No. 590), shall apply to each standby Letter of Credit, and (ii) the rules of the Uniform Customs and Practice for Documentary Credits (International Chamber of Commerce Publication No. 600), shall apply to each commercial Letter of Credit.

(h) In the event of a direct conflict between the provisions of this Section 2.10 and any provision contained in any Issuer Document, it is the intention of the parties hereto that such provisions be read together and construed, to the fullest extent possible, to be in concert with each other. In the event of any actual, irreconcilable conflict that cannot be resolved as aforesaid, the terms and provisions of this Section 2.10 shall control and govern.

2.11   Capital Requirements. If, after the date hereof, Bank determines that (i) the adoption of or change in any law, rule, regulation or guideline regarding capital requirements for banks or bank holding companies, or any change in the interpretation or application thereof by any Governmental Authority charged with the administration thereof, or (ii) compliance by Bank or its parent bank holding company with any guideline, request, or directive of any such entity regarding capital adequacy (whether or not having the force of law), has the effect of reducing the return on Bank's or such holding company's capital as a consequence of Bank's obligations hereunder to a level below that which Bank or such holding company could have achieved but for such adoption, change, or compliance (taking into consideration Bank's or such holding company's then existing policies with respect to capital adequacy and assuming the full utilization of such entity's capital) by any amount deemed by Bank to be material, then Bank may notify Borrower thereof. Following receipt of such notice, Borrower agrees to pay Bank on demand the amount of such reduction of return of capital as and when such reduction is determined, payable within 90 days after presentation by Bank of a statement in the amount and setting forth in reasonable detail Bank's calculation thereof and the assumptions upon which such calculation was based (which statement shall be deemed true and correct absent manifest error). In determining such amount, Bank may use any reasonable averaging and attribution methods.

3. CONDITIONS; TERM OF AGREEMENT.

3.1 **Conditions Precedent to the Initial Extension of Credit.** The obligation of Bank to make the initial extension of credit provided for hereunder on or after the date hereof, is subject to the prior or concurrent fulfillment, to the satisfaction of Bank of each of the following conditions precedent:

3.2 **Conditions Precedent to all Extensions of Credit.** The obligation of Bank to make any Loans or to issue any Letter of Credit hereunder at any time (or to extend any other credit hereunder) shall be subject to the following conditions precedent:

(a) the representations and warranties contained in this Agreement and the other Loan Documents shall be true and correct in all material respects on and as of the date of such extension of credit, as though made on and as of such date (except to the extent that such representations and warranties relate solely to an earlier date); and

(b) no Default or Event of Default shall have occurred and be continuing on the date of such extension of credit, nor shall either result from the making thereof.

3.3 **Effect of Maturity.** On the Maturity Date, all commitments of Bank to provide additional credit hereunder shall automatically be terminated and all of the Obligations immediately shall become due and payable without notice or demand and Borrower shall be required to repay all of the Obligations in full. No termination of the obligations of Bank (other than payment in full of the Obligations and termination of the Revolver Commitment) or termination of this Agreement by Borrower as provided herein shall relieve or discharge Borrower of its duties, obligations, or covenants hereunder or under any other Loan Document and Borrower's Liens in the Collateral shall continue to secure the Obligations and shall remain in effect until all Obligations have been paid in full and the Revolver Commitment has been terminated. When all of the Obligations have been paid in full and Bank's obligations to provide additional credit under the Loan Documents have been terminated irrevocably, Bank will, at Borrower's sole expense, execute and deliver any termination statements, lien releases, discharges of security interests, and other similar discharge or release documents (and, if applicable, in recordable form) as are reasonably necessary to release, as of record, Bank's Liens and all notices of security interests and liens previously filed by Bank.

3.4   Early Termination. Borrower has the option, at any time upon 10 Business Days prior written notice to Bank, to terminate this Agreement and terminate the Revolver Commitments hereunder by repaying to Bank all of the Obligations in full in cash together with the Applicable Prepayment Premium. If Borrower has sent a notice of termination pursuant to the provisions of this Section 3.5, then on the date set forth as the date of termination of this Agreement in such notice, Borrower shall pay to Bank, in cash, the Obligations in full in cash together with the Applicable Prepayment Premium. In the event of a termination of the Revolver Commitment and a prepayment of the Obligations in full prior to the Maturity Date for any other reason, including (a) acceleration of the Obligations as a result of the occurrence of an Event of Default, (b) foreclosure and sale of, or collection of, the Collateral, (c) sale of the Collateral in any Insolvency Proceeding, or (d) the restructure, reorganization, or compromise of the Obligations by the confirmation of a plan of reorganization or any other plan of compromise, restructure, or arrangement in any Insolvency Proceeding, then, in view of the impracticability and extreme difficulty of ascertaining the actual amount of damages to the Bank or profits lost by the Bank as a result of such Prepayment, and by mutual agreement of the parties as to a reasonable estimation and calculation of the lost profits or damages of the Bank, Borrower shall pay to Bank, in cash, the Applicable Prepayment Premium, measured as of the date of such Prepayment.

4. REPRESENTATIONS AND WARRANTIES.

In order to induce Bank to enter into this Agreement, Borrower makes the following representations and warranties to Bank, each of which is true, correct, and complete, in all material respects, as of the date hereof, as of the Closing Date, and as of the date of the making of each Loan (or other extension of credit) made thereafter, as though made on and as of the date of such Loan (or other extension of credit) (except to the extent that such representations and warranties relate solely to an earlier date) and such representations and warranties shall survive the execution and delivery of this Agreement: [remainder to be added by another lawyer]

5. AFFIRMATIVE COVENANTS.

[to be added by another lawyer]

6. NEGATIVE COVENANTS.

[to be added by another lawyer]

7. FINANCIAL COVENANTS.

[to be added by another lawyer]

8. EVENTS OF DEFAULT.

Any one or more of the following events shall constitute an event of default (each, an "Event of Default") under this Agreement

[to be added by another lawyer]

9. BANK'S RIGHTS AND REMEDIES.

9.1   Rights and Remedies. Upon the occurrence, and during the continuation, of an Event of Default, Bank (at its election but without notice of its election and without demand) may do any one or more of the following, all of which are authorized by Borrower:

[to be added by another lawyer]

9.2   Remedies Cumulative. The rights and remedies of Bank under this Agreement, the other Loan Documents, and all other agreements shall be cumulative. Bank shall have all other rights and remedies not inconsistent herewith as provided under the Code, by law, or in equity. No exercise by Bank of one right or remedy shall be deemed an election, and no waiver by Bank of any Event of Default shall be deemed a continuing waiver. No delay by Bank shall constitute a waiver, election, or acquiescence by it.

10.   WAIVERS; INDEMNIFICATION.

10.1   Demand; Protest. Borrower waives demand, protest, notice of protest, notice of default or dishonor, notice of payment and nonpayment, nonpayment at maturity, release, compromise, settlement, extension, or renewal of documents, instruments, chattel paper, and guarantees at any time held by Bank on which Borrower may in any way be liable.

10.2   Bank's Liability for Collateral. Borrower hereby agrees that: (a) so long as Bank complies with its obligations, if any, under the Code, Bank will not in any way or manner be liable or responsible for: (i) the safekeeping of the Collateral, (ii) any loss or damage thereto occurring or arising in any manner or fashion from any cause, (iii) any diminution in the value thereof, or (iv) any act or default of any carrier, warehouseman, bailee, forwarding agency, or other Person, and (b) all risk of loss, damage, or destruction of the Collateral will be borne by Borrower.

10.3   Indemnification. Borrower shall pay, indemnify, defend, and hold the Bank-Related Persons and each Participant (each, an "Indemnified Person") harmless (to the fullest extent permitted by law) from and against any and all claims, demands, suits, actions, investigations, proceedings, liabilities, fines, costs, penalties, and damages, and all reasonable fees and disbursements of attorneys, experts, or consultants and all other costs and expenses actually incurred in connection therewith or in connection with the enforcement of this indemnification (as and when they are incurred and irrespective of whether suit is brought), at any time asserted against, imposed upon, or incurred by any of them (a) in connection with or as a result of or related to the execution and delivery, enforcement, performance, or administration (including any restructuring or workout with respect hereto) of this Agreement, any of the other Loan Documents, or the transactions contemplated hereby or thereby or the monitoring of Borrower's compliance with the terms of the Loan Documents, and (b) with respect to any investigation, litigation, or proceeding related to this Agreement, any other Loan Document, or the use of the proceeds of the credit provided hereunder (irrespective of whether any Indemnified Person is a party thereto), or any act, omission, event, or circumstance in any manner related thereto (each and all of the foregoing, the "Indemnified Liabilities"). The foregoing to the contrary notwithstanding, Borrower shall have no obligation to any Indemnified Person under this Section 10.3 with respect to any

Indemnified Liability that a court of competent jurisdiction finally determines to have resulted from the gross negligence or willful misconduct of such Indemnified Person or its officers, directors, employees, attorneys, or agents. This provision shall survive the termination of this Agreement and the repayment in full of the Obligations. **WITHOUT LIMITATION, THE FOREGOING INDEMNITY SHALL APPLY TO EACH INDEMNIFIED PERSON WITH RESPECT TO INDEMNIFIED LIABILITIES WHICH IN WHOLE OR IN PART ARE CAUSED BY OR ARISE OUT OF ANY NEGLIGENT ACT OR OMISSION OF SUCH INDEMNIFIED PERSON OR OF ANY OTHER PERSON.**

11.   NOTICES.

Unless otherwise provided in this Agreement, all notices or demands by Borrower or Bank to the other relating to this Agreement or any other Loan Document must be in writing and (except for financial statements and other informational documents which may be sent by first-class mail, postage prepaid) must be personally delivered or sent by registered or certified mail (postage prepaid, return receipt requested), overnight courier, electronic mail (at such email addresses as Borrower or Bank, as applicable, may designate to each other in accordance herewith), or telefacsimile to Borrower or Bank, as the case may be, at its address set forth below its signature hereto. Bank and Borrower may change the address at which they are to receive notices hereunder, by notice in writing in the foregoing manner given to the other party. All notices or demands sent in accordance with this Section 11, will be effective on the earlier of the date of actual receipt or 3 Business Days after the deposit thereof in the mail.

12.   CHOICE OF LAW AND VENUE; JURY TRIAL WAIVER.

(a) THE VALIDITY OF THIS AGREEMENT AND THE OTHER LOAN DOCUMENTS (UNLESS EXPRESSLY PROVIDED TO THE CONTRARY IN ANOTHER LOAN DOCUMENT IN RESPECT OF SUCH OTHER LOAN DOCUMENT), THE CONSTRUCTION, INTERPRETATION, AND ENFORCEMENT HEREOF AND THEREOF, THE RIGHTS OF THE PARTIES HERETO AND THERETO WITH RESPECT TO ALL MATTERS ARISING HEREUNDER OR THEREUNDER OR RELATED HERETO OR THERETO, AND ANY CLAIMS, CONTROVERSIES OR DISPUTES ARISING HEREUNDER OR THEREUNDER OR RELATED HERETO OR THERETO SHALL BE DETERMINED UNDER, GOVERNED BY, AND CONSTRUED IN ACCORDANCE WITH THE LAWS OF THE STATE OF CALIFORNIA.

(b) THE PARTIES AGREE THAT ALL ACTIONS OR PROCEEDINGS ARISING IN CONNECTION WITH THIS AGREEMENT AND THE OTHER LOAN DOCUMENTS SHALL BE TRIED AND LITIGATED ONLY IN THE STATE AND, TO THE EXTENT PERMITTED BY APPLICABLE LAW, FEDERAL COURTS LOCATED IN THE COUNTY OF LOS ANGELES, STATE OF CALIFORNIA; PROVIDED, THAT ANY SUIT SEEKING ENFORCEMENT AGAINST ANY COLLATERAL OR OTHER PROPERTY MAY BE BROUGHT, AT BANK'S OPTION, IN THE COURTS OF ANY JURISDICTION WHERE BANK ELECTS TO

BRING SUCH ACTION OR WHERE SUCH COLLATERAL OR OTHER PROPERTY MAY BE FOUND. EACH OF BORROWER AND BANK WAIVE, TO THE EXTENT PERMITTED UNDER APPLICABLE LAW, ANY RIGHT EACH MAY HAVE TO ASSERT THE DOCTRINE OF FORUM NON CONVENIENS OR TO OBJECT TO VENUE TO THE EXTENT ANY PROCEEDING IS BROUGHT IN ACCORDANCE WITH THIS SECTION 12(b).

(c) TO THE MAXIMUM EXTENT PERMITTED BY APPLICABLE LAW, BORROWER AND BANK HEREBY WAIVE THEIR RESPECTIVE RIGHTS, IF ANY, TO A JURY TRIAL OF ANY CLAIM, CONTROVERSY, DISPUTE OR CAUSE OF ACTION DIRECTLY OR INDIRECTLY BASED UPON OR ARISING OUT OF ANY OF THE LOAN DOCUMENTS OR ANY OF THE TRANSACTIONS CONTEMPLATED THEREIN, INCLUDING CONTRACT CLAIMS, TORT CLAIMS, BREACH OF DUTY CLAIMS, AND ALL OTHER COMMON LAW OR STATUTORY CLAIMS (EACH A "CLAIM"). EACH OF BORROWER AND BANK REPRESENT TO THE OTHER THAT IT HAS REVIEWED THIS WAIVER AND THAT IT KNOWINGLY AND VOLUNTARILY WAIVES ITS JURY TRIAL RIGHTS FOLLOWING CONSULTATION WITH LEGAL COUNSEL. IN THE EVENT OF LITIGATION, A COPY OF THIS AGREEMENT MAY BE FILED AS A WRITTEN CONSENT TO A TRIAL BY THE COURT.

(d) BORROWER HEREBY IRREVOCABLY AND UNCONDITIONALLY SUBMITS TO THE EXCLUSIVE JURISDICTION OF THE STATE AND FEDERAL COURTS LOCATED IN THE COUNTY OF LOS ANGELES AND THE STATE OF CALIFORNIA, IN ANY ACTION OR PROCEEDING ARISING OUT OF OR RELATING TO ANY LOAN DOCUMENTS, OR FOR RECOGNITION OR ENFORCEMENT OF ANY JUDGMENT. EACH OF THE PARTIES HERETO AGREES THAT A FINAL JUDGMENT IN ANY SUCH ACTION OR PROCEEDING SHALL BE CONCLUSIVE AND MAY BE ENFORCED IN OTHER JURISDICTIONS BY SUIT ON THE JUDGMENT OR IN ANY OTHER MANNER PROVIDED BY LAW. NOTHING IN THIS AGREEMENT OR ANY OTHER LOAN DOCUMENT SHALL AFFECT ANY RIGHT THAT BANK MAY OTHERWISE HAVE TO BRING ANY ACTION OR PROCEEDING RELATING TO THIS AGREEMENT OR ANY OTHER LOAN DOCUMENT AGAINST BORROWER OR ITS PROPERTIES IN THE COURTS OF ANY JURISDICTION.

(e) NO CLAIM MAY BE MADE BY BORROWER AGAINST BANK, OR ANY AFFILIATE, DIRECTOR, OFFICER, EMPLOYEE, COUNSEL, REPRESENTATIVE, OR ATTORNEY-IN-FACT OF BANK FOR ANY SPECIAL, INDIRECT, CONSEQUENTIAL, OR PUNITIVE DAMAGES IN RESPECT OF ANY CLAIM FOR BREACH OF CONTRACT OR ANY OTHER THEORY OF LIABILITY ARISING OUT OF OR RELATED TO THE TRANSACTIONS CONTEMPLATED BY THIS AGREEMENT OR ANY OTHER LOAN DOCUMENT, OR ANY ACT, OMISSION, OR EVENT OCCURRING IN CONNECTION THEREWITH, AND BORROWER HEREBY WAIVES, RELEASES, AND AGREES NOT TO SUE UPON ANY CLAIM FOR SUCH DAMAGES, WHETHER OR NOT

ACCRUED AND WHETHER OR NOT KNOWN OR SUSPECTED TO EXIST IN ITS FAVOR.

13.   ASSIGNMENTS AND PARTICIPATIONS; SUCCESSORS.

This Agreement shall bind and inure to the benefit of the respective successors and assigns of each of the parties; provided, however, that Borrower may not assign this Agreement or any rights or duties hereunder without Bank's prior written consent and any prohibited assignment shall be absolutely void *ab initio*. No consent to assignment by Bank shall release Borrower from its Obligations. Bank may assign this Agreement and the other Loan Documents and its rights and duties hereunder and thereunder and no consent or approval by Borrower is required in connection with any such assignment.

14.   AMENDMENTS; WAIVERS.

14.1   Amendments and Waivers. No amendment or waiver of any provision of this Agreement or any other Loan Document, and no consent with respect to any departure by Borrower therefrom, shall be effective unless the same shall be in writing and signed by Bank and Borrower and then any such waiver or consent shall be effective only in the specific instance and for the specific purpose for which given.

14.2   No Waivers; Cumulative Remedies. No failure by Bank to exercise any right, remedy, or option under this Agreement or any other Loan Document, or delay by Bank in exercising the same, will operate as a waiver thereof. No waiver by Bank will be effective unless it is in writing, and then only to the extent specifically stated. No waiver by Bank on any occasion shall affect or diminish Bank's rights thereafter to require strict performance by Borrower of any provision of this Agreement. Bank's rights under this Agreement and the other Loan Documents will be cumulative and not exclusive of any other right or remedy that Bank may have.

15.   GENERAL PROVISIONS.

15.1   Effectiveness. This Agreement will be binding and deemed effective when executed by Borrower and Bank.

15.2   Section Headings. Headings and numbers have been set forth herein for convenience only. Unless the contrary is compelled by the context, everything contained in each Section applies equally to this entire Agreement.

15.3   Interpretation. Neither this Agreement nor any uncertainty or ambiguity herein is to be construed against Bank or Borrower, whether under any rule of construction or otherwise. On the contrary, this Agreement has been reviewed by all parties and shall be construed and interpreted according to the ordinary meaning of the words used so as to accomplish fairly the purposes and intentions of all parties hereto.

15.4   Severability of Provisions. Each provision of this Agreement is severable from every other provision of this Agreement for the purpose of determining the legal enforceability of any specific provision.

15.5   Debtor-Creditor Relationship. The relationship between Bank, on the one hand, and Borrower, on the other hand, is solely that of creditor and debtor. Bank has no (or shall be deemed to have any) fiduciary relationship or duty to Borrower arising out of or in connection with the Loan Documents or the transactions contemplated thereby, and there is no agency or joint venture relationship between Bank, on the one hand, and Borrower, on the other hand, by virtue of any Loan Document or any transaction contemplated therein.

15.6   Counterparts; Electronic Execution. This Agreement may be executed in any number of counterparts and by different parties on separate counterparts, each of which, when executed and delivered, shall be deemed to be an original, and all of which, when taken together, shall constitute but one and the same Agreement. Delivery of an executed counterpart of this Agreement by telefacsimile or other electronic method of transmission shall be equally as effective as delivery of an original executed counterpart of this Agreement. Any party delivering an executed counterpart of this Agreement by telefacsimile or other electronic method of transmission also shall deliver an original executed counterpart of this Agreement but the failure to deliver an original executed counterpart shall not affect the validity, enforceability, and binding effect of this Agreement. The foregoing shall apply to each other Loan Document *mutatis mutandis*.

15.7   Revival and Reinstatement of Obligations; Certain Waivers.

(a) If Bank repays, refunds, restores, or returns in whole or in part, any payment or property (including any proceeds of Collateral) previously paid or transferred to Bank in full or partial satisfaction of any Obligation or on account of any other obligation of Borrower under any Loan Document, because the payment, transfer, or the incurrence of the obligation so satisfied is asserted or declared to be void, voidable, or otherwise recoverable under any law relating to creditors' rights, including provisions of the Bankruptcy Code relating to fraudulent transfers, preferences, or other voidable or recoverable obligations or transfers (each, a "Voidable Transfer"), or because such Person elects to do so on the reasonable advice of its counsel in connection with a claim that the payment, transfer, or incurrence is or may be a Voidable Transfer, then, as to any such Voidable Transfer, or the amount thereof that such Person elects to repay, restore, or return (including pursuant to a settlement of any claim in respect thereof), and as to all reasonable costs, expenses, and attorney's fees of such Person related thereto, (i) the liability of Borrower with respect to the amount or property paid, refunded, restored, or returned will automatically and immediately be revived, reinstated, and restored and will exist and (ii) Bank's Liens securing such liability will be effective, revived, and remain in full force and effect, in each case, as fully as if such Voidable Transfer had never been made. If, prior to any of the foregoing, (A) any of Bank's Liens has been released or terminated or (B) any provision of this Agreement has been terminated or cancelled, Bank's Liens, or such provision of this Agreement, will be reinstated in full force and effect and such prior release, termination, cancellation or surrender will not diminish, release, discharge, impair or otherwise affect the obligation of Borrower in respect of such liability or any Collateral securing such liability.

(b) Anything to the contrary contained herein notwithstanding, if Bank accepts a guaranty of only a portion of the Obligations pursuant to any guaranty, Borrower hereby waives its right under Section 2822(a) of the California Civil Code or any similar laws of any other applicable jurisdiction to designate the portion of the Obligations satisfied by the applicable guarantor's partial payment.

15.8   Confidentiality. Bank agrees that material, non-public information regarding Borrower and its operations, assets, and existing and contemplated business plans shall be treated by Bank in a confidential manner, and shall not be disclosed by Bank to Persons who are not parties to this Agreement, except: (a) to attorneys for and other advisors, accountants, auditors, appraisers, and consultants to Bank, (b) to subsidiaries and Affiliates of Bank, provided that any such subsidiary or Affiliate shall have agreed to receive such information hereunder subject to the terms of this Section 15.8, (c) as may be required by regulatory authorities so long as such authorities are informed of the confidential nature of such information, (d) as may be required by statute, decision, or judicial or administrative order, rule, or regulation, (e) as may be agreed to in advance by Borrower or as requested or required by any Governmental Authority pursuant to any subpoena or other legal process, (f) as to any such information that is or becomes generally available to the public (other than as a result of prohibited disclosure by Bank), (g) in connection with any assignment, prospective assignment, sale, prospective sale, participation or prospective participations, or pledge or prospective pledge of Bank's interest under this Agreement, provided that any such assignee, prospective assignee, purchaser, prospective purchaser, participant, prospective participant, pledgee, or prospective pledgee shall have agreed in writing to receive such information hereunder subject to the terms of this Section, (h) in connection with any litigation or other adversary proceeding involving parties hereto which such litigation or adversary proceeding involves claims related to the rights or duties of such parties under this Agreement or the other Loan Documents, and (x) in connection with, and to the extent reasonably necessary for, the exercise of any secured creditor remedy under this Agreement or any other Loan Document.

15.8   Survival. All representations and warranties made by Borrower in the Loan Documents or in the certificates or other instruments delivered in connection with or pursuant to this Agreement or any other Loan Document shall be conclusively presumed to have been relied upon by the other parties hereto and shall survive the execution and delivery of the Loan Documents and the making of any Loans and issuance of any Letters of Credit, regardless of any investigation made by any such other party or on its behalf and notwithstanding that Bank, may have had notice or knowledge of any Default or Event of Default or incorrect representation or warranty at the time any credit is extended hereunder, and shall continue in full force and effect as long as the principal of, or any accrued interest on, any Loan or any fee or any other amount payable under this Agreement is outstanding or unpaid or any Letter of Credit is outstanding and so long as Bank's obligations to make Revolving Loans, issue Letters of Credit or make other extensions of credit to Borrower have not expired or been terminated.

15.9   Integration. This Agreement, together with the other Loan Documents, reflects the entire understanding of the parties with respect to the transactions contemplated hereby and shall not be contradicted or qualified by any other agreement, oral or written, before the date hereof.

IN WITNESS WHEREOF, the parties hereto have caused this Agreement to be executed and delivered as of the date first above written.

_____

a _____

By: _____

Title:

Address:

SURF CITY BANK, N.A.,

a national banking association,

By: _____

Title:

Address: